THE WRITER'S MIND

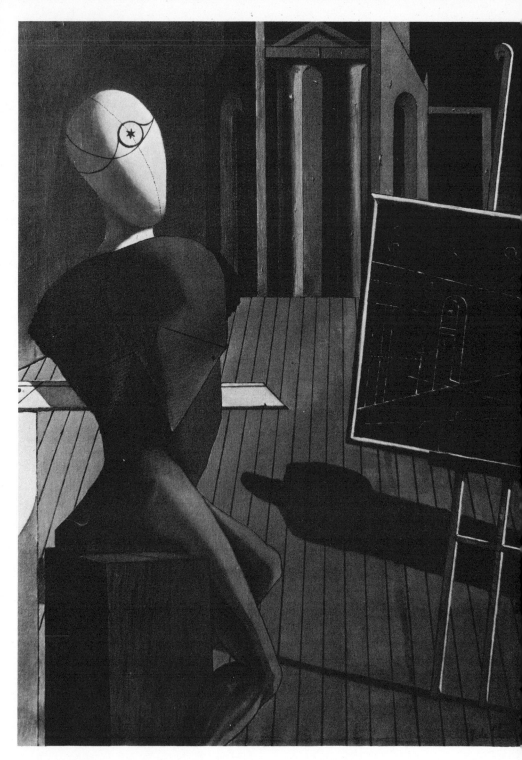

Giorgio de Chirico, THE SEER. Collection James Thrall Soby.

WALLACE KAUFMAN

WILLIAM POWERS

THE WRITER'S MIND

PRENTICE-HALL, INC.
Englewood Cliffs, N. J.

PRENTICE-HALL INTERNATIONAL, INC., *London*
PRENTICE-HALL OF AUSTRALIA, PTY. LTD., *Sydney*
PRENTICE-HALL OF CANADA, LTD., *Toronto*
PRENTICE-HALL OF INDIA PRIVATE LTD., *New Delhi*
PRENTICE-HALL OF JAPAN, INC., *Tokyo*

13-969956-2

Library of Congress Catalog Card No.: 76-112974

Current printing (last number):
10 9 8 7 6 5 4 3 2

for MARK THOMPSON
an unselfish bookman
who put books where
they never were before

What is this book?

This is a book about what happens in a person's mind before he is ready to write effectively. It is based on experiences that have convinced students and teachers that creativity can be learned. But teaching creativity is not to be confused with training commercial talent or mystical creation of genius. We offer concrete ways of exploring and developing the mechanisms of creativity: perception, awareness of relationships, meditation, freedom of thought, and finally judgment.

So long as experience must be edited and words chosen, writing will be a personal act. Any deliberate piece of writing contains a point of view, intimate or detached. Point of view can be an unconscious and imitative refuge for the lazy or timid writer, or it can be the writer's personal commitment. (Ultimately, even the personal commitment may be to someone else's point of view.) We demonstrate how both kinds of point of view happen, but our bias is strongly toward personal commitment.

When we talk about style, organization, forms of writing, and linguistics, we do not discuss these subjects in and of themselves but as actions a writer takes because his mind needs them. And what about literature? The novelists and poets are here. So are architects, biologists, physicists, journalists, artists, politicians, and students. They are here not as men of a trade, but as people who needed to write.

The unity of this book is a continuing and sequentially developed emphasis on the individual writer—why and how he writes.

Who is behind all this?

Every idea has an ancestry or heritage. Also a nourishing environment. This book is a plant growing from many people's actions and ideas. Who knows where the roots of this book are spread? They could not be traced in twice this many pages.

Our own ideas for *The Writer's Mind* began to have shape because of a project conducted by Gordon Rohman and Albert O. Wlecke in 1963 at Michigan State University. From Rohman's and Wlecke's report* to their sponsor, the U.S. Office of Education, we have lifted ideas for exercises and readings as well as the general sequence of lessons.

The hypotheses Rohman and Wlecke tested were, of course, reinforced and refined by writers from many disciplines; for just as writers attend to many subjects, the act

Pre-Writing: The Construction and Application of Models for Concept Formation in Writing.

of writing is also unconfined by narrow intellectual or academic categories. The act of writing does not come from grammar or reading or work or play alone or from the study of any one subject.

The ideas and activities presented in this text were debated, put into practice, judged, revised, put into practice again, and judged and revised again. The instructors who were most helpful in this long process were Elizabeth Rogers, Bethany Sue Strong, Robert Bain, Robert Kirkpatrick, and James "Potifer" Bryan. Jay King was especially fluent with new ideas and sources of material—literary and technical. Newt Smith first used happenings as an effective teaching device rather than a diversionary gimmick of entertainment. His own successes as a teacher and his thorough knowledge of the literature of chance made the happening the key to our demonstration of the principles of order and disorder in the psychology of writing.

We are also grateful to those who have humored us, defended us, or encouraged us as we worked and experimented; our wives, Sally Powers and Sarah Kaufman, and our colleagues in the English Department at the University of North Carolina: Daphne Athas, Max Steele, Fran Saunders, Carroll Hollis, Bernie Harder, Catherine Smith, Fred MacIntosh. John Smith, in person and at the computer, has been a necessary and patient evaluator. As always, among the unnamed are many who should not be omitted: perhaps a hundred graduate instructors at the University of North Carolina at Chapel Hill. Instead of naming them in a lengthy list we admit that they, too, are our co-authors. No book can be shaped in a vacuum, and few courses can be taught without teachers.

Maybe we can express our gratitude to everyone by saying that we have tried to make this a book for teachers as well as for students.

Contents

Symbols

THE WRITER'S MIND

What says what and for whom?

Occasionally the confusion and frustrations around a sensitive person become so strong that he feels his own existence is without meaning. It is as if he had lost his place in the story of his life he had been telling himself.

Some cynical or sophisticated people joke about the person who asks, "Who am I?" The question seems easy yet unanswerable. Perhaps the laughers laugh because they think they know who they are. They may say they are lawyers, doctors, mechanics, teachers—persons who are identified by the jobs they do and the acts they perform. They may have forgotten how important it is to be someone known for himself and not for his role. Their joking may imply that they attach little importance to the development of a person's sense of individuality, his concept of who he is apart from what job he does, how he dresses, or what his "thing" is.

Maybe you do know yourself as a very distinct person, as

an individual. The label "student" added on doesn't help very much. No matter how you think of yourself, at some time you must have been in a situation where you could not say exactly what you meant, even though you had a current word ready. For instance, why do you love your parents (if you do) and not somebody else's parents? Why do you believe strongly in the American form of economy if you admit you know little about economics? Can you say clearly and concretely why you fall in love with one person but not another?

To that last question, a familiar answer might be, "She's different." What does *different* mean? If she is so marvelously different, why isn't she famous, and why isn't anyone else in love with her? Do you really love her or just need her? What's the difference? Perhaps these questions cannot be answered because there are really no reasons. Maybe you love someone only because you are accepting the standards of personality and attractiveness that society has given you. Perhaps you cannot formulate answers because you have not thought about yourself and your situation.

Creating answers in words can be a form of investigation and discovery (if you are honest). Not having words means that in some respects you have not yet discovered yourself. Or having discovered part of yourself, what guarantee do you have that it will not change? Unless you become a mental and emotional fossil, you will always be changing. You will always need new language to communicate to yourself and to other people. Without new language for new situations, no one can be himself.

Language gives shape and boundaries to ideas, thoughts, and feelings and thus to personality. Language itself has inherent forms, however, so that the very tongue our parents give us shapes our personalities. Some languages convey abstract thoughts better than other languages do. Some have more subtle expressions of time (tense). Some are better at combining action and actor.

Munzlinger

The study of language differences and their effects on culture and personality is a relatively new and unexplored field. You will have to turn to the anthropologists and linguists for more information.

Our point is that the individual unconsciously allows language to *shape* him, and sometimes the process handicaps individuality. Most of us know at least one person whose language and personality are made up almost entirely of the phrases and words of a particular group of people.

Before we go any further, let's look at the form of language, just to see what it is and to demonstrate its practical importance. We can begin with the silent language of two cartoons. What parts of the pictures communicate (are their language)? Consider space, light, tradition, position, and so on.

Two questions . . .

1. In each picture, what is communicated by the following:

   Facial expression
   Position (spatial arrangement)
   Dress
   Attitudes
   Setting
   Small detail

   2. Think about what is communicated by the complete picture: a laugh? Is that all?

These pictures may make you laugh (they should—they are jokes), but they also communicate a point of view and an idea and a personality. Try being one of the cartoonists. Speaking or writing as you feel he would, express his cartoon in one sentence. Try to convey his sense of what the whole picture was about—its message—also the tone, mood, and thought that might go with that message.

Now stop to identify the subject, verb, object, and modifiers of your sentence. Of course, you will be describing the sentence grammatically. You may even describe it as a kind of sentence form: compound, complex, or compound-complex.

These pictures, like your sentence, are deliberate arrangements of parts meant for whole communication. Suppose that you exchange the cartoon figures, putting the couple on the bench of the pipe organ and the man in tails on the island. The cartoons will change. If they are still funny, it will be for different reasons, and their meanings will change. Restate or rewrite your sentence defining the meaning of one of the cartoons as you now see it.

Finally, look at the original pictures as silent language and try working out a visual grammar. Identify the parts if you can—subjects, action-carriers, and modifiers. You will find that the pictures have form of their own. Just any form would not make them successful, however. The success of the cartoons will be measured by the way in which their particular form embodies meaning, the cartoonist's fresh sense of life.

The cartoons above provided examples of silent language. Then you followed up the cartoons with words and sentences to communicate something which had first happened as silent language. We were able to make logical sentences from pictures because the pictures and the sentences both were compositions. *A composition is a deliberate arrangement of things which communicate.*

While any given language has shapes that change slowly over centuries, individuals may work within that language to make their own original compositions, to form and project their own beings. Psychologists call this use of language *self-actualization,* making the self real.

Imagine someone who could not use any kind of language. He could not use signs, motions, or sounds. Someone who could not use *any* language would not use facial expressions, gestures, or any muscles. Or he would be as shapeless as a spirit—and he would be as unreal as a ghost.

Being real is dependent upon being known through language of some kind.

Although this book is concerned with writing, we would deny much of the material of the writer if we did not examine the function of silent language. Things we see or feel, which speak to us without language, we often want to write about later on. And sometimes our spoken ideas and our written doctrines can be reinforced by silent language. In practical affairs of everyday life, silent and spoken or written language are often interdependent. We see this below in Saul Alinsky's account of how labor organizers put together a "People's Organization" in the 1930's.

Saul D. Alinsky

Reveille for Radicals

. . . The organizer had already progressed to the point where he had secured the support of the three major parts of the labor movement: the American Federation of Labor, the Congress of Industrial Organizations, and the Railroad Brotherhood.

During the conference the organizer held with the leaders of these representative labor unions, the Negro problem suddenly loomed in the foreground and became a prime issue. It began when one of the Railroad Brotherhood leaders in discussing the arrangements for the mass meeting casually remarked, "And the Niggers will sit up in Nigger Heaven."

The organizer took strong exception to the principle of segregation and was informed by the representatives of the American Federation of Labor as well as the Railroad Brotherhood that this particular town was Jim Crow and as far as they were concerned Jim Crow was right—"After all, a Nigger is a Nigger." The union representatives then went on to point out how "even in our unions the Niggers have their place—and they keep it." The organizer reports the tactics used to solve the issue as well as the ensuing educational process.

"I turned to the C.I.O. leader and said, 'Well, how do you stand on this?' The C.I.O. leader began to hedge around with a lot of general remarks that it wasn't the policy of the C.I.O. to be Jim Crow but after all in a town located so far south they had to respect local traditions and a lot of stuff like that. I realized that I was facing a united front of all three organizations. The first tactic had to be a maneuver to split the ranks of these labor unions. With that in mind I turned to the C.I.O. leader and said, 'Well, now I understand that your constitution has a statement that reads something like this: "regardless of race, color, or creed." Is that right?' The C.I.O. leader began to say, 'Yes—but down south——' I interrupted with, 'Well, don't tell me about that; after all, we have no secrets around here and we aren't doing anything we have to keep under the table. As long as we're not doing anything to be ashamed about, let us make a public announcement of our policy. Now, I have three newspaper reporters outside—one from the *Herald*, one from the *Bugle*, and one from the *Press*. I'll call them in and you tell them.'

"The C.I.O. leader flushed, then muttered, 'Well, you don't have to call any newspapermen in. The C.I.O. has always stood against Jim Crow and that's where we stand.' The split had been accomplished.

From Saul D. Alinsky, *Reveille for Radicals*. Copyright 1946 by Saul D. Alinsky. Reprinted by permission of Random House, Inc.

"I followed through by addressing the A.F. of L. leaders. I began, 'The A.F. of L. is an independent organization and its policies are completely decided by itself—it has its own autonomy and whatever the C.I.O. wants to do is no business of the A.F. of L. Is that right?'

"The A.F. of L leader arose and belligerently said, 'That's right! If the C.I.O. wants to treat Negroes like white men that's their lookout, but by God, whatever the C.I.O. decides on doesn't mean a thing to us.'

"I repeated the same statement to the Railroad Brotherhood and they responded precisely as did the A.F. of L.

"Following these expressions of opinion from all three groups I played my ace-in-the-hole. I said, 'Well, now we're completely agreed that each union runs its own affairs. Since the C.I.O. says that they are against Jim Crow and since the A.F. of L. and the Railroad Brotherhood say that they are for Jim Crow and since this is a democracy, then there is only one thing to do. We'll split the auditorium in half; the C.I.O. will sit on one side with Negroes and whites and the A.F. of L. and the Railroad Brotherhood will sit on the other side and have all the Jim Crow and segregation that they want.'

"There was a momentary silence. The A.F. of L. and Railroad Brotherhood leaders exchanged uncomfortable glances. What was in their eyes was as clear as if it had been spoken. 'What a newspaper picture that would make! Black and white faces on the C.I.O. side of the auditorium and a solid wave of white faces on the Railroad Brotherhood and A.F. of L. side of the hall! What organizational propaganda that picture would serve the C.I.O. in enlisting Negroes into their membership!'

"After a few moments, the A.F. of L. leaders looked down at their hands and blurted, 'Aw, let's throw Jim Crow out the window all together —for *this* meeting, mind you.'

"Although this mass meeting, which would be the first one in this town in which there was no segregation, would be a dramatic step forward, nevertheless, the mass meeting was relatively unimportant compared to the speedly rationalization that followed my meeting with the labor leaders. Not one of these labor leaders would admit to himself that he had been tricked or maneuvered into a progressive position. That would be too much of a blow to their ego. They knew that they had been irrevocably committed to a non-segregation mass meeting. The rationalization process had begun to operate and, *my*, how those people educated themselves! For the next few days, labor leaders who had been bitterly Jim Crow all their lives came to me saying, 'I think we have done right by throwing over Jim Crow. What the hell, we're fighting for the four freedoms, aren't we?' or 'Well, if labor doesn't give the Nigger—excuse me— I mean the Negro a break, where in hell is he going to get it?'

"So it continued and grew—an action which had been taken purely because of tactical reasons. In the weeks following the mass meeting, classes, forums, and other educational programs on race relations were set up within these unions. All of this educational program found its origin in the rationalizing self-education that began when these labor leaders had to prove to themselves that they were right in opposing segregation and had decided to do so on the basis of morality rather than expediency."

In a People's Organization popular education is an exciting and dramatic process. Education instead of being distant and academic becomes a direct and intimate part of the personal lives, experiences, and activities of the people. Committee members find that they must become informed upon the field of activities of their committee; they later discover that in order to be capable of carrying out their own activities they must know about all those other problems and activities which are related to the committee's work. The committee that becomes interested in housing shortly finds itself involved in the fields of planning, health, race relations, and many other issues. Knowledge then becomes an arsenal of weapons in the battle against injustice and degradation. It is no longer learning for learning's sake, but learning for a real reason, a purpose. It ceases to be a luxury or something known under the vague, refined name of culture and becomes as essential as money in the bank, good health, good housing, or regular employment.

WHO SAYS WHAT IN WRITING?

Silent language has an everyday illustrative function; and as demonstrated in Saul Alinsky's writing, it is a vital tool in making belief known. But you cannot rely on silent language alone. Spoken and written words remain the most vital tools of communication. Try thinking without using words: think only in terms of your sense impressions. You will see that you must have more than the silent language of impressions to know your feelings and to make your feelings known.

The authors of this book assume that *who* you think you are is determined by your ability to look at yourself in language by talking to yourself about yourself. So that is the language we start with, the language of imagining, thinking, and writing.

Note the order of the verbals in that last sentence:

imagining, thinking, writing

This is the order we follow in this book. Effective communication is not simply the business or craft of putting words on paper in a form or style similar to something you have been told is good. The first demand of purposeful writing is that you have something to write—not always an answer, but always a wish or feeling or thought. In order to write effectively, you must first want to make something known, and behind the wish to make something known must be a wisher with a sense of *why he* wants to make something known.

Think for a moment about the choices open to you the next time you are assigned to write a paper—any paper in any course. Ask yourself what you want to make known:

That you

- will be satisfied with a "C" and that you have done just enough imitation of conventions in form and style to be labeled "C"?
- are a careless proofreader or that you won't bother to check spelling in a dictionary?
- need help in the mechanics of writing?
- have done your best to make sense of the assignment?
- don't care about the question?
- feel safer repeating what someone else said than thinking for yourself?

Whatever your subject—not just in courses this year but in writing you do for the rest of your life—you will not only demonstrate an approach to a job or to another person, but you will also reveal yourself, exactly as *Life* magazine photographs reveal *Life* and not *The Reader's Digest* or *Escapade* or *Esquire*.

Perhaps, then, that is where the next written assignment should begin, with you, questioning yourself. "Is there anybody there?" asked the Traveller, knocking on the moonlit door."

Those two lines are from Walter de la Mare's poem "The Listeners," and of course the Traveller knocks and shouts again, twice more, and gets no answer from the ghosts inside. The poem builds an eerie tension between the man who speaks and asserts his presence and the "phantom listeners" whose silence is the essence of their unreality.

Who you are is revealed by the words you use. Look at the following list; then describe the person who would use these words and phrases.

childhood and early adolescence

mature . . . mentally developed

love to capacity

person-to-person relationship

basis of communication

height of development

live life to its fullest

slowly advance to maturity

Now, here is the student theme in which the phrases appeared. Try to decide whether the words and phrases were indicative of the kind of person the writer is or wants to be. If not, why did she use them?

WHY I SHOULD NOT BE KILLED

An essential part of life is loving. During late childhood and early adolescence one encounters a series of "crushes?" and considers these love. Yet, only when one is mature, that is mentally developed, one is able to actually love to capacity. There must exist between two people, a person-to-person relationship. A basis of communication must be established.

Since I have not yet achieved this height of development, I am not yet capable of giving myself to anyone. Because I have not had time to live my life to its fullest, I should not die. In a few more years I will slowly advance to maturity and will be able to give completely of myself to someone. I should not be killed and I should not die until after I have fully lived.

Beth Cohan

RALLY 'ROUND THE FLAG, BOYS

Before reading the next theme make a list of the "ringing" words and phrases you often hear associated with student government in high school or college. What are some of the terms used in describing student–faculty problems? Decide whether those words and phrases (or similar ones used in this theme) really refer to any concrete, knowable events and situations. If they do, why didn't the writer use the concrete material? Why does anyone avoid concrete material in favor of abstraction that could be applied to a vast number of people instead of to one individual and his life?

WHAT IS UNIQUE ABOUT ME?

My ability and desire to carry out and participate in school government activities is what makes me unique. In high school I was a member of our student government, and managed to promote and carry out many activities within our school. I have the ability to organize committees and get them started toward accomplishing our goals. Last year I organized and started an honor system in our school, which was very successful and is still in effect this year.

I also took over the office of president of our senior class in the middle of the year, and still accomplished all the goals of our class. I organized several groups to plan and run our graduation exercises last year. I was able to keep these groups working hard, and for the first time in twenty years our graduation was completely organized and carried out by the student government and class officers.

As a freshman at the university I have become a member of the student government and part of a group in charge of arranging for speakers at the university.

Student government is essential to any school. It helps to carry out many activities that the faculty overlooks or can't accomplish alone. It contributes to a better working relationship between students and faculty in accomplishing goals of common interest by giving students a means to express their opinions and viewpoints. I feel that showing an interest in and being able to help fulfill the important activities of student government organizations gives me a unique quality that isn't common to everyone.

Kenneth Bolick

UP
TIGHT

Like many minority groups, students and all young people are constantly victimized by generalizations and clichés. Adults often seem to think they can protect themselves by persuading or forcing younger people to accept their stereotypes of youth. The writer of the following theme begins with that problem. Much of the criticism of youth, he says, is the result of thinking distorted by cliché, abstraction, and generalization, and he lashes out at such thinking, at those who lean on it and seek to impress it on their children.

Read this paper and ask yourself to what extent the writer's own attack is dependent upon, and limited by, the sort of language he condemns. Ask yourself whether the writer seems to have been overcome by his own feelings.

I Am Unique

Everyday we read about the "younger generation" or "the young people of today" in every type of publication. It is amazing how many broad conclusions are made about us. We are stereotyped as the rebellious youth who protest wars and advocate free love. We are purported to be more intelligent but only in respect to academics and not the world and people about us. We are supposedly a bunch of "crazy damn teen-agers." I feel in some ways I fit the above description and vary greatly in others. I feel that a description of myself will reveal that uniqueness which I possess as an individual and also illuminate some of the true feelings of young people today.

I am tired, tired of a world that is constantly in a state of conflict because no one knows what truth is. I know what I would like done and said toward seeking the truth, but no one will listen because I'm too young. I hate middle-class America with its vicariously accepted mores and ethics which you hear much about and see little of. I am neither shocked nor dismayed by homosexuality, pre-marital sex, and/or the decline of Christianity. All of these are products of the lack of truth. The biggest and most truthless group is middle-class America.

I played a violin when I was eight and continued until I was fifteen. Every day I was reminded that normal boys (whatever in hell they are) do not play violin. Normal boys play trumpet very poorly and hate girls in the third grade. I went steady in the third grade. Middle class America was my adversary, and I couldn't fight it so I tried to appease it. I left my violin for a French horn, a guitar, and a combo. I played football, and I dated girls to see how much I could get. I still do. I'm playing their game.

I'm sitting in the main stream of narrow-minded, middle-class America, and yet I see their folly and how I gave up *myself* for lies. I am unique, for I am a fool.

Jeff Moe

Some questions . . .

First, about Jeff Moe's paper:

1. Why does he put some phrases in quotation marks?

2. Are there other phrases which are in fact like the ones in quotation marks?

3. If so, does his inconsistency suggest that he thinks about "middle-class America" in the same way he feels it thinks about him?

4. How much of the paper is written in a language which you think that Jeff Moe, in retrospect, would want to have you examine in making judgments about him as the writer?

5. What does Jeff Moe mean by *unique*? Would his definition be acceptable to most people?

Second, about you:

1. Do you think that in the world around you there are visible products of the thinking Jeff Moe describes and reveals?

2. In your own writing, would you put quotation marks around any or all of these phrases: *Bourgeois taste, middle-class America, decline of Christianity, younger generation, stodgy professor, school spirit, the American Way?*

3. Try defining some of these phrases in terms of concrete actions or situations. Can you find what the phrases mean to *you*? If so, can you use them without quotation marks in your writing?

4. Despite the uncertainty of a phrase like "school spirit," what are some of the reasons you might want to identify yourself with it?

An exercise . . .

First, revise Jeff Moe's paper by striking out the language that seems to have been borrowed from the very adult, "middle-class America" he is attacking.

Second, try making the paper your own by rewriting it but not by writing a new paper from the beginning. Substitute a language of your own for that which is someone else's in his paper, and reshape the paragraphs so that form helps to make feeling understood.

WHAT YOU SAY

On the next page is another picture. Look it over.

In looking at the picture, whether you wanted to use words or not, you probably found some common terms and phrases coming quickly to mind. A first response often comes in language which reveals not simply something about our unconscious but also something about unconscious personal reliance on stereotypes. In this example, the silent language of the picture is employed to help you find a personal meaning in a succession of labels: "Mitzi Gaynor—glamorous motion picture star," "the tan-ables," "a better tan," "a paleface." Thus the sales of cosmetics to men and women often depend not on products themselves but on ideas. The customer does not buy a chemical, he buys an idea of himself. He buys a metaphor to promise himself a nicer, more acceptable self.

When thinking about ourselves, we often do the same thing we did when looking at the picture: we seize words which label something we want to be, feel we ought to be, or are comfortable thinking about. What we often do is let something unlike us stand for us because we disguise our private responses by "buying" other people's vocabularies. In times of civil disorder, we find a great "buying" of a language of public agreement: *patriot, law and order, anti-communist, Black Power, soul brother.* Yet in many an instance, the use of such language reveals someone who is simply putting up a front— "buying" a face.

Let's conclude with a look at how you use the language.

MITZI GAYNOR—glamorous motion picture star

"Coppertone
gives you a better tan"

C'mon, join the tan-ables! Get the fastest tan possible with maximum sunburn protection. That darker, deeper tan...skin that looks and feels satiny smooth, soft. Let Coppertone give you a better tan! More people rely on its exclusive moisturizing-tanning formula than any other suntan product in the world!

Tan, don't burn, use Coppertone.

Coppertone, Shade and Royal Blend are reg. TM's of Plough, Inc. Also available in Canada.

Assignment . . .

1. List your ten favorite words or phrases for describing people. (Think of the words you would use most readily for people you like or dislike.)

   Now list ten words or phrases for describing things which might be owned by people whom you had in mind above.

13

Do the lists overlap? If they do, try finding out why
by determining exactly what the words mean to
you.

> a) Make a list of products you might associate with
>   your favorite words.

b) Make a list of perceptions—of sense feelings—
you would associate with the words.

> Which is more descriptive of your attitude, the
> product or the sense perception?

2. Make a list of "political" words and phrases
   which seem to you to be in the air now.

> Now make a list of people you know well who can
> be clearly classified under one of your "political"
> phrases.

Finally, make a list of people you do not know,
but of whom you have heard or read, and who also
can be classified under one of your "political"
phrases. Is one list longer than the others? Why?

> 3. Define the word *abstraction*. Don't look up
>   the definition in a dictionary. Study the lists which
>   you have made and consider how they might give
>   you the basis for a definition of abstraction. Think
>   back over the chapter. Based on your experience in
>   the past and your present experience with this
>   chapter, what is an abstraction and how does it
>   come into being?

4. Think about how you might define an abstraction without writing a "theme." Create a
   demonstration of an abstraction.

COMMENTARY

Perhaps after looking at the complexity of writing and language you could
be thinking it is all nonsense and that man has gotten along all right for centuries without this kind of analysis and criticism. In the following excerpt,
S. I. Hayakawa (writing as a semanticist, not college president) gives one
view of where all users of language stand today—on the edge of a new
phase in human communication. Who is behind, straddling, or ahead of the
change?

S. I. Hayakawa

from Communications
and Human Community

Next, then, there is the latest stage in the development of human co-operation and communication, which I shall call *The Stage of Organization around Shared Perceptions.* This is perhaps the greatest advance of all in the history of human communication. The basic idea of this new stage was clearly understood to many of the ancient Greeks.

Let me present a communication characteristic of the stage of shared perceptions, quoted from Strato, one of Aristotle's successors in the head-ship of the Lyceum at Athens, who occupied that position from 287 to 269 B.C.:

We must first correct a popular illusion. It must be clearly grasped that vessels which are generally believed to be empty are not really empty but are full of air. Now air, in the opinion of the natural philosophers, consists of minute particles of matter for the most part invisible to us. . . . To prove this make the following experiment. Take a seemingly empty vessel. Turn it upside-down, taking care to keep it vertical, and plunge it into a dish of water. Even if you depress it until it is completely covered no water will enter. This proves that air is a material thing which prevents the water entering the vessel because it has previously occupied all the available space. . . . If . . . you lift the vessel vertically out of the water and turn it up and examine it you will see that the interior of the vessel has remained perfectly dry. This constitutes the demonstration that air is a bodily substance.[5]

What is important to notice in Strato's method of communication is that, instead of saying, "Listen, friend, since I acknowledge the same god as you, you know that you can believe me when I say that air is a material substance," he says, "You don't have to take my word for it; you can see for yourself." As Benjamin Farrington says, in a scientific statement "a confirmatory action is demanded of the listener, a repetition of the experience." Such a statement is what we call in semantics "operational," in that it describes an operation the listener can perform to see for him-self whether or not it is true. No doubt people had been making operational statements for thousands of years before Strato came along, but

[5]Benjamin Farrington, *Greek Science II* (Harmondsworth, Middlesex: Penguin Books, 1949), p. 32.

Reprinted by permission from *ETC.: A Review of General Semantics*, XVI, No. 1. Copyright 1958 by the International Society for General Semantics.

what is important in the Greek scientists, including Aristotle in those writings in which he writes as a scientist, is the fact that they tried *systematically* to make publicly confirmable, and only publicly confirmable, statements about selected areas of experience in order to organize knowledge and make it more readily communicable and usable. These systematic attempts on the part of the ancient Greeks are the foundations of Western science.[6] As we shall see later, Strato and Theophrastus and others like them were 1500 years or more before their time, but without their contributions the scientists of the early Renaissance would have had even less intellectual capital with which to start.

The significant thing about Strato's way of communicating from our point of view is that it transcends local or regional loyalties and makes intercultural communication possible. In other words, what Strato says about air makes equal sense whether addressed to Greeks, Christians, Mohammedans, Hindus, or Australian aborigines. Anybody anywhere who has access to a jug and some water can see for himself whether or not Strato is right. And Strato's example of scientific communication is still, in principle, scientific communication today. The scientist today says, "If you will use the same language I use, perform the operations I have performed, and compute your results by the same mathematical system with which I compute, you will come to the same conclusions I came to. If you do not, let us compare what we did, step by step, and find out what misunderstanding of terms, what differences in the conditions of the experiment, what errors on your part or mine, caused the difference in the results. Then, when we have agreed on our conclusions, let us keep in communication with each other and proceed to other experiments. In this way you and I can help each other to know more and more about the world."

Now the great revolution implied in the transition from the Stage of the Master Symbol to the Stage of Shared Perceptions is that while in the former, agreements at high levels of abstraction (about God, about the Transmigration of Souls, about the Divine Right of Kings, etc.) were the basis of agreements at lower levels of abstraction, in the latter the reverse is the case. In order to share perceptions, we have to agree about obvious and even trivial things before agreeing about more general things. We have to collect verifiable observations about a variety of foods and diets and their effects on thousands of individuals before we can make a general statement about nutrition, and even then, we leave our general statement open to revision in the light of later observation. Systematic agreement about the properties of wood, water, metals, air, gases, has to be established before we can talk about matter in general. True enough,

---

[6]For an insight into some of the *linguistic* reasons for Greek (and Western European) achievements into the systematization of knowledge, the reader is referred to the fascinating and provocative article by Richard Dettering, "What Phonetic Writing Did to Meaning," *ETC.*, XII (1955), 121–136.

science sometimes makes a long extrapolation beyond the confirmable facts, as in the case of the theory of evolution, but that extrapolation is not accepted into the body of science until many more facts are adduced in its support. *Science then, proceeds from agreements at lower levels of abstraction, step by step, to higher levels.*

The caution and the so-called "objectivity" with which science proceeds, far from indicating the amorality of science, indicates its profound sense of social responsibility. The true scientist is so responsible to the rest of human society, including people of nationalities and religions different from his own, that he is unwilling to go beyond what *anybody* similarly trained in observation can confirm. If the scientist holds in check his preference of monogamy over polygamy, of private enterprise over collectivism, of his own national culture over other cultures, he does so not because he is indifferent to these issues, but because he feels that these are subjects about which publicly confirmable statements cannot *yet* be made, and because he wants above all, as a responsible communicator, to maintain the optimum conditions of communication with everybody, including those who may have different preferences as regards marriage customs, economic systems, or patriotic loyalties. He knows that to intrude the preferences of his own culture into his scientific discourse is to cut off his usefulness as a communicator to some segment of humanity. Does this mean that the scientist will forever refrain from making statements about disputed points of conduct or of social organization? Indeed it does not. It means merely that he is waiting until his statements about such matters can be put in confirmable form. Actually, scientists in the psychological and social sciences have already gone quite far in their attempts to throw light on problems of conduct and public affairs formerly settled by habit, intuition, or dogma; for example, in such areas as child care, psychology, psychiatry, criminology, and industrial management, the storehouse of confirmable and confirmed statements is steadily being added to.

The act of communication, says Anatol Rapoport in *Operational Philosophy* (New York: Harper, 1953) is the basic moral act. The morality of the tribal stage insists that by regular participation in appropriate rituals at a common meeting place, you maintain communication and cooperation with all the fellow-members of your tribe.[7] The Morality of the Stage of Master Symbols insists that, by the acknowledgment of more abstract symbols accepted in common by thousands or even millions who share those symbols with you, you maintain communication and cooperation with all your co-religionists. The morality of the Stage of Shared Perceptions insists that you try to maintain communication and cooperation with everybody, by basing your communications on the *similarities in human nervous systems* and the *similarities of the experi-*

---

[7]"Go to church this Sunday!"

ence of those nervous systems in their encounters with the observable world. One begins with the sharing of perceptions about commonplace or even obvious things, so that, with the establishment of myriads of little agreements, larger and larger agreements become possible.[8]

Each of the three stages is moral, in that each is a method of establishing and ensuring cooperation. Each requires the foregoing of egotistic drives in the interests of the larger group. For man is a social creature, which means that he is an incurably moral creature, finding his fulfilment only as he relates meaningfully and is in communication with society.

Today we are largely in transition from concepts of morality inherited from the Stage of Master Symbols to newer concepts of morality and social responsibility implicit in the Stage of Shared Perceptions. This means, then, that the vast struggles going on in the world today are incorrectly thought of if they are described as the struggle of moral people (we) versus immoral people (they)—or, as the children phrase it from watching Westerns on television, the good guys versus the bad guys. What is struggling to emerge out of the great moralities of the Stage of Master Symbols, no longer adequate as principles of human organization in a world suddenly made tiny by technological advances in transportation and communication, is the even more general and all-embracing morality of the Stage of Shared Perceptions.

The emergence of this new morality is slow, because we are all struggling under the weight of sackloads of the holy soil of Israel, unable, like Naaman, to understand that it is possible to love and to pray without them.

---

[8]For the present, I am restricting myself to scientific communication as an example of communication through the sharing of perceptions. I plan to discuss the sharing of perceptions through art, literature, games, and other activities in later sections of this paper to be published in subsequent issues of *ETC*.

Gary Snyder

Milton by Firelight

(Piute Creek, August 1955)

'O hell, what do mine eyes with grief behold?'
Working with an old
Singlejack miner, who can sense
The vein and cleavage
In the very guts of rock, can
Blast granite, build
Switchbacks that last for years
Under the beat of snow, thaw, mule-hooves.
What use, Milton, a silly story
Of our lost general parents, eaters of fruit?

The Indian, the Chainsaw boy,
And a string of six mules
Came riding down to camp
Hungry for tomatoes and green apples.
Sleeping in saddle-blankets
Under a bright night-sky
Han River slantwise by morning.
Jays squall
Coffee boils

In ten thousand years the Sierras
Will be dry and dead, home of the scorpion.
Ice-scratched slabs and bent trees.
No paradise, no fall,
Only the weathering land
The wheeling sky,
Man, with his Satan
Scouring the chaos of the mind.
Oh, Hell!

Fire down
Too dark to read, miles from a road
The bell-mare clangs in the meadow
That packed dirt for a fill-in
Scrambling through loose rocks
On an old trail
All of a summer's day.

Piute Creek

One granite ridge
A tree, would be enough
Or even a rock, a small creek,
A bark-shred in a pool.
Hill beyond hill, folded and twisted
Tough trees crammed
In thin stone fractures
A huge moon on it all, is too much.
The mind wanders. A million
Summers, night air still and the rocks
Warm. Sky over endless mountains.
All the junk that goes with being human
Drops away, hard rock wavers
Even the heavy present seems to fail
This bubble of a heart.
Words and books
Like a small creek off a high ledge
Gone in the dry air.
A clear, attentive mind
Has no meaning but that
Which sees is truly seen.
No one loves rock, yet we are here.
Night chills. A flick
In the moonlight
Slips into Juniper shadow:
Back there unseen
Cold proud eyes
Of Cougar or Coyote
Watch me rise and go.

Gary Snyder, "Milton by Firelight" and "Piute Creek" from *Riprap and Cold Mountain* poems. © 1965 Four Seasons Foundation.

"You may be a recording, baby. But you're all heart."

2

Who nobody is

At one time or another, almost all of us complain of being made into nobodies—names and numbers lost among millions of names and numbers: banks know us as account numbers; universities, as ID numbers; draft boards, as classification numbers. Newspapers carried a story about a young man who even had legally changed his name to Number, so that he could be distinguished as Mr. Number.

We cannot prevent ourselves from being classified by others—Mr. Number will still remain a number. In fact, many persons go a step further and argue that in addition to being classified, all of us continually classify ourselves, and that we should do so. Ben Franklin once sought "moral perfection"—his phrase—by making up a classified list of virtues. He concluded that all moral behavior fell under one of thirteen headings, and he set out to practice one virtue a week for thirteen weeks, hoping thus to master a complete code of moral appearance for himself. He failed. Remarking finally that the task was hopeless from the start, he said that if he had mastered the thirteenth virtue, humility, he could probably have been proud of his humility. Having failed to classify himself Franklin is respected today for his singularity.

It might also be possible to make a list of thirteen or more rules for moral perfection in language and hence arrive at a perfectly clean and standard English. Such a language, however, like Franklin's perfect virtue, would deny the nature of its users. It would be a form of anonymity.

Consider these generalities:

1. Most abstractions and clichés are meaningful because so many people use them.

2. Even if there are a lot of people, I'm still myself—one in a million. That's all I need to know.

3. I'd rather have a number than a name. I like anonymity and the security of being a part of the mass mind.

4. Language doesn't mean much to me and has no relation to how I think about myself as an individual. I can use any convenient language, and my mind will show itself in other ways.

5. The language I use creates an image of me which helps me get along, but it is not the true me.

6. Although I avoid clichés and abstractions, I do imitate the language of people I want to be like: Salinger, Mailer, Hemingway, Vonnegut, Bradbury.

7. I hate myself and therefore must hide from myself behind a mask of language.

An exercise . . .

First. Some of the generalities in this list may make sense to you in explaining your own ways of using the language. Or are they generalities you could ascribe to someone else whom you might describe as a "nobody"?

Make a list of the clichés and abstractions a nobody might use, or write a "nobody" or "nothing" paragraph. What you may see is that a nobody or nothing is visible: he has a vocabulary and a way of acting which you may recognize not as his but as his front, hence as nobody, really.

Second. Some representations of cars and people follow. They date back to the thirties and forties. Ask yourself first whether you see individuals or stereotypes in the illustrations. Then ask yourself whether the ads are out of date or whether they

are like advertising you still see. Is it possible for
this ad form to have become a stereotype or cliché
without any real meaning for real people? If so,
you may argue that the ads use Nobody's language
—both silent and written—to appeal to nobodies.
Analyze both the copy and the pictures for style
and content.

"The picture is so complete"

New Perfected Hydraulic Brakes—*the safest and smoothest ever developed.* . . . . Solid Steel one-piece Turret
Top—*a crown of beauty, a fortress of safety.* . . . . Improved Gliding Knee-Action Ride*—*the smoothest, safest
ride of all.* . . . . Genuine Fisher No Draft Ventilation *in new Turret Top Bodies*—*the most beautiful and comfortable bodies ever
created for a low-priced car.* . . . . High-Compression Valve-in-Head Engine—*the most economical of all fine power plants.* . . . .
Shockproof Steering*—*making driving easier and safer than ever before.* . . . . All these features at Chevrolet's low prices.

CHEVROLET MOTOR COMPANY, DETROIT, MICHIGAN

Available in Master De Luxe models only. Knee-Action, $20 additional

CHEVROLET
A GENERAL MOTORS VALUE

The only complete low-priced car

FOUR PEOPLE?

A person has to be someone, but he may not be a "somebody." Of the following selections, the first three center on machines or things, language, and identity in examining the desire to be "somebody." In reading them, keep in mind the argument that a nobody *is* identifiable: he may be recognized, appealed to, and finally defeated or outwitted by his own language. The fourth selection deals plainly with the ways in which language wrongly used may make a pompous nobody out of someone.

John Keats

The Call of the
Open Road

All advertisements show automobiles in unusual circumstances. They depict smiling, handsome people in evening clothes arriving in glittering hardtops beneath the porte-cocheres of expensive tropical saloons. A polished convertible, top down, filled with laughing young people in yachting costumes, whispers along an idealized shoreline. A ruggedly healthy Mom, Pop, Sis and Buzz smile the miles away as their strangely dustless station wagon shisks over the Rockies. Sometimes, automobiles strangely shine on pedestals; sometimes they slip through astral voids like comets. None of the advertisements show you and me in the automobile as most of us know it—that is, wedged in a fuming line of commuter traffic at 8:30 A.M., or locked in an even worse outbound line at 6 P.M.

A manufacturer, of course, would commit economic hara-kiri if he were to try to sell us a car on truthful grounds, for how could he ask anyone to pay $4,500 for a three-hundred-horsepower contraption on grounds that it would be used only two hours a day for 240 working days a year, and would at all other times—except briefly, on vacations—be parked in an expensive parking lot or sit depreciating at a curb? Would you buy such a car if it were truthfully put to you that the thing would cost you more than $9 an hour to use? No manufacturer in his right mind would plead with you to buy a luggage compartment only slightly smaller than

Delaware in order that you could use part of this space just twice a year. Manufacturers know very well that the American automobile is not primarily a means of transportation and that it cannot be sold as such. Therefore, their advertisements invariably portray the automobile as A Flying Carpet—as a thing to sweep us off to ineffable lotus lands—and this, we discover, in the greatest lie of all. Yet, we cannot plead surprise, because—as a friend remarked—if we now suspect that our automobiles are overblown, overpriced monstrosities built by oafs for thieves to sell to mental defectives, it is only logical to expect that there is not much point in driving them, and that any place an automobile can go probably is not worth visiting. Nevertheless, the advertisements have a certain appeal, because the dream they represent once had substance. There was a time in man's memory when travel was exciting.

It is difficult to say just when the last shred of fun disappeared from the American highway. Some people think it was in 1927, when Henry Ford stopped making the Model T, but other authorities put the date in the late 1930s when the first national restaurant chains spread like plague. Speculation is idle, because we must accept things as they are, and there is no question today but that family travel in America is apt to be one of life's more crashing bores. Let me wipe off the lens a bit for a quick look at two generations of the Foresight family:

Early in the 19th century, Abel Foresight, his wife, Hope, and their children, Prudence, Faith and Jonah, set out from Morgantown, Pennsylvania, in a wagon. They chopped through forests, crept over mountains, forded floods, shot their suppers, struggled with savages, and trusted in God and in their strength to cross an unknown continent. They were more than a year en route, but the Foresight family arrived in California with the look of eagles in their eyes. Theirs was the age of travel adventure.

In the summer of 1958, Roger Foresight followed the path of his longfathers across his native land.

"We take the car it's cheaper," he told his wife June, in the curious English of his day. "You don't see the country you take the train or fly."

Whereupon, Roger gripped the Deep-Dish Command Wheel of his twenty-foot-long Flite-Flo Hacienda Wagon, stirred the Jet-Boom Eight's Power-Plus into life, pressed a master button that wound up all the Saf-T-Tint windows, adjusted the Koolaire to a desired temperature, pushed another button to bring the Flote-Fome seat to its proper level and distance, pressed yet another to cut the Glyde-Ryde Dynamatic Turbomission, and swung away from his Cape Cod Tri-Level's Kar Porte to begin three thousand miles of driving pleasure.

A week later, the Foresights arrived on the opposite coast a little tired from sitting so long on foam rubber, but otherwise they were quite the same people who had left home. There was still that look of vague disappointment in their eyes, because Roger and June Foresight dwell in the tasteless, or Pablum, stage of family travel.

Sinclair Lewis

You Know How
Relatives Are

Well, by golly, it's good to be back. How'd everything go, Mame? Say, how's your brake been acting? That's fine.

Huh? Yuh, sure, I'm fairly certain Walt'll make the loan. But you know how relatives are. I could see he was crazy to make a loan on security like I can give him, but he tried to pretend like he was holding off, and I had to sit around a whole evening listening to his wife and him chewing the rag.

God, how that woman does talk, and say, Walt ain't much better. He insisted on telling me all about a fishing trip he'd made, and of course I wasn't interested—

And curious—say, I never did run into anybody as inquisitive as Walt is, but you know how relatives are. My God, the questions he asked and the hints he threw out! He wanted to know whether you and I ever scrapped or not—

Well, just take an example. I happened to mention Jackie, and he says, "Does Mame allow you to keep him in the house?"

Well, I just looked at him, and I said, kind of cold, "Mame and I have both agreed that the house is no place for a dog, for his own sake, and that he's much better off where he is, out in a doghouse by the garage."

And one thing almost got my goat. He said, "Say, on all these trips you make to New York, haven't you ever picked up a nice little piece of fluff?"

Well, I just looked at him, quietly, and I said, "Walt," I said, "I never could see the necessity for a man that's married to the finest little woman God ever made to even *look* at any other woman. A fellow like that," I said, "he naturally wants to keep all that's finest in him for the one woman who has consented to share his fortunes and keep him happy."

And you might remember that I told Walt that, too—here the way you hint around sometimes and wonder if I don't go taking girls out to dinner when I'm in New York.

And when you consider what I told Walt about Jackie, I'm damned

From Sinclair Lewis, *The Man Who Knew Coolidge.* Copyright 1928 by Harcourt, Brace & World, Inc. Renewed 1956 by Michael Lewis. Reprinted by permission of the publishers.

if I can see any reason why just *once* in a while you can't shut that cat in the kitchen and allow Jackie in the house. But what I'm getting at: I wish you could have listened in and heard me when I was talking to Walt about you. If you heard *some* men gassing about their wives—

But let that pass. I'll just tell you briefly about the trip.

I caught the train all right, with three good minutes to spare, and I had my dinner on the diner—it wasn't such a bad dinner—I remember I had vegetable soup and fried chicken and fried potatoes and corn and a wedge of apple pie with whipped cream on it—say, I wish you could get that Lithuanian to stir her stumps and whip some cream for us once in a while—my God, what does that girl think we're paying her sixty-five good dollars a month for!—and then I went up in the club car and sat down to smoke a cigar, and I got to talking to a gentleman, and he'd been reading a book about "Microbe Hunters," and he told me a lot about germs and bacteria that was very interesting.

Did you know that bacteria multiply at the rate of—I think it's ten thousand an hour—no, a million an hour it is, if I remember; anyway, at a rate of speed that would simply surprise you, and that, you see, explains about a lot of diseases.

And I got to talking to this gentleman, seems he was a lawyer, and he just happened to mention that he came from Brainerd, Minnesota, and I asked him if he happened to know Alec Duplex, of Saint Cloud, Minnesota—you remember the gentleman that we met in California—and say, come to find out, this gentleman was a second cousin of Alec's! Can you beat it!

"Well sir," I says to him, "the world's a pretty small place after all, isn't it!"

Well, along about nine o'clock I thought I'd turn in and try to get a good night's sleep—though it's a funny thing about me; as I may have told you, first night on a sleeper I can't hardly sleep at all; but I thought I'd turn in and try it, and come to find out, the porter had my bed all made up and so I crawled in between the sheets—

But I won't go into details of the trip—there was nothing of especial interest except this remarkable coincidence about this gentleman, a Mr. McLough his name was, that was a cousin of Alec Duplex's, but say, there was one thing:

At breakfast in the morning, I thought I'd try some buckwheat cakes, and I said to the waiter, "I think I'll have some buckwheat cakes," I said. "And syrup."

"Sorry, sir, we ain't got any buckwheat cakes this morning," he says.

"You haven't got any buckwheat cakes?" I says.

"No sir, there ain't any buckwheat cakes on the menu this morning," he says, "but we got corn cakes."

"Well," I says to him, "if you haven't got any buckwheat cakes—"

Max Shulman

Love Is a Fallacy

Cool was I and logical. Keen, calculating, perspicacious, acute and astute—I was all of these. My brain was as powerful as a dynamo, as precise as a chemist's scales, as penetrating as a scalpel. And—think of it!—I was only eighteen.

It is not often that one so young has such a giant intellect. Take, for example, Petey Burch, my roommate at the University of Minnesota. Same age, same background, but dumb as an ox. A nice enough fellow, you understand, but nothing upstairs. Emotional type. Unstable. Impressionable. Worst of all, a faddist. Fads, I submit, are the very negation of reason. To be swept up in every new craze that comes along, to surrender yourself to idiocy just because everybody else is doing it—this, to me, is the acme of mindlessness. Not, however, to Petey.

One afternoon I found Petey lying on his bed with an expression of such distress on his face that I immediately diagnosed appendicitis. "Don't move," I said. "Don't take a laxative. I'll get a doctor."

"Raccoon," he mumbled thickly.

"Raccoon?" I said, pausing in my flight.

"I want a raccoon coat," he wailed.

I perceived that his trouble was not physical, but mental. "Why do you want a raccoon coat?"

"I should have known it," he cried, pounding his temples. "I should have known they'd come back when the Charleston came back. Like a fool I spent all my money for textbooks, and now I can't get a raccoon coat."

"Can you mean," I said incredulously, "that people are actually wearing raccoon coats again?"

"All the Big Men on Campus are wearing them. Where've you been?"

"In the library," I said, naming a place not frequented by Big Men on Campus.

He leaped from the bed and paced the room. "I've got to have a raccoon coat," he said passionately. "I've got to!"

"Petey, why? Look at it rationally. Raccoon coats are unsanitary. They shed. They smell bad. They weigh too much. They're unsightly. They—"

"You don't understand," he interrupted impatiently. "It's the thing to do. Don't you want to be in the swim?"

"No," I said truthfully.

"Well, I do," he declared. "I'd give anything for a raccoon coat. Anything!"

My brain, that precision instrument, slipped into high gear. "Anything?" I asked, looking at him narrowly.

"Anything," he affirmed in ringing tones.

I stroked my chin thoughtfully. It so happened that I knew where to get my hands on a raccoon coat. My father had had one in his undergraduate days; it lay now in a trunk in the attic back home. It also happened that Petey had something I wanted. He didn't *have* it exactly, but at least he had first rights on it. I refer to his girl, Polly Espy.

I had long coveted Polly Espy. Let me emphasize that my desire for this young woman was not emotional in nature. She was, to be sure, a girl who excited the emotions, but I was not one to let my heart rule my head. I wanted Polly for a shrewdly calculated, entirely cerebral reason.

I was a freshman in law school. In a few years I would be out in practice. I was well aware of the importance of the right kind of wife in furthering a lawyer's career. The successful lawyers I had observed were, almost without exception, married to beautiful, gracious, intelligent women. With one omission, Polly fitted these specifications perfectly.

Beautiful she was. She was not yet of pin-up proportions, but I felt sure that time would supply the lack. She already had the makings.

Gracious she was. By gracious I mean full of graces. She had an erectness of carriage, an ease of bearing, a poise that clearly indicated the best of breeding. At table her manners were exquisite. I had seen her at the Kozy Kampus Korner eating the specialty of the house—a sandwich that contained scraps of pot roast, gravy, chopped nuts, and a dipper of sauerkraut—without even getting her fingers moist.

Intelligent she was not. In fact, she veered in the opposite direction. But I believed that under my guidance she would smarten up. At any rate, it was worth a try. It is, after all, easier to make a beautiful dumb girl smart than to make an ugly smart girl beautiful.

"Petey," I said, "are you in love with Polly Espy?"

"I think she's a keen kid," he replied, "but I don't know if you'd call it love. Why?"

"Do you," I asked "have any kind of formal arrangement with her? I mean are you going steady or anything like that?"

"No. We see each other quite a bit, but we both have other dates. Why?"

"Is there," I asked, "any other man for whom she has a particular fondness?"

"Not that I know of. Why?"

I nodded with satisfaction. "In other words, if you were out of the picture, the field would be open. Is that right?"

"I guess so. What are you getting at?"

"Nothing, nothing," I said innocently, and took my suitcase out of the closet.

"Where are you going?" asked Petey.

"Home for the weekend." I threw a few things into the bag.

"Listen," he said, clutching my arm eagerly, "while you're home, you couldn't get some money from your old man, could you, and lend it to me so I can buy a raccoon coat?"

"I may do better than that," I said with a mysterious wink and closed my bag and left.

"Look," I said to Petey when I got back Monday morning. I threw open the suitcase and revealed the huge, hairy, gamy object that my father had worn in his Stutz Bearcat in 1925.

"Holy Toledo!" said Petey reverently. He plunged his hands into the raccoon coat and then his face. "Holy Toledo!" he repeated fifteen or twenty times.

"Would you like it?" I asked.

"Oh yes!" he cried, clutching the greasy pelt to him. Then a canny look came into his eyes. "What do you want for it?"

"Your girl," I said, mincing no words.

"Polly?" he said in a horrified whisper. "You want Polly?"

"That's right."

He flung the coat from him. "Never," he said stoutly.

I shrugged. "Okay. If you don't want to be in the swim, I guess it's your business."

I sat down in a chair and pretended to read a book, but out of the corner of my eye I kept watching Petey. He was a torn man. First he looked at the coat with the expression of a waif at a bakery window. Then he turned away and set his jaw resolutely. Then he looked back at the coat, with even more longing in his face. Then he turned away, but with not so much resolution this time. Back and forth his head swiveled, desire waxing, resolution waning. Finally he didn't turn away at all; he just stood and stared with mad lust at the coat.

"It isn't as though I was in love with Polly," he said thickly. "Or going steady or anything like that."

"That's right," I murmured.

"What's Polly to me, or me to Polly?"

"Not a thing," said I.

"It's just been a casual kick—just a few laughs, that's all."

"Try on the coat," said I.

He complied. The coat bunched high over his ears and dropped all the way down to his shoe tops. He looked like a mound of dead raccoons. "Fits fine," he said happily.

I rose from my chair. "Is it a deal?" I asked, extending my hand.

He swallowed. "It's a deal," he said and shook my hand.

I had my first date with Polly the following evening. This was in the nature of a survey; I wanted to find out just how much work I had to do to get her mind up to the standard I required. I took her first to dinner. "Gee, that was a delish dinner," she said as we left the restaurant. Then I took her to a movie. "Gee, that was a marvy movie," she said as we left the theater. And then I took her home. "Gee, I had a sensaysh time," she said as she bade me good night.

I went back to my room with a heavy heart. I had gravely underestimated the size of my task. This girl's lack of information was terrifying. Nor would it be enough merely to supply her with information. First she had to be taught to *think*. This loomed as a project of no small dimensions, and at first I was tempted to give her back to Petey. But then I got to thinking about her abundant physical charms and about the way she entered a room and the way she handled a knife and fork, and I decided to make an effort.

I went about it, as in all things, systematically. I gave her a course in logic. It happened that I, as a law student, was taking a course in logic myself, so I had all the facts at my finger tips. "Polly," I said to her when I picked her up on our next date, "tonight we are going over to the Knoll and talk."

"Oo, terrif," she replied. One thing I will say for this girl: you would go far to find another so agreeable.

We went to the Knoll, the campus trysting place, and we sat down under an old oak, and she looked at me expectantly. "What are we going to talk about?" she asked.

"Logic."

She thought this over for a minute and decided she liked it. "Magnif," she said.

"Logic," I said, clearing my throat, "is the science of thinking. Before we can think correctly, we must first learn to recognize the common fallacies of logic. These we will take up tonight."

"Wow-dow!" she cried, clapping her hands delightedly.

I winced, but went bravely on. "First let us examine the fallacy called Dicto Simpliciter."

"By all means," she urged, batting her lashes eagerly.

"Dicto Simpliciter means an argument based on an unqualified generalization. For example: Exercise is good. Therefore everybody should exercise."

"I agree," said Polly earnestly. "I mean exercise is wonderful. I mean it builds the body and everything."

"Polly," I said gently, "the argument is a fallacy. *Exercise is good* is an unqualified generalization. For instance, if you have heart disease, exercise is bad, not good. Many people are ordered by their doctors *not* to exercise. You must *qualify* the generalization. You must say exercise is *usually* good, or exercise is good *for most people*. Otherwise you have committed a Dicto Simpliciter. Do you see?"

"No," she confessed. "But this is marvy. Do more! Do more!"

"It will be better if you stop tugging at my sleeve," I told her, and when she desisted, I continued. "Next we take up a fallacy called Hasty Generalization. Listen carefully: You can't speak French. I can't speak French. Petey Burch can't speak French. I must therefore conclude that nobody at the University of Minnesota can speak French."

"Really?" said Polly, amazed. "*Nobody?*"

I hid my exasperation. "Polly, it's a fallacy. The generalization is reached too hastily. There are too few instances to support such a conclusion."

"Know any more fallacies?" she asked breathlessly. "This is more fun than dancing even."

I fought off a wave of despair. I was getting nowhere with this girl, absolutely nowhere. Still, I am nothing if not persistent. I continued. "Next comes Post Hoc. Listen to this: Let's not take Bill on our picnic. Every time we take him out with us, it rains."

"I know somebody just like that," she exclaimed. "A girl back home— Eula Becker, her name is. It never fails. Every single time we take her on a picnic—"

"Polly," I said sharply, "it's a fallacy. Eula Becker doesn't *cause* the rain. She has no connection with the rain. You are guilty of Post Hoc if you blame Eula Becker."

"I'll never do it again," she promised contritely. "Are you mad at me?"

I sighed deeply. "No, Polly, I'm not mad."

"Then tell me some more fallacies."

"All right. Let's try Contradictory Premises."

"Yes, let's," she chirped, blinking her eyes happily.

I frowned, but plunged ahead. "Here's an example of Contradictory Premises: If God can do anything, can He make a stone so heavy that He won't be able to lift it?"

"Of course," she replied promptly.

"But if He can do anything, He can lift the stone," I pointed out.

"Yeah," she said thoughtfully. "Well, then I guess He can't make the stone."

"But He can do anything," I reminded her.

She scratched her pretty, empty head. "I'm all confused," she admitted.

"Of course you are. Because when the premises of an argument contradict each other, there can be no argument. If there is an irresistible force, there can be no immovable object. If there is an immovable object, there can be no irresistible force. Get it?"

"Tell me some more of this keen stuff," she said eagerly.

I consulted my watch. "I think we'd better call it a night. I'll take you home now, and you go over all the things you've learned. We'll have another session tomorrow night."

I deposited her at the girls' dormitory, where she assured me that she had had a perfectly terrif evening, and I went glumly home to my room. Petey lay snoring in his bed, the raccoon coat huddled like a great hairy beast at his feet. For a moment I considered waking him and telling him that he could have his girl back. It seemed clear that my project was doomed to failure. The girl simply had a logic-proof head.

But then I reconsidered. I had wasted one evening; I might as well waste another. Who knew? Maybe somewhere in the extinct crater of her mind, a few embers still smoldered. Maybe somehow I could fan them into flame. Admittedly it was not a prospect fraught with hope, but I decided to give it one more try.

Seated under the oak the next evening I said, "Our first fallacy tonight is called Ad Misericordiam."

She quivered with delight.

"Listen closely," I said. "A man applies for a job. When the boss asks him what his qualifications are, he replies that he has a wife and six children at home, the wife is a helpless cripple, the children have nothing to eat, no clothes to wear, no shoes on their feet, there are no beds in the house, no coal in the cellar, and winter is coming."

A tear rolled down each of Polly's pink cheeks. "Oh, this is awful, awful," she sobbed.

"Yes, it's awful," I agreed, "but it's no argument. The man never answered the boss's question about his qualifications. Instead he appealed to the boss's sympathy. He committed the fallacy of Ad Misericordiam. Do you understand?"

"Have you got a handkerchief?" she blubbered.

I handed her a handkerchief and tried to keep from screaming while she wiped her eyes. "Next," I said in a carefully controlled tone, "we will discuss False Analogy. Here is an example: Students should be allowed to look at their textbooks during examinations. After all, surgeons have X-rays to guide them during an operation, lawyers have briefs to guide them during a trial, carpenters have blueprints to guide them when they are building a house. Why, then, shouldn't students be allowed to look at their textbooks during an examination?"

"There now," she said enthusiastically, "is the most marvy idea I've heard in years."

"Polly," I said testily, "the argument is all wrong. Doctors, lawyers, and carpenters aren't taking a test to see how much they have learned, but students are. The situations are altogether different, and you can't make an analogy between them."

"I still think it's a good idea," said Polly.

"Nuts," I muttered. Doggedly I pressed on. "Next we'll try Hypothesis Contrary to Fact."

"Sounds yummy," was Polly's reaction.

"Listen: If Madame Curie had not happened to leave a photographic plate in a drawer with a chunk of pitchblende, the world today would not know about radium."

"True, true," said Polly, nodding her head. "Did you see the movie? Oh, it just knocked me out. That Walter Pidgeon is so dreamy. I mean he fractures me."

"If you can forget Mr. Pidgeon for a moment," I said coldly, "I would like to point out that the statement is a fallacy. Maybe Madame Curie would have discovered radium at some later date. Maybe somebody else would have discovered it. Maybe any number of things would have happened. You can't start with a hypothesis that is not true and then draw any supportable conclusions from it."

"They ought to put Walter Pidgeon in more pictures," said Polly. "I hardly ever see him any more."

One more chance, I decided. But just one more. There is a limit to what flesh and blood can bear. "The next fallacy is called Poisoning the Well."

"How cute!" she gurgled.

"Two men are having a debate. The first one gets up and says, 'My opponent is a notorious liar. You can't believe a word that he is going to say.' . . . Now, Polly, think. Think hard. What's wrong?"

"I watched her closely as she knit her creamy brow in concentration. Suddenly a glimmer of intelligence—the first I had seen—came into her eyes. "It's not fair," she said with indignation. "It's not a bit fair. What chance has the second man got if the first man calls him a liar before he even begins talking?"

"Right!" I cried exultantly. "One hundred percent right. It's not fair. The first man has *poisoned the well* before anybody could drink from it. He has hamstrung his opponent before he could even start. . . . Polly, I'm proud of you."

"Pshaw," she murmured, blushing with pleasure.

"You see, my dear, these things aren't so hard. All you have to do is concentrate. Think—examine—evaluate. Come now, let's review everything we have learned."

"Fire away," she said with an airy wave of her hand.

Heartened by the knowledge that Polly was not altogether a cretin, I began a long, patient review of all I had told her. Over and over and over again I cited instances, pointed out flaws, kept hammering away without let up. It was like digging a tunnel. At first everything was work, sweat, and darkness. I had no idea when I would reach the light, or even *if* I would. But I persisted. I pounded and clawed and scraped, and finally I was rewarded. I saw a chink of light. And then the chink got bigger and the sun came pouring in and all was bright.

Five grueling nights this took, but it was worth it. I had made a logician out of Polly; I had taught her to think. My job was done. She was worthy of me at last. She was a fit wife for me, a proper hostess for my many mansions, a suitable mother for my well-heeled children.

It must not be thought that I was without love for this girl. Quite the contrary. Just as Pygmalion loved the perfect woman he had fashioned, so I loved mine. I determined to acquaint her with my feelings at our very next meeting. The time had come to change our relationship from academic to romantic.

"Polly," I said when next we sat beneath our oak, "tonight we will not discuss fallacies."

"Aw, gee," she said, disappointed.

"My dear," I said, favoring her with a smile, "we have now spent five evenings together. We have gotten along splendidly. It is clear that we are well matched."

"Hasty Generalization," said Polly brightly.

"I beg your pardon," said I.

"Hasty Generalization," she repeated. "How can you say that we are well matched on the basis of only five dates?"

I chuckled with amusement. The dear child had learned her lessons well. "My dear," I said, patting her hand in a tolerant manner, "five dates is plenty. After all, you don't have to eat a whole cake to know that it's good."

"False Analogy," said Polly promptly. "I'm not a cake. I'm a girl."

I chuckled with somewhat less amusement. The dear child had learned her lessons perhaps too well. I decided to change tactics. Obviously the best approach was a simple, strong, direct declaration of love. I paused for a moment while my massive brain chose the proper words. Then I began:

"Polly, I love you. You are the whole world to me, and the moon and the stars and the constellations of outer space. Please, my darling, say that you will go steady with me, for if you will not, life will be meaningless. I will languish. I will refuse my meals. I will wander the face of the earth, a shambling, hollow-eyed hulk."

There, I thought, folding my arms, that ought to do it.

"Ad Misericordiam," said Polly.

I ground my teeth. I was not Pygmalion; I was Frankenstein, and my monster had me by the throat. Frantically I fought back the tide of panic surging through me. At all costs I had to keep cool.

"Well, Polly," I said, forcing a smile, "you certainly have learned your fallacies."

"You're darn right," she said with a vigorous nod.

"And who taught them to you, Polly?"

"You did."

"That's right. So you do owe me something, don't you, my dear? If I hadn't come along you never would have learned about fallacies."

"Hypothesis Contrary to Fact," she said instantly.

I dashed perspiration from my brow. "Polly," I croaked, "you mustn't take all these things so literally. I mean this is just classroom stuff. You know that the things you learn in school don't have anything to do with life."

"Dicto Simpliciter," she said, wagging her finger at me playfully.

That did it. I leaped to my feet, bellowing like a bull. "Will you or will you not go steady with me?"

"I will not," she replied.

"Why not?" I demanded.

"Because this afternoon I promised Petey Burch that I would go steady with him."

I reeled back, overcome with the infamy of it. After he promised, after he made a deal, after he shook my hand! "The rat!" I shrieked, kicking up great chunks of turf. "You can't go with him, Polly. He's a liar. He's a cheat. He's a rat."

"Poisoning the Well," said Polly, "and stop shouting. I think shouting must be a fallacy too."

With an immense effort of will, I modulated my voice. "All right," I said. "You're a logician. Let's look at this thing logically. How could you choose Petey Burch over me? Look at me—a brilliant student, a tremendous intellectual, a man with an assured future. Look at Petey—a knothead, a jitterbug, a guy who'll never know where his next meal is coming from. Can you give me one logical reason why you should go steady with Petey Burch?"

"I certainly can," declared Polly. "He's got a raccoon coat."

John O'Hayre
The Posture of Pomposity

Big words are not always and necessarily bad. They are bad when the writer is obsessed with them, when he uses them for their own sake, when he uses them to the exclusion of plain words. Then they are pompous.

Of course there's one way of killing this big word bug, and that's to stop talking like a mechanical nobleman who has been stuffed to overflowing with impressive, exotic words, and start talking like the genuine, natural human being you are. It's that simple.

Another writing evil caused by big word pomposity is the evil of falling into error. The more pompous and profound we get, the more we're apt to make mistakes. This pops up in our next sample from a monthly progress report by a state fire officer:

FIRE REPORT: Heavy rains throughout most of the State have given an optimistic outlook for lessened fire danger for the rest of the season. However, an abundance of lightning maintains a certain amount of hazard in isolated areas that have not received an excessive amount of rain. We were pleased to have been able to help Nevada with the suppression of their conflagration.

The curious thing about this stilted, stuffy, unnatural, puffed up and pompous piece is that the fire officer who wrote it is an educated, dignified, uncomplicated, easy-going, unpretentious, plain-talking fellow, who wouldn't be caught dead talking like he writes.

But what happened to him is the same thing that happens to many of us when we pick up a pencil. We become somebody else—and usually that somebody else is an aristocratic dandy of some past century. We just never really look at ourselves as we actually appear in print. If we did, we'd either quit writing or we'd quit writing like we do.

Now let's see how our fog-fighting secretary wrote the pomposity out of the fire officer's memo:

Fire readings are down throughout most of the State. But a few rain-skipped areas are dry, and lightning is a hazard there. We are glad we could send some of our people to help Nevada put out their recent range fire.

The important point here is NOT that our secretary cut down from 60 pompous words to 42 rather simple ones; mere word-cutting is never an end in itself; but that she did make the item simple, natural, and accurate.

As for its accuracy: Our fire officer didn't mean . . . "lightning maintains a hazard in areas that have NOT received an EXCESSIVE amount of rain!" He probably meant . . . "lightning is a hazard in areas that have not received a SUFFICIENT amount of rain;" or, " . . . in areas that ARE EXCESSIVELY dry." Whatever he meant to say, he didn't say it, and he used big, elegant words not saying it.

He did not know how to handle the negative "not." This led him to pick the wrong word in "excessive." However, even this is no real explanation, for you can't explain away a 60-word passel of pomposity by the wrong use of one "not" and one "excessive."

Pomposity isn't that simple. You can't "select it out" by changing a big word here and there; you've got to write it out by rewriting the whole thing. That's because pomposity is more than mere words; it's false tone as well.

It was this false tone that angered Franklin D. Roosevelt when he happened across it. He was convinced that the simple, personal style of writing was the most dignified style for men of importance in government and everywhere else.

Here's a pompous memo that rankled F.D.R. so much he rewrote it and shot it back to the man who pomped it up in the first place. This memo dealt with what Federal workers were to do in case of an air raid:

Such preparations shall be made, as will completely obscure all Federal buildings and non-Federal buildings occupied by the Federal Government during an air raid for any period of time from visibility by reason of internal or external illumination. Such obscuration may be obtained either by blackout construction or by termination of the illumination.

Here's how F.D.R. dignified the memo by giving it simplicity:

Tell them that in buildings where they have to keep the work going to put something over the windows; and, in buildings where they can let the work stop for a while, turn out the lights.

If this kind of unpompous, simple writing means a loss of dignity, then we know a whole lot of readers who wish a lot of writers would lose a lot of "dignity" writing this way. F.D.R. did it all the time. Once, when Frances Perkins was getting a speech ready for him, she wrote this line:

We are endeavoring to construct a more inclusive society.

That night when F.D.R. read the line on the radio, it came out this way:

We are going to make a country in which no one is left out.

Nor did presidential simplicity go out of style with F.D.R.

President Johnson provided this in a State of the Union message. Here's a sample:

Why did men come to this once forbidding land?
They were restless, of course, and had to be moving on. But there was more than that.
There was a dream—a dream of a place where a free man could build for himself and raise his children to a better life—a dream of a continent to be conquered, a world to be won, a nation to be made . . .

This, then, is the state of the Union—free, restless, growing, full of hopes and dreams.
So it was in the beginning.
So it shall always be—while God is willing, and we are strong enough to keep the faith.

That is great writing. It couldn't be simpler or more powerful. That kind of presidential simplicity and charm make us wonder what a Bureau of Land Management (BLM) economist-friend of ours would say. He protested, rather bitterly, that "you can't put economics in simple language without making it cheap."

We know you can write about economics, like you can write about anything else, in a language that's simple enough to suit any audience.

We don't say you can do it easily, but we do say you can do it. And while you're doing it you'll quit worrying over that ethereal thing called "dignity," and start stewing over this solid stuff called "simplicity." You'll also learn that it's easier to be soaring and supernal than it is to be earthy and concrete. You'll learn, too, that readers will love you for the latter. Back now to pomposity in BLM samples:

These original land records, some of which are oriented as far back as 1800, are in a serious state of disrepair and contain many documentary inaccuracies which are detrimental to the effective and efficient determination of land and resource status.

The reaction an ordinary reader has after reading something like that is often something like this:

Ohhhh come off it, fella! If you've got something to say, why don't you come right out and say it, then quit?

Why didn't our writer come right out and say it—maybe like this:

Some of our land records haven't been brought up to date since 1800, and a lot of them are worn out from use. What's more, some have errors in them that keep us from getting accurate status.

Here's another sample:

In numerous instances, the Bureau of Land Management has demonstrated the feasibility of judiciously harvesting timber on municipal watersheds and in drainage tributary to irrigation reservoirs.

Why puff up writing that way when it's so much more genuine written like this:

BLM proves every day it can harvest timber without hurting municipal watersheds or irrigation drainages.

Or, take this pomp from a press release:

The availability of soil survey maps from the Soil Conservation Service for about half of the burned lands was of great assistance to BLM technicians in verifying the information collected by field survey parties in the burned areas.

Why not depomp it like this:

BLM technicians used what maps the SCS had—covering about half of the burned-over-areas—to verify their field findings.

Now here's a stuffy sample from a report that makes it sound like BLM played "indulgent father" to a bunch of uneducated people-kids. See for yourself:

This office's activities during the year were primarily continuing their primary functions of education of the people to acquaint them of their needs, problems and alternate problem solutions, in order that they can make wise decisions in planning and implementing a total program that will best meet the needs of the people, now and in the future.

As so often happens, this kind of pomposity comes from trying to make something that is ordinary and routine sound like something that is ultra-grandiose. This whole thing could have been said very simply and the writer could have maintained his dignity. Perhaps like this:

We spent most of our time last year working with the local people, going over their problems and trying to help them figure out solutions. This way we hoped to help them set up and carry out a program that will solve today's problems and satisfy tomorrow's needs.

And then there's the kind of pomposity that comes from using what we call *persuader* words, words that are nothing more than airy symbols. They are usually used in BLM writing to "important-up" the Bureau or one of its routine jobs. These persuader words are fluff, not fact, air, not action, impressive, not expressive.

The publication of this attractive map is an outstanding example of . . . etc.
This patent was presented at impressive ceremonies held in the Bureau of Land Management State Office . . . etc.
The Board will discuss all of the very difficult problems they will encounter next year . . . etc.
The lease was won after several rounds of spirited bidding, which was highly competitive . . . etc.
As a result, the hearings were completed in record-breaking time and with great savings to the public . . . etc.
The Bureau's case was presented in practically a flawless manner . . . etc.
A huge crowd attended the special installation ceremonies . . .
Fire rehabilitation plans will have to be coordinated very closely with other agencies . . . etc. (You could write the rest of your natural life and not use the word very again. At least not very often!)
Before BLM takes such serious steps, careful consideration is given to . . . etc.

In a move denoting close cooperation between Federal and State agencies, BLM . . . etc.
Mr. So and So retired after giving 33 years of faithful and dedicated service to the Department of the Interior . . . etc.
The distinguished visitors were guests at a BLM orientation meeting this morning in the . . . etc.

And then there's the kind of pomposity that comes from trying to sound "important" when we write "talk." In many ways, this is the worst kind of pomp, for more than anything else, written talk should sound like spoken talk. If it doesn't, if it's pomped up above and beyond naturalness, kill it; then rewrite it. This quote, from a BLM news release, emphasizes the point:

Because the heavy mistletoe infestation in the Kringle Creek area has rendered the residual timber useless for timber production, the ultimate goal is to establish a healthy new stand of Douglas Fir.

That isn't anywhere near plain talk; it's plain pomposity. And it's about time somebody said so.

The mistletoe quote isn't out of the ordinary in BLM writing. Out of 100 BLM quotes we found only 1 that sounded like it might have been said by somebody who talks the way most of us do:

We got everything lined up this morning. Now all we have to take care of is the paper work. Like always, that'll take more time than it should.
But we're all set to push it through as fast as we can. I think we'll be able to wrap it up sometime late next week.

That quote rings true. It sounds like somebody human said it. But it has a sad tale behind it. When the man who said it read it in the newspaper he wasn't happy. He didn't think his "natural" speech sounded "official" enough for a BLM official. He wished he could call his quote back and rewrite it. Had he been able to do so, he would have ruined it, have taken away the thing that made it good: its natural sound, its ring of truth.

This reminds us of the once beautiful woman who had her picture taken when she was pushing 50 and got mad at the photographer because he didn't make her look like she was still pushing 20. The photographer tried to explain that she was still very beautiful, with a beauty that was natural for her age. It was sad she didn't know that.

This is like our language today. It is beautiful because it is natural for our age. And no other style of any other age would fit us quite so well. And it's sad more of us don't know that. Our language, like our clothes, emerges to fit, not only the individual but the society in which he lives. Which one of us would show up for work Monday morning in a Shakespeare cape, a Napoleon cock-hat, or an Al Smith suit? We wouldn't. But that's the way we look when we get pompous in our writing.

We held the next sample until last simply because, in the ways of pomposity, it is the very best.

We'll look at only the first paragraph of this memo, which was pomped up so profoundly it sounded almost frightening in importance:

A basic, although often ignored conservation principle in land treatment practices is the alignment of these practices to contour operations. Contour alignment, manifested in the direction of implement travel, provides an effective and complementary attack on the forces of erosion. When soil surface disturbances run up and down hill, it is easily understood that artificial channels are formed in which runoff accumulates. As the slope of these channels increases, the velocity of the water movement accelerates, with resulting destructive energies.

The pomp proceeds unswervingly for another 400 words, always making little tiny things into great big things, all the way to the very end.

For example, the 80 pompous words in this formalistic paragraph could have been informally said in these rather simple 19:

In doing conservation work, always work on the contour if possible. That is the best way to control erosion.

This may seem like an over-simplified rewrite. If you think it is, go back and analyze the original and see EXACTLY what was said. You'll see that our rather simple 19 words were quite enough, if even they were needed.

Appropriately enough, this memo, like so many we see, called up a couplet written 250 years ago by Alexander Pope, known as the "Wasp of Twickenham," because he buzzed about puncturing pomposity wherever he found it.

> Such labored nothings in so learn'd a style
> Amaze the unlearned and make the learned smile.

Three questions . . .

1. The John Keats selection begins with this sentence: "All advertisements show automobiles in unusual circumstances." He ends by writing that "Roger and Jane Foresight dwell in the tasteless, or Pablum, stage of family travel." What does

nobody's language have to do with his distinction between the unusual and the insipid?

> 2. Why does the speaker in "You Know How Relatives Are" have trouble making a straightforward statement? What has happened to his sense of organization?

3. What does Dobie Gillis mean when, after his first date with Polly, he says to himself, "First she had to be taught to *think*"?

And an exercise . . .

> Here are two paragraphs. Would you define either one as pompous or inflated? Why? If either one seems pompous, think about the audience for which it was written. Perhaps you will agree that writing aimed at somebody is more pompous than writing that comes from someone.

Professor John Dewey, America's most profound philosopher, said the deepest urge in human nature is the "desire to be important." Remember that phrase, "the desire to be important." It is a gnawing and unfaltering human hunger. It was this desire that led the uneducated, poverty-stricken grocery clerk, Abraham Lincoln, to study law; that inspired Dickens to write his immortal novels. It makes you want to wear the latest styles, drive the latest car, and talk about your brilliant children.

As our statement of the problem indicates, we concluded that in order to approach the important question of effective conceptualization, we must fundamentally reconsider the entirety of the writing act, not just that part which appears "above water" on the page. Within the tradition of classical rhetoric, there are coherent, logic-oriented accounts of this earliest stage of the writer's activity. We believed a potentially more inclusive vocabulary could be put together from the accounts of writers and psychologists who have discussed the creative process. One of the major problems we soon encountered, however, was to give conceptual and methodological coherence to scattered and random accounts of creative activity, written in a variety of idioms and with a variety of intentions. To give at least a provisional and minimum definition to our work with conceptualization, we "translated" this great variety of terms into one vocabulary based upon a root organic metaphor. As well as giving us some theoretic and pedagogical coherence in what we attempted to do, this vocabulary seemed more appropriate to describe our own intuitive sense of what goes on in the process of conceptualization. In any event, the process of what we have called "translation" of our problem into a relatively fresh idiom gave us an opportunity to discover possibilities for questions and answers that simply are not potential within the established idiom of classical rhetoric. In a similar way, the English philosopher Weldon, as quoted by Bruner, approaches problem-solving. Weldon distinguishes among difficulties, puzzles, and problems. . . .

Assignments

1.   Draw a sketch of an American "type," or write
a description of him. (Do you want to be serious,
analytical, or humorous? What is the difference?)

2.   Put yourself inside the mind of a "type" and
write any kind of paper that he might write.

WHO SOMEBODY IS

Language dressed in "town ensemble and correct accessories" is not the
only way to effective, contemporary writing. "Correct" language does not
in itself make good writing; neither will slang or informal usage alone guarantee anything. The perennial nature of the problem is illustrated in a 1936
cartoon, which also makes the point that informal dress is as conventional
as the town ensemble and correct accessories. Like soldiers, the students
seem to have dressed according to someone's orders.

Language is like clothing. Use it to suit yourself, and it will be your own;
use it as someone else issues it to you, and it will be a uniform.

Certainly almost all of us will wear a uniform at some time. And certainly
all of us need to be able to use mutually understandable English. In large
part, this book is written in a "standard" English. The question we raise here
is not what kind of English to use but simply how you are to use any English,
and use it as your own.

LANGUAGE, GENTLEMEN, IS BEHAVIOR

You might think about how you behave when you write an essay exam.
Mostly you sit. But writing is also behavior. Your behavior in the exam is
finally described by what is written (*behavior* is even teacher's jargon for exam
results). In writing the exam, you may parrot your lecture notes or pet
phrases. If you do that, you are simply putting on your teacher's linguistic
clothes, and he may pin on a grade classification according to your subtlety
and success. If he likes the way you behave as him—A; if not—F. You may
say that your teacher wants you to behave this way. Who is not flattered by
skillful imitation? You may say that you are trying to show your teacher that
you understand his point of view; again, if it is well done, he will like the
compliment;—and, again, he will classify you as a good student, an A or B.

You might ask yourself about yourself, though. By *learning*, do you mean
trading an old uniform for a new one? It may be desirable at some time to
take off the old uniform and find some new clothes for yourself, and language may be one means of making this change. Suppose, for example, that
you tried to make the exam into an utterance—behavior—of your own. You
might be able to do that if you have formed opinions of your own from the
material provided in the course and if you use language to make your opinions known.

If you wish to lose yourself, adopting another person's language will suppress your own mind as certainly as drugs or alcohol. But if you wish to find yourself, the language may be the mind's stimulant or the means of breaking inhibitions. Consider these propositions:

1. Suppose that you use the language to hide yourself as if you hated yourself. Aren't you using the language as anesthesia, to gas yourself?

2. Can you name anyone else who is exactly like you? If not, can you explain why you should use a language exactly like anyone else's?

3. If you don't think you are unique in person and language, couldn't you eventually marry someone who seeks you because you are like so many other people?

4. If you want to marry someone who respects you for yourself, and if you disapprove of deceit, aren't you compelled to seek a language for expressing your own self?

5. Can you express *yourself* with the language as someone else gives it to you? Or as in auto ads and the example of the essay exam, doesn't repetition lead to loss of identity?

"I DIDN'T KNOW THE GUN WAS LOADED, OFFICER."

We do know that the questions above were loaded, in that they were meant to illustrate again the need for being conscious of the language you use as your own. The problem of finding oneself in language is not a new one. It is not a product of twentieth-century crowds. It has traditionally been the place where the writer has made his beginnings. In the early nineteenth century, Thoreau returned from his stay at Walden Pond and wrote:

I learned this at least, by my experiment; that if one advances confidently in the direction of his dreams, and endeavors to live the life which he has imagined, he will meet with a success unexpected in common hours. He will put some things behind, will pass an invisible boundary; new, universal, and more liberal laws will begin to establish themselves around and within him; or the old laws be expanded, and interpreted in his favor in a more liberal sense, and he will live with the license of a higher order of beings. In proportion as he simplifies his life, the laws of the universe will appear less complex, and solitude will not be solitude, nor poverty poverty, nor weakness weakness. If you have built castles in the air, your work need not be lost; that is where they should be. Now put the foundations under them.

The words and sentences of language may seem like dice waiting to be cast, doing the same job for whoever picks them up and uses them, but language is not a game of chance. Winning numbers come up most often because of the player. Language did not develop by chance nor because it was respectable; it came to be because it fulfilled the human need to be known. It grew out of individuals. In the selections which follow, a constant concern is with writing as something done by someone—as his behavior.

In 1964 Gordon Rohman and Albert Wlecke at Michigan State University carried out a research project that is gradually revising the teaching of writing in many colleges and universities. They began with the premise that writing is the expression of an individual's perspective and that any explanation of how one learns to write must take the individual into account. This selection is from their report.

Gordon Rohman
Albert Wlecke

The Person in the Process

Ours is an age so dominated by machine analogies that we find it difficult to conceive of any process without some mechanism to account for it. But we premise that writing is more like a growing process than a mechanical one. And every growth begins in germination which released the "vitality" that starts the plant growing. Unless we can engage our students as persons in the experience of pre-writing, we have failed in fact to provide them with the key to any subsequent models for concept formation and transference.

By person we mean one who stands at the center of his own thoughts and feelings with the sense that they begin in him. He is concerned to make things happen and not simply to allow things to happen to him; he seeks to dominate his circumstances with words or actions. Rollo May writes, "Any penetrating explanation of the creative process must take it as the expression of the normal man in the act of actualizing himself, not as the product of sickness but representing the highest degree of emotional health." The essential, May continues, "is not the presence or absence of voluntary effort, but the degree of absorption, the degree of intensity . . .; there must be a specific quality of *engagement*."[18] Such engagement or what May calls "encounter," represents a real relationship with the objective world, impossible to anyone not taking himself seriously as a person. This relationship is a continual dialectical process between the world and self, "a process interrelating the person and his world."

In writing, we may say, every occasion for words presents the writer with two interrelations to discover. The first is the interrelation between materials within the "subject matrix," that is, those things about a subject that may be learned inductively, and those ways that we may group these things, according to prior norms of order: cause and effect, definition, narration, etc. But as we have assumed throughout this research, the writer has another, more crucial and primary interrelation to make within the "personal matrix," that assimilation of one's self experienced as a person when confronted with a subject needing expression. Without a successful discovery of this interrelation, we can never have that kind of writing which we have called good: "some perspective that has not already become ordered into a public map."

We make such a point of the role of a person in the writing process because, as teachers of writing, we have so often observed that when students sit down to write, their sense of their reality as persons gets tucked away, and they begin merely to echo all the pat phrases of their culture in essentially meaningless combination. Perhaps because of the excessive emphasis upon extrinsic standards of goodness in writing common to many classrooms, perhaps because of an "other-directed" age, they have not been encouraged or even permitted to experience real involvement in their writing. They have not been taught to believe that it is either possible or desirable to become involved when playing the role of writer. Many who in other roles find self-affirmation and self-acceptance both possible and highly desirable fail to maintain that vitality when engaged in the special behavior known as writing. Both their estimation of their own potential success as writers, and their sense of what goodness in

[18]"The Nature of Creativity," *ETC: A Review of General Semantics*, XVI, No. 3 (Spring, 1959), 264.

writing means ("good manners"), inhibit their chances of self-affirmation and hence of real discovery in their writing. Yet we maintain that such self-affirmation is the "payoff matrix" which germinates the vitality essential to real goodness in writing. Within self-affirmation—the absolute willingness to think one's own thoughts, feel one's own feelings—we find the basis for motivation for any writing that pretends to freshness. We believe that both our culture and our pedagogical methods have encouraged "other-directed" self-images which hinder this kind of writing and which, in fact, hinder any kind of writing. As a result, we have almost a national neurosis about writing, with no object for our anxiety except a vague and increasingly discredited code of "correctness." As one is expected to write acceptable grammar, and as one is expected to choose acceptable diction, so one is expected to think acceptable thoughts, and feel acceptable feelings.

We believe it is both possible and desirable to amend this situation: to give to students some insight into the role they must play when they write if they would hope to discover real possibilities in their subject; and, in addition, to give students some experience of success in playing that role which may, in turn, release that vitality that makes possible real improvement in writing, improvement first in essential pattern, improvement also in external form.

. . . . .

Ours is what might be called an existential approach to composition: in effect, we are seeking an image of man within the process that mobilized the "mechanisms" of problem-solving. Our existential premise is that truth exists for the individual only as he himself produces it in action. Our approach stresses the importance of decision and commitment of the person in the prewriting stages in order that discovery may follow. As we believe there is no truth without participation for the individual, we say also that there is no essential goodness in an essay without evidence of such commitment. The writer comes alive only when he feels the creative process as potential within him, and his essay comes alive only from such an encounter. We do not deny the validity of extrinsic approaches to composition and to writers, with their emphasis upon methods, tradition, conditioning, grammar and the like; we only hold that these alone and these first will never produce good writing defined as fresh perspective. More than that, such approaches can be positively harmful by reducing writing and writers to "things" on machine analogies. They substitute abstractions and concepts for the writer and his composition. Each writer always transcends the mechanisms and experiences discovery in his unique way. The person does not have meaning in terms of the mechanism; the mechanism may have meaning in terms of the person. Essentially our project begins with the existential as a necessary attitude. It then seeks to develop some appropriate techniques to practice that attitude; but the techniques without the attitude are worthless.

Are you a culturally disadvantaged or educationally deprived writer? Don't say no just because you went to prep school or had a two-car family. Read what Herbert Kohl learned about how children learn to write or not write.

Herbert Kohl

from Teaching the Unteachable

Shop with Mom
I love to shop with mom
And talk to the friendly grocer
And help her make the list
Seems to make us closer.
— *Nellie, age 11*

The Junkies
When they are
in the street
they pass it
along to each
other but when
they see the
police they would
run some would
just stand still
and be beat
so pity ful
that they want
to cry
— *Mary, age 11*

Nellie's poem received high praise. Her teacher liked the rhyme "closer" and "grocer," and thought she said a great deal in four lines. Most of all the teacher was pleased that Nellie expressed such a pleasant and healthy thought. Nellie was pleased too, her poem was published in the school paper. I was moved and excited by Mary's poem and made the mistake of showing it to the teacher who edited the school newspaper. She was horrified. First of all, she informed me, Mary couldn't possibly know what junkies were, and, moreover, the other children wouldn't be interested in such a poem. There weren't any rhymes or clearly discernible meter. The word "pityful" was split up incorrectly, "be beat" wasn't proper English and, finally, it wasn't really poetry but just the ramblings of a disturbed girl.

My initial reaction was outrage—what did she know about poetry, or about Mary? But it is too easy to be cruel about the ignorance that is so characteristic of the schools today. That teacher did believe that she knew what poetry was, and that there was a Correct Language in which it was expressed. Her attitude towards the correctness of language and the form of poetry was in a way identical to her attitude towards what sentiments good children's poems ought to express. Yet language is not static, nor is it possible *a priori* to establish rules governing what can or cannot be written any more than it is possible to establish rules governing what can or cannot be felt.

Not long ago when I was teaching a class of remote, resistant children in a Harlem school, as an experiment I asked these children to write. I had no great expectations. I had been told that the children were from one to three years behind in reading, that they came from "deprived" and "disadvantaged" homes and were ignorant of the language of the schools. I had also been told that their vocabulary was limited, that they couldn't make abstractions, were not introspective, oriented to physical rather than mental activity. Other teachers in the school called the children "them" and spoke of teaching as a thankless military task. I couldn't accept this mythology: I wanted my pupils to tell me about themselves. For reasons that were hardly literary I set out to explore the possibilities of teaching language, literature, and writing in ways that would enable children to speak about what they felt they were not allowed to acknowledge publicly. Much to my surprise the children wrote a great deal; and they invented their own language to do so. Only a very small number of the children had what can be called "talent," and many of them had only a single story to write and rewrite; yet almost all of them responded, and seemed to become more alive through their writing. The results of some of this exploration are given here.

I have subsequently discovered other teachers who have explored language and literature with their pupils in this way, with results no less dramatic. The children we have taught ranged from the pre-school years to high school, from lower-class ghetto children to upper-class suburban ones. There are few teaching techniques that we share in common, and no philosophy of education that binds us. Some of these teachers have tight, carefully controlled classrooms; others care less for order and more for invention. There are Deweyites, traditionalists, classicists—a large range of educational philosophies and teaching styles. If there is anything common to our work it is the concern to listen to what the children have to say and the ability to respond to it as honestly as possible, no matter how painful it may be to our teacherly prides and preconceptions. We have allowed ourselves to learn from our pupils and to expect the unexpected.

Children will not write if they are afraid to talk. Initially they suspect teachers and are reluctant to be honest with them. They have had too many school experiences where the loyalty of the staff and the institutional obligations of teachers have taken precedence over honesty. They have seen too much effort to maintain face, and too little respect for justifiable defiance in their school lives. I think children believe that there is a conscious collusion between all of the adults in a school to maintain the impression that the authority is *always* right, and that life is *always* pleasant and orderly. Unfortunately, the collusion is unconscious or at least unspoken. This is dramatically true in slum schools where the pressures of teaching are increased by understaffing and a vague uneasiness about race which is always in the air.

I was assigned to a school in East Harlem in September 1962 and was not sufficiently prepared for the faculty's polite lies about their success in the classroom or the resistance and defiance of the children. My sixth-grade class had thirty-six pupils, all Negro. For two months I taught in virtual isolation from my pupils. Every attempt I made to develop rapport was coldly rejected. The theme of work scheduled by the school's lesson plan for that semester was "How We Became Modern America," and my first lesson was characteristic of the dull response everything received.

It seemed natural to start by comparing a pioneer home with the modern life the children knew—or, more accurately, I thought they knew. I asked the class to think of America in the 1850's and received blank stares, although that presumably was what they had studied the previous year. I pursued the matter.

—Can anyone tell me what was happening around 1850, just before the Civil War? I mean, what do you think you'd see if you walked down Madison Avenue then?

—Cars.

—Do you think there were cars in 1850? That was over a hundred years ago. Think of what you learned last year and try again, do you think there were cars then?

—Yes ... no ... I don't know.
Someone else tried.

—Grass and trees?
The class broke out laughing. I tried to contain my anger and frustration.

—I don't know what you're laughing about, it's the right answer. In those days Harlem was farmland with fields and trees and a few farmhouses. There weren't any roads or houses like the ones outside, or street lights or electricity.

The class was outraged and refused to think. Bright faces took on the dull glaze that is characteristic of the Negro child who finds it less pain-ful to be thought stupid than to be defiant. There was an uneasy drum-ming on desk tops. The possibility of there being a time when Harlem didn't exist had never, could never have occurred to the children. Nor did it occur to me that their experience of modern America was not what I had come to teach about. After two months, in despair, I asked the kids to write about their block.

What a Block!

My block is the most terrible block I've ever seen. There are at least 25 or 30 narcartic people in my block. The cops come around there and tries to act bad but I bet inside of them they are as scared as can be. They even had in the papers that this block is the worst block, not in Manhattan but in New York City. In the summer they don't do nothing except shooting, shabing, and fight-ing. They hang all over the stoops and when you say excuse me to them they hear you but they just don't feel like moving. Some times they make me so mad that I feel like slaping them and stuffing and bag of garbage down their throats. Theres only one policeman who can handle these people and we all call him "Sunny." When he come around in his cop car the people run around the corners, and he wont let anyone sit on the stoops. If you don't believe this story come around some time and you'll find out.

—*Grace, age 11*

My block is the worse block you ever saw people getting killed or stabbed men and women in buildin's taking dope . . .

—*Mary, age 11*

My Neighborhood

I live on 117 street, between Madison and 5th avenue. All the bums live around here. But the truth is they don't live here they just hang around the street. All the kids call it "Junky's Paradise."

—*James, age 12*

My block is a dirty crumby block!

—*Clarence, age 12*

The next day I threw out my notes and my lesson plans and talked to the children. What I had been assigned to teach seemed, in any case, an unreal myth about a country that never has existed. I didn't believe the tale of "progress" the curriculum had prescribed, yet had been afraid to discard it and had been willing to lie to the children. After all I didn't want to burden them or cause them pain, and I had to teach something. I couldn't "waste their time." How scared I must have been when I started teaching in Harlem to accept those hollow rationalizations and use the "curriculum" to protect me from the children. I accepted the myth that the teacher and the book know all; that complex human ques-tions had "right" and "wrong" answers. It was much easier than facing the world the children perceived and attempting to cope with it. I could lean on the teachers' manuals and feel justified in presenting an unambiguously "good" historical event or short story. It protected my authority as a teacher which I didn't quite believe in. It was difficult for me; pontificating during the day and knowing that I was doing so at night. Yet could I cause the class much more pain or impose greater burdens with my lies than they already had? How much time could I have "wasted" even if I let the children dance and play all day while I sought for a new approach. They had already wasted five years in school by the time they arrived in my class.

So we spoke. At first the children were suspicious and ashamed of what they'd written. But as I listened and allowed them to talk they became bolder and angrier, then finally quieter and relieved. I asked them to write down what they would do to change things, and they responded immediately.

If I could change my block I would stand on Madison Ave and throw nothing but Teargas in it. I would have all the people I liked to get out of the block and then I would become very tall and have big hands and with my big hands I would take all of the narcartic people and pick them up with my hand and throw them in the nearest river and oceans. I would go to some of those old smart alic cops and throw them in the Ocians and Rivers too. I would let the people I like move into the projects so they could tell their friends that they live in a decent block. If I could do this you would never see 117 st again.

—*Grace, age 11*

If I could change my block I would put all the bums on an Island where they can work there. I would give them lots of food. But I wouldn't let no whiskey be brought to them. After a year I would ship them to new York and make them clean up junk in these back yard and make them maybe make a baseball diamond and put swings basketball courts etc.

—*Clarence, age 12*

For several weeks after that the children wrote and wrote—what their homes were like, whom they liked, where they came from. I discovered that everything I'd been told about the children's language was irrelevant. Yes, they were hip when they spoke, inarticulate and concrete. But their writing was something else, when they felt that no white man was judging their words, threatening their confidence and pride. They faced a blank page and wrote directly and honestly. Recently I have mentioned this to teachers who have accepted the current analyses of "the language" of the "disadvantaged." They asked their children to write and have been as surprised as I was, and shocked by the obvious fact that "disadvantaged" children will not speak in class because they cannot trust their audience.

Nothing the school offered was relevant, so I read the class novels, stories, poems, brought my library to class and let them know that many people have suffered throughout history and that some were articulate enough to create literature from their lives. They didn't believe me, but they were hungry to know what had been written about and what could be written about.

It was easier for the class to forget their essays than it was for me. They were eager to go beyond their block, to move out into the broader world and into themselves. We talked of families, of brothers and sisters, of uncles, and of Kenny's favorite subject, the Tyranny of Teachers and Moms.

We spoke and read about love and madness, families, war, the birth and death of individuals and societies; and then they asked me permission to write themselves. Permission!

In the midst of one of our discussions of fathers Shiela asked me a question that has become symbolic of my pupils' hunger for concepts. "Mr. Kohl," she said, "if you wanted to write something about your father that was true is there a word for it?" What she meant was that if there was a word for it she would do it, but if there wasn't she would be scared. One names what is permissible, and denies names to what one fears. Shiela led us to talk about biography and autobiography, and she did get to write of her father.

A Biography of My Father
My father was born in California.
He wasn't a hero or anything like that to anyone but to me he was. He was a hard working man he wasn't rich but he had enough money to take care of us. He was mean in a way of his own. But I loved him and he loved me. He said to my mother when he die whe would feel it. My father was a man who loved his work besides if I was a man who worked as a grocery store I would love it to. He wanted his kids to grow up to be someone and be big at name. He wanted a real life. But when he died we started a real life.

The children spoke of themselves as well. They knew what they felt and sometimes could say it. Sharon came into class angry one day and wrote about a fight.

One Day There Was a Big Fight
One day in school a girl started getting smart with a boy. So the boy said to the girl why don't you come outside? The girl said alright I'll be there. The girl said you just wait. And he said don't wait me back. And so the fight was on. One had a swollen nose the other a black eye. And a teacher stoped the fight. His name was Mr. Mollow. I was saying to myself I wish they would mind their own business. It made me bad. I had wanted to see a fight that day. So I call Mr. Mollow up. I called him all kinds of names. I said you ugly skinney bony man. I was red hot. And when I saw him I rolled my eyes as if I wanted to hit him. All that afternoon I was bad at Mr. Mollow.

I tried to talk to her about her paper, tell her that "it make me bad" didn't make any sense. And she explained to me that "being bad" was a way of acting and that down South a "bad nigger" was one who was defiant of the white man's demands. She concluded by saying that being bad was good in a way and bad in a way. I asked the class and they agreed. In the midst of the discussion Louis asked one of his characteristically exasperating questions: "But where do words come from anyway?"

I stumbled over an answer as the uproar became general.

—What use are words anyway?

—Why do people have to talk?

—Why are there good words and bad words?

—Why aren't you supposed to use some words in class?

—Why can't you change words as you like?

I felt that I was being "put on," and was tempted to pass over the questions glibly; there were no simple answers to the children's questions, and the simplest thing to do when children ask difficult questions is to pretend that they're not serious or they're stupid. But the children were serious.

More and more they asked about language and would not be put off by evasive references to the past, linguistic convention and tradition. Children look away from adults as soon as adults say that things are the way they are because they have always been that way. When a child accepts such an answer it is a good indication that he has given up and decided to be what adults would make him rather than himself.

I decided to explore language with the children, and we talked about mythology together.

I thought of Shiela's question and Louis's question, of Shiela's desire to tell a story and her fear of doing it. The children rescued me. Ronald told me one day that Louis was "psyching" him and asked me to do something. I asked him what he was talking about, what he meant by "psyching." He didn't know, and when I asked the class they couldn't quite say either, except that they all knew that Louis was "psyche," as they put it. I said that Louis couldn't be Psyche since Psyche was female. The kids laughed and asked me what I meant, I countered with the story of Cupid and Psyche and the next day followed with readings from Apuleius and C. S. Lewis. Then I talked about words that came from Psyche, psychology, psychic, psychosomatic. We even puzzled out the meaning of psyching, and one of the children asked me if there were any words from Cupid. I had never thought of cupidity in that context before, but it made sense.

From Cupid and Psyche we moved to Tantalus, the Sirens, and the Odyssey. We talked of Venus and Adonis and spent a week on first Pan and panic, pan-American, then pandaemonium, and finally on daemonic and demons and devils.

Some of the children wrote myths themselves and created characters named Skyview, Missile, and Morass. George used one of the words in his first novel:

One day, in Ancient Germany, a boy was growing up. His name was Pathos. He was named after this Latin word because he had sensitive feelings.

The class began a romance with words and language that lasted all year. Slowly the children turned to writing, dissatisfied with mere passive learning. They explored their thoughts and played with the many different forms of written expression. I freed the children of the burden of spelling and grammar while they were writing. If a child asked me to comment on the substance of his work I did not talk of the sentence structure. There is no more deadly thing a teacher can do than ignore what a child is trying to express in his writing and comment merely upon the form, neatness, and heading.[1] Yet there is nothing safer if the teacher is afraid to become involved. It is not that I never taught grammar or spelling; it is rather that the teaching of grammar and spelling is not the same as the teaching of writing. Once children care about writing and see it as important to themselves they want to write well. At that moment, I found, they easily accept the discipline of learning to write correctly. Vocabulary, spelling, and grammar become the means to achieving more precise and sophisticated forms of expression and not merely empty ends in themselves.

The members of big families are often grouped together, rather than separately thought of as individuals. Victor S. Navasky analyzes Robert Kennedy's use of language to distinguish his individual identity.

---

[1]The habit of grading a written exercise according to form, neatness, spelling, punctuation, and heading is not surprising considering that the written part of the examination for the New York City substitute elementary school teaching license is graded that way. Content is irrelevant.

Victor S. Navasky

The Haunting of Robert Kennedy

The Shadow

Robert Kennedy can't just come to town. He comes to town in comparison with his brother John. What other Presidential candidate has ever been plagued by bumper stickers reading "Bobby Ain't Jack"? When a lady standing on the lawn in Beatrice, Neb., turns to her neighbor and says, "He's shorter than I thought," isn't she really saying that he is not as tall as John Kennedy? The candidate himself senses the special shadow in which he acts. When asked why, given his sense of urgency about the war in Vietnam, he waited until after McCarthy's New Hampshire victory to declare, he says, "I probably made a mistake. But at the time I thought people would think it was because of me personally, because of my relationship to John Kennedy."

Upon hearing that President Johnson had taken himself out of the race, Senator McCarthy is reported to have commented, "Until now, Bobby has been running as Jack against Lyndon. Now he's going to have to run as himself against Jack."

By that I take it he meant that Robert would have to emerge from John's shadow, from the Kennedy Administration's penumbra, and among other things explicitly repudiate some New Frontier policies, programs and assumptions. The observation has proved only partly prophetic. Where John Kennedy was preoccupied with the missile gap and the space race ("America must be first . . . not first when, not first if, not first but . . . first period"), Robert now says things like, "It is more important to be able to walk through the ghetto than to walk on the moon," and he would cut back the appropriations for development of the supersonic transport. Also, he has repeatedly acknowledged that when history assesses America's involvement in Vietnam, both he and the Kennedy Administration will bear their "share of the blame, the responsibility."

But readers of his book "To Seek a Newer World" and followers of his Senate career know that long before the campaign he was on record in favor of a post-cold-war, post-New-Frontier liberalism—one which had abandoned anti-Communism as the organizing principle of our foreign policy and had embraced community participation (à la Bedford-

Stuyvesant) as the key to domestic tranquility and progress. The difference is that until March 31, 1968, he was involved in a complicated dialectic, moving from what the New Frontier might have been and what the Great Society never was, toward a vision of his own. Johnson was the usurper, and Robert in William Shannon's useful phrase, was "the heir apparent."

His initial campaign oratory, in which he accused the President of "calling upon the darker impulses of the American spirit," reflected the intensity of his own inner struggle. "He had to get it out of his system," says an aide. But when Johnson withdrew, he took the Vietnam issue with him and shipped it over to Paris in Averell Harriman's attaché case. Now Robert Kennedy had a new problem: in addition to the preservation and definition of his newly emerging identity, he had to build a bridge between the issues which brought him into the compaign and the actions which might win him a majority of the delegates at the Chicago convention.

"The over-all strategy is remarkably like 1960," says Ted Sorenson, who handles day-to-day operations in the informal campaign directorate. "We have to use the primaries to impress the industrial states like Michigan, Illinois, Ohio, Pennsylvania and New Jersey that the people are on our side."

But Kennedy's rhetorical solution has been a kind of intellectual DMZ, where the Old Right meets the New Left. At least in places like Sioux Falls, S. D., Hastings, Neb., Davenport, Iowa, and Crawfordsville, Ind., the noisy code words are conservative, the quiet elaborations are progressive and consistent with positions set forth in "To Seek a Newer World." VIOLENCE, LOOTING, RIOTING, and CRIME IN THE STREETS are UNACCEPTABLE and LAW AND ORDER MUST BE RESTORED (with social justice); THE WELFARE SYSTEM MUST BE REPLACED (by a job system); RUNNING THINGS FROM WASHINGTON IS UNACCEPTABLE and MUST BE REPLACED BY LOCAL CONTROL (under Federal standards); THE FEDERAL GOVERNMENT CAN'T SOLVE THE PROBLEMS OF THE CORE CITY: it needs the help of PRIVATE ENTERPRISE which will come in if given TAX CREDITS and OTHER INCENTIVES. Even on Vietnam the candidate is OPPOSED TO UNILATERAL WITHDRAWAL, but doesn't like to see AMERICAN CASUALTIES CLIMBING WHILE SOUTH VIETNAMESE CASUALTIES GO DOWN (regardless of what happens at the negotiating table). IT IS UNACCEPTABLE THAT AMERICAN BOYS ARE DYING WHILE SOUTH VIETNAMESE BOYS CAN BUY THEIR WAY OUT OF THE DRAFT.

Sorenson's memoirs quote Henry Stimson's observation: "Campaign speeches are not a proper subject for a friendly biographer." That may be true, and a close reading of Robert's off-the-cuff remarks reveals a consistent commitment to decentralization, community participation and equal justice at home, and de-escalation abroad. Nevertheless, a content analysis of his language on the stump might help explain why Robert Kennedy has yet to cast a more clearly defined shadow of his own.

The Image

Lou Harris, who was the official Kennedy pollster in 1960 but who has since parted ways with the family, found as late as May that 57 per cent of those polled nationally feel that Robert is "trying to get elected on his brother's memory." But in Indiana, in the wake of the hard-fought primary, the figure went down to 35 percent . At the same time 52 per cent of the Hoosiers polled thought he had "many of the same qualities as his brother." He had managed to retain a fidelity to John's image while emerging from John's shadow. "He's got one national profile and different state profiles where he has campaigned in the primaries," says Harris. "The question is whether he can bring them into line." "Put bluntly," says a critic, "the question is whether he can spend enough to wrench public attitudes around on a national basis."

Robert Kennedy entered the race trying to convince the voters that he was right about Vietnam. He has ended up trying to convince them that they are wrong about him, that he is not "ruthless," "calculating," "opportunistic." His best arguments are the genuine compassion he displays when in the presence of the very old, the very sick or the very young, and his natural, bantering, non-ruthless question-answering style —considerably looser than the more controlled campaign performance of John, whose sense of humor didn't really surface until after he was President:

At Purdue:
Q.: Can you think of any reason other than your name, money and opportunism that qualifies you to run for President?
R.F.K.: Yes. (*Laughter*)

At Creighton University:
Q.: What's the difference between you and Senator Eugene McCarthy?
R.F.K.: Charm . . . a sense of humor . . . and he's ruthless. I'm only kidding. I don't want to see headlines tomorrow saying, "Kennedy Charges McCarthy Ruthless!"

At Wahoo, Neb., where a reporter from the high school newspaper showed him the results of a student poll and asked if he had any comment:
R.F.K.: Yes. Tell those who voted for me, thank you.
Q.: What about those who voted against you?
R.F.K.: Tell them I'll get them. (*Laughter from the press corps.*)

Across the street from a movie marquee advertising "The Happiest Millionaire":
R.F.K.: (*pointing at the sign*): Make that come true on election day!

E. B. White does write about the language; he uses it to reveal the functionings of bureaucracy and to make himself known.

E. B. White

Two Letters, Both Open

New York, N. Y.
12 April 1951

The American Society for the Prevention of Cruelty to Animals
York Avenue and East 92nd Street
New York 28, N. Y.
Dear Sirs:

I have your letter, undated, saying that I am harboring an unlicensed dog in violation of the law. If by "harboring" you mean getting up two or three times every night to pull Minnie's blanket up over her, I am harboring a dog all right. The blanket keeps slipping off. I suppose you are wondering by now why I don't get her a sweater instead. That's a joke on you. She has a knitted sweater, but she doesn't like to wear it for sleeping; her legs are so short they work out of a sweater and her toenails get caught in the mesh, and this disturbs her rest. If Minnie doesn't get her rest, she feels it right away. I do myself, and of course with this night duty of mine, the way the blanket slips and all, I haven't had any real rest in years. Minnie is twelve.

In spite of what your inspector reported, she has a license. She is licensed in the State of Maine as an unspayed bitch, or what is more commonly called an "unspaded" bitch. She wears her metal license tag but I must say I don't particularly care for it, as it is in the shape of a hydrant, which seems to me a feeble gag, besides being pointless in the case of a female. It is hard to believe that any state in the Union would circulate a gag like that and make people pay money for it, but Maine is always thinking of something. Maine puts up roadside crosses along the highways to mark the spots where people have lost their lives in motor accidents, so the highways are beginning to take on the appearance of a cemetery, and motoring in Maine has become a solemn experience, when one thinks mostly about death. I was driving along a road near Kittery the other day thinking about death and all of a sudden I heard the spring peepers. That changed me right away and I suddenly thought about life. It was the nicest feeling.

You asked about Minnie's name, sex, breed, and phone number. She doesn't answer the phone. She is a dachshund and can't reach it, but she wouldn't answer it even if she could, as she has no interest in outside calls. I did have a dachshund once, a male, who was interested in the telephone, and who got a great many calls, but Fred was an exceptional dog (his name was Fred) and I can't think of anything offhand that he *wasn't* interested in. The telephone was only one of a thousand things. He loved life—that is, he loved life if by "life" you mean "trouble," and of course the phone is almost synonymous with trouble. Minnie loves life, too, but her idea of life is a warm bed, preferably with an electric pad, and a friend in bed with her, and plenty of shut-eye, night and day. She's almost twelve. I guess I've already mentioned that. I got her from Dr. Clarence Little in 1939. He was using dachshunds in his cancer-research experiments (that was before Winchell was running the thing) and he had a couple of extra puppies, so I wheedled Minnie out of him. She later had puppies by her own father, at Dr. Little's request. What do you think about *that* for a scandal? I know what Fred thought about it. He was some put out.

Sincerely yours,
E. B. White

New York, N. Y.
12 April 1951

Collector of Internal Revenue
Divisional Office
Bangor, Maine
Dear Sir:

I have your notice about a payment of two hundred and some-odd dollars that you say is owing on my 1948 income tax. You say a warrant has been issued for the seizure and sale of my place in Maine, but I don't know as you realize how awkward that would be right at this time, because in the same mail I also received a notice from the Society for the Prevention of Cruelty to Animals here in New York taking me to task for harboring an unlicensed dog in my apartment, and I have written them saying that Minnie is licensed in Maine, but if you seize and sell my place, it is going to make me look pretty silly with the Society, isn't it? Why would I license a dog in Maine, they will say, if I don't live there? I think it is a fair question. I have written the Society, but purposely did not mention the warrant of seizure and sale. I didn't want to mix them up, and it might have sounded like just some sort of cock and bull story. I have always paid my taxes promptly, and the Society would think I was kidding, or something.

Anyway, the way the situation shapes up is this: I am being accused in New York State of dodging my dog tax, and accused in Maine of being behind in my federal tax, and I believe I'm going to have to rearrange my life somehow or other so that everything can be brought together, all in one state, maybe Delaware or some state like that, as it is too confusing for everybody this way. Minnie, who is very sensitive to my moods, knows there is something wrong and that I feel terrible. And now *she* feels terrible. The other day it was the funniest thing, I was packing a suitcase for a trip home to Maine, and the suitcase was lying open on the floor and when I wasn't looking she went and got in and lay down. Don't you think that was cute?

If you seize the place, there are a couple of things I ought to explain. At the head of the kitchen stairs you will find an awfully queer boxlike thing. I don't want you to get a false idea about it, as it looks like a coffin, only it has a partition inside, and two small doors on one side. I don't suppose there is another box like it in the entire world. I built it myself. I made it many years ago as a dormitory for two snug-haired dachshunds, both of whom suffered from night chill. Night chill is the most prevalent dachshund disorder, if you have never had one. Both these dogs, as a matter of fact, had rheumatoid tendencies, as well as a great many other tendencies, specially Fred. He's dead, damn it. I would feel a lot better this morning if I could just see Fred's face, as he would know instantly that I was in trouble with the authorities and would be all over the place, hamming it up. He was something.

About the tax money, it was an oversight, or mixup. Your notice says that the "first notice" was sent last summer. I think that is correct, but when it arrived I didn't know what it meant as I am no mind reader. It was cryptic. So I sent it to a lawyer, fool-fashion, and asked him if *he* knew what it meant. I asked him if it was a tax bill and shouldn't I pay pay it, and he wrote back and said, No, no, no, no, it isn't a tax bill. He advised me to wait till I got a bill, and then pay it. Well, that was all right, but I was building a small henhouse at the time, and when I get building something with my own hands I lose all sense of time and place. I don't even show up for meals. Give me some tools and some second-handed lumber and I get completely absorbed in what I am doing. The first thing I knew, the summer was gone, and the fall was gone, and it was winter. The lawyer must have been building something, too, because I never heard another word from him.

To make a long story short, I am sorry about this non-payment, but you've got to see the whole picture to understand it, got to see my side of it. Of course I will forward the money if you haven't seized and sold the place in the meantime. If you have, there are a couple of other things on my mind. In the barn, at the far end of the tieups, there is a goose sitting on eggs. She is a young goose and I hope you can manage everything so as not to disturb her until she has brought off her goslings. I'll give you one, if you want. Or would they belong to the federal government anyway, even though the eggs were laid before the notice was mailed? The cold frames are ready, and pretty soon you ought to transplant the young broccoli and tomato plants and my wife's petunias from the flats in the kitchen into the frames, to harden them. Fred's grave is down in the alder thicket beyond the dump. You have to go down there every once in a while and straighten the headstone, which is nothing but a couple of old bricks that came out of a chimney. Fred was restless, and his headstone is the same way—doesn't stay quiet. You have to keep at it.

I am sore about your note, which didn't seem friendly. I am a friendly taxpayer and do not think the government should take a threatening tone, at least until we have exchanged a couple of letters kicking the thing around. Then it might be all right to talk about selling the place, if I proved stubborn. I showed the lawyer your notice about the warrant of seizure and sale, and do you know what he said? He said, "Oh, that doesn't mean anything, it's just a form." What a crazy way to look at a piece of plain English. I honestly worry about lawyers. They never write plain English themselves, and when you give them a bit of plain English to read, they say, "Don't worry, it doesn't mean anything." They're hopeless, don't you think they are? To me a word is a word, and I wouldn't dream of writing anything like "I am going to get out a warrant to seize and sell your place" unless I meant it, and I can't believe that my government would either.

The best way to get into the house is through the woodshed, as there is an old crocus sack nailed on the bottom step and you can wipe the mud off on it. Also, when you go in through the woodshed, you land in the back kitchen right next to the cooky jar with Mrs. Freethy's cookies. Help yourself, they're wonderful.

Sincerely yours,

E. B. White

Five questions . . .

1. Consider the selection from Rohman and Wlecke, "The Person in the Process." What do you suppose E. B. White had in mind before he began to write?

2. Without looking back, how many of the essays in this group were written in the first person? Would you change any of them to third?

3. The writing of the children Kohl taught shows them as having something to say, but not having a standard English. Which would be more easily understood by their peers: standard English or their own language? What does *bad* mean? How do you keep the quality of a special language or dialect and still communicate outside its limits?

4. Can you make a more effective piece out of some of the children's paragraphs and still keep the concrete quality that is now there?

5. What are your favorite terms when discussing political questions? Do the terms themselves represent you adequately?

Parson Weems Fable by Grant Wood. Collection of Ferry Marquand.

The Artist in His Museum by Charles Willson Peale.
Courtesy The Pennsylvania Academy of the Fine Arts.

An assignment . . .

1. Look for examples of other people's language in use around you. Make a list, card file, a scrapbook—any form you like—of a standard language of contemporary clichés.

2. Search your memory for the language of your childhood. What did you call stickball? What do you remember as the vocabulary of your place and age? Perhaps you can divide it into two sorts, the words that you were taught and the words you found out or made-up. Suppose we say that the language is the expression of self and is also the way to know one's self. What does the language of your self reveal— first, about the world you grew up in: what your parents liked, what they found offensive, what they wanted for you; second, about what you were like: what you did and liked to do, what you disliked, what you felt?

3

Pushbutton language

Think about your idea of Christ. Even if you have no interest in the name at all except as one you have heard, you have probably been exposed to pictures and stories about the name. Write a paragraph or make a list setting out some of the qualities, physical and moral, that you associate with the name *Christ*.

Now read the following news reports. Does your list include any of the qualities which make the Christ of these stories remarkable? Most images of Christ are probably characterized by a Christ stereotype; these stories are characterized by personal discovery of a Christ. Try now writing another paragraph about a being you would like to discover, whatever your present belief.

That New-Time
Religion

Vendors sold Cokes and hot dogs, and a 2,000-voice choir sang softly while people surged toward their seats. As daylight vanished, the arc lights came on to illuminate the playing field of Atlanta Stadium dotted with ten different sets illustrating the life of Christ. The Garden of Gethsemane bloomed near home plate. Pilate's court sat along the third-base line. Calvary loomed in right field. While the baseball diamond provided an unusual backdrop for a Passion play, the 48,000 people who last week jammed the stadium to see "Behold the Man" were attracted by a rarity of a different kind. The choir was thoroughly integrated; so was the 500-member cast. And Christ Himself was black.

"What happened at Atlanta Stadium Sunday night," glowed Atlanta Constitution columnist Jim Rankin, "was the closest thing to a miracle that has happened in this city in many years." Staged so close to the heart of Dixie where religion is as segregated as the courthouse steps, the play was bound to have an impact. "The idea," said white schoolteacher Willard Rustin, who played St. James the Lesser, "is to show the spirit of America, to show that peaceful coexistence between the races is possible."

COOL: Backed by $75,000 from local businessmen as part of Atlanta's keep-it-cool program this summer, the idea for the play itself did not originate with the local liberal establishment. It was written several years ago by a red-bearded Methodist minister named Frank Marshall Roughton as a master's thesis at the University of Georgia. A former small-town rock 'n' roll deejay, Roughton got religion in the late 1950s when he joined a traveling troupe of Passion players. In 1959, he went to Georgia's Candler School of Theology; while there, he continued his theatrical career, and today he still performs in religious plays.

When Roughton talked the Christian Council of Metropolitan Atlanta into sponsoring his show, he made it clear that the cast would be integrated. "It's time," he told the ministers, "you got over the old bugaboo that Negroes can't play any role except a farm hand or a chimney sweep." He told them he even might find a Negro to play Christ. "I'll be a John the Baptist," said the 38-year-old preacher. "I'll see him and see his stature and then look in his eyes, and I'll know he's the man."

Was Jesus an Outsider?

The Anglican clergy who belong to the modern Churchmen's Conference are pledged "to proclaim the Christian Gospel in the light of modern knowledge and in the idiom of today." Last week, the idiom was at least controversial as Canon Hugh Montefiore, a respected theologian, calmly told a conference meeting at Oxford University that Jesus might have been a homosexual. After all, the graying New Testament scholar argued, "women were his friends, but it is men he is said to have loved. The homosexual explanation is one we cannot ignore."

One modern churchman who thought it should be ignored was Dr. Michael Ramsey, Archbishop of Canterbury, who promptly issued a statement affirming that "Christ's dealings with both men and women were those of a perfect man." The canon was also accused by a conference delegate of words that "smear our Lord." But Montefiore, author of such books as "Awkward Questions on Christian Love," defended his suggestion as "serious and reverent." In fact, he believes his theory helps to explain God's efforts, through Jesus, to identify with society's outcasts. "Jesus was identified from conception to death with the outsider. Whether or not we accept the so-called virgin birth, no one can deny that he was born out of wedlock."

Even the most learned scholars offer no absolute evidence of the nature of Christ. Personal experiences of heaven and hell are even less available than the shreds of material and literary evidence about Christ. Yet Jonathan Edwards, an eighteenth-century Puritan minister could say, "The God that holds you over the pit of hell, much as one holds a spider or some loathsome insect over the fire. . . . " And a self-styled preacher of our own decade warned a man, "You are going where there are no ballparks. I had a vision of hell and there were no ballparks in hell." Most people who talk about heaven and hell do not see these places quite so vividly. At best, heaven and hell are very far away, or seem so, which may account for some of the vague writing about them; however, vague and weak writing about the here and now comes from the same use of automatic language ungrounded in experience, from an unawareness of the difference between seeing and just looking.

A good example is a student's theme about being caught in the sweep of an ocean wave. He wrote this final climactic sentence: "Suddenly I was tossed onto the beach out of the moving bowels of the ocean." If his language were being used to describe something he really saw, he certainly was not saying much for himself. Here is another student looking at himself in the mirror the morning after a beer party: "My eyes bore all the earmarks of a hangover." Earmarks are notches or metal tags in the ears of livestock.

Neither the writers nor the classes noticed the grotesque sentences at first. *Bowels* and *earmarks* were simply fancy words for insides and signs. And *insides* and *signs* are not very descriptive of waves or hungover eyes. These clichés not only were no better than relatively abstract words, they also kept the writers from seeing and communicating their experiences.

See what you know about the origins and images involved in the following clichés:

> grease the palm
>
> turn the tables
>
> turn over a new leaf
>
> a stitch in time saves nine
>
> cream of the crop
>
> zero in
>
> give him the sack
>
> corner the market

Why do writers use these phrases when a single word does the same job?

STICKS AND STONES VS. NAMES AND FACES

An old proverb says, "Sticks and stones will break your bones, faces and names can't hurt you." That is not true. Unfortunately, many bigots and tyrants have proven in the mass appeal of their speeches and writing that names and faces do hurt people. They hurt people because they prevent gullible or weary listeners from really seeing something. Stereotypes like Nigger, Yid, fat cop, pig, fascist, hippie, and square keep us from seeing individuals. People get turned into things, and we all know that most things are disposable.

Abstract or general language works the same way. *Law and order* is a very popular political phrase, and most voters never ask to see what a candidate means by it. Law and order was praised by Hitler, but few people today want his law and order. The world and Germany finally saw what *his* words meant.

Few politicians and even fewer men in the street have Hitler's potential for power; however, if they use words that encourage looking instead of seeing, they can undermine other people's ability to think about real lives and events. That, in turn, can undermine a democratic society. If our language habits are like those of Hitler, we harm our society seriously, whether we are talking about a tiddly-winks game or a tea party, clothes or Congress. We form the thought habits of a blind society that will follow an evil vision as easily as a good one.

No one can see all there is to see around him; in addition our biases shape our perceptions—what we see, hear, feel, and taste. Bias in this case may be good or bad. The bias imparted to our perceptions by clichés is usually bad or at least out of date, since clichés by nature take time to solidify.

Not only do we speak and write clichés, but we live in them. Here is a short section of Peter Blake's book, *God's Own Junkyard*. In many cases the junkyard may be the place we are living in.

Peter Blake

Townscape

The two American scenes shown on the opposite page document the decline, fall, and subsequent disintegration of urban civilization in the United States. The two examples are separated by a mere 140 years in time, and by only a few hundred miles in space: at the top, Thomas Jefferson's campus for the University of Virginia, in Charlottesville, started in the 1820's; below, Canal Street, the busiest business street in New Orleans, as it appears in the 1960's.

Jefferson's serene, urban space has been called "almost an ideal city— unique in America, if not in the world." Canal Street, one fervently hopes, has not been called anything in particular in recent times. It is difficult to believe that these two examples of what a city might be were suggested by the same species of mammal, let alone by the same nation. Jefferson called his campus "an expression of the American mind"; New Orleans' Canal Street, and all the other dreary Canal Streets that defile America today, have not been called "expressions of the American mind" by any but this nation's mortal enemies.

On the next several pages are further portraits of the American city today—portraits, not caricatures. They need no identification; for these are the places two-thirds of us call "home." We walk or drive through them each day; this is where we work, shop, and are also born, exist, and die. What manner of people is being reared in these infernal wastelands?

One answer is: people who no longer see. Recently, the Honorable

Photograph by George Cserna.

Photograph by Wallace Litwin.

Mario Cariello, President of the Borough of Queens, one of the five boroughs of New York City, delivered himself of the considered opinion that his Borough "truly represents the full flowering of advanced, urban living." Oh Mario, son of Rome—and of Florence, Siena, Venice, Pisa, possibly even Orvieto—there was once another son of Italy, a man called Leon Battista Alberti, who asked, "How are we moved by a huge, shapeless, ill-contrived pile of stones?" Alas, he lived and died before there was a fully flowering Borough of Queens; and so you may never know his answer.

Language is often touted as being the instrument that lifts man above all other animals. Eugene Ionesco may believe that language has had that historical role. He nevertheless sees that it can become the substance of tragedy.

Eugene Ionesco
The Tragedy of Language

In 1948, before writing my first play, *La Cantatrice Chauve*, I did not want to become a playwright. My only ambition was to learn English. Learning English does not necessarily lead to writing plays. In fact it was because I failed to learn English that I became a dramatist. Nor did I write these plays as a kind of revenge for my failure, although *La Cantatrice Chauve* has been called a satire on the English middle-classes. If I had tried and failed to learn Italian, Russian or Turkish, it would have been quite easy to say that the play resulting from these vain efforts was a satire on Italian, Russian or Turkish society. I feel I should make myself clear. This is what happened: nine or ten years ago, in order to learn English, I bought an English-French Conversation Manual for Beginners. I set to work. I conscientiously copied out phrases from my manual in order to learn them by heart. Then I found, reading them over attentively, that I was learning not English but some very surprising truths: that there are seven days in the week, for example, which I happened to know before; or that the floor is below us, the ceiling above us, another thing that I may well have known before but had never thought seriously about or had forgotten, and suddenly it seemed to me as stupefying as it was indisputably true. I suppose I must have a fairly philosophical turn of mind to have noticed that these were not just simple English phrases with their French translation which I was copying into my exercise-book, but in fact fundamental truths and profound statements.

For all that, I had not yet reached the point of giving English up. And a good thing too, for after these universal truths the author of my manual passed on from the general to the particular; and in order to do so, he expressed himself, doubtless inspired by the Platonic method, in the form of dialogue. In the third lesson two characters were brought together and I still cannot tell whether they were real or invented: Mr. and Mrs. Smith, an English couple. To my great surprise Mrs. Smith informed her husband that they had several children, that they lived in the outskirts of London, that their name was Smith, that Mr. Smith worked in an office, that they had a maid called Mary, who was English too, that for twenty years they had known some friends called Martin, and that their home was a castle because 'An Englishman's home is his castle'.

Of course, I imagine Mr. Smith must have been somewhat aware of all this; but you can never be sure, some people are so absent-minded; besides, it is good to remind our fellows of things they may be in danger of forgetting or take too much for granted. Apart from these particular eternal truths, there were other temporal truths which became clear: for example, that the Smiths had just dined and that, according to the clock, it was nine o'clock in the evening, English time.

Allow me to draw your attention to the nature of Mrs. Smith's assertions, which are perfectly irrefutable truisms; and also to the positively Cartesian approach of the author of my English Manual, for it was his superlatively systematic pursuit of the truth which was so remarkable. In the fifth lesson the Martins, the Smiths' friends, arrived; the conversation was taken up by all four and more complex truths were built upon these elementary axioms: 'The country is more peaceful than big cities', some maintained; 'Yes, but cities are more highly populated and there are more shops', replied the others, which is equally true and proves, moreover, that contrasting truths can quite well coexist.

It was at that moment that I saw the light. I no longer wanted merely to improve my knowledge of the English language. If I had persisted in enlarging my English vocabulary, in learning words, simply in order to translate into another language what I could just as well say in French, without paying any attention to the matter contained in these words, in what they reveal, this would have meant falling into the sin of formalism, which those who nowadays direct our thinking so rightly condemn. I had become more ambitious: I wanted to communicate to my contemporaries the essential truths of which the manual of English-French conversation had made me aware. On the other hand the dialogue between the Smiths, the Martins, the Smiths *and* the Martins, was genuinely dramatic, for drama *is* dialogue. So what I had to produce was a play. Therefore I wrote *La Cantatrice Chauve*, which is thus a specifically didactic work for the theatre. And why is this work called *La Cantatrice Chauve* and not *L'Anglais sans Peine*, which I first thought of calling it, or *L'Heure Anglaise*, which is the title that occurred to me a little later? It would take too long to explain in full: one of the reasons why *La Cantatrice Chauve* received this title is that no prima donna, with or without hair, appears in the play. This detail should suffice. A whole section of the play is made by stringing together phrases taken from my English Manual; the Smiths and the Martins in the Manual are the Smiths and the Martins in my play, they are the same people, utter the same maxims, and perform the same actions or the same 'inactions'. In any 'didactic drama', it is not our business to be original, to say what we think ourselves: that would be a serious crime against objective *truth*; we have only, humbly, to pass on the knowledge which has itself been passed to us, the ideas we have been given. How could I have allowed myself to make the slightest change to words expressing in such an edifying manner the ultimate truth? As it was *genuinely* didactic, my play must on no account be original or demonstrate my own talent!

. . . However, the text of *La Cantatrice Chauve* only started off as a lesson (and a plagiarism). An extraordinary phenomenon took place, I know not how: before my very eyes the text underwent a subtle transformation, against my will. After a time, those inspired yet simple sentences which I had so painstakingly copied into my schoolboy's exercise-book, detached themselves from the pages on which they had been written, changed places all by themselves, became garbled and corrupted. Although I had copied them down so carefully, so correctly, one after the other, the lines of dialogue in the manual had got out of hand. It happened to dependable and undeniable truths such as 'the floor is below us, the ceiling above us'. An affirmation, as categorical as it is sound, such as: the seven days of the week are Monday, Tuesday, Wednesday, Thursday, Friday, Saturday, Sunday, so deteriorated that Mr. Smith, my hero, informed us that the week was composed of three days, which were: Tuesday, Thursday and Tuesday. My characters, my *braves bourgeois*, the Martins, husband and wife, were stricken with amnesia: although seeing each other and speaking to each other every day, they no longer recognised each other. Other alarming things happened: the Smiths told us of the death of a certain Bobby Watson, impossible to identify, because they also told us that three quarters of the inhabitants of the town, men, women, children, cats and ideologists were all called Bobby Watson. Finally a fifth and unexpected character turned up to cause more trouble between the peace-able couple: the Captain of the Fire Brigade. And he told stories which seemed to be about a young bull that gave birth to an enormous heifer, a mouse that begot a mountain; then the fireman went off so as not to miss a fire that had been foreseen three days before, noted in his diary and due to break out at the other side of town, while the Smiths and the Martins took up their conversation again. Unfortunately the wise and elementary truths they exchanged, when strung together, had gone mad, the language had become disjointed, the characters distorted; words, now absurd, had been emptied of their content and it all ended with a quarrel the cause of which it was impossible to discover, for my heroes and heroines hurled into one another's faces not lines of dialogue, not even scraps of sentences, not words, but syllables or consonants or vowels! . . .

. . . For me, what had happened was a kind of collapse of reality. The words had turned into sounding shells devoid of meaning; the char-acters too, of course, had been emptied of psychology and the world ap-peared to me in an unearthly, perhaps its true, light, beyond understand-ing and governed by arbitrary laws.

While writing this play (for it had become a kind of play or anti-play, that is to say a real parody of a play, a comedy of comedies), I had felt genuinely uneasy, sick and dizzy. Every now and then I had to stop working and, wondering what devil could be forcing me on to write, I would go and lie down on the sofa, afraid I might see it sinking into the abyss; and myself with it. When I had finished, I was nevertheless very proud of it. I imagined I had written something like the *tragedy of language*! . . . When it was acted, I was almost surprised to hear the laughter of the audience, who took it all (and still take it) quite happily, considering it a comedy all right, even a sort of rag. A few avoided this mistake (Jean Pouillon for example) and recognised a certain malaise. Others realised that I was poking fun at the theatre of Bernstein and his actors: Nicolas Bataille's cast had already realised this, when they had tried to act the play (especially during the first performances) as if it were a melodrama.

Later, serious critics and scholars analysed the work and interpreted it solely as a criticism of bourgeois society and a parody of Boulevard Theatre. I have just said that I accept this interpretation too: but to my mind there is no question of it being a satire of a *petit bourgeois* men-tality that belongs to any particular society. It is above all about a kind of universal *petite bourgeoisie*, the *petit bourgeois* being a man of fixed ideas and slogans, a ubiquitous conformist: this conformism is, of course, revealed by the *mechanical language*. The text of *La Cantatrice Chauve*, or the Manual for learning English (or Russian or Portuguese), consisting as it did of ready-made expressions and the most threadbare clichés, revealed to me all that is automatic in the language and behavior of people: 'talking for the sake of talking', talking because there is nothing personal to say, the absence of any life within, the mechanical routine of every-day life, man sunk in his social background, no longer able to distinguish himself from it. [The Smiths and the Martins no longer know how to talk because they no longer know how to think, they no longer know how to think because they are no longer capable of being moved, they have no passions, they no longer know how to 'be', they can 'become' anyone or anything, for as they are no longer themselves, in an impersonal world, they can only be someone else, they are inter-changeable.] Martin can change places with Smith and vice versa, no-one would notice the difference. A tragic character does not change, he breaks up; he is himself, he is *real*. Comic characters are people who do not exist.

(The start of a talk given to French Institutes in Italy, 1958)

An exercise . . .

Here are two models of language used to gain a specific end.

Christian Youth Corps

(Anti-Semitic, Anti-Negro, Anti-Catholic Florida-based group)

Each man needs the following basic equipment for GUERRILLA WARFARE OPERATIONS.

(1) Any standard rifle of at least .30 cal.

(2) One good quality hunting knife, 6″ blade.

(3) At least 1000 rounds of ammunition . . .

Rebellion News

(A radical Negro newspaper)

It now appears that it is necessary to defend ourselves with guns and rifles. . . . Right now anyone over 21 can buy a rifle. We recommend buying M-1 carbines or any other high powered semi-automatic weapon. . . . Every black person should own a rifle. . . . BUY YOUR RIFLE NOW!!!

First, make two lists, one for each model, of the words and phrases by which these groups might justify their urging of an arms race.

Second, from your own point of view, look over the words on both lists. Ask yourself whether
a) the two lists should be the same
b) their meaning to you includes "death" in various guises

Third, consider again the nature of clichés. It is the premise of this chapter that the acceptance of clichés is in part responsible for a confrontation of the sort modeled here. Would you agree?

A BRIEF AMPLIFICATION

Here are five more statements issued by groups willing to use violence to solve social problems. Examine their language. Most of these groups wear uniforms of some sort. Is the language here also a kind of uniform?

Extremists on Guns

The following are excerpts from statements and articles by officials of various ultra right-wing and left-wing groups on the subject of guns and gun control legislation. They were cited by the Anti-Defamation League of B'nai B'rith in a report entitled "Extremism, Violence and Guns."

THE MINUTEMEN
(A national semi-military extremist group)

Suppose the reader has no gun at all and is planning to buy one gun only. . . . What shall it be? Though it will surprise many people, my recommendation is a .22 caliber semi-automatic pistol. . . .

It's true that the .22 lacks the "shock" effect of a more powerful cartridge, but this is largely compensated for by the ease of putting a well-placed shot into heart or brain. When needed a second well-aimed shot can be fired quicker from a .22 than from a more powerful weapon. . . .

As a deadly weapon, their effect can be greatly increased by using hollow-point bullets filled with poison. If needed, the hole in the point can be opened up further with a small drill. Sodium or potassium cyanide are two fast acting and easily obtainable poisons. Pharmacists or medical doctors will have ready access to succinyl choline or tubocurarine which are excellent when used in powdered form. If nothing better is available ordinary household lye (thirty cents for a pound can at your local grocery store) will do nicely. . . .

For a small "hideaway" gun, the .25 Browning automatic is unsurpassed. A man wearing slacks and sports shirt can easily carry one of these in his side pants pocket without its ever being noticed.

Don't overlook the potential of .22 long rifles, pistols or rifles, as guerrilla warfare or resistance weapons. These advantages include ready availability, light weight, fast accurate second and third shots, due to absence of recoil, light weight and readily available ammunition, good accuracy, simplicity of care, and comparatively small report when fired. The .22 can be silenced completely with materials that are always available. Although the .22 lacks killing power, this can be readily increased by filling hollow point bullets with poison. . . .

WE URGE YOU TO WRITE AT LEAST FIVE LETTERS TO VARIOUS UNITED STATES SENATORS AND FIVE TO CONGRESSMEN *OPPOSING* ANY FURTHER GUN RESTRICTIONS *OF ANY KIND.* Do this upon receipt of this letter. Then immediately call five of your friends or associates and urge them to do likewise. HURRY!

BREAKTHROUGH
(Detroit-based self-defense group. Speech of its leader, Donald Lobsinger.)

> We have held this meeting to tell our elected officials. . . .
> That we have not surrendered . . . (cheers)
> And we will never surrender. . . . (cheers)
> If another riot comes, we will protect our property. . . . (cheers)
> We will protect our homes. . . . (cheers)
> And we will fire! (wild cheering).

NATIONAL STATES RIGHTS PARTY
(The American Nazi Party)

. . . The N.S.R.P. believes that every White patriot should own and possess sufficient arms and extra large quantities of ammunition. That is necessary because of the red and black revolution that the Jews have unleashed against America. The purpose of Jewish legislation against the right to bear arms is to disarm all law-abiding patriotic citizens so that they will be unable to defend themselves against criminals and revolutionaries. We are exercising our Constitutional right to possess firearms and ammunition and say, "Let the Jews be damned."

PAUL REVERE ASSOCIATED YEOMEN, INC. (PRAY)
(A New Orleans-based rightist organization)

Join the National Rifle Association. . . .

Absolutely REFUSE to register or give up your arms—under ANY circumstances!

Stock up on rifles, shotguns, pistols—all of STANDARD make; with LOTS OF STANDARD ammunition. Arm EVERY member of your family who can shoot a gun to protect his own life!

Consult with your next-door neighbors on HOW best to protect your family and home. Arrange to wear certain kinds of caps or shirts for identification; so you won't be firing at one another in the confusion. DO NOT organize the whole block in your neighborhood, as 10 per cent of the people are probably on the OTHER side—trained for "leadership" of such neighborhood groups, to sell you into do-nothing surrender. Be your OWN LEADER of your own household. . . . and make it an ARMED ARSENAL!

PREPARE yourself and your sons to fight in the streets—in the alleys —in the parks—in public buildings—around the water works—power plants —CITY HALL—TV and radio stations . . . while your wife and daughters protect their lives and your home with gasmasks, shotguns, rifles and pistols.

REMEMBER! The Communists CANNOT subdue an ARMED citizenry!

THE BLACK PANTHERS
(A black nationalist group)

It is . . . mandated as a general order to all members of the Black Panther Party for Self-Defense that all members must acquire the technical equipment to defend their homes and their dependents and shall do so. Any member of the Party having such technical equipment who fails to defend his threshold shall be expelled from the Party for Life.

An assignment . . .

Contradictions are implicit in many of the words in "Extremists on Guns." As clichés or jargon, they seem to mean one thing; in practice, they mean another. Gather a brief vocabulary of such words or phrases in the above relations, then try tracing that vocabulary in publications available to you.

How often do you find this vocabulary used as an almost deliberate means of disguising the ends toward which it may work? You may want to make a small dictionary from your exercise vocabulary or to work up a short report of what you have found.

A problem . . .

We have suggested a contradiction of sorts here: on the one hand, we have provided examples of language used where a uniform group agrees on what is being said; on the other hand, we have suggested that different people or groups looking at the same words will have different responses. Words which communicate precisely within a group therefore fail to communicate precisely between that group and others. Perhaps language is no better than its users. Do you agree? *How would you now begin to define "good" English?*

READING: SOME EXAMPLES

Sydney J. Harris

You Will Never Be
a Writer if You . . .

You'll never be a writer if you refer to a player who "sparked" a rally, to a politician who "spearheaded" a drive, to a committee that "slated" a candidate.

You'll never be a writer if you refer to "optimizing" an opportunity, "enthusing" over a campaign, or "finalizing" a contract.

You'll never be a writer if you refer to Paris as "Gay Paree," to Ireland as the "Emerald Isle," to a lion as the "king of beasts," to a nose as a "proboscis," to death as "passing away."

You'll never be a writer if you refer to a battle "royal," a "foregone" conclusion, a "miscarriage" of justice, a "helping" hand, a diamond "in the rough," an "eagle" eye, a "shadow" of doubt, a sight "for sore eyes."

You'll never be a writer if you refer to an actor as a "thespian," to a poet as a "bard," to a tavern-keeper as a "boniface," to a social leader as a "socialite," to a fireman as a "smoke-eater."

You'll never be a writer if you refer to a "far" cry, a "lap" of luxury, a "pageant" of history, a "square peg" in a round hole, a "sumptuous" meal, a "swank" apartment, a "supreme" sacrifice, a "token" of esteem.

You'll never be a writer if you refer to time as "immemorial," to climate as "halcyon," to truth as "naked," to hearts of "gold" or "stone," to feet of "clay," to a penny as "pretty," to a dollar as "almighty," to opinions as "considered," to plots that "thicken."

You'll never be a writer if you refer to peace offerings as "olive branches," to delicate situations as "hanging by a thread," to any movement out as an "exodus," to the latest possible time as "the eleventh hour," to born in prosperous circumstances as a "silver spoon," to an irrevocable step as "crossing the Rubicon."

You'll never be a writer if you refer to a burdensome possession as a "white elephant," to dancing as "the light fantastic," to a mountain as "coming to Mahomet," to anything selling like "hot cakes" (except hot cakes), to "leaps" that go with bounds and "fits" that go with starts and "hooks" that go with crooks and "bags" that go with baggages and "tooth" that goes with nail and "rack" that goes with ruin and "fast" that goes with loose and "high" that goes with dry and "wear" that goes with tear and . . . .

SILENT MUSIC

Sometimes you suddenly realize you have been hearing music for hours without knowing it. Or have you been hearing it? Why spend a fortune turning hit tunes into music that isn't really supposed to be heard. Here is Kenneth Allsop's analysis of Muzak.

Kenneth Allsop
Music by Muzak

"Just lemme hear some more of that rock-'n'-roll music, Any old way you choose it," sing the Beatles. In fact there is neither rock-'n'-roll beat nor choice in the music with the biggest audience of all. If one definition of pop music is that which reaches the greatest number of ears, the Liverpool sound and rhythm-and-blues, Tamla Motown and soul, city-billy and protest, and all their later Top Ten modifications, are swamped into insignificance by Muzak.

Kenneth Allsop, "Music by Muzak," © 1967 by *Encounter.* Reprinted by permission.

Muzak is the dreamy drizzle you are vaguely conscious of in assembly plant or cocktail bar. Like the ethereal lilt from the pipes on the doves' tails in Shangri-La, it drifts from the air upon you as you cross a hotel lobby and ambushes you again in the lift. It will probably be subliminally hovering above you in the dentist's chair, at the restaurant table, at the factory bench, in the executive suite, in the supermarket, in a bank's vaults, in a zoo reptile house, in the beauty parlour. If you were privileged to fly in a space capsule, cruise in a nuclear submarine, or attend a Pentagon strategic conference, Muzak would be there murmuring into your brain cells. You are now likely to emerge from the womb into a Muzak environment, for many a labour room is wired-up, and as likely to be shot into the crematorium's final annihilating flames to a requiem of Muzak Honey-Rich Strings oozing *Unforgettable*. If you are so moved in the vicinity of Waterloo Station, you will go to the lavatory to Muzak.

Muzak now seeps vapour-like through almost every cranny of urban life. It is the twilight-sleep gas that pervades the atmosphere wherever human beings congregate. It is a plasma of pacification, administered by drip transfusion from concealed grilles. The distinguishing characteristic of Muzak is its indistinguishability: it is seldom possible to remember the tune that creamy ensemble was playing five seconds ago, which floated on the periphery of familiarity, for it is boned, predigested melodious pap, processed to slide down without gulp or taste, and canned for consumption everywhere.

From the endlessly unspooling 550,000 miles of magnetic tape, it is absorbed by sixty million people a day in America alone, its birthplace, and by twice as many again throughout Europe and Asia. The U.S.S.R. is being equipped with its own system. The franchise company in Britain, Planned Music Ltd.—a wholly-owned subsidiary of A.T.V.—already has a 3,000-mile cable network reaching two million listeners a day. But "listener" is a discordant word, for the fundamental idea is that the brainwashed millions do not *listen* to Muzak: they hear it and are blandished by it. It is *Brave New World* spell-binding for our electronic age; sorcery spooned out of *Moon River*, mass mesmerism by *Mary Poppins*.

Needless to say, the Muzak men themselves don't see their product in quite that light, or at least describe it in those terms. Yet they are surprisingly candid about their aims and achievements, which are paraded with an innocent ardour. In the New York headquarters on Park Avenue South, in a custom-tailored Muzak heaven (silky indirect lighting, apricot walls, frondy tendrils, ceramic lamps, and, natch, the faint purl of a mellifluous *pot-pourri*, as pastel-shaded and blank as the walls) I got the straight pitch.

"Muzak is music to be heard but not listened to," explained a young executive. "Once you're conscious of it there's something wrong. No, I wouldn't agree that it's soporific. On the contrary, it's euphoric. It creates a feeling of well-being where people work in conditions of stress or monotony. Muzak gives workers a cohesive feeling of belonging. They share the mood created by Muzak, whether it's in a hospital or a foundry, but it also gives a good sense of privacy and separation. There's now this total environment concept—ergonomics—which figures out how to provide people with the right functional furniture, atmosphere, spatial lighting and colour climate, and Muzak is architected in, just as routine as air-conditioning.

"Every big building going up in New York has the Muzak system as a basic requisite. No community in the United States of more than fifty thousand population is now without Muzak. This is scientifically programmed background music. But what we're really marketing is a technique for motivating people in boring or tense situations. We put a smile on the face; we pick up morale; we improve efficiency."

A member of the sales staff had just been dealing with a finicky customer, who, finding that Hawaiian medleys hadn't stimulated appetites with South Sea island magic, had asked for a replacement of standard Muzak in his café—and was now "as happy as a clam." Standing in the transmission studio, beside banks of huge reels silently unwinding their eight hours of happiness into the ether, the sales director explained that if a hitch occurred the computerised control threw the automation into an emergency programme. "So really," he added with serene satisfaction, "nothing can stop Muzak."

Don O'Neill, the programme chief who organises the fortnightly recording sessions with the fifty-five arranger-conductors and the groups ranging from sextets to orchestras thirty-strong, talked of the art of tempering Muzak to exact requirements. "It stresses melody and simplicity," he said. "It has no tricks or colour. Of course, carried to an extreme this could be uninteresting, vapid, without character. Programmes aren't designed for entertainment, but to eliminate monotony and boredom. You couldn't do that if the music itself was boring, so we try to find a line between that and music that dominates or distracts.

"No crescendos, no runs from pianissimo to fortissimo—that would interfere with the worker's concentration on his task. Nor must it be too loud. A lot of brass is used, but we score it to be non-intrusive, discreet, with mutes or delicate playing, so that we get the tonal quality without the powerful impact. We never put on voices. That doesn't go over too well. They stop to listen. We couldn't use the Rolling Stones or Elvis Presley."

Behind Mr. O'Neill hung large coloured graphs: the *Mood Stimulus Charts*. It should not be supposed that Muzak dribbles over infinite mud flats of sameness. It is far more subtly constructed, a mosaic dove-tailed from aerial reconnaissance of the human spirit. Mr. O'Neill guided me along the first diagram, a roller-coaster of the *Industrial Efficiency Curve*. The zig-zagging red line illustrated how the typical worker arrives at the factory in moderately chipper shape, to nose-dive into a steep slump around ten-thirty. As lunch-time approaches, his morale and output rev upward, a glow sustained until early afternoon. Then, wham again—down at about three-thirty into the deepest pit of lassitude and blues, with a distinct recovery as the clock nears knock-off time. Alongside, the *Muzak Stimulus Curve* disclosed how these treacherous human vagaries are manipulated and ironed out, so that each veer on the first chart is neatly complemented and counterbalanced. Between 8 a.m. and 9 a.m. the worker is gently bombarded with a Muzak that is "*Moderate*: to instil cheerful attitude at start of first half of workday." Between 9 a.m. and 10 a.m.: "*Moderate to bright*: to combat onset of potential tension." Between 10 a.m. and 11 a.m.: "*Bright*: to counter maximum potential tension at period of morning when most critical." Between noon and 1 p.m.: "*Mild and restful*: to provide midday relief." A similar cycle is dialled for the afternoon, except that the brightness is brighter.

In its pioneer infancy, Muzak made such blunders as programming Brazil with sambas and tangos, which proved too aggressively attention-bothering. Thereafter, the identical American-styled tapes were distributed globally: "All music is functional. There is no difference anywhere how people respond to Muzak." In the Muzak world the whole human race can be plugged into the same circuit. The circuit also pumps out silence. "Research studies reveal a law of diminishing returns," continued Mr. O'Neill. "You can play too much music. If you keep it going continuously it becomes part of the monotony of the job and production rates drop. We alternate fifteen minutes of music with a fifteen-minute interlude. This produces the effect of breaking-up the day. We sell silence."

Nor is the old record incessantly rehashed. Mr. O'Neill is in charge of the Muzak Tune Treasury, a ten million dollar punch-card library from which computers retrieve and juggle 365 programmes a year with no tune repeated more than once every nine days on any premises. "People don't really know they're hearing it, but they scream if it's turned off," Mr. O'Neill said with business-like wizardry.

Those upon whom Muzak has impinged will hazily recall that it calibrates from Victor Sylvester-ish buoyant to Melachrinoesque swoony, adjusted to whether it is intended for, say, high-school examination rooms or that Atlanta motel swimming pool with underwater Muzak, which leaves you with the desperate thought that you couldn't escape it even by drowning yourself. The menu is schemed out with astute relevance to its egress point. *Stormy Weather* and *I Don't Stand a Ghost of a Chance* are banned on airlines. Presumably *It Can't Be That Bad* and *Scarlet Ribbons* have been excised from the tapes for the Houston operating theatre where the Duke of Windsor had hum-along abdominal surgery, and *I've Got a Feeling I'm Falling* from the programmes for President Johnson's ranch. Certainly classical music has been altogether scrubbed. "I love Mozart, Beethoven, Brahms," said another Muzak man, "but I couldn't work to that stuff. Hindemith felt that music could be put to some everyday use but wasn't sure what it could be. Muzak did it. As a matter of fact, if we could invent a subsonic signal that could have the same influence over work-people that Muzak has, we'd broadcast that."

Frank though the spokesmen are, there is an even balder philosophy in Muzak's printed literature. This unashamedly exhorts the employer to boost his profits and stealthily soothe his staff. A Muzak booklet entitled *The Science of Music* says:

Music arouses varied emotional and physical responses in people, both on a conscious and subconscious level. Muzak puts this powerful effect to work for business. . . . In the early 1930s Muzak psychologists and musicologists began harnessing the emotional power of music for the specific purpose of creating pleasant and profitable business environment. Unlike most other forms of music, music by Muzak was designed to be unobtrusive and to require no active listening. Years of research resulted in the present-day Muzak concept of "functional programming," a technique for motivating people with precisely timed and planned musical conditioning. . . Transmitted via modern communications channels, music by Muzak is employed as a technique of realistic profit-minded management in outstanding businesses throughout the world.

It carries on:

Every year industry loses countless millions of productive hours to inefficiency, mistakes, and absenteeism, most of which start with boredom and monotony. Every year, thousands upon thousands of restaurants and stores fail to reach their potential sales level—because of customer tension and irritation from noise, crowds, long waits, or cold atmosphere. Muzak creates an atmosphere beneficial to workers, and produces a sense of well-being among customers and patrons. . . . It puts people in a relaxed frame of mind and enhances their buying moods. . . . Accurate timing is crucial to the Muzak concept, for the music must always be in phase with the emotional needs of its audience. Muzak has invested millions of dollars for research into accurate, automatic, and foolproof timing methods.

Another promotional leaflet emphasises: "The very nature of functional background music requires that it is not a noticeable factor to those 'hearing' it. It follows that people do not realise the way music is used today or appreciate the size and scope of the industry at work behind the loudspeaker. . . . As each tune is played there is an increase in stimulus value, giving workers a psychological sense of moving forward—making work seem easier and time pass faster." *Can Music Increase the Efficiency of Your Office By Ten Per Cent?* asks one booklet. It describes how Muzak can "create a work mood." Pointing out that all the "ten best-

managed companies" and "over eighty per cent of America's largest life
insurance companies and banks" shimmer with Muzak, it declares: "When
personnel become tense or feel frustrated, they develop an indifference
which often results in costly errors, accidents, absenteeism, lateness and
non-productive activities such as early departures, idle conversation and
daydreaming." Muzak "enhances a company's image, combats tension and
fatigue with timed psychological lifts, and masks distracting machine
noise, conversation or cold silence."

Testimonials are presented from realistic, profit-minded and silence-
hating businessmen. Edward S. Godlewski, of the Levi Case Company,
Schenectady, confides: "Our plant is as noisy as ever, but our employees
don't realise it." Frank A. Gunther, of Radio Engineering Laboratories
Inc., New York, reports: "Increased efficiency, fewer errors, eased tensions, happy, contented employees, and a reduction in absenteeism—a
major profit factor." The Muzak Marketing Memos, for internal circula-
tion among the sales force, yield some interesting attitudes: "Profit-
minded hotel managers know Muzak warms a cold, impersonal atmosphere, keeps guests on the premises with money to spend. Check-out
bills are fatter." A Memphis school principal finds Muzak has "pleasing
effects on young children during the cafeteria period when they are somewhat uninhibited." One Marketing Memo introduces Irving Wexler, Mi-
ami Beach franchise vice-president, a completely "Muzakated" man. "He
lives the product he sells. He believes in it. He has Music by Muzak
in his home, in every room, and it plays twenty-four hours a day. 'I know
Muzak has therapeutic, psychological value,' Irving says. 'We sleep with
it on, watch television with it on. I never permit it to be shut off.'" Even
Irving's "fiery red Thunderbird convertible" is on the beam. "Muzak programming is played continuously on the special automobile tuner."

Yet another Marketing Memo discusses *Togetherness: The Bad Side*:

Proxemics, the study of human behavior at varying degrees of proximity, gives
Muzakmen another opportunity to show how Muzak programming has proved
highly successful as the solution to problems caused by overcrowding or isolation in offices. The new science concerned with spatial relationships among
office workers reveals clearly that employee performance can suffer if workers
are packed too close together, or, conversely, if they are too widely separated
or isolated. A crowded office atmosphere leads to worker tensions evidenced
sooner or later in tardiness, early departures, absenteeism, idle chatter, water-
cooler visits, rest-room lounging, protracted personal telephone calls and a
high rate of turnover. Conversely, employees situated too far apart tend to develop feelings of loneliness, being lost. . . . Unobtrusive Muzak programming
forms a kind of screen in the crowded atmosphere, separates workers with an
invisible curtain of melody and reduces substantially feelings of fear and oppression. . . . Also it gives isolated employees a sense of belonging, a unified
and cohesive feeling of working together, because background music by Muzak
acts as an invisible but unifying force.

There is also a British publication entitled *Muzak In Industry*. Its glossy pages are lucent with smiling, contented hands. There are many quotes, straight from the fraternal factory floor: "Muzak takes your mind off your own personal worries." "When we had *Housewives' Choice* the women sang with the records and tended to skylark about. Muzak stopped that." "It seems to pass the time away. When the first quarter of an hour is over there is always the next one to look forward to."

However, this is all rah-rah-rah material for the front-line salesmen. Hardcore Muzak tactics can be tracked down in duller documents, such as *Effects of Muzak on Industrial Efficiency* and *Effects of Muzak on Office Personnel*. These are jingly with diagrams and mathematical equations: sections headed "Calculation of Significance of Performance Change in Test Department," "Manual Dexterity Speed Scores and Productivity Changes with Muzak," and "Percentage Increase Before Muzak and With Muzak." Even more fascinating is the *Vigilance With Background Music* report prepared by the Human Engineering Laboratories at the Aberdeen Proving Ground, Maryland. This instructs how to conduct music-while-you-press-the-button tests for missile system personnel. The examiner is advised to get it across this way:

Alertness is very important in a lot of military situations—your life, and maybe your buddies' lives, too, can depend on how alert you are. The task you're to do is based on what the officer in charge of a missile site might have to do. . . . The colour of the light tells you what the target's identification is: green—friendly; yellow—unidentified; red—enemy. You press a key to tell the missile system what to do.

Then the examiner switches on Muzak.

It may come as a relief to the civilian population barred from this special Muzak intimacy to learn that the overwhelming majority of missile button-pressers approve of background music while responding alertly to the coloured flashes. In fact most said: "The music was really great." What worries me is the small, but possibly vital, percentage who sulked: "I didn't like the tunes." I hope they work out a programme that keeps them permanently pleased.

In point of fact, this recalcitrant minority isn't confined to Minutemen control centres. Muzak has a problem. There is a last ditch awkward squad who won't be human-engineered. Melvin Cohen, Muzak's research manager, concedes that there are "negative responses from three to five per cent of the population: elderly spinster ladies, just-plain-contrary people and individualists who won't accept any music that others have chosen for them. . . ." One can see how infuriating they must be to Muzak. But my impression was that Muzak feels they can ride this small irritation: they *know* which is the winning side.

Edwin A. Roberts, Jr.

Fantacy: Rhetoric
for the Moon

The whole world seems to agree that the attempt to land a man on the moon boggles the mind. It is the greatest adventure story in all of history, a scientific expedition that makes the deeds of earlier explorers look like the groping of children. A man has a right to be boggled by the thought of it.

Luckily, everything will be put into perspective by the columnists of the daily press, who have the knack of sorting things out for the average reader. But suppose, just suppose, that this tremendous event was beyond even the analytical resources of the columnists. Suppose they were so overwhelmed by the fact of a lunar landing that they too were boggled. They would then be forced to face their typewriters armed only with the familiar music of their styles.

It will never happen, of course, but imagine, just imagine. . . .

James Reston: "The central fact about the moon is not that it lacks people, but that it is uninhabited, and it is this phenomenon that has Washington wondering. It is difficult enough to promote political stability in a populated area; in an unpopulated area the problem is complicated by the absence of even the most primitive form of social organization. Thus the question is not whether popular elections are possible, but whether representative democracy for the moon is attainable."

Joseph Alsop: "While the newspaper that claims pre-eminence has been considering the immediate implications of man's first lunar landing, the larger problem has been deliberately ignored. The earth and moon have been encircling the sun for millions of years, but there is no reason to believe this mechanism will continue to function indefinitely. Indeed, there is persuasive evidence that it is only a matter of time before the earth and its satellite leave their courses and hurtle sunward to a fiery doom."

Rowland Evans and Robert Novak: "A significant aspect of the feat of Apollo 11 is its impact on the heated battle now being waged in the 14th ward of South Amboy, N.J. In a little noticed development, labor leader Cookman ("Cookie") Baker has been knocking on doors in the predominantly Serbian section of the city, drumming up support for

Edwin A. Roberts, "Fantasy: Rhetoric for the Moon," reprinted from *The National Observer*.

Jacob ("Jack") Armstrong in the contest for game warden. What Baker hopes to do, according to sources close to South Amboy politics, is cash in on the Armstrong name now that Neil Armstrong is in the headlines. If he is successful, the implications for 1972 are clear."

William F. Buckley, Jr.: "While fatuous critics of the lunar effort are now in hiding, reasonable men can ponder the synodic, anomalistic, nodal, and sidereal ramifications of the silvery ball. Considering what is known about the evection and parallactic inequality of the moon's longitude, one may reasonably conclude—I dare say *must* conclude—that, pending untoward planetary perturbations, the stars are right for the nation's long-delayed return to first principles."

Drew Pearson: "This column has learned that several months before man's first lunar flight, some 300,000 acres of prime moon real estate (much of it bordering on the Sea of Tranquility) was purchased by the entire United States Senate. The deal was arranged on the Senate's personal behalf by the Moonbeam Foundation, whose board of directors includes the nine justices of the Supreme Court. The property is to be sold to the House of Representatives which will then lease it to President Nixon. The President is anxious to build a golf course on the moon, figuring his wood shots will be improved by the low lunar gravity."

Well, that's what some of the nation's best-known columnists might write if the landing on the moon turned out to be too much to cope with. But they are all experienced hands, and they have seen so much on earth that an astronaut's visit to a heavenly body is unlikely to cause any of them to break stride.

The worst of it is that the crew of Apollo 11 doesn't include a columnist, someone to recount the experience with precision and in his own style. For his readers it would be like having an old friend on board, describing his perhaps not-so-brave feelings as the space craft departed earth, accelerated into the void, and finally settled down amid the craters of the moon.

One good choice for the assignment would be Jimmy Breslin, former columnist and former politician. His story would make history. After a Moon dateline he might begin: "This place is dry as dust, so if you come up here bring your own."

STRIP DOWN FOR POPULARITY

Clichés are very popular, or they would not be clichés. Can we therefore expect to find that the so-called popular arts are really clichés of art forms? Abraham Kaplan is a philosopher specializing in behavioral science. Art is of course a form of human behavior and has consequences like most forms of behavior.

Abraham Kaplan

The Aesthetics of the Popular Arts

Aesthetics is so largely occupied with the good in art that it has little to say about what is merely better or worse, and especially about what is worse. Unremitting talk about the good, however, is not only boring but usually inconsequential as well. The study of *dis*-values may have much to offer both aesthetics and criticism for the same reasons that the physiologist looks to disease and the priest becomes learned in sin. Artistic taste and understanding might better be served by a museum of horribilia, presented as such. It is from this standpoint that I invite attention to the aesthetics of the popular arts.

I

By the popular arts I do not mean what has recently come to be known as pop art. This, like junk art and some of the theater of the absurd, is the present generation's version of dada. In some measure, no doubt, it serves as a device for enlarging the range of artistic possibilities, exploring the beauty in what is conventionally dismissed as meaningless and ugly, as well as the ugliness in what is conventionally extolled as beautiful. Basically, it is a revolt against the artistic establishment, a reaction against the oppressiveness of the academic and familiar. As such, it is derivative as though to say, "You call *this* junk?" If it is lacking in artistic virtue, its vice is like that of watching a voyeur—the sins of another are presupposed. It is what pop art presupposes that I am calling *popular art.*

Second, I do not mean simply *bad art,* neither the downright failures nor those that fall just short of some set of critical requirements. It is a question of *how* they fail and, even more, to what sort of success they aspire. Popular art may be bad art, but the converse is not necessarily true. It is a particular species of the unaesthetic that I want to isolate.

Similarly, I set aside what may be deprecated as merely minor art. Its products are likely to be more popular, in the straight-forward sense, than those which have greatness. The *Rubaiyat* may be more widely read than *De rerum natura,* and *The Hound of the Baskervilles* more than *Crime and Punishment,* but each is excellent after its own kind. A work of minor art is not necessarily a minor work. Greatness, that is to say, is a distinctive aesthetic attribute—a matter of scope or depth and so forth; the word is not just a designation for the highest degree of artistic value. The lack of greatness may be a necessary condition for popular art, but most surely it is not a sufficient condition.

The *kind* of taste that the popular arts satisfy, and not how widespread that taste is, is what distinguishes them. On this basis, I provisionally identify my subject as *midbrow art,* to be contrasted with what appeals to either highbrow or lowbrow tastes. Popular art is what is found neither in the literary reviews nor in the pulp magazines, but in the slicks; neither in gallery paintings nor on calendars, but on Christmas cards and billboards; neither in serious music nor in jazz, but in Tin Pan Alley. The popular arts may very well appeal to a mass audience, but they have characteristics that distinguish them from other varieties of mass art, and distinctive contexts and patterns of presentation. A work of popular art may be a best seller, but it is not assigned in freshman English nor reprinted as a comic. It may win an Academy Award, but it will be shown neither at the local Art Cinema nor on the late, late show.

Many social scientists think that these symptoms—for they are no more than that—provide an etiology of the disease. Midbrow art, they say, is more properly designated *middle-class art.* It is a product of the characteristic features of modern society: capitalism, democracy, and technology. Capitalism has made art a commodity, and provided the means to satisfy the ever widening demands for the refinements of life that earlier periods reserved to a small elite. Democracy, with its apotheosis of majorities and of public opinion, has inevitably reduced the level of taste to that of the lowest common denominator. The technology of the mass media precludes the care and craftsmanship that alone can create works of art. For a time it was fashionable to lay these charges particularly at American doors, to view the popular arts as the distinctive features of American culture; but by now, I think, most of those who take this line see popular art more generally, if not more generously, as only "the sickness of the age."

My thesis is this: that popular art is not the degradation of taste but its immaturity, not the product of external social forces but produced by a dynamic intrinsic to the aesthetic experience itself. Modern society, like all others, has its own style, and leaves its imprint on all it embraces. But this is only to say that our popular art is *ours,* not that it is our sole possession. Popular art is usually said to stem from about the beginning of the eighteenth century, but in its essence it is not, I think, a particularity of our time and place. It is as universal as art itself.

II

We might characterize popular art first, as is most often done, with respect to its *form*. Popular art is said to be simple and unsophisticated, aesthetically deficient because of its artlessness. It lacks quality because it makes no qualifications to its flat statement. Everything is straightforward, with no place for complications. And it is standardized as well as simplified: one product is much like another. But it is just the deadly routine that is so popular. Confronted with that, we know just where we are, know what we are being offered, and what is expected of us in return. We can respond with mechanical routines ourselves, and what could be simpler and more reliably satisfying?

Yet this account of the matter is itself too simple to be satisfactory. For why should simplicity be unaesthetic? Art always strips away what is unessential, and purity has always been recognized as a virtue. Put the adjective *classic* before it and simplicity becomes a term of high regard. What is simple is not therefore simple-minded. Art always concentrates, indeed it owes its force to the power of interests that have been secured against distraction and dissipation. Art, we may say, does away with unnecessary complications. We can condemn popular art for treating as expendable the *necessary* complications, but nothing has been added to our aesthetic understanding till we have been given some specification of what complexity is necessary and what is not.

There is a similar lack in the condemnation of popular art as being standardized. One Egyptian statue is much like another, after all, just as there are marked resemblances among Elizabethan tragedies or among Italian operas. Such works are not for that reason assigned the status of popular art. The standardization of popular art does not mean that forms are stylized but that they are *stereotyped*. The failing does not lie in the recurrence of the forms but in deficiencies even in the first occurrence. The characters and situations of the usual movie, words and music of popular songs, the scenes and sentiments of magazine illustrations are all very much of a piece, each after its own kind. What makes them stereotypes is not that each instance of the type so closely resembles all the others, but that the type as a whole so little resembles anything outside it.

The stereotype presents us with the blueprint of a form, rather than the form itself. Where the simplifications of great art show us human nature in its nakedness, the stereotypes of popular art strip away even the flesh, and the still, sad music of humanity is reduced to the rattle of dry bones. It is not simplification but schematization that is achieved; what is put before us is not the substance of the text but a reader's digest. All art selects what is significant and suppresses the trivial. But for popular art the criteria of significance are fixed by the needs of the standardization, by the editor of the digest and not by the author of the reality to be grasped. Popular art is never a discovery, only a reaffirmation. Both producer and consumer of popular art confine themselves to what fits into their own schemes, rather than omitting only what is unnecessary to the grasp of the scheme of things. The world of popular art is bounded by the limited horizons of what we think we know already; it is two-dimensional because we are determined to view it without budging a step from where we stand.

The simplification characteristic of popular art amounts to this, that we restrict ourselves to what *already* comes within our grasp. Every stereotype is the crystallization of a prejudice—that is, a prejudgment. Even the inanimate materials of its medium have been type-cast.

Popular art is dominated throughout by the star system, not only in its actors but in all its elements, whatever the medium. Every work of art, to be sure, has its dominant elements, to which the rest are subordinate. But in popular art it is the dominant ones alone that are the objects of interest, the ground of its satisfaction. By contrast, great art is in this sense pointless; everything in it is significant, everything makes its own contribution to the aesthetic substance. The domain of popular art is, paradoxically, an aristocracy, as it were: some few elements are singled out as the carriers of whatever meaning the work has while the rest are merged into an anonymous mass. The life of the country is reduced to the mannered gestures of its king. It is this that gives the effect of simplification and standardization. The elements of the schema, of course, need not be characters in the strict sense; action, color, texture, melody, or rhythm may all be simplified and standardized in just this way.

What popular art schematizes it also abstracts from a fully aesthetic context. Such an abstraction is what we call a *formula*; in formula art the schema is called upon to do the work of the full-bodied original, as though a newspaper consisted entirely of headlines. The abstraction can always be made, as is implied in the very concept of style, and of specific stylistic traits. We can always apply formulas to art; the point is that popular art gives us the formula but nothing to apply it to. Popular art uses formulas, not for analysis but for the experience itself. Such substance as it has is only the disordered residue of other more or less aesthetic experiences, themselves well on the way towards schematization. Popular art is thus doubly derivative: art first becomes academic and then it becomes popular; as art achieves style it provides the seeds of its own destruction.

Thus popular art may be marked by a great emphasis on its newness—it is first-run, the latest thing. Prior exposure diminishes whatever satisfactions it can provide. Alternatively, it may be endlessly repeated: familiarity gives the illusion of intimacy. Most often, popular art is characterized by a combination of novelty and repetition: the same beloved star appears in what can be described as a new role. The novelty whips up a flagging interest. At the same time the repetition minimizes the demands made on us: we can see at a glance what is going on, and we know already how it will all turn out. Curiosity is easily satisfied, but suspense may be intolerable if we must join in the work of its resolution. We are really safe on the old, familiar ground. Popular art tosses baby in the air a very little way, and quickly catches him again.

In sum, what is unaesthetic about popular art is its formlessness. It does not invite or even permit the sustained effort necessary to the creation of an artistic form. But it provides us with an illusion of achievement while in fact we remain passive.

More specifically, there is work undone on both perceptual and psychodynamic levels.

As to the first, aesthetic *perception* is replaced by mere *recognition*. Perceptual discrimination is cut off, as in most nonaesthetic contexts, at the point where we have seen enough to know what we are looking at. Moreover, the perception is faithful, not to the perceptual materials actually presented, but to the stereotyped expectations that are operative. We perceive popular art only so as to recognize it for what it is, and the object of perception consists of no more than its marks of recognition. This is what is conveyed by the designation *kitch*: an object is kitch when it bears the label *Art* (with a capital "A"), so disposed that we see and respond only to the label.

On the psychodynamic level, the aesthetic *response* is replaced by a mere *reaction*. The difference between them is this: a reaction, in the sense I intend it, is almost wholly determined by the initial stimulus, antecedently and externally fixed, while a response follows a course that is not laid out beforehand but is significantly shaped by a process of self-stimulation occurring then and there. Spontaneity and imagination come into play; in the aesthetic experience we do not simply react to signals but engage in a creative interpretation of symbols. The response to an art object shares in the work of its creation, and only thereby is a work of art produced. But in popular art everything has already been done. Thus the background music for the popular movie signalizes the birth of love with melodious strings and the approach of death by chords on the organ; contrast these signals with the demanding substance of, say, Prokofieff's music for Eisenstein's *Alexander Nevsky*. To vary the metaphor, popular art is a dictatorship forever organizing spontaneous demonstrations and forever congratulating itself on its freedoms.

In the taste for popular art there is a marked intolerance of ambiguity. It is not just that we shrink from doing that much work—the work, that is, of creative interpretation. At bottom, aesthetic ambiguity is frightening. Popular art is a device for remaining in the same old world and assuring ourselves that we like it, because we are afraid to change it.

At best, popular art replaces ambiguity by some degree of complexity. This is most clearly demonstrated by the so-called *adult Western*, which has moved beyond the infantilism of "good guys" and "bad guys," by assigning virtues and vices to both heroes and villains. But the moral qualities themselves remain unambiguous in both sign and substance. The genre, for the most part, is still far from the insight into the nature of good and evil invited, say, by Melville's Captain Ahab or, even more, by his Billy Budd. Yet, *High Noon* is undeniably a far cry from *The Lone Ranger*.

In short, popular art is simple basically in the sense of easy. It contrasts with art in the markedly lesser demands that it makes for creative endeavor on the part of its audience. An artistic form, like a life form, is a creation, and like the living thing again, one which demands a cooperative effort, in this case between artist and audience. We cannot look to popular art for a fresh vision, turn to it for new direction out of the constraints of convention. Unexplored meanings call for their own language, which must be fashioned by a community with the courage and energy of pioneers. But for a new language there must be something new to say; what the pioneer can never do without is—a frontier.

III

Quite another approach to the analysis of popular art is by way of feeling rather than form. Popular art may be characterized by the kinds of emotions involved in it, or by its means of evoking or expressing them.

Thus there is a common view that popular art is merely *entertainment*, in a pejorative sense. It does not instruct, does not answer to any interests other than those aroused then and there; it is just interesting in itself. Popular art offers us something with which to fill our empty lives; we turn to it always in quiet desperation. It is a specific against boredom, and is thus an inevitable concomitant of the industrial civilization that simultaneously gives us leisure and alienates us from anything that might make our leisure meaningful.

Whatever merits this view may have as sociology, as aesthetics I do not find it very helpful. That the interests satisfied by popular art are self-contained is hardly distinctive of the type. All art has inherent value, independent of its direct contributions to extra-aesthetic concerns. And all art has a certain intrinsic value, affording delight in the form and color of the aesthetic surface, independent of depth meaning. That something is entertaining, that it gives joy to the beholder without regard to more serious interests, so-called, is scarcely a reason therefore, for refusing it artistic status. It is surely no more than snobbery or a perverted puritanism to disparage entertainment value, or to deny it to art.

The question still remains, What makes popular art entertaining? To invoke a contrast with boredom is not of much help, for that is a descriptive category, not an explanatory one; as well say that work is an antidote to laziness. Indeed, I think the claim might be more defensible that popular art, far from countering boredom, perpetuates and intensifies it. It does not arouse new interests but reinforces old ones. Such satisfaction as it affords stems from the evocation in memory of past satisfactions, or even from remembered fantasies of fulfillment. What we enjoy is not the work of popular art but what it brings to mind. There is a nostalgia characteristic of the experience of popular art, not because the work as a form is familiar but because its very substance is familiarity.

The skill of the artist is not in providing an experience but in providing occasions for reliving one. In the experience of popular art we lose ourselves, not in a work of art but in the pools of memory stirred up. Poetry becomes a congeries of poetic symbols which now only signalize feeling, as in the lyrics of popular songs; drama presents dramatic materials but does not dramatize them—brain surgery, or landing the crippled airliner; painting becomes illustration or didactic narrative from Jean Greuze to Norman Rockwell.

Conventions are, to be sure, at work; the associations aroused are not wholly adventitious and idiosyncratic. But *convention* is one thing and *style* is another. One is extrinsic to the materials, giving them shape; the other is the very substance of their form. The difference is like that between a railroad track and a satellite's orbit: convention is laid down beforehand, guiding reactions along a fixed path, while style has no existence antecedent to and independent of the ongoing response itself. For this reason popular art so easily becomes dated, as society changes its conventional associations; seen today, [the melodramatic play] *A Father's Curse* surely evokes laughter rather than pity or fear. On the other hand, a work of art may become popular as its expressive substance is replaced by associations—Whistler's "*Mother*" is a case in point.

Popular art wallows in emotion while art transcends it, giving us understanding and thereby mastery of our feelings. For popular art, feelings themselves are the ultimate subject matter; they are not present as a quality of the experience of something objectified, but are only stimulated by the object. The addiction to such stimuli is like the frenzied and forever frustrated pursuit of happiness by those lost souls who have never learned that happiness accrues only when the object of pursuit has its own substance. Popular art ministers to this misery, panders to it, we may say. What popular art has in common with prostitution is not that it is commercialized; art also claims its price, and the price is often a high one. The point is that here we are being offered consummations without fulfillment, invited to perform the gestures of love on condition that they remain without meaning. We are not drawn out of ourselves but are driven deeper into loneliness. Emotion is not a monopoly of popular art, as Dickens, Tschaikovsky, or Turner might testify; but these artists do not traffic in emotion. Popular art, on the contrary, deals in nothing else. That is why it is so commonly judged by its impact. To say truly that it is sensational would be high praise; what we usually get is an anaesthetic.

IV

There is yet another reason for questioning whether popular art provides relief from boredom, bringing color into grey lives. The popular audience may be chronically bored, but this is not to say that it is without feeling. On the contrary, it is feeling above all that the audience contributes to the aesthetic situation and that the popular artist then exploits. Popular art does not supply a missing ingredient in our lives, but cooks up a savory mess from the ingredients at hand. In a word, feelings are usually lacking in *depth*, whatever their intensity. Popular art is correspondingly shallow.

Superficial, affected, spurious—this is the dictionary meaning of *sentimental*. So far as feeling goes, it is sentimentality that is most distinctive of popular art. There is a sense, I suppose, in which we could say that all feeling starts as sentiment: however deep down you go you must begin at the surface. The point is that popular art leaves our feelings as it finds them, formless and immature. The objects of sentiment are of genuine worth—cynicism has its own immaturity. But the feelings called forth spring up too quickly and easily to acquire substance and depth. They are so lightly triggered that there is no chance to build up a significant emotional discharge. Sentimentality is a mark always of a certain deficiency of feeling; it is always just words, a promise that scarcely begins to move toward fulfillment.

Yet it is only an excess of a special kind that is in question here. We must distinguish sentimentality from sensibility, that is, a ready responsiveness to demands on our feelings. Art has no purchase at all on insensibility. Unless a man is capable of being moved, and moved deeply, in circumstances where his antecedent interests are not engaged, art has nothing for him. Sensibility becomes sentimental when there is some disproportion between the response and its object, when the response is indiscriminate and uncontrolled. Emotion, Beethoven once said, is for women, and I think we all understand him; but we are to keep in mind the difference between such women as Elizabeth Bennett and her mother.

It is this difference that we want to get at. Dewey comes very near the mark, I believe, in characterizing sentimentality as "excess of receptivity without perception of meaning." It is this lack of meaning, and not intensity of feeling, that makes the receptivity excessive. Popular art is not sentimental because it evokes so much feeling, but because it calls for so much more feeling than either its artist or audience can handle. The trouble is not too much feeling but too little understanding; there is too little to be understood.

Sentimentality, then, moves in a closed circle around the self. The emotions released by a stimulus to sentiment satisfy a proprietary interest, and one which is directed inward. The important thing is that they are *my* feelings, and what is more, feelings about *me*. The prototype of sentimentality is self-pity. Popular art provides subjects and situations that make it easy to see ourselves in its materials. Narcissus, W. H. Auden conjectured, was probably a hydrocephalic idiot, who stared into the pool and concluded, "On me it looks good!" The self-centeredness of popular art is the measure of our own diminishing.

V

Perhaps the most common characterization of popular art is that it is *escapist*. There is no doubt that it can produce a kind of narcosis, a state of insensibility arresting thought and feeling as well as action—in a word, a trance. We do not look at popular art, we stare into it, as we would into flames or moving waters. I think it not accidental that the most popular media, movies and television, are viewed in the dark. The medium is such stuff as dreams are made on.

Popular art seeks to escape ugliness, not to transform it. There is nothing like a pretty face to help you forget your troubles, and popular art can prettify everything, even—and perhaps especially—the face of death. It provides an escape first, therefore, by shutting out the reality, glossing over it.

But popular art is said to do more; it seems to provide an escape not only *from* something but also *to* something else, shuts out the real world by opening the door to another. We do not just forget our troubles but are reminded of them to enjoy the fantasy of overcoming them. Popular art is as likely to relieve anxiety as boredom.

The world of popular art is unreal not just in the sense that it consists of symbols rather than realities—"it's only a movie." Science, too, replaces things by abstract representations of them, but it is not for that reason derogated as an escape from reality. But what makes it science, after all, is that it is capable of bringing us back to the realities, however far from them it detours in its abstractions. Whether symbols are essentially an escape depends at bottom on what they symbolize. Popular art is unreal, not as being sign rather than substance, but because what it signifies is unreal. All art is illusion, inducing us as we experience it to take art for life. But some of it is true to life, illusory without being deceptive. Popular art is a tissue of falsehoods.

Popular art depicts the world, not as it is, nor even as it might be, but as we would have it. Everything in it is selected and placed in our interest. It is a world exhausted in a single perspective—our own—and it is peopled by cardboard figures that disappear when viewed edgewise. We are not to ask whether the rescued maiden can cook, nor do we see the gallant knight through the eyes of the dragon, who is after all only wondering where his next meal will come from. In real drama, said [the nineteenth-century German dramatist] Friedrich Hebbel, all the characters must be in the right. That is how God sees them, which is to say, how they are. Art, like science, raises us up to divine objectivity; popular art is all too human.

It must be admitted that popular art is more sophisticated today than it was a generation or so ago. But often its realism is only another romantic pose. In popular art, it is a matter of taking over the shapes of realism but not the forms. The modern hero of popular art is given a generous admixture of human failings; but no one is really fooled—he is only superman in disguise. Indeed, the disguise is so transparent that it can be discarded: we have come full circle from Nick Carter through Sam Spade to James Bond.

Yet, is not all art fantasy, not the symbolic replication of reality but the fulfillment of a wish? To be sure! But what is wish-fulfilling is the art itself, and not the world it depicts.

For this reason popular art could well be said to suffer from too little fantasy as too much: it does not do enough with its materials. Its imagination is reproductive rather than creative. When it comes to breaking out of the constraints of reality, what better examples are there than *Midsummer Night's Dream* and *The Tempest*, the paintings of Hieronymous Bosch, or the sculpture of the Hindu pantheon? But popular art is so bound to reality it gives us nowhere to escape *to*, save deeper within a self that is already painfully constricted. The eighteenth century usefully distinguished between fancy and imagination, according to whether fantasy has worked far enough to confer reality on its own products. Popular art is all fancy. If it sees the world as a prison, it contents itself with painting on the walls an open door.

Though all art is fantasy, there is a mature as well as an infantile process. Art may be produced for children—Lewis Carroll and Robert Louis Stevenson—or with a childlike quality—Paul Klee and Joan Miro—but it is not therefore childish. It is this childishness, however, that characterizes popular art: the fairy tale is retold for adult consumption, but stripped of just those qualities of creative imagination in which lies the artistry of the original.

In mature fantasy both the reality principle and the pleasure principle are at work. Popular art is concerned only with the pleasure, and for just this reason it can provide only immature satisfactions. In responding to popular art we do not escape from reality—we have not yet attained to the reality. Beneath the pleasure in popular art is the pathos of the note lying outside the orphanage wall: "Whoever finds this, I love you!"

VI

Now, after all, what makes popular art so popular? The usual reply follows the account that conceives of popular art in terms of distinctive features of modern society. The major premise is the alienation and deracination of modern man; the minor premise is that popular art serves to counter these forces, providing a basis for at least an ersatz community. Popular art reaches out to the lowest common denominator of society; it provides the touch of nature that makes all men kin, or, at least, all men who share the conventions of a common culture.

In so far as the function of popular art today is to be explained in terms of social conditions rather than psychic processes, the situation seems to be the reverse of what the previous account relies on. It is not man who is alienated and uprooted, but art. In our time art has become increasingly dissociated from the cultural concerns with which it has been so intimately involved throughout most of its history—religion, love, war, politics, and the struggle for subsistence. Art today is, in Dewey's brilliant phrase, "the beauty-parlor of civilization." Popular art at least pretends to a social relevance, and is not only willing but eager to find a place for itself outside the museum.

Popular art today is neither worse nor more common than it always has been. There is a wider audience today for art of every kind: the mass of the Athenian population were slaves, and not much more than that in Renaissance Italy or Elizabethan England. There may be more poor stuff produced today because there are more people to consume it, but this is even more true, proportionately, for the superior product. Nor do I sympathize with the view that ours is an age of barbarism to be defined, according to Ortega y Gasset, as "the absence of standards to which appeal can be made." What is absent, to my mind, is only a cultural elite that sets forth and enforces the standards; and I say, so much the better! It is ironic that popular art is taken as a sign of barbarism; every real development in the history of art, and not only the modern movement, was first greeted as a repudiation of aesthetic standards. My objection to popular art is just the contrary, that it is too rigidly bound to the standards of the academy. Kitch is the homage paid by popular art to those standards: Oscar and Emmy are avatars of the muse.

Art is too often talked about with a breathless solemnity, and viewed with a kind of religious awe; if high art needs its high priests, I hope that aesthetics will leave that office to the critics. To put it plainly, there is much snobbery in the aesthetic domain, and especially in the contempt for popular art on no other basis than its popularity. We speak of popular art in terms of its media (paperbacks, movies, television) as though to say, "Can any good come out of Nazareth?"; or else by the popular genres (western, mystery, love story, science fiction) as though they can be condemned wholesale. For audiences, art is more of a status symbol than ever; its appearance in the mass media is marked by a flourish of trumpets, as befits its status; the sponsor may even go so far as to omit his commercials. Even where popular art vulgarizes yesterday's art, it might anticipate tomorrow's—baroque once meant something like kitch. I am willing to prophesy that even television has art in its future.

But if not, what then? Aesthetic judgment is one thing and personal taste another. The values of art, like all else aesthetic, can only be analyzed contextually. There is a time and a place even for popular art. Champagne and Napoleon brandy are admittedly the best of beverages; but on a Sunday afternoon in the ballpark we want a coke, or maybe a glass of beer. "Even if we have all the virtues," Zarathustra reminds us, "there is still one thing needful: to send the virtues themselves to sleep at the right time." If popular art gives us pleasant dreams, we can only be grateful—when we have wakened.

WHOSE STEREOTYPING?

Language can be manipulated to suit the purposes of a group or an individual, and sometimes the manipulation is so successful that it becomes unconscious. It also expands without effort. In the following selection, a black journalist explores the nature of racism and the stereotyped images of the black man.

Bob Teague

Charlie Doesn't Even
Know His Daily Racism
Is a Sick Joke

If you look at the racial problem from a black man's point of view, you can see the jokes as well as the injustices. Which is to say that you can then understand this: The underlying syndrome that must be attacked is much more subtle than a white policeman's nightstick. It's more like a topsy-turvy vaudeville routine in which all the funny lines come from the straight men.

A favorite comic theme among the "concerned and enlightened" elements of white society is "Let's Stamp Out Racial Hatred." Hoo boy! Hatred has very little to do with the central problem, Charlie. What is done to and withheld from black folk day by day in this country is based on neither hate nor horror. On the contrary. It is coldly impersonal. Like the brains of precocious computers.

Simply put, it seems to me that white folk are convinced, deep in their bones, that the way they run this melting pot—with black folk unmelted at the bottom—is nothing more than the natural order of things.

What happens quite naturally, for example, is that a black *bon vivant* who shows up in a clean shirt at a posh restaurant is approached by white customers who beg him to get them a good table, please. There is nothing malicious about it. They simply think of black men in clean shirts as waiters.

Similarly, a black man caught on foot near a public parking lot is likely to be buttonholed by a pale proud patrician who wants his limousine fetched in a hurry.

And even the most militant white egalitarians are prone to compliment one another by saying, "That's real white of you, Edgar." Obviously, the notion that anything white is inherently superior to its black counterpart is built into the white American idiom, and thus into the white American mind.

Do you think it's accidental that the bad guys in Western movies are the ones in black sombreros?

This is not to suggest that white folk don't feel a respectable amount of guilt now and then, here and there. What the hell. They're human, too. In fact, I personally witnessed a veritable orgy of private and public breast-beating among whites early this year—that is, after they had recovered from the initial shock of learning from the President's Commission on Civil Disorders that "the main cause of black violence in the ghettos last summer was white racism."

Although I had reached a similar conclusion by the time I was 10 years black, I nevertheless judged the President's commission to be somewhat crude. You shouldn't spring a thing like that on 180 million unsuspecting suspects without warning. They didn't even have time to consult their lawyers.

Fortunately for the white masses, however—before their breasts had been pounded into lily-white pulp—a nationally famous Washington ventriloquist intervened. Through a captive puppet, he delivered a one-line joke that helped to bring white America back to normal. "It would be a mistake," the straight man said, "to condemn a whole society."

The implication was clear: Perhaps only a small minority of misguided whites were the culprits.

The collective sigh of relief was still in the air when a black civic leader, a former city councilman, died in East St. Louis. Naturally, since the natural order had been restored, the Valhalla Cemetery refused the corpse—on the ground that "everybody else buried in Valhalla is white." Who said the people who run cemeteries have no sense of humor?

A popular variation of the Valhalla skit was played this summer in the Republican political arena. Bold headlines stirred up a fuss around the two leading contenders for the G.O.P. Presidential nomination because each belonged to a private club, in different states, that bars black folk from membership—as if nearly all white folk don't belong to a Society of, a Committee to, a Council for or a Convention on that maintains the same standards of purity.

I am exposed to the same basic joke almost every time I walk into an all-white apartment building to keep an appointment with a friend. I see panic in the eyes of the pale residents coming out as I go in—trying to recall whether they locked their doors. And the doorman himself seems to be trying to remember the standard procedure for What to Do Until the Cops Come.

Although it has taken me many years to reach this point of view— perhaps because I managed a getaway of sorts from the ghetto—I understand now that neither the Valhalla Cemetery nor the doorman and the rest of white America are motivated by hate. To their way of thinking, the business of keeping black folk at a comfortable distance is not a matter of racism, not a choice between right and wrong. It's like fearing the bomb, saluting the flag and sending a card on Mother's Day. It's an automatic reflex action. In other words, no emotion of any kind is necessarily involved.

Consider, for example, those magazine and newspaper advertisements for "flesh-colored" bandages. The color they mean blandly ignores the color of most flesh on this planet. Mine in particular. But the top bananas who dreamed up that bit would be sorely aggrieved if someone called them racists. Some of those chaps are probably card-carrying fellow-travelers in the N.A.A.C.P., and their wives probably sent food to the poor people's shantytown in Washington. Their "flesh-colored" bandages are merely a profitable manifestation of a common assumption among white folk: White skin is what human flesh is *supposed* to look like. Anything else—black skin certainly—is irrelevant. Sort of a whimsical goof by Mother Nature.

How else can a black man explain those ubiquitous cosmetic ads showing a pale proud beauty using the facial lotion that promises to give her "the natural look"? The joke here is that this same beauty, and those who swear by "flesh-colored" bandages spend as much time in the sun as possible to darken their natural looks. They even buy chemical tans in bottles. And did you ever hear a commercial Goldilocks say, "Goodness gracious, my tan is much too dark"?

A spin-off joke from that particular farce is the honest pretense among whites that only their backward brothers—way down yonder in Mississippi—are hypersensitive to color. The white liberal party says in effect that truly civilized whites regard black skin as a rather flamboyant costume for humankind, but nonetheless legitimate.

This is self-deception, of course. My experience has been that most white folk are so caught up in the seductive *mystique* of White Power that their brains are rarely brushed by the notion that the "natural order" in this country is in any way forced and unnatural.

Only last week one of my white friends—to be known here as Charlie —called my attention to one of those "flesh-colored" ads. Although Charlie is well past 35 and literate and had read similar ads over the years, he was seeing it clearly for the first time.

"Man, look at this," he said, wearing an embarrassed grin. "They even insult you in the ads, don't they?"

Charlie's insight is not yet complete, however. If it ever is, he'll say "we" instead of "they."

How could good old Charlie have missed the point of that joke for so many years and thus become an accessory to the largely unconscious white conspiracy? It was easy. Just as it is for white gossip columnists to report regularly that the the sexy movie queen who appears to be nude on the screen is actually hiding the goodies in a "flesh-colored" bra. They wouldn't dream of explaining such illusions in terms of "a bra that virtually matched her skin." Those gossip columnists, by God, know "flesh color" when they see it.

All of which is to say that white folk are immersed in such a totally racist climate that—like fish born in the ocean—they have no reason to suspect for a moment that they might be all wet. Wherever they look in this society, there are white institutions, habits, signs, symbols, myths and realities that reinforce their notion that black folk rank somewhere between King Kong and Frankenstein's monster on the scale of lower forms of life.

I recently read a best-selling novel which was not about the race problem. Yet the hero and his adversaries made the point again and again in passing that the busty blond heroine was clearly depraved and lost beyond recall since, between sexual acrobatics with the good guys, she allowed a "boogey" into her boudoir. That novel has sold more than 900,000 copies in the hard-cover editions, and more than two million more in paperback. I am not saying that its success is based in any way on its casual racial insults. The point is, it's a typical visual aid in the process of white indoctrination.

Television is even more effective in that respect. Here again, of course, white folk control both the medium and the message.

If a superintelligent visitor from another planet were to deduce, strictly from television, the nature of the 22 million black pariahs who exist in the crevices of this society, he undoubtedly would get an impression that was 99 44/100 per cent pure nonsense. From the electronic evidence of omission, projected around the clock, the visitor might gather that black women are rather dull and sexless creatures. Apparently nothing known to science or Madison Avenue can help black girls to develop "the skin you love to touch." With scarcely a blond hair to call their own, they obviously are not the kind of broads who "have more fun." And without one toothbrush among them, they have no interest in the leading toothpaste that "gives your mouth sex appeal."

Black men are equally irrelevant among the fauna of the natural TV order. It is tacitly suggested, for instance, that they are socially backward—black Square Johns, so to speak. Otherwise they would be seen driving "the low-priced luxury car" to seduce more swinging chicks.

It's true that black satellites are sometimes seen in TV dramatic series, but usually as cardboard characters with virtually no lives of their own. They are perpetually in orbit around the full-blooded white supermen who perform brain surgery, fall in love, bounce children on their knees and worry about middle-aged spread.

My impression is that many white folk would like to portray black people in a more sophisticated manner. But, alas, they cannot forget all those Tarzan movies of their youth. These made it official that black folk are naturally spear carriers, dangerous savages and beasts of the white man's burdens.

Then, too, there are all those cannibal cartoons in the slick magazines put out by and for white folks. Who wouldn't be somewhat repelled by a black gourmet whose favorite entree is fricassee of Charlie?

Such examples of how black folk are systematically misrepresented or shut out from the stuff that the American Dream is made of are virtually endless. The smiling faces on greeting cards are never black faces. Department-store manikins don't resemble anyone you are likely to meet in the ghetto. And all plastic angels who symbolize the Christmas spirit are pink.

The net effect of these deceptions is that each tailor-made reality buttresses the other in the minds of whites. This explains in large measure why so many white folk are genuinely baffled by the grumbling and violence in the ghettos. Which is the basis for the popular white joke that ends with the punch line: "What do you people want?"

When black folk bother to spell out the answer to that riddle—with expectations that can only be described as naive—the consistent white responses add up to rather predictable pranks: another study of black frustration; another conference on brotherhood; another million-dollar crash program to tear down an old ghetto and replace it with a new ghetto.

As one of the best buffoons in the Federal Government observed after the riots last summer: "The very existence of the ghetto is un-American." But that line was much too oblique for most of white America to comprehend.

I am not suggesting that white folk don't even try. On the contrary. They conscientiously integrate a school here and there—even if it means doing something silly, like busing half the youngsters from A to Z and the other half vice versa. At the same time, however, they automatically prevent black families from buying or renting homes near the school in question. And they bar black folk from the jobs that pay the kind of money that would enable them to afford such a pristine neighborhood.

But getting back to how hard white people try, I witnessed one of their truly valiant efforts against insuperable odds this year. The occasion was the hint dropped by the President's Commission on Civil Disorders that the "ghetto is created by whites, maintained by white institutions and condoned by white society."

Most white folk were truly sorry about that. They rushed from their enclaves of affluence to the nearest ghetto to make amends. However, once in the wilds of Harlem and its scattered subdivisions, they simply could not resist telling corny jokes. Like the one Hitler told as he toured a concentration camp: "Jews stink."

What the Führer was smelling, of course, was Nazism. And in America the heady aroma of racism is equally confusing to the thin straight noses of the master race. Otherwise it would not be possible for those dead-pan middle-class comedians to come up with such boffos as: "Why can't the black man pull himself up by his bootstraps like the other minorities have done?" While guarding the boots with bulldog tenacity day and night.

Admittedly, that is a rather large generalization. I have no doubt that some white skeptics will challenge me to prove it. My answer is this: Regard me as sort of a black J. Edgar Hoover. You didn't ask him to prove his public generalization that "Martin Luther King is one of the most notorious liars in the country."

Furthermore, I am prepared to generalize again. From my experience with white storekeepers over the years, I judge that many white merchants make a special hard-sell effort when a black customer shows up—to unload whatever raunchy merchandise they have in stock.

Example: One of my soul sisters overheard a white housewife chewing out a white butcher for putting rotten meat on display. "Can't you see it's not fit to eat?" she demanded.

"Lady, this is not for you," the butcher said matter-of-factly. "It's for them. Believe me, they don't know any better. They're like pigs."

Although black folk are reluctant to admit it in this age of militant reassessment of their position, they do feel a certain amount of pity for white folk now and then. Like Sam Bowers, who resigned this year as Grand Dragon of the United Ku Klux Klans in Georgia. Sam said he wanted "to work for a united America where black men and white men stand shoulder to shoulder."

When I broadcast that item last spring, I couldn't help thinking: What grievous tortures poor old Sam must have suffered upon discovering the joke of white supremacy.

Another public confession was made recently at the opposite end of the spectrum by a self-declared white liberal—a Northern youth who had risked his life as a field worker in the civil-rights movement in Mississippi. Out of curiosity, he said, he took a trip on the LSD express. And the jig was up. Under the influence of the so-called mind-expanding drug, he realized for the first time that, in the Deep South of his soul, he honestly believed that black people were not now, never had been and never could be as deserving as whites. The immediate result of his insight was a nervous breakdown.

That young man was neither the first nor the last of his breed. The mass media these days are overpopulated with white liberals who portray themselves as "champions of the inarticulate masses." The sick joke here is that the masses—especially the black masses—are not at all inarticulate. They tell it like it is and like it ought to be—with precision, persistence and profanity.

But white society can't grasp the meaning of all that yammering—being too busy washing brains, their victims' and their own. They therefore have no real difficulty in maintaining their cool and the status quo in the face of massive protest and violence.

Being highly inventive jesters, white folk entertain themselves with a monologue that says, in effect, black folk are too stupid to realize that something phony is going on here. It goes like this: "It's the Communist agitators and Communist dupes who are behind all this violence."

One-liners like that are probably what killed vaudeville.

If black folk don't laugh out loud at such routines, it is because their funny bones are dulled from the same old stale material. Real comedy depends on surprises. So why should a black man chuckle over the annual Congressional Follies built around civil-rights legislation, for example? He knows in advance that the new Civil Rights Act is going to wind up like the so-called Open Housing Act of 1866—unenforced and soon forgotten.

Enforcement, he is told, would "infringe on the rights" of the white minority. That's a good one, too. But it is as familiar as, "Why does a fireman wear red suspenders?"

As for the sight gags in white society's repertoire, these too have worn thin from overexposure. How many times can an individual black man be amused by the blind-cabdriver routine? After the 37th time, it no longer strikes him as suitable material for a laff-in.

Did I say "individual black man"? Actually, there is scarcely any such animal as far as white eyes can see. They recognize "the first Negro who" and "the only Negro to," but not as individuals—instead, as freaks or symbols. Which is to say that white folks have a habit of arbitrarily assigning a rather standard personality to a black man. His real self is like an iceberg, deeply submerged in a sea of white assumptions.

One of my soul brothers was recently promoted to an executive position with a giant corporation in New York City. He had earned it by bringing in more sales orders over the last five years than anyone else in his department. You can imagine how chagrined he was when several of his white colleagues dismissed his personal achievement with humorless jokes like this: "It pays to be black these days. Man, you've got it made."

Such an attitude is not founded primarily on jealousy, as it might appear on the surface. White folks are simply incapable of seeing a black man as anything beyond his blackness.

At least twice a year, for instance, I am approached for an interview by one national magazine or another. My experience as a newspaper reporter and television news broadcaster has provided me with a wealth of interesting material from face-to-face encounters with four Presidents, a half-dozen princesses, scores of prizefighters, hundreds of politicians, assorted pimps, paragons and pin-up queens. But not one white interviewer ever shows the slightest interest in anything except my blackness.

"What is the role of the black newsman?" they want to know.

"The role of a black man," I tell them off the record, "is or ought to be the same as it is for everybody else in his profession; in this case, to gather the facts and report them with as much integrity, clarity and objectivity as he can muster." End of interview.

I am also rather weary of getting letters from white television fans that read like this one:

"When you first began broadcasting the news on television, I watched you every night, but I realize now, years later, that I was so conscious of the fact that you were black that I didn't hear a word you said about the news. Now, I am happy to say, I still watch you every night, but only because you are a damn good newscaster. . . ."

What I'm getting at here is that white folks are generally flabbergasted by a black man who can fly a plane, mix a martini, speak unbroken English or shoot a round of golf. Such a black man is something like the celebrated dog that could walk on its hind legs unassisted.

About the only realm of this society which seems to be perhaps one-third of the way toward the verge of catching the spirit of this thing called the free democratic society is professional sports. Even here a string of qualifying exceptions must be taken into account. To mention just a few: Boxing is obsessed by the search for a "white hope"; football is convinced that a black quarterback could not lead his team to the goal line; and baseball, like all the others, shuts out black men from the managerial and decision-making level. And besides all that, there is a great deal of friction and apartheid on the so-called integrated teams.

But baseball still deserves a better grade than white Americans generally. In the first place, black players are no longer required to be supermen like Jackie Robinson. If you watch baseball these days, you see black men fumbling routine grounders, dropping flies, striking out with the bases loaded and winding up the season with microscopic batting averages. Just like whites. And no one suggests that such derelictions are peculiar to one race or another.

Furthermore, if a white interviewer shows up in the locker room, he is full of questions about the spitball or the squeeze play that didn't quite work in the ninth. After all, why should a third baseman, even a black one, be limited to discussing racial jokes?

So how long is it going to take the rest of this country to evolve even as little as baseball? In my judgment, another 100 years at the very least, if this society manages to survive that long.

Why so much time? Well, it seems to me that while one side of those split personalities called white Americans is striving with all its might to open their minds and their society, the other side is being pulled in the opposite direction by what white Americans accept and automatically maintain as the natural order. As you can see for yourself, it is something of an unequal race.

Four assignments . . .

1. Write your personal experience with some person who is a member of a group often stereotyped.

2. Go out and watch a stranger for a few minutes. Do not make your attention known. Try to find out something revealing and write about your discovery.

3. Select a street, landscape, campus, room, or any scene and describe it so that you reveal inherent design clichés or lack of sensitivity. Choose something susceptible but not too obvious.

4. Punch a hole in a piece of paper. Look through it at someone or something. Write about the difference in what you see when you focus through that hole and what you see without it.

COMMENTARY

Robert Frost

Why Wait for Science?

Sarcastic Science she would like to know,
In her complacent ministry of fear,
How we propose to get away from here
When she has made things so we have to go
Or be wiped out. Will she be asked to show
Us how by rocket we may hope to steer
To some star off there say a half light-year
Through temperature of absolute zero?
Why wait for Science to supply the how
When any amateur can tell it now?
The way to go away should be the same
As fifty million years ago we came—
If anyone remembers how that was.
I have a theory, but it hardly does.

Neither Out Far nor In Deep

The people along the sand
All turn and look one way.
They turn their back on the land.
They look at the sea all day.

As long as it takes to pass
A ship keeps raising its hull;
The wetter ground like glass
Reflects a standing gull.

The land may vary more;
But wherever the truth may be—
The water comes ashore,
And the people look at the sea.

They cannot look out far.
They cannot look in deep.
But when was that ever a bar
To any watch they keep?

4

Whose way is right?

Although most of us would agree that old and accepted ways of looking at the world are by no means the only ways of looking, many of us have the attitude that nevertheless those old ways are probably correct or true. Underlying a willingness to experiment with new ways of looking is often a surrender to the strength of old ways. Often this surrender is no more than an anchor in security, and the strength of the old way is little more than the self-righteousness and numerical strength of those who hold the old ways of looking.

The real argument is not whether an old way or a new way is correct or true but whether "correct" and "true" are suitable words to describe any point of view. We need to ask whether any man ever sees his world fully and correctly or whether any human knowledge is absolute. In Chapter 3, we dealt with how different individuals will arrive at different ways of seeing, even see different things, though they all start with the same concrete surroundings.

Does this mean that anything goes, that anything one says can be as valid as anything someone else says? Or is it that this disparity exists because we are not capable or patient enough to be *objective*? If we had the time, ability, and industry to speak and write scientifically, would we then be using the one really accurate, objective form of composition? (Scientific investigation and discovery is, after all, a kind of composition like our cartoons in Chapter 1 and like your sentences, paragraphs, and whole essays.)

Look at the ink blots. What do you see? Ask some friends what they see. Ask why each person gives his particular answer and keep track of the different reasons. You know that inkblots like these are often used in personality tests, which ask "What do you see there?" or "How often do you see that shape around you?" Answers to those require a highly personal use of the language. Let's reverse the test: can you employ a "purely" scientific or objective language to describe this inkblot? First, you must decide whose "pure" language you mean to use: the printer's? the draftsman-artist's? the mathematician's? But will such a language be a "pure" one, or will it simply be someone else's?

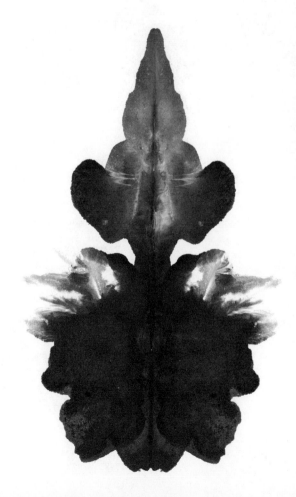

Those inkblots were complex with all their curves, lines, shades, empty spaces, and symmetry, but the world we walk through every day is infinitely more complicated. Not even with all the electronic and chemical gadgetry at our command can we see all there is to see, even in a small segment of time. All composition is the process of selecting and arranging those things we see or choose to see in our world. Whether or not you view language as an extension of man or as a mechanical tool will depend on whether you believe a man may look at the world in his own way or whether you accept its shape as forced upon the man.

By examining the writer's and thinker's process of selection and by showing how experience first becomes language and why, we will try to demonstrate in this chapter that all imaginative acts of composition are subjective acts. Art or writing may imitate nature, but it can never duplicate or be nature. Every act in composition contains the mind of a composer as well as a vision and experience of his subject. If you understand this, then you will understand why skill in using language is indispensable to *being* an individual, why an awareness and control of individuality is so important to good writing.

A LOOK AT "OBJECTIVITY"

We often think of good newspaper stories as being objective, telling only what happened and scrupulously avoiding any interference by the author. Is that true of the following articles?

Kathleen Morner

The Percussionist Will
Now Go Berserk

Lukas Foss rushed onto the stage of the auditorium at Northern Illinois University in De Kalb. "We are going to make a piece of instant composition," he said to four startled music students. The clarinetist nervously ran his fingers over his instrument. "Let's see," Foss continued briskly. "It's 12:30 and the concert is at 2. That should give us just enough time."

Kathleen Morner, "The Percussionist Will Now Go Berserk." Reprinted with permission from *The Chicago Sun-Times*.

The composer sat down at the piano and began to pound out the Bach D minor concerto. "I will play selections of this concerto. Not the whole work. Not necessarily in any order. And you must create a wall of interference."

The organist landed on his electronic instrument with both fists, producing a reasonably impenetrable sound.

"That's the idea," said Foss, "but it would be even better like this." He climbed on the organ bench and collapsed onto the keyboard, elbows out and head down.

"Don't be timid. Don't allow your respect for Bach to get into your way."

"This piece of ours will be a sort of Bach dream. We will annihilate Bach at the same time that we show our love for him."

The double-bass player scratched his head with his bow.

"By using the dream mood, we can show an attitude toward tradition. Stockhausen likes to think of the contemporary composer as the knight who set out from home to seek whatever it is that knights seek— happiness or the philosopher's stone. The one requirement is that he can't look back.

"But the important thing is that he must be aware that there is something to look back to; he may avoid Bach consciously, but then in his dream Bach sneaks in the back door. I often have dreams in which Bach sixteenth notes come flooding over me, choking me, laughing at me."

Foss darted back to the piano. "This dream will move from nothing to something back to nothing. You must begin playing almost inaudibly until called upon to emerge. Follow me. Get in between my registers. Walk around me. Create an envelope for me.

"The idea of composing this kind of music first struck me last September when we—my chamber players and I—when we were making a broadcast tape in Denmark on our way to the Warsaw Festival," said Foss, over his shoulder to a reporter. "The tape was ten minutes short, so we created this piece of instant composition with the Bach.

"When we repeated it in Warsaw, there was a great stir over the idea—the idea of anonymous music. It's a team idea. The composer gives up his ego as if he were in therapy. The composer and performers then work together with the same heart and mind and aims. I call it nonimprovisation. The composer tells the performers what to do, but he only tells them the essentials. And he tells them it's their piece."

As the Bach slow movement unfolded, the students began to add sounds, with Foss calling encouragement. "This is soft, sad. Make moans. Stick something in your clarinet so that you can bend the pitch in a long wail."

"Now the dream becomes a nightmare." Foss gazed around. His eyes stopped suddenly on the percussion player. "The percussionist will go berserk. I could write a very complicated set of instructions for the percussionist: Now you hit the Glockenspiel, now you rap twice on the bongos, quick the triangle, back to the bongos. The poor guy would kill himself practicing these precise movements at high speed.

"If I tell him just to create clamor, he can get a similar effect without having to practice a nonessential.

"This is nonimprovisation because the performers are given very well defined tasks. I originally used improvisation as a pedagogical device when I was teaching at UCLA.

"But I am no longer interested in improvisation because I think that what I can dream up in my lonely chamber is much wider. Improvisation relies too much on traffic controls, on insurance policies, little ways of playing safe so everyone comes out together. I prefer to control the result in more significant ways."

Foss launched into the concerto's finale while the percussionist madly attacked his instruments. The clarinet turned into a siren. The bass player dug his bow into his strings, spraying the stage with resin. And the organist took a loud nap on his keyboard. Bach was all but destroyed.

The nightmare was suddenly over. Bach emerged again but more quietly. The other instruments faded with the piano. As the piece came to an end, Foss seemed to be mumbling some strange incantation.

"Oh, it doesn't matter what the pianist says," he explained. "I happened to be saying 'metamorphosis, metamorphosis' over and over again. But you could say 'Dellapiccola, Dellapiccola.' Whatever you like."

It was after 2 o'clock. The audience had assembled. A student pianist had just performed Four (conservative) Two-Part Inventions by Lukas Foss. The program notes announced that Foss had written them when he was 15.

Foss came on stage smiling. "It was ingenious of the concert committee to present first the crimes of my youth and then one of my recent crimes. But my name should not be on the program after this next piece. I am not the composer. It is anonymous nonimprovisation. These students will create interference while I play Bach by performing very well-defined tasks that they learned two hours ago when we met. It's a kind of Bach dream. Don't listen to this as normal music, just close your eyes and dream. . ."

The voice was continuing as I put on my coat and slipped out the side door.

Aspen Hippies Sue, Demanding Police Halt 'Harassment'

Special to The New York Times

ASPEN, Colo., Aug. 17—The members of the hippie community in this jet-set ski and cultural center have filed suit in Federal District Court in Denver demanding a halt in what they charge is police harassment.

The seven plaintiffs in the lawsuit, which is scheduled for a preliminary hearing in Denver Tuesday, are also asking that Aspen municipal ordinances, mainly the laws on vagrancy and loitering, be declared unconstitutional.

Backing the seven plaintiffs in the action is the Aspen chapter of the American Civil Liberties Union and a growing number of townspeople who have expressed criticism of harsh treatment of hippies, especially since July 15 when a "get tough" petition was presented to the City Council signed by 87 residents.

The police policy since then, the hippies charged, has resulted in orders to "get out of town" for some new arrivals, several 90-day jail sentences on what they call trumped-up charges and a series of illegal searches and seizures.

For several years businessmen here have complained of "undesirable transients" who have arrived in Aspen.

First came long-haired and boisterous surfers who had left the ocean beaches for the ski slopes, and more recently long-haired hippies appeared.

One of the most outspoken of the critics has been Guido Meyer, a restaurant owner, who keeps a sign in his window with the warning, "No beatniks allowed."

Until recently Mr. Meyer was a police magistrate. He could pass legal judgment on the hippies coming before him for violations of municipal ordinances.

However, on Aug. 6, the City Council, responding to a demand by the Pitkin County Bar Association, removed Mr. Meyer from office.

If journalism or "reporting" is not objective, if it really is shaped by an individual, why try to pretend otherwise? Nat Hentoff doesn't. To the reader who wants the security of thinking his traditional news story is the absolute unbiased truth, Hentoff says:

Nat Hentoff

Behold the New Journalism — It's Coming After You!

Mailer's new book shows the way to a personal style in which the writer puts himself at the center of his story, powering it with feeling as well as intellect to blast through the reader's wall of apathy.

I saw it begin to happen in my own work several years ago. I was no longer the "visitor" to whom the person I was writing about spoke. (You know the old style: "I'm going to kill myself," Roberta Himmelfarb said to a visitor as she jumped out the window.) During my early years as a journalist, I wrote many long pieces without a single "I" in them. In traditional journalism, it was bad form to put yourself in. You might be accused of lack of "objectivity," and stripped, like Dreyfus, of press cards, copy paper, and big, soft black pencils while your former colleagues jeered, "He thought he was more important than the story!"

Sure, there were a few "personal journalists" in the 1950's. I don't mean political analysts, but rather working reporters who not only got the story but told you how they felt as they were getting it, what was still missing, and how the story affected *them*. They, however, were considered special cases. They were a bonus in the paper, but for the real, hard news, you had to read the *Times*.

Well, the times, they have changed—though not the paper of that name nearly enough. Aside from the continuing collected works of Murray Kempton, the best single model of the rapidly increasing new personal journalism is Norman Mailer's *The Armies of the Night*—first published in *Harper's* and *Commentary*, and now a New American Library book. An account of Mailer's participation in the October, 1967 peace demonstrations in Washington, the work could hardly be more personal and yet it simultaneously digs more deeply into the essences— and some of the putrescences—of the way we live now than the total wordage moved by AP and UPI during the past year.

Two examples. First, Mailer describing the club-swinging Marshals: ". . . the hollows in their faces spoke of men who were rabid and toothless, the tenderness had turned corrosive, the abnegation had been replaced by hate, dull hate, cloud banks of hate, the hatred of failures who had not lost their greed. So he [Mailer] was reminded of a probability he had encountered before: that, nuclear bombs all at hand, the true war party of America was in all the small towns, even as the peace parties had to collect in the cities and the suburbs. Nuclear warfare was dividing the nation. The day of power for the small-town mind was approaching— who else would be left when atomic war was done would reason the small-town mind, and in measure to the depth of their personal failure, would love Vietnam, for Vietnam was the secret hope of a bigger war, and that bigger war might yet clear the air of races, faces, in fact— technologies—all that alienation they could not try to comprehend."

Secondly, there is Mailer, in jail, wanting OUT, and seeing Tuli Kupferberg refuse to agree to stay away from the Pentagon for six months and thereby condemned to serve his five days: "Kupferberg was not particularly happy; with his beard and long hair, he did not think it was going to be altogether routine when the majority of the Pentagon protestors were gone, and he was then dropped in with the regular prison population. But he did not see any way out of it. To agree not to return to the Pentagon for six months was to collaborate with the government— what then had they been protesting?"

Herewith the new journalism: "Seen from one moral position . . . prison could be nothing but an endless ladder of moral challenges. Each time you climbed a step, as Kupferberg just had, another higher, more disadvantageous step would present itself. Sooner or later, you would have to descend. It did not matter how high you had climbed. The first step down in a failure of nerve always presented the same kind of moral nausea. Probably, he [Mailer] was feeling now like people who had gone to the Pentagon, but had chosen not to get arrested, just as such people, at their moment of decision, must have felt as sickened as all people who should have marched from Lincoln Memorial to the Pentagon, but didn't. The same set of emotions could be anticipated for all people who had been afraid to leave New York. One ejected oneself from guilt by climbing the ladder—the first step back, no matter where, offered nothing but immersion into nausea. No wonder people hated to disturb their balance of guilt. To become less guilty, then weaken long enough to return to guilt was worse than to remain cemented in your guilt."

Now, there, right there, is what the new journalism is all about. It is not only that Mailer is so personally, so vulnerably involved in the events he is reporting, but also *his* involvement draws *you* in as no traditional news account possibly could. If you're not entirely anesthetized, reading that passage is bound to have an unlocking effect on you, quite beyond those particular events at the Pentagon. That passage brings you the news about the rest of your life.

Obviously this kind of journalism is by no means pervasive as yet. Clifton Daniel, managing editor of the *New York Times*, still says—and God save the mark, still believes!—that "newspapers—this one included—hold up a mirror to the world." The reporter must not get "involved."

And this past March, Dr. Lincoln Gordon, President of Johns Hopkins University, told 5,000 student journalists meeting in New York that it is a "bizarre notion" and a "disastrous myth to assume that objectivity is impossible and therefore, . . . not worth striving for. Write the news not how it feels, but how it is happening."

What is bizarre is Dr. Gordon's omission of the fact that a reporter does feel. What is he to do with that feeling? Bill Moyers, of all people, has quite different advice for journalists. When Moyers was at the White House, manipulating the news, he once told a free-lance writer, "That must be great—to be your own man." Now that Moyers is publisher of *Newsday*, he apparently feels better, and is certainly thinking more clearly.

During an interview on a Public Broadcasting Laboratory (PBL) television show on the press, Moyers spoke for the new journalism: "For a long time, there's been a myth about journalism, a myth shared by people who read us and view us, and a myth shared by those of us who are in the profession. That myth has been that newspapers are . . . simply mirrors of the world . . . that we simply reflect what is happening in the world." In the process of discarding that myth, Moyers went on to say that we're on the edge of "a major development in the history of journalism in this country because there really is no such thing, in journalism, as an innocent bystander. If a man is a bystander, he isn't innocent, and to really understand what's going on so that he can make sense to the reader, he has to be part of it and see it as a participant, and record what he feels."

"You do not have to accept it," Moyers concluded, "if you're the reader. You do not have to subscribe to it, but you do have to get a feeling that here's a man trying to do his best to tell you, another man, what he has seen and felt about something that has happened, and this will open the creative processes of journalism in a way that writing the five W's of the old traditional newslead will never do."

For this to happen to any significant extent in the dailies there'll have to be a new generation of editors, successors to the Clifton Daniels. But it is already happening in the underground press, in magazines such as this one, in Mailer's body of journalistic work (look back on some of the reporting in *Cannibals and Christians*). And the result is that a new generation of young readers is being brought into the news in ways that make more and more of them realize that they need not remain only voyeurs of living history. The new journalism, because it is powered by feeling as well as intellect, can help break the glass between the reader and the world he lives in. A citizen has to be more than informed; he has to act if he is to have some say about what happens to him; and the new journalism can stimulate active involvement.

It can, that is, if it continues to grow and if it extends much more deeply than it has so far to television and to films. The fundamental affliction of this society—what William Sloane Coffin defines as "original sin"—is that we do not feel. On a very basic, pragmatic level, if not enough of the citizenry, for example, feel urgently about the waste of black people, their elected representatives engage in the ritual dance of rhetoric but do not reallocate resources and redistribute power. Martin Luther King, Jr. is mourned pietistically by public officials but the dull beat of white auto-anesthesia goes on.

I have often wondered how the *Times* would look on any given day if it were edited and written by people from Bedford-Stuyvesant. Norman Mailer, in *The Armies of the Night*, tells of a similar fantasy: "He would buy a television station, and a commentator would read the news each day, and a chorus of street kids would give comments."

Neither of these fantasies is about to become real. But for the best of the younger journalists, the old ways are dead. And if institutions like the *Times* do not open themselves to the new journalism—a start has been made in the *Times* with Tom Wicker's column—they will no longer attract the best of the younger journalists. And this new generation of readers will increasingly turn to other sources of real news.

When Adlai Stevenson was ending his life telling lies for his country at the United Nations, nearly all the reportage on his disintegration missed the marrow of the story because the journalists then did not allow their own feelings to become part of what they were writing. They knew he was telling lies, but they hardly ever said so, and never directly. And so most of the citizenry *didn't* know he was telling lies. The reporters, many of them, felt the pathos of this man deadening himself to the last of the life within him, but they didn't write about it. And so most of the citizenry was unaware of a prototypical tragedy of this time. It would not happen that way now across the journalistic board. The wire services and many of the dailies would still be "objective," but a sizable number of papers and reporters—among them Tom Wicker—could no longer pretend to be innocent bystanders.

Admittedly, the new journalism has a long way to go, but as a sometime journalist, I'm convinced there has not for decades been a better time than now to practice the profession. The subtitle of *The Armies of the Night* is: *History as a Novel/The Novel as History*. The novel, Mailer says, "is, when it is good, the personification of a vision which will enable one to comprehend other visions better; a microscope if one is exploring the pond; a telescope upon a tower if you are scrutinizing the forest."

And so is history, when it is good—Gibbon, for instance. Journalism, too, because it is living history. Of course, as a journalist, you still get all the facts you can. But then you tell what the facts mean to you, how you react to them. And in that way you can bring the reader into living history. The new journalist, then, will have to have something of the novelist's eye and ear, the novelist's ability to project himself into the head and viscera of others, the novelist's cauterizing skill at self-exploration. This does not mean he has to be able to write novels. Mailer is unusual, to say the least. A clearer paradigm is Murray Kempton. He is entirely a journalist, but with a novelist's creative vision.

To be personal—and how could I not be in *this* piece?—I'll keep on writing novels because I enjoy the total unpredictability of that act. But increasingly I find that much of the freedom of feeling I have in fiction can also be part of journalism, and so I intend to continue being a journalist too. However, that "visitor," that faceless, note-taking onlooker has gone from my nonfiction articles. It's I who am there; it's I telling you where I've been, what I've seen, how I felt about it, what changes it made and did not make in me. As Bill Moyers says, "You don't have to subscribe to it; you don't have to accept it." The way journalism is going is the way it has to go, and if I'm any good at all, you're going to react to what I write with your feelings.

Like the Beatles say, "I read the news today oh boy." And as they say it, they feel, you feel, "God, it is, it could be, about me."

Many people have a stereotype of Albert Einstein as a typical scientist: withdrawn, abstract, a little unintelligible and cold, like a mathematical equation. No one doubts he had a brilliant scientific mind. Here are some of that scientist's thoughts about science.

Albert Einstein
On Science

I believe in intuition and inspiration. . . . At times I feel certain I am right while not knowing the reason. When the eclipse of 1919 confirmed my intuition, I was not in the least surprised. In fact, I would have been astonished had it turned out otherwise. Imagination is more important than knowledge. For knowledge is limited, whereas imagination embraces the entire world, stimulating progress, giving birth to evolution. It is, strictly speaking, a real factor in scientific research.

The basis of all scientific work is the conviction that the world is an ordered and comprehensive entity, which is a religious sentiment. My religious feeling is a humble amazement at the order revealed in the small patch of reality to which our feeble intelligence is equal.

✿   ✿   ✿   ✿   ✿

By furthering logical thought and a logical attitude, science can diminish the amount of superstition in the world. There is no doubt that all but the crudest scientific work is based on a firm belief—akin to religious feeling—in the rationality and comprehensibility of the world.

✿   ✿   ✿   ✿   ✿

Music and physical research work originate in different sources, but they are interrelated through their common aim, which is the desire to express the unknown. Their reactions are different, but their results are supplementary. As to artistic and scientific creation, I hold with Schopenhauer that their strongest motive is the desire to leave behind the rawness and monotony of everyday life, so as to take refuge in a world crowded with the images of our own creation. This world may consist of musical notes as well as of mathematical rules. We try to compose a comprehensive picture of the world in which we are at home and which gives us a stability that cannot be found in our external life.

* * * * *

Science exists for Science's sake, like Art for Art's sake, and does not go in for special pleading or for the demonstration of absurdities.

* * * * *

A law cannot be definite for the one reason that the conceptions with which we formulate it develop and may prove insufficient in the future. There remains at the bottom of every thesis and of every proof some remainder of the dogma of infallibility.

* * * * *

In every naturalist there must be a kind of religious feeling; for he cannot imagine that the connections into which he sees have been thought of by him for the first time. He rather has the feeling of a child, over whom a grown-up person rules.

* * * * *

We can only see the universe by the impressions of our senses reflecting indirectly the things of reality.

* * * * *

Among scientists in search of truth wars do not count.

* * * * *

There is no universe beyond the universe for us. It is not part of our concept. Of course, you must not take the comparison with the globe literally. I am only speaking in symbols. Most mistakes in philosophy and logic occur because the human mind is apt to take the symbol for the reality.

If we admit the element of individual shaping and choosing in all kinds of composition, we are giving writers more responsibility and opportunity. If we value creativity, then we are prepared to find it in all writing. This is what John DeWitt McKee of New Mexico Institute of Mining and Technology explains.

John DeWitt McKee

All Good Writing
Is Creative

In the degree of creativity they demand, there is no real difference between the work of an objective writer and the work which is principally subjective, nor between the writer who deals primarily in fact and the one whose production begins with imagination.

The writer of any piece of clear exposition is no less creative—at least he should not be—than the writer of a poem, a short story, a novel, or a play. *War and Peace* is no more a work of the creative imagination than is *The Descent of Man.* And the newspaper story which Stephen Crane wrote and upon which he later based *The Open Boat* is as much a creation as the fiction that grew out of it.

The great pieces of reporting, from the histories of Thucydides and Herodotus—war correspondence after the fact—to the late Meyer Berger's recreation of the burning of the French liner *Normandy,* from Isaac Newton's *Phaenomena of Colours* to the in-depth reporting of a network news special, are all creations as surely as are *Ode to a Grecian Urn* and *Moby Dick.* They all depend on the creative ability of the writer to select and order particular experiences, with the prospect of drawing one or more universals from such shaping.

All communications—even the attempted communication of chaos, as in the "theater of the absurd" and the "aliterature" of those authors who purport to be mere recording machines—is in the very nature of language a matter of selecting and ordering detail. In fact, are not the creation and apprehension of order the chief reasons for any intellectual activity? Building a structure of thought, emotion, and intuition in which the otherwise unintelligible babble of impressions can be made comprehensible is in turn the basic reason for any kind of writing.

Still, there exists an undeniable difference between the exposition of objective fact and the subjective interpretation of experience. While the writer of fiction—including, in this context, poetry and drama—can and must *use* fact as the base of his fiction, the expositor and interpreter of physical, historical, or social phenomena must *limit* himself to the facts.

In psychology, and more particularly in psycho-analysis, science has made its one attempt to combine the ways of fact and fiction. At one extreme, in "The Jet-Propelled Couch," Robert Lindner makes the ex-

John DeWitt McKee, "All Good Writing Is Creative," *College Composition and Communication,* XVIII, No. 1 (Feb., 1967), pp. 32–34. Reprinted with the permission of the National Council of Teachers of English and John DeWitt McKee.

perience fit the symbol. At the other extreme, Marie Bonapart puts Poe's stories on the couch and analyzes him through them.

Such an approach is open to question, whether the subject be considered as literary criticism or as psychiatric case material, from both a literary and a scientific point of view. To interpret a man's literary output solely for the psychological import of that production as it applies to the writer does not allow for sufficient distance between the art and the artist. Art consists largely of shaping material toward an integration of experience. That shaping is almost always a critical function rather than creative. What a writer dredges up from his memory, what he captures out of the bombardment of instantaneous experience, what fleeting visions he dreams or melodies he imagines—these may be subject to psychoanalysis. When they have been shaped into an artistic expression, however, they have been structured by something which is as much outside the psyche as pipefitting or running a count on a meteorite fall. To say, in effect, "If I analyze a man's production, I shall have analyzed the man," is unfair to both the man and his production. On the other hand, as reporting, the resultant case study makes interesting fiction.

If the reporter—be he scientist, historian, or journalist—is limited to observable phenomena, the writer of fiction has at his disposal all the findings of all the sciences and all interpretations of observable phenomena. He may even violate the logic of those findings if by so doing he can create a more understandable world for himself and his readers. In fact, he can sometimes do more with those findings and interpretation in reporting on the human condition than can the objective reporter who is limited to the gathering and ordering of facts.

The writer of fiction must, however, remain within whatever framework gives his production the illusion of actuality. That is to say, he cannot ignore "fact" any more than can the writer who deals in nonfiction. No writer who is any good writes solely from the contemplation of his navel. He must *know*, either through personal experience or through research. The interesting thing about this necessity is that, as a researcher, the writer of fiction does the same job, and goes about it in the same general way, as does the writer of nonfiction.

Someone once said, "There is no such thing as a true generalization, including this one," but we can come pretty close to a true generalization when we say that *every writer must be first a reporter*. The desire to report his findings is one of the things that makes an artist function. He has to organize and order experience to create an understandable world for himself; but if he is an artist, he must also communicate that organization and that order. He must do this first to objectify the picture for himself, and second, to go running through the streets like Archimedes, crying, "Eureka!"

The history of Western thought shows that the process is the same for a scientist as for a poet. Ptolemy created a universe; so did Dante, and Copernicus, and Milton, and Newton, and Goethe, and Einstein. These names come easily to mind because each of these men, whether reporters of physical phenomena or explorers of the human heart and character in the context of those phenomena, performed prodigious feats of creative imagination.

It is folly for the poet to say of the true scientist that all he does is to label and bin the raw material for the making of the world. The true scientist, as opposed to the test-tube technician, is not only an analyst; he is also a synthesist; and synthesis results from the application of creative imagination to the raw material of creation.

It is equally folly for the scientist—or for any writer who flatters himself that he is an absolutely objective reporter—to say that the poet deals only with subjective and unverifiable evidence. Werner Heisenberg's principle of indeterminacy indicates that when it comes to knowing ultimate reality, the poet and the physicist are in the same leaky boat. Heisenberg says that the very observation of a physical phenomenon changes the character of that phenomenon, so that in the end there may not even be any such thing as observable reality.

In short, what our world looks like to us depends on where we stand to do our looking. It does not matter really whether our vehicle is science or history, fiction, fantasy or fact. Our world is literally what we make it. It is our creation, and it is a creation regardless of the intellectual discipline we use in its building.

Most of us, unfortunately, are not equipped to build an entire universe in the manner of Milton or Newton. But we can till our own not-quite-galactic fields. We can cut a chunk from the conglomerate of chaos and shape it to our understanding. And our cutting tool, whether we be poet or scientist, novelist or reporter, is the creative imagination.

Every child knows that being creative can also get you into trouble. Man's creativity with language has been both benefit and bane. Philosopher Susanne Langer goes back to the origins of language to explain what it is, why we create and recreate it, and how it is at the center of today's most serious domestic and international problems. As you read Langer, try to take the opposing view, that language is not a subjectively created tool.

Susanne K. Langer

The Lord of Creation

The world is aflame with man-made public disasters, artificial rains of brimstone and fire, planned earthquakes, cleverly staged famines and floods. The Lord of Creation is destroying himself. He is throwing down the cities he has built, the works of his own hand, the wealth of many thousand years in his frenzy of destruction, as a child knocks down its own handiwork, the whole day's achievement, in a tantrum of tears and rage.

What has displeased the royal child? What has incurred his world-shattering tantrum?

The bafflement of the magnificent game he is playing. Its rules and its symbols, his divine toys, have taken possession of the player. For this global war is not the old, hard, personal fight for the means of life, *bellum omnium contra omnes*, which animals perpetually wage; this is a war of monsters. Not mere men but great superpersonal giants, the national states, are met in combat. They do not hate and attack and wrestle as injured physical creatures do; they move heavily, inexorably, by strategy and necessity, to each other's destruction. The game of national states has come to this pass, and the desperate players ride their careening animated toys to a furious suicide.

These moloch gods, these monstrous states, are not natural beings; they are man's own work, products of the power that makes him lord over all other living things—his mind. They are not of the earth, earthy, as families and herds, hives and colonies are, whose members move and fight as one by instinct and habit until a physicial disturbance splits them and the severed parts reconstitute themselves as new organized groups. The national states are not physical groups; they are social symbols, profound and terrible.

They are symbols of the new way of life, which the past two centuries have given us. For thousands of years, the pattern of daily life—working, praying, building, fighting, and raising new generations—repeated itself with only slow or unessential changes. The social symbols expressive of this life were ancient and familiar. Tribal gods or local saints, patriarchs, squires, or feudal lords, princes and bishops, raised to the highest power in the persons of emperors and popes—they were all expressions of needs and duties and opinions grounded in an immemorial

Reprinted from the January, 1944 issue of Fortune Magazine by special permission. © 1944 Time Inc.

way of life. The average man's horizon was not much greater than his valley, his town, or whatever geographical ramparts bounded his community. Economic areas were small, and economic problems essentially local. Naturally in his conception the powers governing the world were local, patriarchal, and reverently familiar.

Then suddenly, within some two hundred years, and for many places far less than that, the whole world has been transformed. Communities of different tongues and faiths and physiognomies have mingled; not as of old in wars of conquest, invading lords and conquered population gradually mixing their two stocks, but by a new process of foot-loose travel and trade, dominated by great centers of activity that bring individuals from near and far promiscuously together as a magnet draws filings from many heaps into close but quite accidental contact. Technology has made old horizons meaningless and localities indefinite. For goods and their destinies determine the structure of human societies. This is a new world, a world of persons, not of families and clans, or parishes and manors. The proletarian order is not founded on a hearth and its history. It does not express itself in a dialect, a local costume, a rite, a patron saint. All such traditions by mingling have canceled each other, and disappeared.

Most of us feel that since the old controlling ideas of faith and custom are gone, mankind is left without anchorage of any sort. None of the old social symbols fit this modern reality, this shrunken and undifferentiated world in which we lead a purely economic, secular, essentially homeless life.

But mankind is never without its social symbols; when old ones die, new ones are already in process of birth; and the new gods that have superseded all faiths are the great national states. The conception of them is mystical and moral, personal and devotional; they conjure with names and emblems, and demand our constant profession and practice of the new orthodoxy called "Patriotism."

Of all born creatures, man is the only one that cannot live by bread alone. He lives as much by symbols as by sense report, in a realm compounded of tangible things and virtual images, of actual events and ominous portents, always between fact and fiction. For he sees not only actualities but meanings. He has, indeed, all the impulses and interests of animal nature; he eats, sleeps, mates, seeks comfort and safety, flees pain, falls sick and dies, just as cats and bears and fishes and butterflies do. But he has something more in his repertoire, too—he has laws and religions, theories and dogmas, because he lives not only through sense but through symbols. That is the special asset of his mind, which makes him the master of earth and all its progeny.

By the agency of symbols—marks, words, mental images, and icons of all sorts—he can hold his ideas for contemplation long after their original causes have passed away. Therefore, he can think of things that are not presented or even suggested by his actual environment. By associating symbols in his mind, he combines things and events that were never together in the real world. This gives him the power we call imagination. Further, he can symbolize only part of an idea and let the rest go out of consciousness; this gives him the faculty that has been his pride through-out the ages—the power of abstraction. The combined effect of these two powers is inestimable. They are the roots of his supreme talent, the gift of reason.

In the war of each against all, which is the course of nature, man has an unfair advantage over his animal brethren; for he can see what is not yet there to be seen, know events that happened before his birth, and take possession of more than he actually eats; he can kill at a distance; and by rational design he can enslave other creatures to live and act for him instead of for themselves.

Yet this mastermind has strange aberrations, for in the whole animal kingdom there is no such unreason, no such folly and impracticality as man displays. He alone is hounded by imaginary fears, beset by ghosts and devils, frightened by mere images of things. No other creature wastes time in unprofitable ritual or builds nests for dead specimens of its race. Animals are always realists. They have intelligence in varying degrees—chickens are stupid, elephants are said to be very clever—but, bright or foolish, animals react only to reality. They may be fooled by appearance, by pictures or reflections, but once they know them as such, they promptly lose interest. Distance and darkness and silence are not fearful to them, filled with voices or forms, or invisible presences. Sheep in the pasture do not seem to fear phantom sheep beyond the fence, mice don't look for mouse goblins in the clock, birds do not worship a divine thun-derbird.

But oddly enough, men do. They think of all these things and guard against them, worshiping animals and monsters even before they con-ceive of divinities in their own image. Men are essentially unrealistic. With all their extraordinary intelligence, they alone go in for patently impractical actions—magic and exorcism and holocausts—rites that have no connection with common-sense methods of self-preservation, such as a highly intelligent animal might use. In fact, the rites and sacrifices by which primitive man claims to control nature are sometimes fatal to the performers. Indian puberty rites are almost always intensely painful, and African natives have sometimes died during initiations into honorary societies.

We usually assume that very primitive tribes of men are closer to animal estate than highly civilized races; but in respect of practical atti-tudes, this is not true. The more primitive man's mind, the more fantastic it seems to be; only with high intellectual discipline do we gradually approach the realistic outlook of intelligent animals.

Yet this human mind, so beclouded by phantoms and superstitions, is probably the only mind on earth that can reach out to an awareness of things beyond its practical environment and can also conceive of such notions as truth, beauty, justice, majesty, space and time and creation.

There is another paradox in man's relationship with other creatures: namely, that those very qualities he calls animalian—"brutal," "bestial," "inhuman"—are peculiarly his own. No other animal is so deliberately cruel as man. No other creature intentionally imprisons its own kind, or invents special instruments of torture such as racks and thumbscrews for the sole purpose of punishment. No other animal keeps its own brethren in slavery; so far as we know, the lower animals do not commit anything like the acts of pure sadism that figure rather largely in our newspapers. There is no torment, spite, or cruelty for its own sake among beasts, as there is among men. A cat plays with its prey, but does not conquer and torture smaller cats. But man, who knows good and evil, is cruel for cruelty's sake; he who has a moral law is more brutal than the brutes, who have none; he alone inflicts suffering on his fellows with malice aforethought.

If man's mind is really a higher form of the animal mind, his morality a specialized form of herd instinct, then where in the course of evolution did he lose the realism of a clever animal and fall prey to subjective fears? And why should he take pleasure in torturing helpless members of his own race?

The answer is, I think, that man's mind is *not* a direct evolution from the beast's mind, but is a unique variant and therefore has had a meteoric and startling career very different from any other animal history. The trait that sets human mentality apart from every other is its preoccupation with symbols, with images and names that *mean* things, rather than with things themselves. This trait may have been a mere sport of nature once upon a time. Certain creatures do develop tricks and interests that seem biologically unimportant. Pack rats, for instance, and some birds of the crow family take a capricious pleasure in bright objects and carry away such things for which they have, presumably, no earthly use. Perhaps man's tendency to see certain forms as *images*, to hear certain sounds not only as signals but as expressive tones, and to be excited by sunset colors or starlight, was originally just a peculiar sensitivity in a rather highly developed brain. But whatever its cause, the ultimate destiny of this trait was momentous; for all human activity is based on the appreciation and use of symbols. Language, religion, mathematics, all learning, all science and superstition, even right and wrong, are products of symbolic expression rather than direct experience. Our commonest words, such as "house" and "red" and "walking," are symbols; the pyramids of Egypt and the mysterious circles of Stonehenge are symbols; so are dominions and empires and astronomical universes. We live in a mind-made world, where the things of prime importance are images or words that embody ideas and feelings and attitudes.

The animal mind is like a telephone exchange; it receives stimuli from outside through the sense organs and sends out appropriate responses through the nerves that govern muscles, glands, and other parts of the body. The organism is constantly interacting with its surroundings, receiving messages and acting on the new state of affairs that the messages signify.

But the human mind is not a simple transmitter like a telephone exchange. It is more like a great projector; for instead of merely mediating between an event in the outer world and a creature's responsive action, it transforms or, if you will, distorts the event into an image to be looked at, retained, and contemplated. For the images of things that we remember are not exact and faithful transcriptions even of our actual sense impressions. They are made as much by what we think as by what we see. It is a well-known fact that if you ask several people the size of the moon's disk as they look at it, their estimates will vary from the area of a dime to that of a barrel top. Like a magic lantern, the mind projects its ideas of things on the screen of what we call "memory"; but like all projections, these ideas are transformations of actual things. They are, in fact, *symbols* of reality, not pieces of it.

A symbol is not the same thing as a sign; that is a fact that psychologists and philosophers often overlook. All intelligent animals use signs; so do we. To them as well as to us sounds and smells and motions are signs of food, danger, the presence of other beings, or of rain or storm. Furthermore, some animals not only attend to signs but produce them for the benefit of others. Dogs bark at the door to be let in; rabbits thump to call each other; the cooing of doves and the growl of a wolf defending his kill are unequivocal signs of feelings and intentions to be reckoned with by other creatures.

We use signs just as animals do, though with considerably more elaboration. We stop at red lights and go on green; we answer calls and bells, watch the sky for coming storms, read trouble or promise or anger in each other's eyes. That is animal intelligence raised to the human level. Those of us who are dog lovers can probably all tell wonderful stories of how high our dogs have sometimes risen in the scale of clever sign interpretation and sign using.

A sign is anything that announces the existence or the imminence of some event, the presence of a thing or a person, or a change in a state of affairs. There are signs of the weather, signs of danger, signs of future good or evil, signs of what the past has been. In every case a sign is closely bound up with something to be noted or expected in experience. It is always a part of the situation to which it refers, though the reference may be remote in space and time. In so far as we are led to note or expect the signified event we are making correct use of a sign. This is the essence of rational behavior, which animals show in varying degrees. It is entirely realistic, being closely bound up with the actual objective course of history—learned by experience, and cashed in or voided by further experience.

If man had kept to the straight and narrow path of sign using, he would be like the other animals, though perhaps a little brighter. He would not talk, but grunt and gesticulate and point. He would make his wishes known, give warnings, perhaps develop a social system like that of bees and ants, with such a wonderful efficiency of communal enterprise that all men would have plenty to eat, warm apartments—all exactly alike and perfectly convenient—to live in, and everybody could and would sit in the sun or by the fire, as the climate demanded, not talking but just basking, with every want satisfied, most of his life. The young would romp and make love, the old would sleep, the middle-aged would do the routine work almost unconsciously and eat a great deal. But that would be the life of a social, superintelligent, purely sign-using animal.

To us who are human, it does not sound very glorious. We want to go places and do things, own all sorts of gadgets that we do not absolutely need, and when we sit down to take it easy we want to talk. Rights and property, social position, special talents and virtues, and above all our ideas, are what we live for. We have gone off on a tangent that takes us far away from the mere biological cycle that animal generations accomplish; and that is because we can use not only signs but symbols.

A symbol differs from a sign in that it does not announce the presence of the object, the being, condition, or whatnot, which is its meaning, but merely *brings this thing to mind*. It is not a mere "substitute sign" to which we react as though it were the object itself. The fact is that our reaction to hearing a person's name is quite different from our reaction to the person himself. There are certain rare cases where a symbol stands directly for its meaning: in religious experience, for instance, the Host is not only a symbol but a Presence. But symbols in the ordinary sense are not mystic. They are the same sort of thing that ordinary signs are; only they do not call our attention to something necessarily present or to be physically dealt with—they call up merely a conception of the thing they "mean."

The difference between a sign and a symbol is, in brief, that a sign causes us to think or act *in face of* the thing signified, whereas a symbol causes us to think *about* the thing symbolized. Therein lies the great importance of symbolism for human life, its power to make this life so different from any other animal biography that generations of men have found it incredible to suppose that they were of purely zoological origin. A sign is always embedded in reality, in a present that emerges from the actual past and stretches to the future; but a symbol may be divorced from reality altogether. It may refer to what is *not* the case, to a mere idea, a figment, a dream. It serves, therefore, to liberate thought from the immediate stimuli of a physically present world; and that liberation marks the essential difference between human and nonhuman mentality. Animals think, but they think *of* and *at* things; men think primarily *about* things. Words, pictures, and memory images are symbols that may be combined and varied in a thousand ways. The result is a symbolic structure whose meaning is a complex of all their respective meanings, and this kaleidoscope of *ideas* is the typical product of the human brain that we call the "stream of thought."

The process of transforming all direct experience into imagery or into that supreme mode of symbolic expression, language, has so completely taken possession of the human mind that it is not only a special talent but a dominant, organic need. All our sense impressions leave their traces in our memory not only as signs disposing our practical reactions in the future but also as symbols, images representing our *ideas* of things; and the tendency to manipulate ideas, to combine and abstract, mix and extend them by playing with symbols, is man's outstanding characteristic. It seems to be what his brain most naturally and spontaneously does. Therefore his primitive mental function is not judging reality, but *dreaming his desires*.

Dreaming is apparently a basic function of human brains, for it is free and unexhausting like our metabolism, heartbeat, and breath. It is easier to dream than not to dream, as it is easier to breathe than to refrain from breathing. The symbolic character of dreams is fairly well established. Symbol mongering, on this ineffectual, uncritical level, seems to be instinctive, the fulfillment of an elementary need rather than the purposeful exercise of a high and difficult talent.

The special power of man's mind rests on the evolution of this special activity, not on any transcendently high development of animal intelligence. We are not immeasurably higher than other animals; we are different. We have a biological need and with it a biological gift that they do not share.

Because man has not only the ability but the constant need of *conceiving* what has happened to him, what surrounds him, what is demanded of him—in short, of symbolizing nature, himself, and his hopes and fears—he has a constant and crying need of *expression*. What he cannot express, he cannot conceive; what he cannot conceive is chaos, and fills him with terror.

If we bear in mind this all-important craving for expression we get a new picture of man's behavior; for from this trait spring his powers and his weaknesses. The process of symbolic transformation that all our experiences undergo is nothing more nor less than the process of *conception*, which underlies the human faculties of abstraction and imagination.

When we are faced with a strange or difficult situation, we cannot react directly, as other creatures do, with flight, aggression, or any such simple instinctive pattern. Our whole reaction depends on how we manage to conceive the situation—whether we cast it in a definite dramatic form, whether we see it as a disaster, a challenge, a fulfillment of doom, or a fiat of the Divine Will. In words or dreamlike images, in artistic or religious or even in cynical form, we must *construe* the events of life.

There is great virtue in the figure of speech. "I can *make* nothing of it," to express a failure to understand something. Thought and memory are processes of *making* the thought content and the memory image; the pattern of our ideas is given by the symbols through which we express them. And in the course of manipulating those symbols we inevitably distort the original experience, as we abstract certain features of it, embroider and reinforce those features with other ideas, until the conception we project on the screen of memory is quite different from anything in our real history.

Conception is a necessary and elementary process; what we do with our conceptions is another story. That is the entire history of human culture—of intelligence and morality, folly and superstition, ritual, language, and the arts—all the phenomena that set man apart from, and above, the rest of the animal kingdom. As the religious mind has to make all human history a drama of sin and salvation in order to define its own moral attitudes, so a scientist wrestles with the mere presentation of "the facts" before he can reason about them. The process of *envisaging* facts, values, hopes and fears underlies our whole behavior pattern; and this process is reflected in the evolution of an extraordinary phenomenon found always, and only, in human societies—the phenomenon of language.

Language is the highest and most amazing achievement of the symbolical human mind. The power it bestows is almost inestimable, for without it anything properly called "thought" is impossible. The birth of language is the dawn of humanity. The line between man and beast— between the highest ape and the lowest savage—is the language line. Whether the primitive Neanderthal man was anthropoid or human depends less on his cranial capacity, his upright posture, or even his use of tools and fire, than on one issue we shall probably never be able to settle—whether or not he spoke.

In all physical traits and practical responses, such as skills and visual judgments, we can find a certain continuity between animal and human mentality. Sign using is an ever evolving, ever improving function throughout the whole animal kingdom, from the lowly worm that shrinks into his hole at the sound of an approaching foot, to the dog obeying his master's command, and even to the learned scientist who watches the movements of an index needle.

This continuity of the sign-using talent has led psychologists to the belief that language is evolved from the vocal expressions, grunts and coos and cries, whereby animals vent their feelings or signal their fellows; that man has elaborated this sort of communion to the point where it makes a perfect exchange of ideas possible.

I do not believe that this doctrine of the origin of language is correct. The essence of language is symbolic, not signific; we use it first and most vitally to formulate and hold ideas in our own minds. Conception, not social control, is its first and foremost benefit.

Watch a young child that is just learning to speak play with a toy;

he says the name of the object, e.g.: "Horsey! horsey! horsey!" over and over again, looks at the object, moves it, always saying the name to himself or to the world at large. It is quite a time before he talks to anyone in particular; he talks first of all to himself. This is his way of forming and fixing the *conception* of the object in his mind, and around this conception all his knowledge of it grows. *Names* are the essence of language; for the *name* is what abstracts the conception of the horse from the horse itself, and lets the mere idea recur at the speaking of the name. This permits the conception gathered from one horse experience to be exemplified again by another instance of a horse, so that the notion embodied in the name is a general notion.

To this end, the baby uses a word long before he *asks for* the object; when he wants his horsey he is likely to cry and fret, because he is reacting to an actual environment, not forming ideas. He uses the animal language of *signs* for his wants; talking is still a purely symbolic process—its practical value has not really impressed him yet.

Language need not be vocal; it may be purely visual, like written language or even tactual, like the deaf-mute system of speech; but it *must be denotative*. The sounds, intended or unintended, whereby animals communicate do not constitute a language, because they are signs, not names. They never fall into an organic pattern, a meaningful syntax of even the most rudimentary sort, as all language seems to do with a sort of driving necessity. That is because signs refer to actual situations, in which things have obvious relations to each other that require only to be noted; but symbols refer to ideas, which are not physically there for inspection, so their connections and features have to be represented. This gives all true language a natural tendency toward growth and development, which seems almost like a life of its own. Languages are not invented; they grow with our need for expression.

In contrast, animal "speech" never has a structure. It is merely an emotional response. Apes may greet their ration of yams with a shout of "Nga!" But they do not say "Nga" between meals. If they could *talk about* their yams instead of just saluting them, they would be the most primitive men instead of the most anthropoid of beasts. They would have ideas, and tell each other things true or false, rational or irrational; they would make plans and invent laws and sing their own praises, as men do.

The history of speech is the history of our human descent. Yet the habit of transforming reality into symbols, of contemplating and combining and distorting symbols, goes beyond the confines of language. All *images* are symbols, which make us think about the things they mean.

This is the source of man's great interest in "graven images," and in *mere appearances* like the face of the moon or the human profiles he sees in rocks and trees. There is no limit to the meanings he can read into natural phenomena. As long as this power is undisciplined, the sheer enjoyment of finding meanings in everything, the elaboration of concepts without any regard to truth and usefulness, seems to run riot; superstition and ritual in their pristine strength go through what some anthropologists have called a "vegetative" stage, when dreamlike symbols, gods and ghouls and rites, multiply like the overgrown masses of life in a jungle. From this welter of symbolic forms emerge the images that finally govern a civilization; the great symbols of religion, society, and selfhood.

What does an image "mean"? Anything it is thought to resemble. It is only because we can abstract quite unobvious forms from the actual appearance of things that we see line drawings in two dimensions as images of colored, three-dimensional objects, find the likeness of a dipper in a constellation of seven stars, or see a face on a pansy. Any circle may represent the sun or moon; an upright monolith may be a man.

Wherever we can fancy a similarity we tend to see something represented. The first thing we do, upon seeing a new shape, is to assimilate it to our own idea of something that it resembles, something that is known and important to us. Our most elementary concepts are of our own actions, and the limbs or organs that perform them; other things are named by comparison with them. The opening of a cave is its mouth, the divisions of a river its arms. Language, and with it all articulate thought, grows by this process of unconscious metaphor. Every new idea urgently demands a word; if we lack a name for it, we call it after the first namable thing seen to bear even a remote analogy to it. Thus all the subtle and variegated vocabulary of a living language grows up from a few roots of very general application; words as various in meaning as "gentle" and "ingenious" and "general" spring from the one root "ge" meaning "to give life."

Yet there are conceptions that language is constitutionally unfit to express. The reason for this limitation of our verbal powers is a subject for logicians and need not concern us here. The point of interest to us is that, just as rational, discursive thought is bound up with language, so the life of feeling, of direct personal and social consciousness, the emotional stability of man and his sense of orientation in the world are bound up with images directly given to his senses: fire and water, noise and silence, high mountains and deep caverns, the brief beauty of flowers, the persistent grin of a skull. There seem to be irresistible parallels between the expressive forms we find in nature and the forms of our inner life; thus the use of light to represent all things good, joyful, comforting, and of darkness to express all sorts of sorrow, despair, or horror, is so primitive as to be well-nigh unconscious.

A flame is a soul; a star is a hope; the silence of winter is death. All such images, which serve the purpose of metaphorical thinking, are *natural symbols*. They have not conventionally assigned meanings, like words, but recommend themselves even to a perfectly untutored mind, a child's or a savage's, because they are definitely articulated *forms*, and to see something expressed in such forms is a universal human talent. We do not have to learn to use natural symbols; it is one of our primitive activities.

The fact that sensuous forms of natural processes have a significance beyond themselves makes the range of our symbolism, and with it the horizon of our consciousness, much wider and deeper than language. This is the source of ritual, mythology, and art. Ritual is a symbolic rendering of certain emotional *attitudes*, which have become articulate and fixed by being constantly expressed. Mythology is man's image of his world, and of himself in the world. Art is the exposition of his own subjective history, the life of feeling, the human spirit in all its adventures.

Yet this power of envisagement, which natural symbolism bestows, is a dangerous one; for human beings can envisage things that do not exist, and create horrible worlds, insupportable duties, monstrous gods and ancestors. The mind that can see past and future, the poles and the antipodes, and guess at obscure mechanisms of nature, is ever in danger of seeing what is not there, imagining false and fantastic causes, and courting death instead of life. Because man can play with ideas, he is unrealistic; he is inclined to neglect the all-important interpretation of signs for a rapt contemplation of symbols.

Some twenty years ago, Ernst Cassirer set forth a theory of human mentality that goes far toward explaining the vagaries of savage religions and the ineradicable presence of superstition even in civilized societies: a symbol, he observed, is the embodiment of an idea; it is at once an abstract and a physical fact. Now its great emotive value lies in the concept it conveys; this inspires our reverent attitude, the attention and awe with which we view it. But man's untutored thought always tends to lose its way between the symbol and the fact. A skull represents death; but to a primitive mind the skull *is* death. To have it in the house is not unpleasant but dangerous. Even in civilized societies, symbolic objects— figures of saints, relics, crucifixes—are revered for their supposed efficacy. Their actual power is a power of *expression*, of embodying and thus revealing the greatest concepts humanity has reached; these concepts are the commanding forces that change our estate from a brute existence to the transcendent life of the spirit. But the symbol-loving mind of man reveres the meaning not *through* the articulating form but *in* the form so that the image appears to be the actual object of love and fear, supplication and praise.

Because of this constant identification of concepts with their expressions, our world is crowded with unreal beings. Some societies have actually realized that these beings do not belong to nature, and have postulated a so-called "other world" where they have their normal existence and from which they are said to descend, or arise, into our physical realm. For savages it is chiefly a nether world that sends up spooks; for more advanced cults it is from the heavens that supernatural beings, the embodiments of human ideas—of virtue, triumph, immortality—descend to the mundane realm. But from this source emanates also a terrible world government, with heavy commands and sanctions. Strange worship and terrible sacrifices may be the tithes exacted by the beings that embody our knowledge of nonanimalian human nature.

So the gift of symbolism, which is the gift of reason, is at the same time the seat of man's peculiar weakness—the danger of lunacy. Animals go mad with hydrophobia or head injuries, but purely mental aberrations are rare; beasts are not generally subject to insanity except through a confusion of signs, such as the experimentally produced "nervous breakdown" in rats. It is man who hears voices and sees ghosts in the dark, feels irrational compulsions and holds fixed ideas. All these phantasms are symbolic forms that have acquired a false factual status. It has been truly said that everybody has some streak of insanity; i.e., the threat of madness is the price of reason.

Because we can think of things potential as well as actual, we can be held in nonphysical bondage by laws and prohibitions and commands and by images of a governing power. This makes men tyrants over their own kind. Animals control each other's actions by immediate threats, growls and snarls and passes; but when the bully is roving elsewhere his former domain is free of him. We control our inferiors by setting up symbols of our power, and the mere idea that words or images convey stands out to hold our fellows in subjection even when we cannot lay our hands on them. There is no flag over the country where a wolf is king; he is king where he happens to prowl, so long as he is there. But men, who can embody ideas and set them up to view, oppress each other by symbols of might.

The envisagements of good and evil, which make man a moral agent, make him also a conscript, a prisoner, and a slave. His constant problem is to escape the tyrannies he has created. Primitive societies are almost entirely tyrannical, symbol-bound, coercive organizations; civilized governments are so many conscious schemes to justify or else to disguise man's inevitable bondage to law and conscience.

Slowly, through ages and centuries, we have evolved a picture of the world we live in; we have made a drama of the earth's history and enhanced it with a backdrop of divinely ordered, star-filled space. And all this structure of infinity and eternity against which we watch the pageant of life and death, and all the moral melodrama itself, we have wrought by a gradual articulation of such vast ideas in symbols—symbols of good and evil, triumph and failure, birth and maturity and death. Long before the beginning of any known history, people saw in the heavenly bodies, in the changes of day and night or of the seasons, and in great beasts, symbolic forms to express those ultimate concepts that are the very frame of human existence. So gods, fates, the cohorts of good and evil were conceived. Their myths were the first formulations of cosmic ideas. Gradually the figures and traditions of religion emerged; ritual, the overt expression of our mental attitudes, became more and more intimately bound to definite and elaborate concepts of the creative and destructive powers that seem to control our lives.

Such beings and stories and rites are sacred because they are the great symbols by which the human mind orients itself in the world. To a creature that lives by reason, nothing is more terrible than what is formless and meaningless; one of our primary fears is fear of chaos. And it is the fight against chaos that has produced our most profound and indispensable images—the myths of light and darkness, of creation and passion, the symbols of the altar flame, the daystar, and the cross.

For thousands of years people lived by the symbols that nature presented to them. Close contact with earth and its seasons, intimate knowledge of stars and tides, made them feel the significance of natural phenomena and gave them a poetic, unquestioning sense of orientation. Generations of erudite and pious men elaborated the picture of the temporal and spiritual realms in which each individual was a pilgrim soul.

Then came the unprecedented change, the almost instantaneous leap of history from the immemorial tradition of the plow and the anvil to the new age of the machine, the factory, and the ticker tape. Often in no more than the length of a life-time the shift from handwork to mass production, and with it from poetry to science and from faith to nihilism, has taken place. The old nature symbols have become remote and have lost their meanings; in the clatter of gears and the confusion of gadgets that fill the new world, there will not be any obvious and rich and sacred meanings for centuries to come. All the accumulated creeds and rites of men are suddenly in the melting pot. There is no fixed community, no dynasty, no family inheritance—only the one huge world of men, vast millions of men, still looking on each other in hostile amazement.

A sane, intelligent animal should have invented, in the course of ten thousand years, or more, some sure and obvious way of accommodating indefinite numbers of its own kind on the face of a fairly spacious earth. Modern civilization has achieved the highest triumphs of knowledge, skill, ingenuity, theory; yet all around its citadels, engulfing and demolishing them, rages the maddest war and confusion, inspired by symbols and slogans as riotous and irrational as anything the "vegetative" stage of savage phantasy could provide. How shall we reconcile this primitive nightmare excitement with the achievements of our high, rational, scientific culture?

The answer is, I think, that we are no longer in possession of a definite, established culture; we live in a period between an exhausted age—the European civilization of the white race—and an age still unborn, of which we can say nothing as yet. We do not know what races shall inherit the earth. We do not know what even the next few centuries may bring. But it is quite evident, I think, that we live in an age of transition, and that before many more generations have passed, mankind will make a new beginning and build itself a different world. Whether it will be a "brave, new world," or whether it will start all over with an unchronicled "state of nature" such as Thomas Hobbes described, wherein the individual's life is "nasty, brutish, and short," we simply cannot tell. All we know is that every tradition, every institution, every tribe is gradually becoming uprooted and upset, and we are waiting in a sort of theatrical darkness between the acts.

Because we are at a new beginning, our imaginations tend to a wild, "vegetative" overgrowth. The political upheavals of our time are marked, therefore, by a veritable devil dance of mystical ideologies, vaguely conceived, passionately declared, holding out fanatic hopes of mass redemption and mass beatitudes. Governments vie with each other in proclaiming social plans, social enterprises, and demanding bloody sacrifices in the name of social achievements.

New conceptions are always clothed in an extravagant metaphorical form, for there is no language to express genuinely new ideas. And in their pristine strength they imbue the symbols that express them with their own mystery and power and holiness. It is impossible to disengage the welter of ideas embodied in a swastika, a secret sign, or a conjuring word from the physical presence of the symbol itself; hence the apparently nonsensical symbol worship and mysticism that go with new movements and visions. This identification of symbolic form and half-articulate meaning is the essence of all mythmaking. Of course the emotive value is incomprehensible to anyone who does not see such figments as expressive forms. So an age of vigorous new conception and incomplete formulation always has a certain air of madness about it. But it is really a fecund and exciting period in the life of reason. Such is our present age. Its apparent unreason is a tremendous unbalance and headiness of the human spirit, a conflict not only of selfish wills but of vast ideas in the metaphorical state of emergence.

The change from fixed community life and ancient local custom to the mass of unpedigreed human specimens that actually constitutes the world in our industrial and commercial age has been too sudden for the mind of man to negotiate. Some transitional form of life had to mediate between those extremes. And so the idol of nationality arose from the wreckage of tribal organization. The concept of the national state is really the old tribe concept applied to millions of persons, unrelated and different creatures gathered under the banner of a government. Neither birth nor language nor even religion holds such masses together, but a mystic bond is postulated even where no actual bond of race, creed, or color may ever have existed.

At first glance it seems odd that the concept of nationality should reach its highest development just as all actual marks of national origins—

language, dress, physiognomy, and religion—are becoming mixed and obliterated by our new mobility and cosmopolitan traffic. But it is just the loss of these things that inspires this hungry seeking for something like the old egocentric pattern in the vast and formless brotherhood of the whole earth. While mass production and universal communication clearly portend a culture of world citizenship, we cling desperately to our nationalism, a more and more attenuated version of the old clan civilization. We fight passionate and horrible wars for the symbols of our nations, we make a virtue of self-glorification and exclusiveness and invent strange anthropologies to keep us at least theoretically set apart from other men.

Nationalism is a transition between an old and a new human order. But even now we are not really fighting a war of nations; we are fighting a war of fictions, from which a new vision of the order of nature will someday emerge. The future, just now, lies wide open—open and dark, like interstellar space; but in that emptiness there is room for new gods, new cultures, mysterious now and nameless as an unborn child.

An assignment: be what you will . . .

Select a traditional news story from a newspaper. Write three or more versions of it, each from a different kind of experience or witness. You might try different points of view or different methods of selecting detail. Stick as closely as possible to the raw materials presented in the original article or facts reasonably inferred from the original.

COMMENTARY

It was very tough on my wife, but I decided I was going to try to hold a moratorium on speech for myself. So for approximately two years I didn't allow myself to use words. I thought I would see if by doing that I could force myself back to the point where I would really understand what it was I was thinking and be sure that when I made a sound that I really meant to make that sound—that it wasn't something I was parroting and that was just coming off my tongue. I had learned how facile I was at popping off things that someone else gave me.

All this was pretty difficult for my wife because we were in Chicago and didn't have any money. We had an apartment in the least expensive fireproof tenement I could find, because we did have our baby. I really did stop all sounds, and then gradually started wanting to use a particular sound. I was finally pretty sure I would know what the effects would be on my fellow man if I made a particular sound. I wanted to be sure that when I did communicate that I really meant to communicate thusly and that this was *me* communicating and not somebody else.*

*Buckminster Fuller, *Ideas and Integrities*, ed. by Robert W. Marks (Englewood Cliffs, N.J.: Prentice-Hall, Inc., 1963), p. 47.

5

How to see again

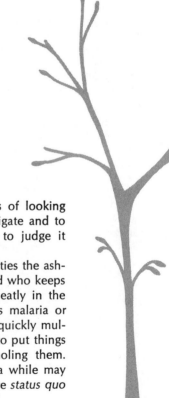

The first problem in breaking out of old ways of looking at things is to know *how* to see, how to investigate and to experience something, rather than to rush in, to judge it and label it.

Many people live like the housewife who empties the ashtray each time someone stubs out a butt in it and who keeps all the bookshelves filled and the magazines neatly in the rack. A little disorder wouldn't give her guests malaria or dysentery, but she is afraid a little disorder will quickly multiply. So in other areas of life, people are quick to put things in order by categorizing, labeling, or pigeonholing them. That keeps things arranged in ways which for a while may prove secure, at least if no one relates that secure *status quo* to any of the troubles in the "changing world."

As Susanne Langer wrote in "Lord of Creation," new ways of seeing the world do not just happen; they come in response to a need. They are man's response to a sense of disorder in his world. Our old systems of order—scientific, political, social—were created in this way. As the world changes and as we change, we sense new relationships or create new systems of order. And this means we must be *willing* to see disorder. If we are to be creative, our response to the first hint of disorder cannot be a reflex reversion to an old system of order.

Anarchy is no way to run a family, a community, or the world, but only when we are willing to allow our thoughts and perceptions a kind of temporary anarchy or chaos can we arrive at new ideas and ways of seeing. Few of us could live for long with people who never make sense or who constantly complain of being mixed up and unable to see any clear choices or course of action. However, too often the words *illogical, confused, mixed up* and *irrational* are hurled around like verbal stones. Their users do not really know that the subjects of the epithets are thinking chaotically. In such instances the users are simply showing their own fear of disorder, their unwillingness to abandon an old order even in a temporary search for new meaning.

The inkblots in Chapter 4 were a kind of disorder or confusion out of which most people created their own order. If one of those inkblots were shaped like the drawing below, with YALE stamped on it, the viewer would say, "It's a key." Lacking the initial confusion of the less definite inkblots, he could not see it in his *own* way.

Look at the following photos; remember your first and later reactions.

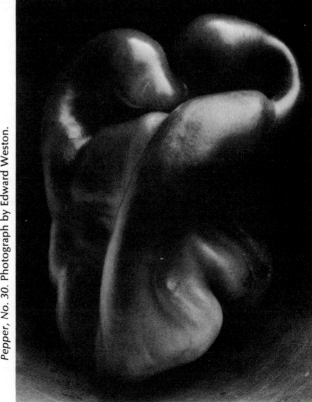

Pepper, No. 30. Photograph by Edward Weston.

The mind and the eye . . .

If you did not immediately recognize the subjects, what interfered?

What aspect of the pictures first struck you? When you recognized the subject, did that first aspect remain with you to give you a new sense of the subject?

What old notions did the photographer have to cast aside in order to see his subject as he did?

If you did not like the photographs, why? If you liked the photographs, think of someone who would not. What would be his reasons?

What new aspect or sense of the subject is emphasized by each picture? Could that sense be made as strong in a traditional picture?

Is there any intellectual, emotional, or practical value in looking at these subjects in this unorthodox way?

As the photographers have seen these subjects, do they at all resemble something else? Is this intentional? What is the result?

All valuable writing makes sense and order out of disorder, so naturally the writer must first experience disorder. Merely to repeat old ideas, however valuable, in moving prose is to do little more than push buttons on our emotional responses. (To present old ideas in new words and images is a different matter and recreates our sense of how important those old things are. We *rediscover* the old things, not simply *reaffirm* our own sentiments.)

Although writers are generally dedicated to the creation of order, many of them have written well about chaos. That is where their writing often begins, and that is where this section of the text begins. The following poem, "Prime" by W. H. Auden, explores a brief and limited experience with chaos. Auden starts with the momentary lack of identity at the point of waking.

W. H. Auden
Prime

Simultaneously, as soundlessly,
  Spontaneously, suddenly
As, at the vaunt of the dawn, the kind
  Gates of the body fly open.
To its world beyond, the gates of the mind,
  The horn gate and the ivory gate
Swing to, swing shut, instantaneously
  Quell the nocturnal rummage
Of its rebellious fronde, ill-favored,
  Ill-natured and second-rate,
Disenfranchised, widowed and orphaned
  By an historical mistake:
Recalled from the shades to be a seeing being,
  From absence to be on display,
Without a name or history I wake
  Between my body and the day.

Holy this moment, wholly in the right,
  As, in complete obedience

To the light's laconic outcry, next
  As a sheet, near as a wall,
Out there as a mountain's poise of stone,
  The world is present, about,
And I know that I am, here, not alone
  But with a world and rejoice
Unvexed, for the will has still to claim
  This adjacent arm as my own,
The memory to name me, resume
  Its routine of praise and blame
And smiling to me is this instant while
  Still the day is intact, and I
The Adam sinless in our beginning,
  Adam still previous to any act.

I draw breath; this is of course to wish
  No matter what, to be wise,
To be different, to die and the cost,
  No matter how, is Paradise
Lost of course and myself owing a death:
  The eager ridge, the steady sea,
The flat roofs of the fishing village
  Still asleep in its bunny,
Though as fresh and sunny still are not friends
  But things to hand, this ready flesh
No honest equal, but my accomplice now
  My assassin to be, and my name
  Stands for my historical share of care
  For a lying self-made city,
Afraid of our living task, the dying
  Which the coming day will ask.

"Law and order" is a familiar cry. Almost everybody wants it. Writing and thinking, like law, are forms of control over disorder. By looking at how Washington, D.C., children reacted to a riot after the murder of Martin Luther King, John Mathews and Ernest Holsendorph reveal some interesting things about people and disorder.

John Mathews and Ernest Holsendorph

The Children Write
Their Own Postscript

Harold, aged 11, a black boy who lives on a slum block a couple of miles from the White House, walked past rifle-bearing troops and shells of burned-out buildings on his way to school on Monday, April 8. In his sixth-grade classroom at the Bundy Elementary School, on the edge of the Seventh Street business area devastated in riots the previous weekend, Harold drew vivid pictures of troops, firemen and looters, then wrote this composition:

"My weekend was not fine at all. Friday night [the people] of P St. and Bates St. broke in the corner store Katz. Katz is a Jew store they shoped and hit everything. My mother told my family not to go to that store. She said her self that she hope they got that store. They also got the liquor store. And they took all the achol from it."

At Cardozo High School, a block from wrecked 14th Street, Alice, a junior, could see from her classroom window smoldering fires that partly obscured the Capitol dome in the distance. She wrote this statement:

"I believe that the riot that recently occurred can be justified . . . I am sorry that it took the burning of his store, etc. in order for him to listen, but in my opinion that's the price you have to pay. It has been made clear these past few days that the Negro isn't going to let Mr. Whiteman push him around any longer. And I cannot blame this generation the least bit."

In the days following the assassination of Dr. Martin Luther King Jr. in Memphis and the weekend rioting, Harold, Alice and thousands of their classmates, mainly in Washington's overwhelmingly Negro inner-city schools, produced an unusual record of their reactions to the shattering events. The record, an outpouring of drawings, compositions, answers to questionnaires and classroom discussions, was inspired by the District of Columbia's Model School Division, an experimental subsystem in the central city. Norman W. Nickens, assistant superintendent who heads the division, had given these instructions to ghetto-area teachers after the assassination:

"REMEMBER, CLASSES SIMPLY CANNOT GO ON AS USUAL. Unusual events have occurred, and your children are preoccupied with these. In times of crisis, children learn rapidly. Therefore, make use of the events of the April 5 weekend to help them learn. Do NOT FAIL THEM BY LECTURING WHEN THEY NEED TO TALK."

The discussions, compositions and pictures showed that fear and a feeling that the adult world was spinning out of control were prevalent emotions. The younger children's drawings are filled with swirls of smoke and curtains of fire. Helpless little figures are often pictured in burning buildings, crying out in comic-strip balloons, "Help me!"

Some pupils in the fourth, fifth and sixth grades described their fears this way:

"I thought the world was coming to an end . . . I felt like a man in a house of fire . . . I really thought the world was in motion . . . Right now, I want to saved from the riot and live in another city . . . I would like to forget Black Power, 'soul' and all the burning of stores . . . I want to be in another country."

A particularly distraught child summed up many of his classmates' feelings when he wrote:

"Right now, I want to have a chance to forget ever thing thats happen in the last 6 days. Right now I want to change the way the world is acting. Right now I want to remember the way the world be. Right now I want to forget ever thing thats happened."

Reactions of fear and insecurity were not confined to younger children. A brilliant high school senior on his way to an Ivy League college next fall expressed his "utter despair of learning of Dr. King's death." A few hours after the assassination, he wrote this personal account:

"I am suspended in hell on this pale chill night, the harsh raggedness of knife-edged rock sweeping endlessly into the sky, a heartless wash of pale green lumin. The ground is black, pits and craters and twisted frozen magma, dully lit, shadows like holes of blindness, creeping over the wolf-jawed rim of hills within the quiet, blank, airless emptiness . . .

"The world, so lively once, is now a sprawl of fire and ice, wheeling overhead an unthinkable distance away . . . This land erupted into a blaze of black flame under the harsh sharp stars.

"I kneel under a sky that is flashing ice and bitter dark, the thin radiance creeping over blackened tumbled cities of ruinous desolation. With the slowness of fleeing through clinging mud a shocked mind and body become responsive to reasoned reflex. We are tense, like the coil of desperation that has already struck out, that in a flash of steel made a martyr."

Fear sometimes was mixed with elation. "When I heard 14th and 7th were on fire I got excited and sat very quiet. I hardly breath," wrote one child. A classmate added: "Friday was the biggest day of my life. Children and people from everywhere came for the looting."

The excitement and elation appeared to be based on what the children recognized as a new fact of life. Before troops arrived in force, masses of black people controlled the streets and, for once, it was truly safe to be black.

"A soul brother is protection," one child observed. "I was not scared this weekend because I was brown," wrote another. A fifth-grader said: "A colored person won't bother a colored person. They are the same colored. Right now I want to be colored."

A high-school student combined her feelings of elation and security at being black with what she saw as a remarkable unity among Negroes:

"I would like to say that I actually felt good watching my people being so happy. I was so happy I could have cried. They were get thing they never had before and would probably never get again. Everyone was calling each other sister and brother. They were helping each other carry things. I never saw and I doubt if I will ever see agains such unity as there was among those people."

The sense of unity, pride in blackness and at least temporary personal security can also be seen in the children's understanding, expressed in their drawings, that "Soul Brother" scrawled on a store window generally provided insurance against damage. The drawings are filled with scenes showing white-owned stores in flames or being looted, while the "Soul Brother" establishment is unharmed. But the drawings also show that not all the destruction was rationally planned. Some children clearly depict white stores in flames and Negroes living in apartments above them trapped and burned out of their homes.

The Model School Division suggested to teachers that they stimulate discussion of the ghetto-originated term "soul." Some simple definitions were: "A soul brother is a man with a lot sence and nerve . . . black power . . . a person who love each other . . . a person who is hipped to everything . . . person waiting for the time to break into stores and take things that does not belong to them."

A more moralistic definition of "soul" was expressed by a seventh-grader: "A soul brother is a person who treats his neighbor as he would want his neighbor to treat him. Not a person who wears loud chottle [clothes] or has long hair tight pants or short short dresses, but is a person who has a religious feeling inside him."

Some responses dwelt on style as a measure of "soul": "They call us soul brother because we are all mostly of the same race. Were hip to the same and we dig the same . . . its all in your mind and soul dig it. You have to dress in style and have a reputation not a bad reputation a good one . . ."

For many, "soul" had no meaning outside the racial context: "A soul brother is a black person who is proud of being black. He or she is not afraid of Honkies . . ."

In the second-grade classroom of a white teacher in a predominantly Negro school, children wrote "Soul Sister" on the blackboard the day after Dr. King's assassination.

The teacher recalled that her pupils were unusually affectionate and protective, even advising her to go home early because the streets were unsafe for whites.

The test many Negro children established for the admission of whites to "soul brotherhood" seemed to be the white's acknowledgement of Negro equality.

But a Negro student at integrated Western High School saw some practical problems. "You know, I got white friends, but last week, out in the street, I can see how you can just get to hating all whites," he said in a classroom discussion. "If you were out on 14th Street and say I'm with you and I know that mentally you're with me, that won't work."

Students who argued that whites could not be "soul brothers" often cited the King murder as a reason: "Can a white person be a soul brother? No, because a white man killed the KING so if a white person put soul brother on their car Negroes will hit it." Another student wrote: "A soul brother is a Negro who loved Martin Luther King who had pride for Negros . . . Soul brothers are Negroes who had pride for Lincoln, Kennedy and King."

A sixth-grade pupil seemed to be saying that Negro "soul," as epitomized by Dr. King, represented a superior value system. Whites "don't realy care about being a soul brother," he wrote. "They don't care if there houses get burend but we color people care because the are not as sick as white people but we don't care about money. Money are not as important as our lives are. All white people care about is money."

Many students ascribed to Dr. King's life and death a variety of meanings. To some he was the savior: "He wanted to take us to the promised land with him . . ." Others saw him as the prophet of nonviolence and the champion of both races: "He stuck his neck out for white and color." And many recognized him as the pre-eminent Negro leader, calling him "Our King" or the "President of the Negroes."

Perhaps transmitting the views of their parents and teachers, many students cited Dr. King's nonviolent teaching as the basis for condemning the rioting. A typical reaction was that of a high-school student who wrote: "In my impartial opinion the riots were a direct negation to what Martin Luther King was doing and they dishonored him." But other students felt strongly that the only appropriate reaction to the killing of the symbol of nonviolence was retribution: "If we protested the dead of Dr. MLK by boycotting, etc., there would hardly be any attention being payed. But when you rioted you let people know you mean business."

The minority of school children who participated in the riots did so only by looting. Widespread looting on Seventh Street began as students were dismissed early from public schools the day after the assassination.

"I took things because everybody did and we did not have anything so we took what we wanted," said one paper.

"I felt happy but I just don't know what it was. They were burning stores down. I went over to the liquor store with my sisters and brothers and I got two fifths of rum and my sister got 4 cases of beer and my father drank the scotch. He gave some to a friend and put the rest in his cabinet."

"I went up 14th St. and we came back with candy, cookies, food, tools. We saw mothers coming down the street with hats, money, ham and chicken."

A 10th-grade student at Lincoln Junior High School defined looting this way in a class discussion: "Lootin' is different from stealin.' If you steal it's individual, you steal by yourself; but lootin' is when a group of people steal together."

Another saw looting as a consumers' revolt: "They were fighting stores." Looting was a revolt of the poor masses, a third student thought: "Some people are right to take that stuff because they never had a $30 pair of shoes. It's right for those who needed it, but those dudes who came out with loads of stuff, that's wrong."

Students of a wide age range often expressed bitter feelings against particular stores. A high-school girl told of her animosity toward a large downtown department store that escaped the riots unscathed: "They're very prejudiced. My girl friend went down there and they told her where she could get the cheapest things. But she wanted to buy something real expensive for her father, but because she was Negro they figured she was poor." A classmate corroborated her statement: "Yeah, if you have the slightest tint in your skin they ask, 'Do you have a charge account?' I told him, 'I'm in high school, man, I don't have no charge account.' So I'd rather go somewhere else."

Some students argued that the looting was a rational program directed at stores that cheated and overcharged in the ghetto. Others disagreed, maintaining that only white stores were attacked, with no distinctions made about customer policies.

"On my block there's this Jew white man and he was very nice," said one girl. "He'd give credit and all that . . . and there's this woman with five or six kids, and she got no husband and he used to give her milk for the kids, and I saw her right in there pulling out everything she could . . . There's this Negro store right across the street and he has a big sign—'No Credit'—but nothing happened to him."

A distinction was made between looting and burning, which was considered an extreme step. One high-school composition said: "I feel that it was good to a certain point. I felt that stealing was one thing and burning buildings was another thing. The burning was totally unnecessary. The burning of buildings left some people jobless, homeless and businesses were lost."

Some participants in a high-school discussion saw the looting as self-defeating: "You say hit whitey in the pocketbook. Just who do you think will now have to pay higher prices to cover whitey's losses during the riot? Who do you think is going to pay $50 for a $10 suit to make it up?"

"Riots gained respect for us," said one high-school militant. "They woke us up, too." Another saw the riots as part of an American tradition: "You know, this rebellion was sort of like the American Revolution or the Boston Tea Party, except the brothers didn't bother to dress up like Indians. And you could compare Stokely Carmichael to Paul Revere when he said, 'Go home and get your guns.'"

A discussion at predominantly Negro Eastern High School included this exchange:

"If I were a white man, watching all that stuff on TV, I think I would conclude that my ways are wrong. But I don't expect that most white people will change overnight, if at all. I suppose a few are more aware now, if only because they were frightened by all those burnt-out buildings."

"Our parents had to be good niggers, but we don't. That was the lesson I got by the events."

"Yeah, looting and violence are the only ways to let white people know we need something."

Across the city at Western High School, a Negro girl said: "I think whites are now scared. . . . But I don't know. . . . Maybe if they are scared they won't take so much advantage of Negroes. . . . Oh, I really don't know."

"In the suburbs there isn't going to be any change. The riot just hasn't affected them," a white girl said emphatically.

"If they keep pushing back whites, the whites will come out and fight," a Negro girl added. "Negroes always think they can fight off anything."

A white boy proposed his solution: "The only way I can see to get out of the problem is to cut out anybody over 30, with few exceptions. They got us into the whole mess . . . If the antiwar people, the student power and the black-power people got together, there'd be plenty of power. The only way I see out is for young people to get together and take over."

"What's wrong is that a lot of people are always separate," a Negro girl said. "Like here at Western, in the cafeteria you see a white table, a black table, a Chinese table, a foreign table. If I were President, I'd destroy all the cities and build new houses all in a row, with a white house, a Negro house, a Chinese house . . ."

The younger children were asked to draw pictures of their neighborhoods on Friday—the day after the assassination; on Monday—after the riots—and in the future. The Friday scenes are usually pictures of fire and looting. The post-riot pictures show broken windows, shells of buildings and the military occupation. But the drawings of the future are the most illuminating.

Many depict a completely nonurban scene: the city block suddenly transformed into a television-and-magazine suburbia of single-family houses, trees, flowers. Other pictures, though, show the same city block, with the same stores reopened and restocked and many of the same people with unchanged, tense, drawn faces.

Some people are shocked by the toleration of disorder in our society. Others pay to experience disorder. Robert Kotlowitz joined the paying group, and he tells what happened at "Murray the K's World."

Robert Kotlowitz

Pleasure Dome '66:
The World of Murray The K

A celebrated disc jockey has created a "total theater" in an old hangar where 1,500 teen-agers at a time can dance, look at movies, slides, and TV, and simultaneously see themselves as the focal point of the universe.

Deep in Long Island's Nassau County, where Garden City shades into Mineola and West Hempstead is indistinguishable from Westbury, stretches a weather-beaten complex of old airplane hangars. In 1927 Lindbergh rolled the *Spirit of St. Louis* out of one and took off for Paris. During World War II, they served the Army as Roosevelt Air Field, and in the 'fifties a theatrical producer named Michael Myerberg set up film production on the base, making a puppet movie there of *Hansel and Gretel.* This spring, Roosevelt Air Field went through another metamorphosis when Myerberg transformed Lindy's old hangar into a teen-age entertainment center called "Murray the K's World." I am telling you about it, because in one variation or another The World may be coming your way.

Murray the K is a New York disc jockey whose last name is Kaufman. He is most celebrated for a national television program he produced last year designed to promote the Job Corps and keep adolescents from dropping out of school; Murray the K's sponsor was the United

States government. The morning after the show, which consisted of pop singers, mostly rock 'n' roll, performing their big hits in unlikely settings (all of them real, including slum streets), several Congressmen reacted with a Philistine zeal excessive even for elected officials. The music on the show, they complained, was a desecration of our way of life; was this what American culture was coming to? They should have known better. Murray the K is not Leonard Bernstein. He is not even Lawrence Welk, nor has he ever pretended to be. The government received value for its money if it really intended the program to reach teen-agers. Mr. K is a force in the teen-age world and the music he offered on television that night was exactly what most teen-agers want to hear. It is hard to reach potential dropouts with a Bach Brandenburg.

I recently visited "Murray the K's World," not unwillingly. I had been intrigued by the press announcements that preceded its opening. "A new concept of total theater . . . large enough to accommodate 3,000 visitors on the 5,000 square foot dance floor," they described it, going on to explain that "the traditional entertainment of today—movies, theater, radio, television, rock 'n' roll shows—all channel our interest to a single focal point, whether it be audio or visual, or even a combination of both. We are always reacting to this 'focal point' and never allowed to be part of it—to be at the center— as is the case in real life. The central concept of Murray the K's World is that the individual *is* the 'focal point' . . . you are the center, and everything is happening around *you*! . . . Are you ready for the fantastic?" The fact is that I am always ready for the fantastic, ready, I should say, to a fault; I also enjoy watching adolescents at play, especially when their toys are music and dancing.

There is room on Roosevelt Field alongside Murray the K's World to park one thousand automobiles, and on weekends it is filled. (To enter the World at night, when alcohol is served, you must be eighteen; during the afternoon, at "kiddie matinees," the age limit is sixteen.) On the night I went, a line about a hundred yards long, made up of yawning teen-agers, stretched in front of the hangar. It moved slowly; each person paid $2.50 to get in. As I entered the lobby, a young girl dressed in purple and orange bell-bottom slacks and a blouse to match, blew cigarette smoke gently into my face. "Are you sure you're over eighteen?" she asked. "Alas," I said, "I am." She laughed good-naturedly and pointed the way inside. Heading through the lobby I noticed a sign that read, "Occupancy by more than 1,580 persons illegal," and alongside it another: "Anyone entering these premises gives unqualified approval to the management to photograph—televise—exhibit and transmit their image for profit."

Inside the hangar it was dark, but instantaneously I was overwhelmed by a quick series of visual and aural images, all of them registering almost at the same time. Straight ahead, across the hangar floor, was a bar running the width of the building and over it a huge screen showing a shadowed, grainy picture of teen-agers dancing. It was closed circuit TV, I was told, on which the dancers can look at themselves looking at themselves. Flanking the screen on each side were three smaller movie screens, all showing variations of World War I fighter planes in action; dogfights and crashes filled the wall. The same theme was picked up on eighteen or so slide-film screens on both the right and left walls of the hangar. Lindy could be seen waving goodbye to the camera on his way to Europe; instantly he was replaced by a picture of a Parisian crowd mobbing him. More crashes followed, some of them comic; no blood was shed.

Directly in front of me, caught by stroboscopic lights or plain spots, close to 1,580 teen-agers were dancing, getting ready to, or looking for someone to dance with. The recorded music bounced solidly against the hangar walls, producing a constant ricochet of echoes and reverberations; a trio called The Supremes sounded like six voices, then nine, and during her solos, Diane Ross, their leader, rang like a huge, amplified bell. Close by, I saw a pretty girl, her face dead-white and sharp, wearing a suit with slacks, all of it covered with a pink-and-red diamond pattern; on her feet were red boots, the toes pointed as a dagger. She was dancing with a blond young man, forelock hanging over his forehead, in a navy-blue blazer and ascot. They were surrounded by a small, admiring circle of other young people who applauded every now and then; while they never touched, they made a fiercely poised couple, dancing smoothly and sometimes beautifully together. Here and there, one dateless young girl danced with another, each an unmistakable Long Island Mod, and at one point I caught a swift, startling glimpse of a young man in a tan satin shirt with puffed sleeves, over which he was wearing a sleeveless brown suede jacket; no one gave him a second look.

Words drifted through the air. He (feigning surprise): "What are *you* doing here?" She (feigning surprise): "What am *I* doing here? What are *you* doing here?" (They go off together.) One girl to another: "Where's Murray the K?" Second girl: "I'm sure he's on the way."

I moved up a curved staircase to "The VIP Balcony," sat down at a small table, and looked out over The World. Around us on three sides were the TV, slide, and movie screens; the latter were still showing World War I dogfights. Another balcony was set over a refreshment bar on the left-hand wall; there the music was electronically programmed and the decibel level controlled. On the right wall was still another balcony, dark now, on which "live" singing groups, as well as Murray the K and four girl dancers, were to perform later. From dead center below the ceiling hung a final balcony from which all the TV, film, and slide pictures were projected. Beneath this control center, young girls sat on a circular platform in the middle of the dance floor looking disdainful or frightened, while embarrassed clumps of boys unaggressively circled them; most of them looked as though they were in great pain. From my table upstairs I could see a tall girl with stringy hair performing a quiet, reticent dance with her plump girlfriend. One of the boys cut in and took her off for himself; as they danced together, she made him suit his style to hers.

"Where's Murray the K?" I asked a waiter.

"Don't worry, he's coming," he said.

LIBERTY DEFROCKED

I suddenly became aware that the Statue of Liberty was being magically transformed into a nude on one of the movie screens. First her grimy robes dropped off. Then her crown disappeared. Finally the torch went, leaving an undressed woman in its place. The song that was playing was called "Love Makes the World Go Round." Thin, bony models from *Vogue* and *Harper's Bazaar* flashed on the screen. Following the Statue of Liberty, they looked vaguely diseased. Then strong men wearing tights showed off their biceps. Color slides of insects came on and off in swift motion; some were whole, some halved, others quartered. It seemed that the insects were doing mating dances. I saw the white-faced girl in the pink-and-red suit moving fast on the dance floor; her partner was sweating in a spotlight. The Statue of Liberty became a nude again. A strong man in a Tarzan costume showed off his biceps. "Love, suhweet luh-hu-huv," the lyrics went. Stroboscopic lights played on and off. A spot caught me at my table; I looked up and saw myself—a "focal point" if there ever was one—on the TV screen.

The music changed. This time it was The Beach Boys, an aggregation of boy sopranos in their early twenties, singing "Sloop John B." On one of the screens, a girl with long, Alice-in-Wonderland hair danced on the deck of a sailboat, first fast, then in slow motion. Up and down she floated, her hair undulating like seaweed. Film clips of teen-age sports followed. Cheerleaders jumped up and down in front of the crowd, arching their backs and waving fake chrysanthemums in the air. Athletic kids in sweatshirts somersaulted around the screen. A football team ran onto a field, looking terrifically gung ho.

The music changed again: "Turn, Turn, Turn," with lyrics from Ecclesiastes. Some of the teen-agers on the dance floor began to sing along quietly. I counted twenty-seven customers at the bar across the hall; it was about sixty feet long and gaping with unmanned bar space. Everybody was dancing. Details from Hieronymus Bosch and Peter Breughel paintings flashed on the slide screens, repeating themselves, six, eight, a dozen times. There they were, goblins, monsters, grotesques, the war wounded, infinitely bigger than their canvas selves. The crowd below swayed together with the music. Some continued to sing: "There's a Time for War and a Time for Peace. . . ." Corpses, witches, and dwarfs covered the walls, and strobe lights played over the floor.

A half-dozen other songs followed, then another half-dozen. I saw the girl in the pink-and-red suit and her boyfriend wearily dancing back to front now like two tarnished spoons. One couple danced in each other's arms. From the loudspeakers, I heard, "To hold you and keep you and kiss you to my dying day. . . ." And again: "To hold you and keep you. . . ." Then I heard it a third and fourth time. Clips from television commercials filled the movie screens—quick cuts of soap ads (lovely middle-class ladies in their bathtubs and housewives with their hands in the kitchen sink). Nearby, someone called out, "The Vagrants are coming." A sudden wild tune was accompanied by a film of Britain's Royal Family touring Africa; it subtly segued into an anti-Jim Crow film, all of it over and done with in a little over two minutes. The dancing was faster now; the bar space filled up with another dozen teen-agers. Lights began to go on over the balcony on which the "live" acts were to appear. Someone alongside me said, "It's The Vagrants." A small cheer went up and a John Lennon hat was tossed into the air. I noticed that the card on my table said that a Coca-Cola cost one dollar.

"Where's Murray the K?" I asked.

"He's stuck in traffic."

What is the difference between being absurd and just funny? Absurdity has been so intriguing that some dramatists have created the *theater of the absurd*. London producer and director Martin Esslin explores the psychology and value of dramatic absurdity.

Martin Esslin

The Significance
of the Absurd

When Nietzsche's Zarathustra descended from his mountains to preach to mankind, he met a saintly hermit in the forest. This old man invited him to stay in the wilderness rather than go into the cities of men. When Zarathustra asked the hermit how he passed his time in his solitude, he replied:

From *The Theatre of the Absurd*, by Martin Esslin. Copyright © 1961 by Martin Esslin. Reprinted by permission of Doubleday & Company, Inc.

I make up songs and sing them; and when I make up songs, I laugh, I weep, and I growl; thus do I praise God.

Zarathustra declined the old man's offer and continued on his journey:

But when he was alone, he spoke thus to his heart: "Can it be possible! This old saint in the forest has not yet heard that God is dead!"

Zarathustra was first published in 1883. The number of people for whom God is dead has greatly increased since Nietzsche's day, and mankind has learned the bitter lesson of the falseness and evil nature of some of the cheap and vulgar substitutes that have been set up to take His place. And so, after two terrible wars, there are still many who are trying to come to terms with the implications of Zarathustra's message, searching for a way in which they can, with dignity, confront a universe deprived of what was once its center and its living purpose, a world deprived of a generally accepted integrating principle, which has become disjointed, purposeless—absurd.

The Theatre of the Absurd is one of the expressions of this search. It bravely faces up to the fact that for those to whom the world has lost its central explanation and meaning, it is no longer possible to accept art forms still based on the continuation of standards and concepts that have lost their validity; that is, the possibility of knowing the laws of conduct and ultimate values, as deductible from a firm foundation of revealed certainty about the purpose of man in the universe.

In expressing the tragic sense of loss at the disappearance of ultimate certainties the Theatre of the Absurd, by a strange paradox, is also a symptom of what probably comes nearest to being a genuine religious quest in our age: an effort, however timid and tentative, to sing, to laugh, to weep—and to growl—if not in praise of God (whose name, in Adamov's phrase, has for so long been degraded by usage that it has lost its meaning), at least in search of a dimension of the Ineffable; an effort to make man aware of the ultimate realities of his condition, to instill in him again the lost sense of cosmic wonder and primeval anguish, to shock him out of an existence that has become trite, mechanical, complacent, and deprived of the dignity that comes of awareness. For God is dead, above all, to the masses who live from day to day and have lost all contact with the basic facts—and mysteries—of the human condition with which, in former times, they were kept in touch through the living ritual of their religion, which made them parts of a real community and not just atoms in an atomized society.

The Theatre of the Absurd forms part of the unceasing endeavor of the true artists of our time to breach this dead wall of complacency and automatism and to re-establish an awareness of man's situation when confronted with the ultimate reality of his condition. As such, the Theatre of the Absurd fulfills a dual purpose and presents its audience with a two-fold absurdity.

On the one hand, it castigates, satirically, the absurdity of lives lived unaware and unconscious of ultimate reality. This is the feeling of the deadness and mechanical senselessness of half-unconscious lives, the feeling of "human beings secreting inhumanity," which Camus describes in *The Myth of Sisyphus*:

In certain hours of lucidity, the mechanical aspect of their gestures, their senseless pantomime, makes stupid everything around them. A man speaking on the telephone behind a glass partition—one cannot hear him but observes his trivial gesturing. One asks oneself, why is he alive? This malaise in front of man's own inhumanity, this incalculable letdown when faced with the image of what we are, this "nausea," as a contemporary writer calls it, also is the Absurd.

This is the experience that Ionesco expresses in plays like *The Bald Soprano* or *The Chairs*, Adamov in *La Parodie*, or N. F. Simpson in *A Resounding Tinkle*. It represents the satirical, parodistic aspect of the Theatre of the Absurd, its social criticism, its pillorying of an inauthentic, petty society. This may be the most easily accessible, and therefore most widely recognized, message of the Theatre of the Absurd, but it is far from being its most essential or most significant feature.

Behind the satirical exposure of the absurdity of inauthentic ways of life, the Theatre of the Absurd is facing up to a deeper layer of absurdity —the absurdity of the human condition itself in a world where the decline of religious belief has deprived man of certainties. When it is no longer possible to accept simple and complete systems of values and revelations of divine purpose, life must be faced in its ultimate, stark reality. That is why, in the analysis of the dramatists of the Absurd in this book, we have always seen man stripped of the accidental circumstances of social position or historical context, confronted with the basic choices, the basic situations of his existence: man faced with time and therefore waiting, in Beckett's plays or Gelber's, waiting between birth and death; man running away from death, climbing higher and higher, in Vian's play, or passively sinking down toward death, in Buzzati's; man rebelling against death, confronting and accepting it, in Ionesco's *Tueur Sans Gages*; man inextricably entangled in a mirage of illusions, mirrors reflecting mirrors, and forever hiding ultimate reality, in the plays of Genet; man trying to establish his position, or to break out into freedom, only to find himself newly imprisoned, in the parables of Manuel de Pedrolo; man trying to stake out a modest place for himself in the cold and darkness that envelop him, in Pinter's plays; man vainly striving to grasp the moral law forever beyond his comprehension, in Arrabal's; man caught in the inescapable dilemma that strenuous effort leads to the same result as passive indolence—complete futility and ultimate death —in the earlier work of Adamov; man forever lonely, immured in the prison of his subjectivity, unable to reach his fellow man, in the vast majority of these plays.

Concerned as it is with the ultimate realities of the human condition, the relatively few fundamental problems of life and death, isolation and communication, the Theatre of the Absurd, however grotesque, frivolous, and irreverent it may appear, represents a return to the original, religious function of the theatre—the confrontation of man with the spheres of myth and religious reality. Like ancient Greek tragedy and the medieval mystery plays and baroque allegories, the Theatre of the Absurd is intent on making its audience aware of man's precarious and mysterious position in the universe. . . .

In the "literary" theatre, language remains the predominant component. In the anti-literary theatre of the circus or the music hall, language is reduced to a very subordinate role. The Theatre of the Absurd has regained the freedom of using language as merely one—sometimes dominant, sometimes submerged—component of its multidimensional poetic imagery. By putting the language of a scene in contrast to the action, by reducing it to meaningless patter, or by abandoning discursive logic for the poetic logic of association or assonance, the Theatre of the Absurd has opened up a new dimension of the stage.

In its devaluation of language, the Theatre of the Absurd is in tune with the trend of our time. As George Steiner has pointed out in two radio talks entitled *The Retreat from the Word*, the devaluation of language is characteristic not only of the development of contemporary poetry or philosophical thought but, even more, of modern mathematics and the natural sciences. "It is no paradox to assert," Steiner says, "that much of reality now begins *outside* language. . . . Large areas of meaningful experience now belong to non-verbal languages such as mathematics, formulae, and logical symbolism. Others belong to 'anti-languages' such as the practice of nonobjective art or atonal music. The world of the word has shrunk." Moreover, the abandonment of language as the best instrument of notation in the spheres of mathematics and symbolic logic goes hand in hand with a marked reduction in the popular belief in its practical usefulness. Language appears more and more as being in contradiction to reality. The trends of thought that have the greatest influence on contemporary popular thinking all show this tendency.

Take the case of Marxism. Here a distinction is made between *apparent* social relations and the social *reality* behind them. Objectively, an employer is seen as an exploiter, and therefore an enemy, of the working class. If an employer therefore says to a worker; "I have sympathy with your point of view," he may himself believe what he is saying, but objectively his words are meaningless. However much he asserts his sympathy for the worker, he remains his enemy. Language here belongs to the realm of the purely subjective, and is thus devoid of objective reality.

The same applies to modern depth psychology and psychoanalysis. Every child today knows that there is a vast gap between what is consciously thought and asserted and the psychological reality behind the words spoken. A son who tells his father that he loves and respects him is objectively bound to be, in fact, filled with the deepest Oedipal hatred of his father. He may not know it, but he means the opposite of what he says. And the subconscious has a higher content of reality than the conscious utterance.

The relativization, devaluation, and criticism of language are also the prevailing trends in contemporary philosophy, as exemplified by Wittgenstein's conviction in the last phase of his thinking, that the philosopher must endeavor to disentangle thought from the conventions and rules of grammar, which have been mistaken for the rules of logic. "A *picture* held us captive. And we could not get outside it, for it lay in our language, and language seemed to repeat it to us inexorably. . . . Where does our investigation get its importance from, since it seems only to destroy everything interesting; that is, all that is great and important? (As it were, all the buildings, leaving behind only bits of stone and rubble.) What we are destroying is nothing but houses of cards, and we are clearing up the ground of language on which they stand." By a strict criticism of language, Wittgenstein's followers have declared large categories of statements to be devoid of objective meaning. Wittgenstein's "word games" have much in common with the Theatre of the Absurd.

But even more significant than these tendencies in Marxist, psychological, and philosophical thinking is the trend of the times in the workaday world of the man in the street. Exposed to the incessant, and inexorably loquacious, onslaught of the mass media, the press, and advertising, the man in the street becomes more and more skeptical toward the language he is exposed to. The citizens of totalitarian countries know full well that most of what they are told is double-talk, devoid of real meaning. They become adept at reading between the lines; that is, at guessing at the reality the language conceals rather than reveals. In the West, euphemisms and circumlocutions fill the press or resound from the pulpits. And advertising, by its constant use of superlatives, has succeeded in devaluing language to a point where it is a generally accepted axiom that most of the words one sees displayed on billboards or in the colored pages of magazine advertising are as meaningless as the jingles of television commercials. A yawning gulf has opened between language and reality.

Apart from the general devaluation of language in the flood of mass communications, the growing specialization of life has made the exchange of ideas on an increasing number of subjects impossible between members of different spheres of life which have each developed its own specialized jargon. As Ionesco says, in summarizing and enlarging on the views of Antonin Artaud:

As our knowledge becomes separated from life, our culture no longer contains ourselves (or only an insignificant part of ourselves), for it forms a "social" context into which we are not integrated. So the problem becomes that of bringing our life back into contact with our culture, making it a living culture once again. To achieve this, we shall first have to kill "the respect for what is written down in black and white" . . . to break up our language so that it can be put together again in order to re-establish contact with "the absolute," or, as I should prefer to say, "with multiple reality"; it is imperative to "push human beings again toward seeing themselves as they really are."

That is why communication between human beings is so often shown in a state of breakdown in the Theatre of the Absurd. It is merely a satirical magnification of the existing state of affairs. Language has run riot in an age of mass communication. It must be reduced to its proper function—the expression of authentic content, rather than its concealment. But this will be possible only if man's reverence toward the spoken or written word as a means of communication is restored, and the ossified clichés that dominate thought (as they do in the limericks of Edward Lear or the world of Humpty Dumpty) are replaced by a living language that serves it. And this, in turn, can be achieved only if the limitations of logic and discursive language are recognized and respected, and the uses of poetic language acknowledged.

The means by which the dramatists of the Absurd express their critique—largely instinctive and unintended—of our disintegrating society are based on suddenly confronting their audiences with a grotesquely heightened and distorted picture of a world that has gone mad. This is a shock therapy that achieves what Brecht's doctrine of the "alienation effect" postulated in theory but failed to achieve in practice—the inhibition of the audience's identification with the characters on the stage (which is the age-old and highly effective method of the traditional theatre) and its replacement by a detached, critical attitude. . . .

The madness of the times lies precisely in the existence, side by side, of a large number of unreconciled beliefs and attitudes—conventional morality, for example, on the one hand, and the values of advertising on the other; the conflicting claims of science and religion; or the loudly proclaimed striving of all sections for the general interest when in fact each is pursuing very narrow and selfish particular ends. On each page of his newspaper, the man in the street is confronted with a different and contradictory pattern of values. No wonder that the art of such an era shows a marked resemblance to the symptoms of schizophrenia. But it is not, as Jung has pointed out in an essay on Joyce's *Ulysses*, the artist who is schizophrenic: "The medical description of schizophrenia offers only an analogy, in that the schizophrenic has apparently the same tendency to treat reality as if it were strange to him, or, the other way around, to estrange himself from reality. In the modern artist, this tendency is not produced by any disease in the individual but as a manifestation of our time."

The challenge to make sense out of what appears as a senseless and fragmented action, the recognition that the fact that the modern world has lost its unifying principle is the source of its bewildering and soul-destroying quality, is therefore more than a mere intellectual exercise; it has a therapeutic effect. In Greek tragedy, the spectators were made aware of man's forlorn but heroic stand against the inexorable forces of fate and the will of the gods—and this had a cathartic effect upon them and made them better able to face their time. In the Theatre of the Absurd, the spectator is confronted with the madness of the human condition, is enabled to see his situation in all its grimness and despair, and this, in stripping him of illusions or vaguely felt fears and anxieties, enables him to face it consciously, rather than feel it vaguely below the surface of euphemisms and optimistic illusions. And this, in turn, results in the liberating effect of anxieties overcome by being formulated. This is the nature of all the gallows humor and *humour noir* of world literature, of which the Theatre of the Absurd is the latest example. It is the unease caused by the presence of illusions that are obviously out of tune with reality that is dissolved and discharged through liberating laughter at the recognition of the fundamental absurdity of the universe. The greater the anxieties and the temptation to indulge in illusions, the more beneficial is this therapeutic effect—hence the success of *Waiting for Godot* at San Quentin. It was a relief for the convicts to be made to recognize in the tragicomic situation of the tramps the hopelessness of their own waiting for a miracle. They were enabled to laugh at the tramps—and at themselves.

As the reality with which the Theatre of the Absurd is concerned is a psychological reality expressed in images that are the outward projection of states of mind, fears, dreams, nightmares, and conflicts within the personality of the author, the dramatic tension produced by this kind of play differs fundamentally from the suspense created in a theatre concerned mainly with the revelation of objective characters through the unfolding of a narrative plot. The pattern of exposition, conflict, and final solution mirrors a view of the world in which solutions are possible, a view based on a recognizable and generally accepted pattern of an objective reality that can be apprehended so that the purpose of man's existence and the rules of conduct it entails can be deduced from it.

This is true even of the lightest type of drawing room comedy, in which the action proceeds on a deliberately restricted view of the world —that the whole purpose of the characters involved is for each boy to get his girl. And even in the darkest pessimistic tragedies of the naturalistic or Expressionist theatres, the final curtain enables the audience to go home with a formulated message or philosophy in their minds: the solution may have been a sad one, but it was a rationally formulated conclusion nevertheless. This, as I pointed out in the introduction, applies even to the theatre of Sartre and Camus, which is based on a philosophy of the absurdity of human existence. Even plays like *Huis Clos (No Exit),*

Le Diable et le Bon Dieu (Lucifer and the Lord), and *Caligula* allow the audience to take home an intellectually formulated philosophical lesson.

The Theatre of the Absurd, however, which proceeds not by intellectual concepts but by poetic images, neither poses an intellectual problem in its exposition nor provides any clear-cut solution that would be reliable as a lesson or an apothegm. Many of the plays of the Theatre of the Absurd have a circular structure, ending exactly as they began; others progress merely by a growing intensification of the initial situation. And as the Theatre of the Absurd rejects the idea that it is possible to motivate all human behavior, or that human character is based on an immutable essence, it is impossible for it to base its effect on the suspense that in other dramatic conventions springs from awaiting the solution of a dramatic equation based on the working out of a problem involving clearly defined quantities introduced in the opening scenes. In most dramatic conventions, the audience is constantly asking itself the question "What is going to happen next?"

In the Theatre of the Absurd, the audience is confronted with actions that lack apparent motivation, characters that are in constant flux, and often happenings that are clearly outside the realm of rational experience. Here, too, the audience can ask, "What is going to happen next?" But then *anything* may happen next, so that the answer to this question cannot be worked out according to the rules of the ordinary probability based on motives and characterization that will remain constant throughout the play. The relevant question here is not so much what is going to happen next but what *is* happening? "What does the action of the play represent?" . . .

Ultimately, a phenomenon like the Theatre of the Absurd does not reflect despair or a return to dark irrational forces but expresses modern man's endeavor to come to terms with the world in which he lives. It attempts to make him face up to the human condition as it really is, to free him from illusions that are bound to cause constant maladjustment and disappointment. There are enormous pressures in our world that seek to induce mankind to bear the loss of faith and moral certainties by being drugged into oblivion—by mass entertainments, shallow material satisfactions, pseudo-explanations of reality, and cheap ideologies. At the end of that road lies Huxley's Brave New World of senseless euphoric automata. Today, when death and old age are increasingly concealed behind euphemisms and comforting baby talk, and life is threatened with being smothered in the mass consumption of hypnotic mechanized vulgarity, the need to confront man with the reality of his situation is greater than ever. For the dignity of man lies in his ability to face reality in all its senselessness; to accept it freely, without fear, without illusions—and to laugh at it.

That is the cause to which, in their various individual, modest, and quixotic ways, the dramatists of the Absurd are dedicated.

Whatever value disorder or chaos or the absurd may have, we cannot live our lives in them, at least not more than one or two of us at a time. Walter Kerr, a drama critic, looks at the "now" theater and tries to see what it means in the context of our society.

Walter Kerr

Now — Is There Nothing but Now?

It suddenly strikes me that one whole strand of the current experimental theater is entirely superfluous. It is straining desperately to get us where we already are.

It is trying to give us the sense that we are *there*—there where the action is, there at the precise moment the happening happens, there where immersion in the immediate is total, there under bombardment, there on the spot, there before thought has had a chance to tidy things up.

We are at the center of the melee, with impromptu voices calling over our shoulders to "tell it like it is, man," caught between forces that have not yet become coherent, subject to violation by sound track and players, part of the script before the script has been written, participants in an action that no one has quite planned.

Advocates of this kind of theater are in passionate earnest, and they have a premise. The theater we have known bores us because it displays a dead life, life cut and trimmed and dumped on the meat counter where it has already gathered flies. The only alternative is to enter a live life, before the callous and merely money-minded butchers have got at it. Catch life before anyone else has caught it and codified it, killed it, for you.

Working from the premise, one such advocate has already announced that last year's march on the Pentagon was last year's only genuine *play*. Those who marched had met and mingled with drama instead of observing, distantly and indifferently, its interment on a stage. Those who were unable, or who failed, to march on the Pentagon may be able to take up the slack by marching, or being marched upon, in auditorium or garage. The important thing is that, wherever you are, it's *now*.

From *The New York Times*, Sept. 8, 1968.

But the one wrestler's grip that life has already got on us, the one awareness no modern man is without, is the grip of the now, the actual and unyielding pressure of the instantly present. I'm not going to re-catalogue McLuhanisms for you here, or talk about Telstar making a global village of us all, sharing the anger of Prague before Prague can quite clear its head of bewilderment. One needed only to flick a television set on—and off—during the Democratic National Convention of a week ago to deal with nowness directly.

Flicking it off said as much about the living instant as flicking it on. Here was a speech in progress, not a film. An empty speech, a speech making its way through ritual, unfelt motions. (The living *now* can be as mummified in its immediacy as the dead *then*.) It was going to go on for a while, stretch into a new, not yet counted, nowness. Snap it off, for now. I have a *now* of my own: I can speak to someone, write a check, write a letter, while waiting for nowness in Chicago to catch up with mine here. Half the time I am ahead of it, so fast does my world go.

When I snap it on again, I am there—as those old record albums used to say—while helmeted police maul ministers and hurl them into waiting wagons. No blood is dry yet, no scalps are stitched. The shocked faces of bystanders are my shock, coinciding in time. They have not re-flected, I have not reflected, we are joined, locked in simultaneity. Some-one in my house went to the bathroom and missed seeing Dan Rather knocked down. No, not seeing. *Being* at the knocking down. The dizzy totality spins on, and we are breathless from it. Multiply it by a ringing telephone—another *now* message—and we scarcely know which way to turn. Chances are the caller will say "Are you looking at what's happen-ing *now*?"

More than the television image is blurred in the frantic swing of the camera to catch what has never been rehearsed, what cannot be predicted. The eyes blur, comprehension blurs, the antennae of the senses blur (what is that sound, a gavel at the convention or someone banging on the front door?). In time—and this is very much what some theatrical experimentalists are after—the distinction between the rehearsed and the unrehearsed blurs. You may have read, in a recent New Yorker, a neck-snapping account of a motion picture actor, an actor who had appeared in "The Dirty Dozen" and similar films, getting out of his car on the highway, smilingly approaching the driver behind who'd lightly touched his bumper, and clouting the driver full in the face, drawing his finger-nails across the man's eyes for good measure. Sincere experimentalists would have to approve the actor and the action. He was not confined to dead film, the film was *now*.

We are all of us in it all of the time and a sniper may tag us on the Long Island Rail Road. In our homes, in our cars, on trains and on the telephone, we are centers of a thousand trajectories, hostile, friendly, de-manding, beneficent, irrational, logical, random. We have been pushed up forward, and that is where we try to cope. We speed-read the signals, and have no time to look back. We no longer have to look at our watches. We are everywhere the second-hand is, when it is.

That is already our experience. The attempt to reproduce it in the theater—to reproduce it as it is, man—exposes the theater to three swift self-denials. The attempt, quite literally, is to make the theater indistinguishable from life—as in calling the march on the Pentagon a play. This deprives the theater of an identity of its own. Life goes on, the theater does not. To the degree that such theater succeeds in duplicating the precise conditions of our lives, it also becomes superfluous. Why go to the theater when we are already there? And, lastly, it becomes synthetic. The process, trying hard not to be a manufacture but a continuation of fact, remains a manufacture: the sounds are manufactured, the sights are manufactured, the performers are only performers, feeble alongside the sniper, the cop, the shocked bystander, the real bore. We have duplicated what did not need duplicating, and in general duplicated it lamely.

This is not a pitch for evasion of the real. It is a pitch for understanding of the real. Obviously the moment of least comprehension is the moment of greatest inundation. Even as we watch bodies being clubbed on television, even as we are caught up—our heads swimming—in the violent, unfocused, swerving, jarring immediacy of it all, we want to stand back. Stand back just a little, just for a moment. We want to *see* what we are seeing, see it in its wholeness, its shape, its meaning. We want to know what orders were given, where and by whom. We want to know, at the very least, which victims may have deserved a tenth of what they are getting, which have deserved nothing at all. We want to relate the action *now* to the actions that preceded it, and we want to grasp its implications for action that will follow tomorrow. We want the event to take form, and only distancing will do that for us.

Form—through distancing—is of course what the theater has always been about. It has never denied *now*; it has simply put it in the intelligible perspective of *and then*. It may have sometimes, it may have very often, falsified the *and then*; but even when it was clumsily falsifying it was not losing sight of its function. If we are rebelling in the theater now, it may be a good idea to ask what we are rebelling against: the act of distancing itself, or a merely outmoded method of distancing, one we have come to see through and one which may very well be replaced by a better.

The issue seems to me critical just now. It may be that this is the very time when we most need the theater on its own terms. The more we are plunged into nowness in our lives, the farther we are pushed toward an unfamiliar and even incomprehensible frontier, the more we are desperately engaged with unexpected blows struck by an invisible hand at an unpredictable hour, the more desperately do we need a space in which we *may* stand back, or even sit down. Standing there, or sitting there, we need accept no lies about shape. But unless we have a reflective, judging, distancing place in which shaping may be attempted, or even experienced, we won't be able to tell a lie from a truth.

What were all those people talking about?

1. In Auden's poem, what is man's relation to disorder and chaos?

2. The Washington, D.C., assistant superintendent talked about unusual events and rapid learning coinciding. Is this true in your experience? What is it about "unusual" events that might speed learning?

3. What did the kids learn from the local chaos? Did they have any new insights into familiar words and phrases?

4. Why do people go to a place like Murray the K's World?

5. What is the difference between the absurdity Martin Esslin talks about and something that is just funny?

6. What is the difference between theater of the absurd and just plain disorder?

7. Would Walter Kerr feel that theater of the absurd should fade away? Why or why not?

8. Could theater of the absurd and traditional theater be useful to each other in any way? Explain.

Two assignments . . .

1. Cut out or copy down twenty-five newspaper headlines and arrange them any way you want. Try to have some sense in your arrangement. Now show them to someone else and see if your arrangement gets across to him.

2. Write a paper of two or three pages in which you relate a brief event in your life that confused you at least momentarily. Do not moralize about the event. Limit yourself to concrete description, but try to write so that the reader is not confused by the writing.

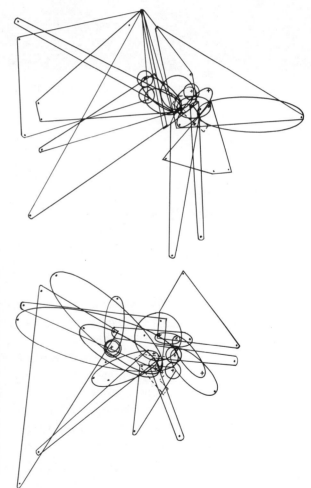

Household activity patterns of two types of activities. Interviews with a simple, random sample of people in households flanking downtown Durham, N.C., revealed recreations patterns shown in top figure and visiting patterns shown in bottom figure. The activity places are indicated by black dots, and places of residence are indicated by plus signs. (From F. Stuart Chapin, Jr., *Urban Land Use Planning*, rev. ed. Urbana: University of Illinois Press, 1965. Reproduced by permission.)

Gymnastics in a refugee camp, Punjab, India, 1947. © Henri Cartier-Bresson-Magnum.

Peter Dale

Single Ticket

The train rattles through the night.
That face opposite. More sallow now
yet still that hair mists into light,
the skin more mobile on the brow—
A lapse of memory. Or time.
Gone that sidelong
glance her eyes had, green as lime.
Caught in scrutiny of a face
they lowered like a dog's in disgrace.
Now tears rim those eyes once strong.

Peter Dale, "Single Ticket" from *The Storms* (Chester Springs, Pa.: Dufour Editions Inc., 1968), pp. 18–19.

Time and again she glances my way
Unsure, I wonder whether she tries
to place me or returns the stray
stares I prolong to recognize
her features. I turn to the dusty pane
and there's her face
wrinkled and weeping in the driving rain.
Illness or years might make her look
like this. I nod back to my book
returning through years to the old place.

A trick of memory, commonsense
insists. There's a ring on her hand.
Too much depends on coincidence
for one homecoming in years to land
me on this branch of the local line
in the same train
with her, however changed those fine
features, the laughter corded round
the lips. I stare again as if bound
to catch some trait clinchingly plain.

The battered case offers no clue,
no name, no label. Travelling alone
she troubles me like one I knew
by sight those years ago, the tone
of her voice unheard. I do not speak
and nor does she.
If we'd once broken week after week
of silence we might have joined this train
together, and her eyes not show such pain.
I doubt it, though. She stares at me.

My stop. She gets out further down
the corridor and runs as once she ran
when late to catch her train to town—
or any woman runs to dodge a man
who eyes her too intently. I walk
the other way
and two miles home rehearsing talk
to come. Her heels tick into night.
More faces to re-shape at sight,
their recognitions to outstare next day.

6

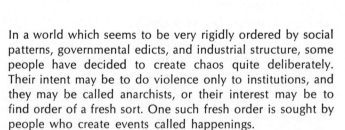

Chaos and beyond

In a world which seems to be very rigidly ordered by social patterns, governmental edicts, and industrial structure, some people have decided to create chaos quite deliberately. Their intent may be to do violence only to institutions, and they may be called anarchists, or their interest may be to find order of a fresh sort. One such fresh order is sought by people who create events called happenings.

For our purposes we shall define a happening as the deliberate simulation of spontaneous and random events. The primary effect of a successful happening is a disordering of perception and expectation, in order to create the sense of a strange environment and to place the spectator within that environment. Surroundings do not behave as we usually see them and expect them to behave, and voluntarily or involuntarily we are set free of the structures and patterns of the everyday world.

Here are twenty-five directions for twenty-five persons in

a short happening which has been used to demonstrate the experience of chaos in a classroom.

1. Go to the door and open it and shut it. Go to the window and do the same. Keep repeating this cycle.

2. Go to the blackboard and place your palms on it. Move all around the board; push on it as if you expect one panel to open.

3. Go to the front right corner of the room and hide your head in it. Keep counting to yourself and on every third number say loudly (don't shout) "Home."

4. Walk around the room and knock dum-dum de dum-dum slowly on each desk or chair.

5. Go up to the front of the room and face the class. Count to yourself, and each time you reach five say, "If I had the wings of an angel."

6. Sit in your seat and watch the person facing you from the front of the room. Each time he says "Angel" you clap. Don't look anywhere else.

7. Put your head down on the desk and close your eyes and don't open them until it is all over.

8. Count to eight over and over to yourself. Each time you reach eight say out loud, "This is English 2W class."

9. Each time you hear no one talking say "Silence!" as if you had just discovered it.

10. Stand by your seat and face the back of the room. Each time you count to ten, raise your hands above your head and make an effort to fly by flapping your hands.

11. Go to the blackboard and draw doors of all sizes. Try to make them recognizable doors, but don't spend much time on any one picture.

12. On a piece of paper, keep writing "I am, I am, I am . . ."

13. Keep your head down on your desk. The instant the happening starts say, "Stop, stop, stop." When the instructor ends the happening say, "Go, go, go."

14. Sit at your desk and pretend you are counting money in $2 bills. Each time you have a stack worth $30, gather it up and throw it in the air and say, "Thirty dollars."

15. Walk around to everyone in the room and pat him or her on the back lightly and say, "It's all right." Stop occasionally and ask, "Who, me?"

16. Look at your feet, but don't ever move them or look up or anywhere else in the room.

17. Gently tap your forehead against your desk. Keep doing this without looking around.

18. Draw a big circle on a sheet of paper, then a smaller one inside, then another and so on. Each time you complete a circle hold up the paper so everyone can see. Say "Circle" as you hold up the paper. When you put it down again, say "Square."

19. Each time someone stands up and mentions anything about money, you ask "Where are you from?" Every time the time is announced, ask "What time is it?"

20. Be an ice cream cone; change flavor.

21. Announce from the back, "Mr. Balaban is an ice cream cone."

22. Be Emmett Kelly.

23. Be a child playing guns.

24. Be the timekeeper. We have four minutes. Count slowly to 60.
    Announce: Three minutes to time. Count slowly to fifty.
    Announce: Two minutes to time. Count slowly to forty.
    Announce: One minute to time. Count slowly to thirty.
    Announce time. Say, "Hurry up, please. It's time."

25. Be the head of a draft board. Look around you. Announce: "1-A, Fort Benning, Georgia; 4-F, New York Jets."

Obviously this happening was unlike anything that goes on in any room full of people. Classes, cocktail parties, movies, dances, lectures all have their own traditional patterns in which we feel more or less comfortable. At least we do not expect a new experience very often at a movie or dance, any more than we do at a parade. Student reactions to the happening above were mixed. Most started off hesitantly, then began to enjoy the novelty and nonconformity. But quite a few also became increasingly disturbed as they began to feel more and more ridiculous. More important than these two reactions is the way most students wrote about the happening when asked to write a paragraph describing their experience.

1. I was walking around the room telling everyone individually "It's all right." At first I did not think much of it. That was my job. But soon I began to feel like I wanted them to respond and no one would. I was a stupid optimist in a world of completely morbid and isolated people. Pretty soon I wanted to shake somebody up, especially the boy who was banging his head on his desk.

2. I kept saying "If I had the wings of an angel." Well I know the next line too, "I'd fly o'er these prison walls." I didn't think I was in a prison, at least not a criminal prison. It was like being with any group of people who don't know what they are doing. And of course I began to realize I was being escapist. No one can have the wings of an angel.

3. I kept waiting for no one to be talking so I could say "Silence!" Once I waited too long and ended up saying it amidst a lot noise. Saying it was not the hard part, but waiting to say it. It was sort of like trying to get a word into a fast conversation, except I really wasn't interested in this conversation. I was only interested in when it stopped.

These three statements reveal a common psychology. When trying to talk about chaos or confusion, when trying to communicate something about the experience of chaos, the writers all looked for some unifying *concept*. The simplest form of order was to call the happening a *mad house*. That is what most of the students did. However confusing and undesirable a mad house is, we all know what to expect of it. Mad house is a category, a pattern into which we finally put something that fits nowhere else, or which we will willfully refuse to understand.

This use of mad house to make some sense out of disorder is what we call *conceptualizing*. Human beings conceptualize all the time unless, of course, they simply shut out all the incoming data. Since we are now talking about a fairly deep psychological idea, and since your authors are not psychologists, here is a psychologist's explanation of *concept*, followed by a poet's demonstration.

Lyle E. Bourne

Human Conceptual Behavior

The term "concept" has a multitude of meanings. Most of us have used or applied it in a myriad of ways, and among these uses there may not be a great deal of obvious similarity. For example, "concept" is commonly used as a synonym for idea, as when we say, "Now he seems to have the concept," in reference to someone who has finally caught onto a message. Or we may talk of an abstract state of affairs, such as freedom, and call it a concept. On other occasions, a concept seems to be akin to a mental image, as in the case of trying to conceptualize (visualize) an unfamiliar object or event from a verbal description. Undoubtedly, each of these examples captures in part the meaning of "concept." But clearly, it would be difficult (or impossible) to formulate an unambiguous definition from them.

In experimental psychology the term "concept" has come to have a rather specialized meaning, which may not encompass all its various ordinary uses. Psychology is the scientific investigation of the behavior of organisms, which includes as a subarea the study of how organisms (human beings and lower animals) learn and use concepts. In such an undertaking, explicit, communicable definitions of terms are an absolute necessity. "Concept" is no exception.

As a working definition we may say that a concept exists whenever two or more distinguishable objects or events have been grouped or classified together and set apart from other objects on the basis of some common feature or property characteristic of each. Consider the class of "things" called dogs. Not all dogs are alike. We can easily tell our favorite Basset from the neighbor's Great Dane. Still all dogs have certain features in common, and these serve as the basis for a conceptual grouping. Furthermore, this grouping is so familiar and so well defined that few of us have any difficulty calling a dog (even an unfamiliar dog) by that name when we encounter one. There is then the concept "dog"; similarly, the class of all things called "house" is a concept, and the class of things called "religion."

Each of us carries around a fairly large number of concepts. Most of them we have learned at some earlier time and use in everyday behavior, but we do continue to learn new concepts when the occasion demands. It is probably true that much, if not most, of the interaction between an individual organism and his environment involves dealing with classes or categories of things rather than with unique events or objects. This is fortunate. If an individual were to utilize fully his capacity for distinguishing between things and were to respond to each event as unique, he would shortly be overcome by the complexity and unpredictability of his environment. Categorizing is not only an easy way but also a necessary way of dealing with the tremendous diversity one encounters in everyday life. Concepts code things into a smaller number of categories and thus simplify the environment to some degree.

The bases upon which things may be grouped as a concept are legion. Perhaps the simplest is sheer physical identity or similarity among the instances. For example, we may think of all "red houses" as members of a concept. Here redness and the various observable characteristics of inhabitable dwellings serve as common features. On a different plane common or similar function may provide the basis for grouping. To illustrate, consider the concept "food." There is little physical similarity between a grapefruit and a beefsteak, but the use to which each is put links them together. Other bases . . . are even less obvious or more complex. Whatever the underlying principle is, however, it is usually logical, rational, and understandable.

We may note at this point that grouping things together means, in a certain sense, that all members of the group are responded to in the same way. For human beings the nature of this response is often wholly or in part verbal. Thus, most concepts are associated with a general descriptive name or label—as must be obvious for the foregoing examples.

Psychologists are primarily interested in the ways in which organisms acquire and use concepts rather than in any deep philosophical analysis of the nature and meaning of particular concepts. We may dub such activities of an organism as conceptual behavior. What are some of these activities? First of all, concepts just do not come into existence suddenly and spontaneously. Although the bases for a concept may exist in the environment, in the form of things which illustrate it, and although the organism may have the intellectual capacity to "understand" the concept, some learning process has to take place before the concept exists for the organism. Most concepts, if not all, are acquired. Many concepts, such as "roundness," are so simple and familiar that it is sometimes difficult for adults to imagine that learning was ever necessary. But empirical studies clearly demonstrate that even the simplest of groupings are often difficult for the young or naïve organism. The process of learning a new concept is one important form of conceptual behavior and is usually termed "concept formation."

Equally important, and perhaps more common for the adult human being, is a task or problem which requires the use of concepts which are already known. For example, the subject may have to search for, identify, and use in any given situation one from a collection of several alternative, familiar concepts. This aspect of conceptual behavior, which as we shall see has been given somewhat more attention in psychological research, is called here "concept utilization."

Theodore Roethke

Dolor

I have known the inexorable sadness of pencils,
Neat in their boxes, dolor of pad and paper-weight,
All the misery of manilla folders and mucilage,
Desolation in immaculate public places,
Lonely reception room, lavatory, switchboard,
The unalterable pathos of basin and pitcher,
Ritual of multigraph, paper-clip, comma,
Endless duplication of lives and objects.
And I have seen dust from the walls of institutions,
Finer than flour, alive, more dangerous than silica,
Sift, almost invisible, through long afternoons of tedium,
Dropping a fine film on nails and delicate eyebrows,
Glazing the pale hair, the duplicate gray standard faces.

Conceptualizing is vital to our survival. Whether we like it or not, the world around us is essentially like a happening: disordered, random, confusing.

Look again at the student paragraphs and the directions for the happening. Very different meanings and concepts emerge because of the random coming together of unrelated events. Somebody is probably already screaming, "What about science; what about God?" Okay, what about them? Science is characterized by its uncertainty and by the unknown and not the known. Einstein made that point. And how many people can agree on the way in which God has set things up? Not the Pope and the bishops, not Baptist and Zen Buddhist, not you and your family, not your two authors. Maybe this is an orderly universe, but no man has been smart enough or big enough to discover what that order is.

The world is as confusing as a happening if we really look at it. When I drive to work in the morning I conceptualize that I am on a *town street*. That concept assures me that people will not turn somersaults in front of me or cast fishing nets into the intersections. Of course most of us agree that the place I am driving *is* a town street. We agree on that concept and all it contains. But that agreement does not *make* the place a town street. We cannot legislate reality with words. We can only make it understandable to ourselves. Suppose people were rioting at the moment I drove through. Would the concept battleground or the concept town street be more accurate? Here is a description of the Detroit streets as a war scene.

The trouble burst on Detroit like a firestorm and turned the nation's fifth biggest city into a theater of war. Whole streets lay ravaged by looters, whole blocks immolated in flames. Federal troops—the first sent into racial battle outside the South in a quarter century—occupied American streets at bayonet point. Patton tanks—machine guns ablaze—and Huey helicopters patrolled a cityscape of blackened brick chimneys poking out of gutted basements. And suddenly Harlem 1964 and Watts 1965 and Newark only three weeks ago fell back into the shadows of memory. Detroit was the new benchmark, its rubble a monument to the most devastating race riot in U.S. history—and a symbol of a domestic crisis grown graver than any since the Civil War.*

Concepts may not *be* reality, but concepts alone could still get me into trouble. Suppose on a normal day my concept of town street was battleground or hell or ocean. I would be locked up on a drug charge or sent to a hospital—if I lived that long. You may have heard of the "War of the Worlds" radio broadcast of the late 1930s. Many listeners thought they were hearing an account of an actual invasion of earth by Martians. What had been an ordinary night was abruptly filled with frightening sounds and sights for those persons. Many fled in panic, and women were hurt, some died.

The concepts we are allowed to keep or want to keep are those which help us to act usefully, safely, or pleasurably. But that is getting ahead of ourselves. For now we are concerned only with the world as a happening, not with what we do to the happening.

Unless you can find some order, system, or pattern in the world and prove its absolute existence, then the world for you, as for most of us, is a happening. You cannot know all there is to know, so you must admit even your most carefully documented decisions are biased by selectivity. They are merely extensions of your concepts of the world happening.

Because happenings are disturbing, even when planned and controlled, we avoid seeing the world as a happening. We paper it over with ready-made concepts, including many whose emotional tones show a certain desperation and rigidity. Look back in Chapter Three at stereotypes. Aren't these ready-made concepts? Many people very early in life become adept at this papering over, and they never change concepts. If we are to keep abreast of change, we must be willing to see the world as a happening from time to time and then see if new concepts are more enlightening and useful than the old ones. This is especially true if the old concepts we used were formed by someone else's view and experience of the world happening. When you say that Mr. Frissyfritter is still living in the nineteenth century, you may mean that he is using century-old concepts to see the present scene. Only a coward runs from a puff of air into the nearest house without waiting to see if the breeze means storm, night, cool weather, snow, rain, or just a passing cloud.

While we are talking about creativity and chaos, we might as well begin at the beginning. Here is John Milton's description of the Chaos from which God made all things. Satan has just had the doors of Hell thrown open and beholds what lies between him and Heaven.

John Milton

from Paradise Lost *Book II*

> Before thir eyes in sudden view appear
> The secrets of the hoarie deep, a dark
> Illimitable Ocean without bound,
> Without dimension, where length, breadth, and highth,
> And time and place are lost; where eldest Night
> And *Chaos*, Ancestors of Nature, hold
> Eternal *Anarchie*, amidst the noise
> Of endless warrs, and by confusion stand.
> For hot, cold, moist, and dry, four Champions fierce
> Strive here for Maistrie, and to Battel bring
> Thir embryon Atoms; they around the flag

Of each his faction, in thir several Clanns,
Light-arm'd or heavy, sharp, smooth, swift, or slow,
Swarm populous, unnumber'd as the Sands
Of *Barca* or *Cyrene's* torrid soil,
Levied to side with warring Winds, and poise
Thir lighter wings. To whom these most adhere,
Hee rules a moment; *Chaos* Umpire sits,
And by decision more imbroiles the fray
By which he Reigns: next him high Arbiter
Chance governs all. Into this wilde Abyss,
The Womb of nature and perhaps her Grave,
Of neither Sea, nor Shore, nor Air, nor Fire,
But all these in thir pregnant causes mixt
Confus'dly, and which thus must ever fight,
Unless th' Almighty Maker them ordain
His dark materials to create more Worlds,
Into this wilde Abyss the wary fiend
Stood on the brink of Hell and look'd a while,
Pondering his Voyage; for no narrow frith
He had to cross. Nor was his eare less peal'd
With noises loud and ruinous (to compare
Great things with small) then when *Bellona* storms,
With all her battering Engines bent to rase
Som Capital City, or less then if this frame
Of Heav'n were falling, and these Elements
In mutinie had from her Axle torn
The stedfast Earth. At last his Sail-broad Vannes
He spreads for flight, and in the surging smoak
Uplifted spurns the ground, thence many a League
As in a cloudy Chair ascending rides
Audacious, but that seat soon failing, meets
A vast vacuitie: all unawares
Fluttring his pennons vain plumb down he drops
Ten thousand fadom deep, and to this hour
Down had been falling, had not by ill chance
The strong rebuff of som tumultuous cloud
Instinct with Fire and Nitre hurried him
As many miles aloft: that furie stay'd
Quencht in a Boggie *Syrtis*, neither Sea,
Nor good dry Land: nigh founderd on he fares,
Treading the crude consistence, half on foot,

Half flying; behoves him now both Oare and Saile.
As when a Gryfon through the Wilderness
With winged course ore Hill or moarie Dale,
Pursues the *Arimaspian*, who by stelth
Had from his wakeful custody purloind
The guarded Gold: So eagerly the fiend
Ore bog or steep, through strait, rough, dense, or rare,
With head, hands, wings, or feet pursues his way,
And swims or sinks, or wades, or creeps, or flyes:
At length a universal hubbub wilde
Of stunning sounds and voices all confus'd
Born through the hollow dark assaults his eare
With loudest vehemence: thither he plyes,
Undaunted to meet there what ever power
Or Spirit of the nethermost Abyss
Might in that noise reside, of whom to ask
Which way the neerest coast of darkness lyes
Bordering on light; when strait behold the Throne
Of *Chaos*, and his dark Pavilion spread
Wide on the wasteful Deep; with him Enthron'd
Sat Sable-vested Night, eldest of things,
The consort of his Reign; and by them stood
Orcus and *Ades*, and the dreaded name
Of *Demogorgon*; Rumor next and Chance,
And Tumult and Confusion all imbroild,
And Discord with a thousand various mouths.
   T' whom *Satan* turning boldly, thus. Ye Powers
And Spirits of this nethermost Abyss,
Chaos and *ancient Night*, I come no Spie,
With purpose to explore or to disturb
The secrets of your Realm, but by constraint
Wandring this darksome desart, as my way
Lies through your spacious Empire up to light,
Alone, and without guide, half lost, I seek
What readiest path leads where your gloomie bounds
Confine with Heav'n; or if som other place
From your Dominion won, th' Ethereal King
Possesses lately, thither to arrive
I travel this profound, direct my course;
Directed, no mean recompence it brings
To your behoof, if I that Region lost,

All usurpation thence expell'd, reduce
To her original darkness and your sway
(Which is my present journey) and once more
Erect the Standerd there of *ancient Night*;
Yours be th' advantage all, mine the revenge.
   Thus *Satan*; and him thus the Anarch old
With faultring speech and visage incompos'd
Answer'd. I know thee, stranger, who thou art,
That mighty leading Angel, who of late
Made head against Heav'ns King, though overthrown.
I saw and heard, for such a numerous host
Fled not in silence through the frighted deep
With ruin upon ruin, rout on rout,
Confusion worse confounded; and Heav'n Gates
Pourd out by millions her victorious Bands
Pursuing. I upon my Frontieres here
Keep residence; if all I can will serve,
That little which is left so to defend
Encroacht on still through our intestine broiles
Weakning the Scepter of old Night: first Hell
Your dungeon stretching far and wide beneath;
Now lately Heaven and Earth, another World
Hung ore my Realm, link'd in a golden Chain
To that side Heav'n from whence your Legions fell:
If that way be your walk, you have not farr;
So much the neerer danger; goe and speed;
Havock and spoil and ruin are my gain.
   He ceas'd; and *Satan* staid not to reply,
But glad that now his Sea should find a shore,
With fresh alacritie and force renew'd
Springs upward like a Pyramid of fire
Into the wilde expanse, and through the shock
Of fighting Elements, on all sides round
Environ'd wins his way; harder beset
And more endanger'd, then when *Argo* pass'd
Through *Bosporus* betwixt the justling Rocks:
Or when *Ulysses* on the Larbord shunnd

Charybdis, and by th' other whirlpool steard.
So he with difficulty and labour hard
Mov'd on, with difficulty and labour hee;
But hee once past, soon after when man fell,
Strange alteration! Sin and Death amain
Following his track, such was the will of Heav'n,
Pav'd after him a broad and beat'n way
Over the dark Abyss, whose boiling Gulf
Tamely endur'd a Bridge of wondrous length
From Hell continu'd reaching th' utmost Orbe
Of this frail World; by which the Spirits perverse
With easie intercourse pass to and fro
To tempt or punish mortals, except whom
God and good Angels guard by special grace.
But now at last the sacred influence
Of light appears, and from the walls of Heav'n
Shoots farr into the bosom of dim Night
A glimmering dawn; here Nature first begins
Her fardest verge, and *Chaos* to retire
As from her outmost works a brok'n foe
With tumult less and with less hostile din,
That *Satan* with less toil, and now with ease
Wafts on the calmer wave by dubious light
And like a weather-beaten Vessel holds
Gladly the Port, though Shrouds and Tackle torn;
Or in the emptier waste, resembling Air,
Weighs his spread wings, at leasure to behold
Farr off th' Empyreal Heav'n, extended wide
In circuit, undetermined square or round,
With Opal Towrs and Battlements adorn'd
Of living Saphire, once his native Seat;
And fast by hanging in a golden Chain
This pendant world, in bigness as a Starr
Of smallest Magnitude close by the Moon.
Thither full fraught with mischievous revenge,
Accurst, and in a cursed hour he hies.

Wallace Stevens' poem sets an act of man against the natural landscape. The result is a clear statement about not only this act but man and nature.

Wallace Stevens

Anecdote of the Jar

I placed a jar in Tennessee,
And round it was, upon a hill.
It made the slovenly wilderness
Surround that hill.

The wilderness rose up to it,
And sprawled around, no longer wild.
The jar was round upon the ground
And tall and of a port in air.

It took dominion everywhere.
The jar was gray and bare.
It did not give of bird or brush,
Like nothing else in Tennessee.

If each individual must find or create his own sense of order to prove himself alive, then life is really an art. Philosopher Irwin Edman argues this idea and explains the two chief acts of all art—intensification and clarification.

Irwin Edman

Art and Experience

Whatever life may be, it is an experience; whatever experience may be, it is a flow through time, a duration, a many-colored episode in eternity. Experience may be simple as it is among babies and simple people; it may be complex as it is in the case of a scientist or poet or man of affairs. It may range from the aimless movement of a baby's hands and the undisciplined distraction of its eyes to the controlled vision and deliberate movements of the champion marksman. It may move from the beholding and manipulation of physical things to the invention and organization of ideas tenuous and abstract. But between birth and death, this much may be averred of life, it is the stimulation and response of a living body, of "five little senses startling with delight," of muscle twitching to answer with action, of hands eager and restless, of a tongue moved to utterance and a mind provoked to thought. Portions or aspects of that experience may be remembered and recorded. Totally considered, it may be aimless or purposeful. It may be merely the veil or revelation of something behind or beyond experience itself. It may be merely a systematic transient delusion. It may be a nightmare or a dream. Philosophers and poets have espoused at one time or another all these hypotheses.

But whatever experience may portend or signify, veil or reveal, it is irretrievably there. It may be intensified and heightened or dulled and obscured. It may remain brutal and dim and chaotic; it may become meaningful and clear and alive. For a moment in one aspect, for a lifetime in many, experience may achieve lucidity and vividness, intensity and depth. To effect such an intensification and clarification of experience is the province of art. So far from having to do merely with statues, pictures, and symphonies, art is the name for that whole process of intelligence by which life, understanding its own conditions, turns them to the most interesting or exquisite account. An art, properly important, would be, as Aristotle pointed out, politics. Its theme would be the whole of experience, its materials and its theater the whole of life.

Such a comprehensive art is still the statesman's dream. The conditions of life, especially of life together, are as complex as they are precarious. We do not know enough about them to be sure of our touch, nor has any man enough power to be sure his touch is translated into action. An artist bent on turning the whole of life into an art would have to be at once a universal despot and a universal genius, a Goethe, a Newton, and an Alexander rolled into one. The art of life is an aspiration and a prophecy, not a history or a fact.

The artist de facto has had to deal with segments of experience, though he may suggest or imply it all. Experience, apart from art and intelligence, is capricious and confused. It is matter without form, movement without direction. The passing sounds are a vague noise unattended or undesired; the colors and shapes about us are unnoticed or unpleasant. The words we hear are signals to action; if they are that. Now to a certain extent life has achieved form. As we shall try to point out in the succeeding chapter, civilization itself is an art form, highly successful and fortuitous, but none the less an art.

To the extent that life has form, it is an art, and to the extent that the established disorder of civilization has some coherence, it is a work of art. All that goes by the name of custom or technique or institution is the working of intelligence or its perhaps dilapidated heritage. The realm of art is identical with the realm of man's deliberate control of that world of materials and movements among which he must make his home, of that inner world of random impulses and automatic processes which constitute his inner being. The breaking of a stick, the building of a hut, a skyscraper, or a cathedral, the use of language for communication, the sowing or the harvesting of a crop, the nurture and education of children, the framing of a code of law or morals, the weaving of a garment, or the digging of a mine—all these are alike examples of art no less than the molding of a relief or the composition of a symphony.

It is for purely accidental reasons that the fine arts have been singled out to be almost identical with Art. For in painting and sculpture, music and poetry, there is so nice and so explicit a utilization of materials, intelligence has so clear and complete a sway over materials at once so flexible and delightful, that we turn to examples of these arts for Art and in them find our aesthetic experience most intense and pure. But wherever materials are given form, wherever movement has direction, wherever life has, as it were, line and composition, there we have intelligence and there we have that transformation of a given chaos into a desired and desirable order that we call Art. Experience, apart from art and intelligence, is wild and orderless. It is formless matter, aimless movement.

It is difficult to realize how much of our diurnal experience is what William James called it, "a big blooming buzzing confusion." It is hard to realize how much of it is a semistupor. Life has often enough been described as a waking dream. But not much of it has the vividness, though a great deal of it may have the incoherence or the horror of a dream. For most people most of the time it is a heavy lethargy. They have eyes, yet they do not, in any keen and clear sense, see. They have ears, yet they do not finely and variously hear. They have a thousand provocations to feeling and to thought, but out of their torpor comes no response. Only the pressure of some animal excitement, instant and voluminous, rouses them for a moment to an impulsive clouded answer. Life is for most of us what someone described music to be for the un-initiate, "a drowsy reverie, interrupted by nervous thrills."

How is this dazed basking in the sun, or this hurried passage from an unwilled stimulus to an uncontrolled response, transformed? How does an artist remake experience into something at once peaceful and intense, domestic and strange? What does the artist do to the world to render it arresting? What part do the arts play in our experience that gives them a special seduction and delight?

Ordinary experience, that of practical or instinctive compulsion, is at once restless and dead. Our equipment of habits and impulses is such that we see and hear just so much of objects, partake imaginatively just so much in events as is necessary for the immediate satisfaction of im-pulses or the fulfillment of practical intentions. Our instincts and our necessities hasten us from object to object. From each we select just as much as is requisite to our desires or to our purposes, the bare minimum of all that to free and complete aesthetic apprehension would be there. Just as meat to the dog is something to be eaten, and the cat simply something to be chased, so the chair to a tired man or an executive is simply something to be sat on; and to the thirsty man water, however lovely its flow or sparkle, simply something to be drunk. The man of affairs intent upon future issues or the next step, the scientist interested in some special consequence of the combination of two elements, the hungry or the lustful intent upon the fulfillment of one absorbing and immediate desire—all these hasten from moment to moment, from object to object, from event to event. Experience is a minimum and that mini-mum is bare. Only one aspect of its momentary practical or impulsive urgency is remembered; all else is forgotten or more precisely ignored.

It is one of the chief functions of the artist to render experience ar-resting by rendering it alive. The artist, be he poet, painter, sculptor, or architect, does something to objects, the poet and novelist do something to events, that compel the eye to stop and find pleasure in the beholding, the ear to hear for the sheer sake of listening, the mind to attend for the keen, impractical pleasure of discovery or suspense or surprise. The chair ceases to be a signal to a sitter; it becomes a part and a point in a com-position, a focus of color and form. It becomes in a painting pictorially significant; it becomes alive. That passing face is not something to be persuaded or conquered or forgotten. It is to be looked at; it is an object of pictorial interest, at once satisfying and exciting. It ceases to be an in-cident or an instrument; it is not a precipitate to action, a signal to anger or to lust. It is a moment crowded with vitality and filled with order; it is knowledge for its own sweet sake of something living and composed; it is beautiful, as we say, to look at, and its beholding is a pleasure.

Painters sometimes speak of dead spots in a painting: areas where the color is wan or uninteresting, or the forms irrelevant and cold. Experience is full of dead spots. Art gives it life. A comprehensive art, as has been intimated, would render the whole of life alive. The daily detail of doing or undergoing would be delightful, both in its immediate quality, and for the meaning that it held. Our relations with others would all have something of the quality of friendship and affection; what we did would be stimulating as it is stimulating to a writer to write or to a painter to paint. What we encountered would be like an encounter with music or with painting or poetry. To live would be a constant continuum of creative action and aesthetic appreciation. All that we did would be an art, and all that we experienced would be an appreciation and a delight. Living would be at once ordered and spontaneous, disciplined and free.

There are a dozen reasons why that perfect functioning which would be an art of life is the philosopher's blueprint and the poet's dream rather than a fact. In the life of the individual, a thousand factors of health and fatigue, of external circumstance, of poverty and responsibility, combine to defeat the deployment of resilient energies with exquisite wisdom. Pure spirit must rely on poor matter; the clearest intelligence on a body and world which are at once its matrix and its materials. The dead spots in experience are not avoidable. As life is constituted in a disorganized world, much that has to be done is incidental and instrumental. We work for leisure and we rush for peace. The work is not sweet nor the pursuit calm. A lowering of vitality clips the wings of youth and exuberance. The presence of dull people turns conversation into ennui. The ugliness of our streets, our houses, and our cities is a realistic interruption of what might, ideally speaking, be perpetual delight.

That is one reason among a thousand others why the artist and the aesthete flee to the fine arts. It is one reason, too, why art is regarded so often and has so repeatedly been described as a flight from life. The fine arts are in two senses a flight from reality. For the artist they provide a realm where his intelligence can function freely over tractable materials. The technical problems of the poet or musician may be difficult, but they are solvable, and their solving is itself a tantalizing kind of felicity. The musician, like the mathematician, lives in a complex but tractable realm. It is vast, airy, and metaphysical, but in it his intelligence can freely function, and his faculties can find their peace.

It is often remarked that artists are helpless in practical life. Its problems are to them dull or baffling or both; in its helter-skelter miscellany, their intelligence, disciplined to one sphere, as fine as it is small, cannot feel at home. It is not to be wondered at that the world finds the artist often foolish in affairs, any more than that the artist should find the affairs of the world foolish. What is a mind fastidious and precious to do with the awkward grossness of things and events? What is a spirit to whom a discord is an evil to make of the jangle of politics and morals? So many poets have been romanticists and visionaries because their sensibilities, quick and nervous, could not bear to live in the world of facts. Poets of the first water, it is true, have been prepared to look steadily upon all that existed under the sun, and celebrate things, as André Gide well said, by enumeration. Painters as different as Rembrandt and Degas have learned to look at things in their immediacy ugly and distressing, a tired worker, an aged woman, and, through some magic of line and light, turn them into a beautiful peace. But for artists, gifted in their power but restricted in their range and courage, the arts have been escapes from a reality they could not bear, to a section of color and light, of sound, of imaginative reverie, which was not only bearable but beautiful.

Shelley turns from the cruelty and stupidity of nineteenth-century England to a Utopia, Platonic in its spiritual beauty and classic in its marmoreal precision. Beethoven in his deafness and suffering listens, in the choral finale movement of the Ninth Symphony, to his own concluding paean to the world as pure fellowship and joy.

The impulses that go to the making of the romantic artist go to the formation, too, of romantic appreciation. For many lovers of the arts find in music, poetry, painting, and the novel escapes, as narcotic as they are delightful, from the pressures and exigencies in which we are involved by our health, our finances, and our affections. The shopgirl's novel has been the *locus classicus* in illustration of the theory of art as an escape. In its pages, the drab little person can move in luxury with princes, duchesses, and movie stars. She can possess vicariously beauty and freedom. The clerk tied to his desk can move in adventure novels, through the open spaces, and be, in the person of a robust romantic figment, a hero all strength and chivalry.

But the novel is not the only art that yields escape. It does so by its vicarious leading of the imagination through paths we have longed to tread but have never trodden, through lands we have never known, including palaces that never were on land or sea. Other arts offer subtler escapes. Schopenhauer pointed them out with classic persuasion, many years ago. Aesthetic interest is itself detachment, though it is not the kind of detachment that it is commonly supposed to be. But any perusal of a painting by the eye is a kind of release from our normal habits. For that moment at least we are looking at things for, and only for, themselves, not for their promise or their portent. It is the color of the apple in a still life that engages us, it is something to be seen vividly, not to be grasped at in hunger. The aesthetic is substituted for the practical vision; in Schopenhauer's language, knowledge, for the moment, comes to predominate over will. It is notable how in the late nineteenth century a romantic pessimism and a romantic aestheticism were allied. The hungry will might never find its satisfaction or its peace in a world that was doomed never to satisfy it. Life might be an eternity between two oblivions, a vast anacoluthon, a sentence without a meaning. Be it so. In that brief interval one might, as Pater suggests in his famous conclusion to *The Renaissance,* be filled with light and color and music. One could escape from the defeats of the intellect and the emotions to an exquisite Epicureanism. As far as possible, as far as one can live in the aesthetic experience itself, make life a continuum of roses and raptures. One can escape the times that are out of joint, like Richard II, in a harmonious music. In the still perfection of marble, in the fine modeling of a face in a painting, or of the shadows on a wall, one can escape into a realm of eternity. In music, too, emotions finer and subtler than any ever experienced can be enjoyed. And in literature, even pain and distress may be experienced at arm's length and in the garb of beauty. For the observer, one function of the fine arts is certainly to provide the peace of beauty and the escape of detachment. Broadly speaking it is not the practical functions but the eternal essences of things that the arts provide. To behold an essence is to behold something in and for itself. The purely aesthetic observer has for the moment forgotten his own soul, and has gained the world, that is to say, the world of art.

This theory and ideal of aesthetic appreciation has a particular following among those in whom sensibility is combined with disillusion. The aesthete is a melancholy exquisite loitering among the gleams in a fading world. There is no doubt that the arts must for many be nothing more than such a flight. The saint flees to his desert, the aesthete to his tower of ivory. One finds his peace in God, the other in form.

The fact is, however, that this theory of art as escape fails to take into account much that is true of aesthetic experience, and is an insult to the more rich and positive aspects of aesthetic enjoyment and production. It abstracts the Aesthetic Man much as the early nineteenth century abstracted the Economic Man. No one is ever, or ever for long, an aesthetic observer, and part of aesthetic enjoyment is the rendition, vivid and revealing, of the world we know and the nature we are. The eye of the beholder is the eye of a human being, with all the vast reverberation of human interests and emotions. The ear of a listener is the ear of one to whom sounds have associations and of one who has listened to words for their meaning as well as for their tintinnabulation. The arts may be, in many instances and for many observers, flights into a compensatory dream or into a Paradise of forms, lucid and satisfying, in which the apprehension is satisfied and the conflicts of experience are lulled.

There is a more melodramatic sense, too, in which the arts may be escapes. Nietzsche pointed out in *The Birth of Tragedy* the elements, complementary and apparently contradictory, in Greek tragedy, and in all moving art. These he defined as the Apollonian, the element of repose, and the Dionysian, the element of passion and vitality. The arts do more than bring or bestow peace; they communicate fire. In the high climaxes of the fine arts, the psyche, condemned in the ordinary circumstances of living to be diffident and constrained, finds a provocation, an outlet, and an excuse for those fires which are ordinarily banked. Nietzsche was for a time peculiarly seduced by Wagner because he felt in the urgency and flow of that romantic musician precisely the Dionysian element which was for him the lifeblood of the arts. "Literature," says Anatole France, "is the opium and hasheesh of the modern world." Rather it might be said to be music. One has but to gaze at the faces of a modern concert audience to see how, in the swelling tide of some orchestral climax, passions are finding their release that have found no other utterance; music is saying unashamed what most of its listeners would be as ashamed of as they would be unable to say in words.

Nor is it only the madder moments of passionate assertion that find their expression in the arts. Nuances of feeling, subtleties of thought that practical experience keeps us too gross or too busy to observe, that words are too crude to express, and affairs too crude to exhaust, have in the arts their moment of being. For these reasons, too, for the observer, they are absorbing flights from life. But they may—in major instances they do —clarify, intensify, and interpret life.

First, as to the intensification: our senses, we learn from the biologists, are adaptations to a changing and precarious environment. They were developed in the long animal history of the race, as instruments by which a troubled animal might adjust itself to a constantly shifting experience. A pigmented spot sensitive to light becomes eventually the eye. That organ enables the animal to estimate at a distance the dangerous and desirable object too far removed for touch. The ear, similarly the product of a long evolutionary history, likewise originated as an instrument that rendered the animal advertent to the dangers and promises in a mysterious and uncertain environment. Smell, in its animal origin, was likewise a warning of the noxious, a signal of edible or otherwise promising things. Taste, too, developed as a rough guide to the poisonous and the nourishing. Touch began as that near and immediate sensitivity closely bound up with self-preserving and procreative lusts.

In their origin our senses are thus practical, not aesthetic. They remain in diurnal living, essentially practical still. There is, as it were, a myopia to which we are all subject. Rather we are all subject to a blindness, instinctive and compulsive. We become anaesthetic to all phases of objects save those in which our immediate fortunes or actions are concerned.

The artist's function, the success of a work of art, are both partly measurable by the extent to which our senses become not signals to action but revelations of what is sensibly and tangibly there. Somewhere Stephen Crane has a story of three men shipwrecked in a small boat on a wide and stormy sea. The first sentence is, "They did not see the color of the sky." So intent were they upon the possibilities of being saved that they had no time, interest, or impulse for seeing the color of the sky above them.

In the fine arts, then, the experience becomes intensified by the arresting of sensations. We become aware with tingling pleasure of the colors and shapes on a canvas, of the sounds of a voice or a violin. The other senses too, have their possible aesthetic exploitation, but touch, taste, and smell are not as finely manipulable, not as easily incorporated in objects or detached from practical biological interests as are sight and sound. The peculiar function of the fine arts lies, therefore, chiefly in the realm of these two subtle and finely discriminated organs, the eye and the ear. Color, which for practical purposes is usually the most negligible aspect of an object, is the painter's special material. Differences in rhythm and tone, negligible in practical communication, become for the musician the source of all his art, for the music lover the source of all his pleasure. The senses from being incitements to action are turned into avenues of delight.

It is in this respect that the basis and the ultimate appeal of all art is sensuous. We become engaged, as it were, by the amiable and intensified surfaces of things. The charm of a still life is certainly in its composition, but it is the blues and greens and yellows of the fruit that arrest us; our body becomes alive to what the senses present. Those moralists who have regarded art as a sensuous distraction have sourly stated the truth. Eyes dulled and routinated become keen again in the observation of painting; the ear becomes a subtilized organ of precise and intense sensation. We move in painting and in music not among the abstract possibilities of action but among the concrete actualities of what is there to be seen and heard.

The arts do more, however, than simply intensify sensations. In the routine of our lives, successively similar situations have produced successively similar emotional reactions. We become dulled emotionally as well as sensuously. In the clear and artful discipline of a novel or a drama our emotions become reinstated into a kind of pure intensity. It might appear on the surface that the actualities of life, the impingements of those so very real crises of birth and death and love, are more intense than any form of art provides. That is true. But we do not live always amid crises, and the ordinary run of our experiences gives us only emotions that are dull and thin. A tragedy like *Hamlet*, a novel like *Anna Karénina*, clarify and deepen for us emotional incidents of familiar human situations. For many people, it is literature rather than life that teaches them what their native emotions are. And ideas themselves, which in the abstractions of formal reasoning may be thin and cold and external, in the passionate presentation of poetry and drama may become intimate and alive. Those would fall asleep over Godwin's *Political Justice* who might be inflamed to passion by the political poetry of Shelley. Whom the formulas of friendship enunciated by Aristotle leave cold, would be stirred to living emotion by dialogues gracious and humane in which Plato illuminates that amiable theme.

The second function of the arts noted above was the clarification of experience. This holds true likewise from the direct level of the senses to that of speculation and reflection. Our experience, through the pressure of impulses on the one hand, and the conditions of living on the other, is conventionalized into logical and practical patterns; we are likely to forget how diverse and miscellaneous experience in its immediacy is. It consists of patches of color and fragments of form; it lives as a moment transient and confused in a vanishing flux. Our senses, our instincts, and our world give some form to the undiscriminated blur. Were there no pattern at all to follow we could not live. Every blur of vision forms itself into some kind of landscape: the chaos of impressions and impulses at any moment has for that moment some coherency and shape. Our habits and our institutions canalize life. Even insanity has its own, if irrelevant, kind of order. Except in drowsiness or semistupor, and hardly even there, absolute chaos does not exist.

But in works of art sensations are more profoundly and richly clarified through some deliberate and explicit pattern; emotions are given a sequence and a development such as the exigencies of practical life scarcely or rarely permit. Our reveries, amiable and wandering, are disciplined to the pathway of some controlled logical sequence.

An illustration of each may be of service. Others than painters of still life have seen fruit in a bowl on a table. But it requires a Cézanne or a Vermeer to organize the disordered sensations of color and form into something lucid and harmonious and whole. Everyone has experienced the blindness of human pride or the fatal possessiveness of love. But it requires a Sophocles to show him the tragic meaning of the first in such a play as *Oedipus*, a Shakespeare to exhibit to him the latter in *Othello*. Even the most unreflective have at some time or other harbored scattered and painful thoughts on the vanity of life or the essential beauty and goodness of Nature. A few have formulated these scattered insights into a system. But a poet like Lucretius can turn that vague intuition into a major and systematic insight; Dante can exhibit the latter in a magnificent panorama of life and destiny. The kaleidoscope of our sensations falls into an eternal pattern; a mood half articulate and half recognized in its confused recurrence becomes, as it were, clarified forever in a poem or a novel or a drama. A floating impression becomes fixed in the vivid system of music or letters.

In a sense, therefore, all art is idealization, even where it pretends to be realistic. For no experience could possibly have the permanent order, the pattern, the changeless integration of a work of art. The mere permanence of a painting as compared with the vision of a passing moment, the mere dramatic logic of a drama as compared with the incongruous juxtapositions of life are illustrations of the point. But the idealization which is art has the benefit of holding a clarifying mirror up to Nature. It shows us by deliberate artifice what is potentially in Nature to be seen, in life to be felt, in speculation to be thought.

Now, to return to the interpretation of experience. Psychologists and logicians are fond of pointing out how much of what seems to be mere and sheer sensation is a matter of judgment and inference. We do not see cabbages and kings; we thus interpret blurs of vision. Our intelligence and our habits are, in their way, artists. They enable us to respond to things not simply as sheer physical stimuli but as meanings. The fine arts simply accentuate the process or perhaps merely italicize the process which all intelligence exemplifies. Those separate spots of color become significant items in the total pattern in a painting, the pattern itself is significant of a face, the face of some passion or its tragic frustration. In a novel the words are significant as well as vibrant: they tell with significant detail of some life, some experience, some destiny.

All the arts in one way or another, to some greater or lesser extent, interpret life. They may "interpret" nothing more than the way in which a bowl of fruit "appears" to the ordered imagination of a painter. They may "interpret" nothing more than sensation. Or they may interpret, as *Hamlet* does, or *War and Peace*, or *Ode on the Intimations of Immortality from Recollections of Early Childhood*, the confused intuitions of millions of men, bringing to a focus an obscure burden of human emotion. A poem like *The Divine Comedy* or Goethe's *Faust* may be a commentary upon the whole human scene, its nature, its movement, and its destiny. When Matthew Arnold defined poetry as a criticism of life, he might well have extended his definition to the whole of the fine arts. For criticism is a judgment upon, an interpretation of, a given section of life. Explicit interpretation, of course, is to be found chiefly in literature. But a statue by Michelangelo or Rodin, a piece of music by Beethoven or Debussy, is by virtue of its comprehensive and basic quality, its mood, its tempo, and its essential timbre, an interpretation of experience. One hears more than an arrangement of sounds in Beethoven's Fifth Symphony. One hears the comment of a great spirit on the world in which it lives. In Rembrandt's pictures of old rabbis, or El Greco's of Spanish grandees, there is more than meets the simply pictorial eye. These works are the language of men who not only saw and heard with the external eye and ear, but put into sound a hearing, into canvas a vision of what life essentially meant to them.

These three functions, intensification, clarification, and interpretation of experience, the arts fulfill in various degree. For many observers the arts are simply sensuous excitements and delights. For many they are the language in which the human spirit has clarified to itself the meanings of its world. For many the arts are the sensuously enticing and emotionally moving vehicles of great total visions of experience. The arts, in fragments as it were, suggest the goal toward which all experience is moving: the outer world of things, the inner world of impulse mastered thoroughly by intelligence, so that whatever is done is itself delightful in the doing, delightful in the result. The Utopia of the philosopher of which Plato dreamed is foreshadowed in those moments of felicity which the fine arts at moments provide. A symphony in its ordered perfection, a drama in its tragic logic, a poem in its sensuously moving grace, is a foretaste of what an ordered world might be. Art is another name for intelligence, which in an ordered society would function over the whole of men's concerns, as it functions happily now in those scattered works we call beautiful, in those happy moments we call aesthetic pleasure.

Synectics means joining apparently unrelated things. Researchers have developed synectics into a creative approach to seeing and solving problems of all kinds. William J. Gordon, a researcher, explains the difference between creative and noncreative thinking as seen in the mechanisms of synectics.

William J. J. Gordon

The Operational Mechanisms

Synectics defines creative process as the mental activity in problem-stating, problem-solving situations where artistic or technical inventions are the result. I use the expression "problem-stating, problem-solving" rather than merely "problem-solving" in order to include the definition and understanding of the problem. The operational mechanisms of Synectics are the concrete psychological factors which support and press forward creative process. The mechanisms do not pertain to the motivations for creative activity, nor are they intended to be used to judge the ultimate product of an esthetic or technical invention. Psychological states such as empathy, involvement, play, detachment, and use of irrelevance are (as we have seen) basic to creative process but they are not operational. The Synectics mechanisms are intended to induce appropriate psychological states and thus promote creative activity.

Words like intuition, empathy, and play are merely names put to complex activities in the hope that the naming of the activity will in fact describe it. Experience has shown it to be most difficult to feed back into a problem-stating, problem-solving situation such nominalistic abstractions. When dealing with an individual or a group faced with problem-stating and problem-solving, it is ineffectual to attempt to persuade the individual to be intuitive, to empathize, to become involved, to be detached, to play, or to tolerate apparent irrelevance. However, in our research experience the Synectics mechanisms effectively increase the probability of success when creativity is called for. They draw the individual into the psychological states.

The Synectic process involves:

(i) making the strange familiar;
(ii) making the familiar strange.

Making the strange familiar: In any problem-stating, problem-solving situation, the first responsibility of individuals involved is to understand the problem. This is essentially an analytical phase where the ramifications and the fundamentals of the problem must be plumbed. However, if only this analytical step is taken, no novel solution is possible. For work on a problem to get started, some concrete assumptions must be made, although in the course of the problem-stating, problem-solving process, the understanding of the problem may change. It is the function of the mind, when presented with a problem, to attempt to make the strange familiar by means of analysis. The human organism is basically conservative, and any strange thing or concept is threatening to it. When faced with strangeness the mind attempts to engorge this strangeness by forcing it into an acceptable pattern or changing its (the mind's) private geometry of bias to make room for the strangeness. The mind compares the given strangeness with data previously known and in terms of these data converts the strangeness into familiarity.

This is, of course, an obvious part of problem-solving. However, Synectics is an attempt to describe those conscious, preconscious and subconscious psychological states which are present in any creative act. Therefore, it would be an omission not to mention the analytical, the making-the-strange-familiar mechanism. The great pitfall, the traditional danger, in making the strange familiar is in becoming so buried in analysis and detail that these become ends in themselves, leading nowhere. The process of making the strange familiar, if used alone, yields a variety of superficial solutions; but basic novelty demands a fresh viewpoint, a new way of looking at the problem. Most problems are not new. The challenge is to view the problem in a new way. This new viewpoint in turn embodies the potential for a new basic solution.

Making the familiar strange: To make the familiar strange is to distort, invert, or transpose the everyday ways of looking and responding which render the world a secure and familiar place. This pursuit of strangeness is not a blasé's search for the bizarre and out-of-the-way. It is the conscious attempt to achieve a new look at the same old world, people, ideas, feelings, and things. In the "familiar world" objects are always right-side-up; the child who bends and peers at the world from between his legs is experimenting with the familiar made strange. (One sees the familiar tree as a collection of solids in an otherwise empty space. The sculptor consciously may invert his world and see the tree as a series of voids or holes carved within the solid block of the air.)

Owen Barfield quotes a South Sea Islander's pigeon-English description of a three-masted, screw steamer with two funnels: "Thlee-pieces bamboo, two-pieces puff-puff, walk-along inside, no-can-see."[1] In our terms, the conceptions which frame the steamship are firmly established in the realm of the familiar. Here, the familiar Western concept of steamship is juxtaposed with the strange pigeon-English version. Barfield says, "Now when I read the words, 'Thlee-pieces bamboo, two-pieces puff-puff, walk-along inside, no-can-see,' I am for a moment transported into a totally different kind of consciousness. I see the steamer, not from my own eyes, but through the eyes of a primitive South Sea Islander. His experience, his *meaning* is quite different from mine, for it is the product of different concepts. This he reveals by his choice of words; and the result is that, for a moment, I shed Western civilization like an old garment and behold my steamer in a new and strange light."[2] The steamer seen by the Western mind in this light is reconstituted and presented as alive and malleable to the imagination.

These several mechanisms for making the familiar strange are not a collection of mental tricks for the achievement of superficial novelty. They have been developed and are used in the several Synectics groups as a systematic way of solving actual invention problems. Thus, Barfield's "new look" at the familiar steamer could be the starting point for considering propulsion. Combined with technical competence it could in turn lead to a new viewpoint for the development of a new invention.

The attempt to make the familiar strange involves several different methods of achieving an intentionally naive or apparently "out of focus" look at some aspect of the known world. And this look can transpose both our usual ways of perceiving and our usual expectations about how we or the world will behave. The experience of sustaining this condition can provoke anxiety and insecurity. But maintaining the familiar as strange is fundamental to disciplined creativity. All problems present themselves to the mind as threats of failure. For someone striving to win in terms of a successful solution, this threat evokes a mass response in which the most immediate superficial solution is clutched frantically as a balm to anxiety. This is consistent with the natural impulse to master the strange by making it familiar. Yet if we are to perceive all the implications and possibilities of the new we must risk at least temporary ambiguity and disorder. Human beings are heir to a legacy of frozen words and ways of perceiving which wrap their world in comfortable

---

[1]Owen Barfield, *Poetic Diction* (London: Faber & Faber, 1957), p. 49.
[2]*Ibid.*

familiarity. This protective legacy must be disowned. A new viewpoint depends on the capacity to risk and to understand the mechanisms by which the mind can make tolerable the temporary ambiguity implicit in risking.

Trying out the reading . . .

1. Choose any work of art, perhaps a reading or picture in this book, and show by what specific methods it intensifies and clarifies experience.

2. Using one sentence or as much as a paragraph, make something familiar into something strange.

3. Like Stevens' jar, what other acts or creations of man bring some meaning to nature?

Three assignments . . .

1. Look at a modern penny and pretend that you are an intelligent visitor from outer space. You know nothing of earth, but you do have an advanced scientific technology. What things can you say with absolute certainty about the penny? Make a list. In class or on your own, you can test this list against your instructor's or another student's. How many subjective statements did you make? What unconscious conceptions interfered with your "objectivity"? In other words, how often did you unknowingly make statements using your biases as a human who knows about earth and money?

2. Look long and hard at any familiar scene until you begin to see it as a kind of happening. Write a short description while you still see it from this perspective. In a final paragraph, try to apply some new concept to the scene; e.g., people on campus become messengers and data banks in a communications system.

3. Go any place where there is a crowd—a movie, a sporting event, or a street corner. Search out order in the group. You will find it centered on the film or game part of the time, but you will also find persons there making an order of their own apart from what is happening in front of them. Describe what you see.

Opposite page: Ordinary matter is represented by the atoms that made the luminous spots in this field-ion micrograph of an iridium crystal. Each spot corresponds to a single atom. Micrograph was made by Erwin W. Müller and O. Nishikawa, Pennsylvania State University. © 1967 by Müller and Nishikawa. Reprinted by permission.

A BEGINNING

Think about the last time your feelings were hurt or the last time you were angry at someone; how badly were you hurt or how angry were you? You cannot make sense of that feeling by trying to register degrees of intensity: hurt, very hurt, most hurt. A writer would record that feeling by putting it into a place or action. Here is how Norman Mailer described his response to the battle at the Democratic Convention, Chicago, 1968.

The police cut through the crowd one way, then cut through them another. They chased people into the park, ran them down, beat them up; they cut through the intersection at Michigan and Balbo like a razor cutting a channel through a head of hair, and then drove columns of new police into the channel who in turn pushed out, clubs flailing, on each side, to cut new channels, and new ones again. As demonstrators ran, they reformed in new groups only to be chased by the police again. The action went on for ten minutes, fifteen minutes, with the absolute ferocity of a tropical storm, and watching it from a window on the nineteenth floor, there was something of the detachment of studying a storm at evening through a glass, the light was a lovely gray-blue, the police had uniforms of sky-blue, even the ferocity had an abstract elemental play of forces of nature at battle with other forces, as if sheets of tropical rain were driving across the street in patterns, in curving patterns which curved upon each other again. Police cars rolled up, prisoners were beaten, shoved into wagons, driven away. The rain of police, maddened by the uncoiling of their own storm, pushed against their own barricades of tourists pressed on the street against the Hilton Hotel.*

Later in the account, Mailer acknowledged that what he had witnessed was the growth of fear in himself. He was made afraid by a series of events and experiences. The sight of the "ferocious" and "elemental" struggle in the streets of Chicago was a center where he came to recognize some of that fear.

Think again about your own feelings. Write about a feeling, about the feeling itself inside you, but in the way it shaped or colored what you saw around you, even as Mailer saw razors and a storm.

AND A CONTINUATION

We have been treating writing as a threefold act: experiencing, understanding, and recording. In Mailer's paragraph, he draws on both experience and understanding in the recording. In order to write well, one must pay attention to what precedes the act of writing as much as to the act itself. A journal or a writer's notebook allows its writer freely to explore the nature of his experience. For professional writer or student, the journal will provide a source of "captured" and partially organized material which may later be shaped in more deliberate or formal writing, exactly as Mailer's Chicago experience later acquired the shape of his understanding.

Basically, the writer's notebook is a daily record of thoughts and experiences, but it is not a diary of times and places. It is a record of experience and impression. Perhaps we should recall that this chapter has included a description of experience as "happening." We should then describe the journal as the record of the individual's struggle with chaos. It may not be the place where one will create firm order, but it should be the place where the experience of disorder is recorded and examined, later to be understood and written about again. The simplest first step in a journal is to recognize disorder and record clearly the interesting detail. Do not immediately worry about final answers.

Here are three entries from the journal of the American Puritan and Governor of the Massachusetts Bay Colony, John Winthrop. From the journal for the year 1642:

Mr. Larkam of Northam, alias Dover, suddenly discovering a purpose to go to England, and fearing to be dissuaded by his people, gave them his faithful promise not to go, but yet soon after he got on ship board, and so departed. It was time for him to be gone, for not long after a widow which kept in his house, being a very handsome woman, and about 50 years of age, proved to be with child, and being examined, at first refused to confess the father, but in the end she laid it to Mr. Larkam.

From the journal for 1643:

About this time Captain Daniel Patrick was killed at Stamford by a Dutchman, who shot him dead with a pistol. This captain was entertained by us out of Holland (where he was a common soldier of the Prince's guard) to exercise our men. We made him a captain, and maintained him. After, he was admitted a member of the church of Watertown and a freeman. But he grew very proud and vicious, for though he had a wife of his own, a good Dutch woman and comely, yet he despised her and followed after other women; and perceiving that he was discovered, and that such evil courses would not be endured here, and being withal of a vain and unsettled disposition, he went from us, and sat [down] within twenty miles of the Dutch, and put himself under their protection, and joined to their church, without being dismissed from Watertown: but when the Indians arose in those parts, he fled to Stamford and there were slain. The Dutchman who killed him was apprehended, but made an escape; and this was the [fruit] of his wicked course and breach of covenant with his wife, with the church, and with that state who had called him and maintained him, and he found his death from that hand where he sought protection. It is observable that he was killed upon the Lord's day in the time of afternoon exercise (for he seldom went to the public assemblies). It was in Captain Underhill's house. The Dutchman had charged him with treachery, for causing 120 men to come to him upon his promise to direct them to the Indians, etc., but deluded them. Whereupon the captain gave him ill language and spit in his face, and turning to go out, the Dutchman shot him behind in the head, so he fell down dead and never spake. The murderer escaped out of custody.

From the journal for 1644:

Two of our ministers' sons, being students in the college, robbed two dwelling houses in the night of some 15 pounds. Being found out, they were ordered by the governours of the college to be there whipped, which was performed by the president himself—yet they were about 20 years of age; and after they were brought into the court and ordered to twofold satisfaction, or to serve so long for it. We had yet no particular punishment for burglary.

In these entries Winthrop records disorder in the settlement, despite its religious dedication. Later he came to terms with this disorder in his now famous "Little Speech on Liberty," of July, 1645.

For the other point concerning liberty, I observe a great mistake in the country about that. There is a twofold liberty, natural (I mean as our nature is now corrupt) and civil or federal. The first is common to man with beasts and other creatures. By this, man, as he stands in relation to man simply, hath liberty to do what he lists; it is a liberty to evil as well as to good. This liberty is incompatible and inconsistent with authority and cannot endure the least restraint of the most just authority. The exercise and maintaining of this liberty makes men grow more evil, and in time to be worse than brute beasts. This is that great enemy of truth and peace, that wild beast, which all the ordinances of God are bent against, to restrain and subdue it. The other kind of liberty I call civil or federal, it may also be termed moral, in reference to the covenant between God and man, in the moral law, and the politic covenants and constitutions, amongst men themselves. This liberty is the proper end and object of authority, and cannot subsist without it; and it is a liberty to that only which is good, just, and honest. This liberty you are to stand for, with the hazard (not only of your goods, but) of your lives, if need be. Whatsoever crosseth this, is not authority, but a distemper thereof. This liberty is maintained and exercised in a way of subjection to authority; it is of the same kind of liberty wherewith Christ hath made us free.

Most writers do not feel compelled to keep journals for the good of a community, as Winthrop did, yet most writers keep notebooks and journals of some kind. Why? The easiest answer is that a journal helps a writer remember. But if the journal were only a memory aid, quite likely it would be little more than brief outline notes, like somebody's telephone pad or a bus station departure and arrival board.

Journal writing is informal and often disorderly, but it is usually writing and not just notes. Remember that all language has form or order. So recreating experience, even in a sentence fragment, means shaping experience. Writers keep journals to satisfy their curiosity. They want to see what possible shapes experience might take. Sometimes the writer pursues one possibility, sometimes many. The key word is *possibility*. Finding new perspectives means withholding final judgment while trying to see clearly—both what is and what might be.

The following excerpts show the variety of ways journals have served writers past and present.

SELECTIONS FROM THE
JOURNALS OF SEVEN WRITERS

Nathaniel Hawthorne

A week ago last Monday, Herman Melville came to see me at the Consulate, looking much as he used to do (a little paler, and perhaps a little sadder), in a rough outside coat, and with his characteristic gravity and reserve of manner. He had crossed from New York to Glasgow in a screw steamer, about a fortnight before, and had since been seeing Edinburgh and other interesting places. I felt rather awkward at first; because this is the first time I have met him since my ineffectual attempt to get him a consular appointment from General Pierce. However, I failed only from real lack of power to serve him; so there was no reason to be ashamed, and we soon found ourselves on pretty much our former terms of sociability and confidence. Melville has not been well, of late; he has been affected with neuralgic complaints in his head and limbs, and no doubt has suffered from too constant literary occupation, pursued without much success, latterly; and his writings, for a long while past, have indicated a morbid state of mind. So he left his place at Pittsfield, and has established his wife and family, I believe, with his father-in-law in Boston, and is thus far on his way to Constantinople. I do not wonder that he found it necessary to take an airing through the world, after so many years of toilsome pen-labor and domestic life, following upon so wild and adventurous a youth as his was. I invited him to come and stay with us at Southport, as long as he might remain in this vicinity; and accordingly, he did come, the next day, taking with him, by way of baggage, the least little bit of a bundle, which, he told me, contained a night-shirt and a tooth-brush. He is a person of very gentlemanly instincts in every respect, save that he is a little heterodox in the matter of clean linen.

He stayed with us from Tuesday till Thursday; and, on the intervening day, we took a pretty long walk together, and sat down in a hollow among the sand hills (sheltering ourselves from the high, cool wind) and smoked a cigar. Melville, as he always does, began to reason of Providence and futurity, and of everything that lies beyond human ken, and informed me that he had 'pretty much made up his mind to be annihilated'; but still he does not seem to rest in that anticipation; and, I think, will never rest until he gets hold of a definite belief. It is strange how he persists—and has persisted ever since I knew him, and probably long before—in wandering to-and-fro over these deserts, as dismal and monotonous as the sand hills amid which we were sitting. He can neither believe nor be comfortable in his unbelief; and he is too honest and courageous not to try to do one or the other. If he were a religious man, he would be one of the most truly religious and reverential; he has a very high and noble nature, and better worth immortality than most of us.

from Hawthorne's English Notebooks

❖ ❖ ❖ ❖ ❖

A sketch to be given of a modern reformer—a type of the extreme doctrines on the subject of slaves, cold water, and other such topics. He goes about the streets haranguing most eloquently, and is on the point of making many converts, when his labors are suddenly interrupted by the appearance of the keeper of a madhouse, whence he has escaped. Much may be made of this idea.

There is evil in every human heart, which may remain latent, perhaps, through the whole of life; but circumstances may rouse it to activity. To imagine such circumstances. A woman, tempted to be false to her husband, apparently through mere whim—or a young man to feel an instinctive thirst for blood, and to commit murder.

from Hawthorne's American Notebooks

Ralph Waldo Emerson

Herschel said, chemistry had made such progress that it would no longer be that men would perish of famine, for sawdust could be made into food. And yet men in Sligo and Cape Verde and New York have been dying of famine ever since. 'Tis answered, yes, you can convert woolen and cotton rags into sugar, but 'tis very expensive and 'tis like the Duke of Sussex's recommendation, that the poor should eat curry.

I find it easy to translate all Napoleon's technics into all of mine, and his official advices are to me more literary and philosophical than the *Memoires* of the Academy. See in *Atlantis* for February, 1856, p. 118, how Carnot translated mechanics into politics.

'Until man is able to compress the ether like leather, there will be no end of misery, except through the knowledge of God.'—*Upanishad.* . . . "He (Brahma, or the Soul) does not move; is swifter than the mind: not the gods (the senses) did obtain him, he was gone before. Standing, he outstrips all the other gods, how fast soever they run. 'He moves, he does not move. He is far, and also near.'

Song of the Soul (Brahma)

If the red slayer think he slays,
Or if the slain think he is slain,
They know not well the subtle ways
I keep, and pass, and turn again.

Far or forgot to me is near;
Shadow and sunlight are the same;
The vanished gods not less appear;
And one to me are shame and fame.

They reckon ill who leave me out;
When me they fly, I am the wings;
I am the doubter and the doubt,
And I the hymn the Brahmin sings.
The strong gods pine for my abode,
And pine in vain the sacred Seven;
But thou, meek lover of the good!
Find me, and turn thy back on heaven.

from Emerson's Journals

Henry David Thoreau

Jan. 4 p.m.—The weather still remarkable warm; the ice too
soft for skating. I go through by the Andromeda Ponds and down
river from Fair Haven. I am encouraged by the sight of men fishing
in Fair Haven Pond, for it reminds me that they have animal spirits
for such adventures. I am glad to be reminded that many go a-
fishing. When I get down near to Cardinal Shore, the sun near setting, its light is wonderfully reflected from a narrow edging only
two or three feet wide, and the stubble but a few inches high. (I
am looking east.)

It is remarkable because the ice is but a dull lead-color (it is so soft
and sodden), reflecting no light, and the hill beyond is a dark russet,
here and there patched with snow, but this narrow intermediate
line of stubble is all aglow. I get its true color and brightness best
when I do not look directly at it, but a little above it toward the
hill, seeing it with the lower part of my eye more truly and ab-

stractly. It is as if all the rays slid over the ice and lodged against and were reflected by the stubble. It is surprising how much sunny light a little straw that survives the winter will reflect.

The channel of the river is open part of the way. The *Cornus sericea* and some quite young willow shoots are the red-barked twigs so conspicuous now along the riversides. That bright and warm reflection of sunlight from the insignificant edging of stubble was remarkable. I was coming downstream over the meadows, on the ice, within four or five rods of the eastern shore. The sun on my left was about a quarter of an hour above the horizon. The ice was soft and sodden, of a dull-lead color, quite dark and reflecting no light as I looked eastward, but my eyes caught by accident a singular border of stubble only three or four inches high (and as many feet wide perhaps) which rose along the edge of the ice at the foot of the hill. It was not a mere brightening of the bleached stubble, but the warm and yellow light of the sun, which, it appeared, it was peculiarly fitted to reflect. It was that amber light from the west which we sometimes witness after a storm, concentrated on this stubble, for the hill beyond was merely a dark russet spotted with snow. All the yellow rays seemed to be reflected by this insignificant stubble alone, and when I looked more generally a little above it, seeing it with the under part of my eye, it appeared yet more truly and more bright; the reflected light made its due impression on my eye, separated from the proper color of the stubble, and it glowed almost like a low, steady, and serene fire. It was precisely as if the sunlight had mechanically slid over the ice, and lodged against the stubble. It will be enough to say of something warmly and sunnily bright that it glowed like lit stubble. It was remarkable that, looking eastward, this was the only evidence of the light in the west.

Here and there in the meadow, etc., near springy places, you see where the thinner ice has been pushed up tentwise ⋀ or ⋀⟍⟍ and cracked, either for want of room, two fields crowding together, or expanding with heat from below.

from Thoreau's Journal

Albert Camus

It is always useless to try to cut oneself off, even from other people's cruelty and stupidity. You can't say: "I don't know about it." One either fights or collaborates. Three is nothing less excusable than war, and the appeal to national hatreds. But once war has come, it is both cowardly and useless to try to stand on one side under the pretext that one is not responsible. Ivory towers are down. Indulgence is forbidden—for oneself as well as for other people.

It is both impossible and immoral to judge an event from outside. One keeps the right to hold this absurd misfortune in contempt only by remaining inside it.

One individual's reaction has no intrinsic importance. It can be of some use, but it can justify nothing. The dilettante's dream of being free to hover above his time is the most ridiculous form of liberty. This is why I must try to serve. And, if they don't want me, I must accept the position of the "despised civilian." In both cases, I am absolutely free to judge things and to feel as disgusted with them as I like. In both cases, I am in the midst of the war, and have the right to judge it. To judge it, and to act.

Novel about women: One theme. Sincerity.

"Oh my soul, do not aspire to immortal life, but exhaust the limits of the possible." Pindar, *Pythian* iii.

Characters.

The old man and his dog. Eight years of hatred.

The other man, and his verbal mannerism: "He was charming and, moreover, very pleasant."

"A deafening noise, and, moreover, one that made you jump."

"It's eternal and, moreover, human."

A.T.R.

A morning spent with bare bodies and sunlight. A shower, then light and heat.*

---

*From *Notebooks 1935–1942*, by Albert Camus, trans. by Philip Thody. © Copyright 1963 by Hamish Hamilton Ltd. and Alfred A. Knopf, Inc. Reprinted by permission of Alfred A. Knopf, Inc.

Edwin Way Teale

October 15, 1952.

Again, the dawn mist is smoky gray beneath the trees, shining, silver gray in the open. As I wander through the Insect Garden, I come upon a woolly bear spangled and starred with droplets of moisture. A little wild cherry beside the trail is adorned like a Christmas tree. Its dead branches are spider-trimmed with ropes and webs and dew-decorated spangles. Above me, a cheery "perchicory!" call marks the passage of a goldfinch, invisible in the vapor. As I approach the swamp stream, out of the autumn fog phragmites and cattails suddenly seem to step forward.

For a decade and a half now, I have watched the silent battle between these two. Slowly the phragmites have extended their foothold. These high, plumed reeds have less food value for wildlife than the cattails. But . . . in Milburn Swamp, their chief value is as a shelter for blackbirds, grackles and starlings. Each day, at sunset, I see the great starling flocks come in to roost for the night. As I stand in the chill morning vapor, looking into the phragmites—gray and wavering in the gray mist—I begin to imagine what it must be like within that dense stand of canes when the starling hosts pour down from the sky. . . . Tomorrow, before sunset, I will return and secrete myself in the heart of the phragmites and watch homecoming birds descend around me.

October 16.

A little before five P.M., wearing long boots, old army pants, a leather jacket and an ancient felt hat, I push my way into the jungle of the phragmites. The day has been warm for mid-October. But a chill rises early from the swamp. In the heart of the stand, I tramp out a little hollow. Here I await the returning birds and here I set down the following notes:

5:01 P.M. I can see only four or five feet, at most, into the tangle around me. Here and there, by the laws of chance, the stems are arranged into corridors that open for several feet high, thin corridors barred at the end by a maze of upright stems. The interior of the canebrake is so like pictures of bamboo jungles of the Orient that a tiger or cobra would hardly seem out of place. Over my head, eight or nine feet above the floor of the swamp, wave the plumes of the phragmites. Each stem is hardly thicker than my little finger.

5:05 P.M. Each time a breeze sweeps across the swamp, there is a creaking of stems and a dry rustle of leaves. The fall is a time of growing brittleness.

5:07 P.M. The first bird to arrive is a redwing. I hear its monosyllabic "Check! Check!" as it alights in the willow and then flies down to the far side of the phragmites.

5:09 P.M. Birds are assembling in the swampside maples. The sun is going down and the flocks are coming in. I can hear the mingled calling of many birds.

5:12 P.M. After five minutes of this bird bedlam, my ears feel weary and battered and deafened. There are alarm notes, quarreling notes, excitement, discontent, gossiping, the hubbub of hundreds of birds around me.

5:20 P.M. The uproar reaches a crescendo. Then there is, suddenly, silence. A perfect hush falls on the multitude of birds. It is followed by a silken whirring, a mighty fluttering, and the plumes of the phragmites wave in the wing-formed wind as the birds rise in unison into the air. For a moment, all the stems around me rock as in a breeze.

5:22 P.M. Beyond the swamp stream, the birds have alighted in another and larger stand of phragmites where they will spend the night. I hear their confused clamor muted by distance. I also hear the voices of a new concentration of starlings building up in the maples.

5:31 P.M. The chill is growing. Shadows have engulfed the phragmites.

5:42 P.M. Now the second wave breaks over the plumed reeds. The deserted phragmites are again filled with life. The concentration and the vast tumult builds up with each new addition to the flock. A redwing—one of those still to migrate—alights close behind my head. Its surprised "Check!" rings loud in my ears. There are little pauses, from time to time, in the vast tumult of bird voices beating against my ears. And in one of them a single starling, almost overhead, imitates a snatch of the sweet, plaintive song of the white-throat.

5:51 P.M. Again there is the sudden hushing of the din, the sudden mounting "Wooosh!" of wings, the swaying of the plumes above my head. These birds, too, cross the stream to the larger stand of phragmites for the night.

6:07 P.M. The individual reed stems are merging together in the gloom. The chill of the night, the smell of the swamp, the feel of mist is in the air.

6:39 P.M. No more birds have come. Outside I hear the flutter and splash of two ducks alighting on the swamp stream. The thronging birds in the far phragmites have fallen quiet. Now, even the steely hum of a mosquito sounds large in my ears. . . . Darkness is all around. The homecoming of the birds is over.

from *Circle of the Seasons*

Gerard Manley Hopkins

Sept. 24. First saw the Northern Lights. My eye was caught by beams of light and dark very like the crown of horny rays the sun makes behind a cloud. At first I thought of silvery cloud until I saw that these were more luminous and did not dim the clearness of the stars in the Bear. They rose slightly radiating thrown out from the earthline. Then I saw soft pulses of light one after another rise and pass upwards arched in shape but waveringly and with the arch broken. They seemed to float, not following the warp of the sphere as falling stars look to do but free though concentrical with it. This busy working of nature wholly independent of the earth and seeming to go on in a strain of time not reckoned by our reckoning of days and years but simpler and as if correcting the preoccupation of the world by being preoccupied with and appealing to and dated to the day of judgment was like a new witness to God and filled me with delightful fear.

from *The Journals and Papers of Gerard Manley Hopkins*

Thomas Merton

July 11.

We have a new mechanical monster on the place called a D-4 Trax-cavator which is enormous and rushes at the earth with a wide-open maw and devours everything in sight. It roars terribly, especially when it is hungry. It has been given to the laybrother novices. They feed it every day and you can't hear yourself think in the monastery while the brute is at table. It is yellow and has a face like a drawbridge and is marked all over with signs saying it comes from the Whayne supply company in Louisville, but really, as I know from secret information, it was born on a raft in Memphis, Tennessee. There, the hippopotamus abounds: which this instrument greatly resembles.

Also we have bought fans. They are exhaust fans. You make a hole in the building and put the fans there and they draw all the hot air out of the dormitory. Nobody knows what happens after that. My guess is that the hot air that went out through the fan is then replaced by the hot air that comes in through the windows. The fans are not yet running because the laybrother novices have not yet made the holes in the building. However, they have begun. They have a scaffold up on the roof of the infirmary and they have been blasting at the gable of that wing with jack-hammers, and two frail novices who are very young were posted down on the ground floor near the doorways with artistic signs which read "Falling Bricks." At first one of them was standing at the precise spot where all the falling bricks would land on his head. He was saying the rosary in an attitude of perfect abandonment. Afterwards he got a stool and moved inside the cloister and propped up the sign in his lap and took to reading the immortal masterpiece of Father Garrigou-Lagrange, *Christian Perfection and Contemplation.*

November 24.

. . . It was raining and there was a wind. I went out to the wagon shed. You could still see the hills in the distance, not too much rain for that—many black clouds, low and torn, like smoke from a disaster, flying angrily over the wide open ruin of the old horsebarn, where I now love to walk alone. On sunny days it does not have this Castle of Otranto look about it. Today, first I was full of a melody that might have been related to something in Stravinsky's "Firebird" which I have nevertheless forgotten. This was mostly my own and I sang it to God, along with angels. Then the melody went away and I sat on a stone.

December 27. Feast of Saint John.

Yesterday Father Cellarer lent me the jeep. I did not ask for it, he just lent it to me out of the goodness of his heart, so that I would be able to go out to the woods on the other side of the knobs. I had never driven a car before. Once or twice at Saint Bonaventure's I took lessons. Father Roman tried to teach me to drive a little broken-down Chevvie he had there. Yesterday I took the jeep and started off gaily all by myself to the woods. It had been raining heavily. All the roads were deep in mud. It took me some time to discover the front-wheel drive. I skidded into ditches and got out again, I went through creeks, I got stuck in the mud, I bumped into trees and once, when I was on the main road, I stalled trying to get out of the front-wheel drive and ended up sideways in the middle of the road with a car coming down the hill straight at me. Thank heaven I am still alive. At the moment I didn't seem to care if I lived or died. I drove the jeep madly into the forest in a rosy fog of confusion and delight. We romped over trestles and I sang "O Mary I love you," went splashing through puddles a foot deep, rushed madly into the underbrush and backed out again.

Finally I got the thing back to the monastery covered with mud from stem to stern. I stood in choir at Vespers, dizzy with the thought: "I have been driving a jeep."

Father Cellarer just made me a sign that I must never, never, under any circumstances, take the jeep out again. . . .

December, 1950. Feast of Saint Lucy.

I remember Gray Street, Louisville. A black carnival mask with broken elastic lying in the dirty snow in front of one of those ancient ornate houses. Gray Street must look nice in spring when the sun comes shining through the sycamores. . . .

I am aware of silence all around me in the country as of a world that is closed to men. They live in it and yet its door is closed to them. This silence, it is everywhere. It is the room Jesus told us to enter into when we pray.

from *The Sign of Jonas*

DEMONSTRATION

The Principle of Inversion

Clarke
owned a store.
Business on the first floor
was excellent.
Business on the second floor
was bad.
Business on the third floor
was terrible.
Clarke said to Al,
the engineer,
"I have to do something

Published with the hope it will remind some Americans of their basic responsibilities.
For reprints write: Director, Responsibility Series, Newsweek, 444 Madison Avenue,
New York, N.Y. 10022.
Reprinted from *Newsweek*.

about floors two and three."
Al said, "I am not just an
engineer. I am a mystic.
I get my ideas from the
prophets.
"Clarke, your customers
won't go upstairs because
they are varicose, asthmatic,
bunioned, tired, lazy.
"A wise man said, 'If you
cannot move Mohammed to the
mountain, move the mountain
to Mohammed.'
"If your customers won't walk
up the stairs, let them stand
still and move the stairs."
Thus
was born
the escalator.
The principle?
Inversion.
If you have a business, family,
social or economic problem
and can't find the answer in
"A"
concentrate on "B."
If your problem won't walk
up the stairs,
let the stairs do the walking.

Assignment . . .

Begin a journal of your own. There are no prohibitions on style or grammar or spelling. Make at
least one entry each day. The important thing is to
avoid cliché and abstraction. They will only lead
you in circles or have you repeating things other
people have already said.

Take your journal to class every day. It may not be
collected; but when it is collected, your instructor
will know that you have been keeping up and did
not just pull up to date when he asked you to bring
in your journal.

7

Who creates order?

Someone who considers himself a nonwriter may say "I know a great story. If I could write, I'd write about what happened to Samantha and me last week." He may be right in judging that he cannot write for publication. But he is wrong if he assumes that because he cannot write his story for *Playboy* or *Evergreen Review* or *Harper's*, he cannot be creative as a writer. Too often we think that either we *are* creative or we *are not*. "Either you've got it or you haven't." We reinforce this idea with a cliché, "He's a born writer."

Inheritance versus development—nature versus nurture —is an unresolved problem; however, we know that creativity is something most people can develop. There may be inborn limits, but these limits do not deny all creativity. Few people are ever professional novelists, journalists, poets or essayists, but everyone can behave creatively.

One reason many people limit themselves as writers is that they try to begin their creative act in the wrong place—

on a piece of paper. Put simply, a written page is the result of two other processes.

First, a writer must have some form of experience. Something enters his nervous system and brain.

Second, his mind does something to that experience. He feels it out by classifying, categorizing, comparing, contrasting, organizing, extending possibilities, playing, simplifying, meditating, and so on.

Third, he expresses something. He writes words, sentences, and paragraphs that tell what he wants to communicate about the past experience.

Step two is where creativity really functions. Of course, creative people often seek out experiences (step one), and they often have a wider variety of experience than uncreative people. However, everyone has experiences—*experience is what happens.*

The creative writer cannot simply be a wild man gleaning strange experiences and spewing them back out. He would be doing little more than reporting in a very uncontrolled way. He would not be much different from a complex hybrid of camera, tape recorder, and phonograph. Nor can someone pass as a writer simply by rewriting very common experience in fancy language. Merely having "a way with words" does not make a person a writer.

Really effective and imaginative writing combines all three steps. Creative writing is therefore a way with the mind, not a way with words, and not a bohemian life.

Many writers have talked about the way of the mind in writing, and many psychologists have experimented with teaching people to use their minds creatively. The results are positive. Creativity is not entirely a have or have not condition. It can be developed.

In earlier chapters on chaos and concept-making, we dealt with some reasons people shun disorder and fall back on ready-made conceptions. Disorder is frightening whether it occurs in the confusion of sleepy awakening or in a voting booth. But all responses to apparent disorder need not be stereotyped order. Just as we can consciously avoid new ways of thinking, we can also create them.

Experience or what our senses harvest of the world is always the raw material of thinking, unless you decide the mind can experience itself apart from any external world. In order to experience the world fully, we must shed certain fears and inhibitions (to whatever limits we feel we can risk). We must shed our instinctive and persistent tidying up. This involves a whole set of character traits or *learned responses*.

Creativity is in many ways a matter of personality. There *are* creative personalities and noncreative personalities. Shall the twain ever meet? Let us look at creative personalities from several points of view. What we want to do is to identify creative traits or modes of thought. You can determine if you think these things can be acquired or learned and to what degree.

Dorothy Parker, as novelist, story writer, and poet, could always look at painful things with humor. She was also an unceasing writer, and the following poem reveals what writing was like for her.

Dorothy Parker

Portrait of the Artist

Oh, lead me to a quiet cell
    Where never footfall rankles,
And bar the window passing well,
    And gyve my wrists and ankles.

Oh, wrap my eyes with linen fair,
    With hempen cord go bind me,
And, of your mercy, leave me there,
    Nor tell them where to find me.

Oh, lock the portal as you go,
    And see its bolts be double. . . .
Come back in half an hour or so,
    And I will be in trouble.

H. L. Mencken was always interested in the personalities of nations and groups. As a writer, he was a prolific journalist and essayist. Here are his comments on the personalities of writers.

H. L. Mencken

The Author at Work

If authors could work in large, well-ventilated factories, like cigar-makers or garment-workers, with plenty of their mates about and a flow of lively professional gossip to entertain them, their labor would be immensely lighter. But it is essential to their craft that they perform its tedious and vexatious operations *a cappella*, and so the horrors of loneliness are added to stenosis and their other professional infirmities. An author at work is continuously and inescapably in the presence of himself. There is nothing to divert and soothe him. Every time a vagrant regret or sorrow assails him, it has him instantly by the ear, and every time a wandering ache runs down his leg it shakes him like the bite of a tiger. I have yet to meet an author who was not a hypochondriac. Saving only medical men, who are always ill and in fear of death, the literati are perhaps the most lavish consumers of pills and philtres in this world, and the most assiduous customers of surgeons. I can scarcely think of one, known to me personally, who is not constantly dosing himself with medicines, or regularly resorting to the knife.

It must be obvious that other men, even among the intelligentsia, are not beset so cruelly. A judge on the bench, entertaining a ringing in the ears, can do his work quite as well as if he heard only the voluptuous rhetoric of the lawyers. A clergyman, carrying on his mummery, is not appreciably crippled by a sour stomach: what he says has been said before, and only scoundrels question it. And a surgeon, plying his exhilarating art and mystery, suffers no professional damage from the wild thought that the attending nurse is more sightly than his wife. But I defy anyone to write a competent sonnet with a ringing in his ears, or to compose sound criticism with a sour stomach, or to do a plausible love scene with a head full of private amorous fancies. These things are sheer impossibilities. The poor literatus encounters them and their like every time he enters his work-room and spits on his hands. The moment the door bangs he begins a depressing, losing struggle with his body and his mind.

Why then, do rational men and women engage in so barbarous and exhausting a vocation—for there are relatively intelligent and enlightened authors, remember, just as there are relatively honest politicians, and even bishops. What keeps them from deserting it for trades that are less onerous, and, in the eyes of their fellow creatures, more respectable? One reason, I believe, is that an author, like any other so-called artist, is a man in whom the normal vanity of all men is so vastly exaggerated that he finds it a sheer impossibility to hold it in. His overpowering impulse is to gyrate before his fellow men, flapping his wings and emitting defiant yells. This being forbidden by the police of all civilized countries, he takes it out by putting his yells on paper. Such is the thing called self-expression.

In the confidences of the literati, of course, it is always depicted as something much more mellow and virtuous. Either they argue that they are moved by a yearning to spread the enlightenment and save the world, or they allege that what steams them and makes them leap is a passion for beauty. Both theories are quickly disposed of by an appeal to the facts. The stuff written by nine authors out of ten, it must be plain at a glance, has as little to do with spreading the enlightenment as the state papers of the late Chester A. Arthur. And there is no more beauty in it, and no more sign of a feeling of beauty, than you will find in the décor of a night-club. The impulse to create beauty, indeed, is rather rare in literary men, and almost completely absent from the younger ones. If it shows itself at all, it comes as a sort of afterthought. Far ahead of it comes the yearning to make money. And after the yearning to make money comes the yearning to make a noise. The impulse to create beauty lingers far behind. Authors, as a class, are extraordinarily insensitive to it, and the fact reveals itself in their customary (and often incredibly extensive) ignorance of the other arts. I'd have a hard job naming six American novelists who could be depended upon to recognize a fugue without prompting, or six poets who could give a rational account of the difference between a Gothic cathedral and a Standard Oil filling-station.

The thing goes even further. Most novelists, in my experience, know nothing of poetry, and very few poets have any feeling for the beauties of prose. As for the dramatists, three-fourths of them are unaware that such things as prose and poetry exist at all. It pains me to set down such inconvenient and blushful facts. If they ought to be concealed, then blame my babbling upon scientific passion. That passion, today, has me by the ear.

Poets are often considered a breed of writer quite separate from all other writers. In the two following selections, Stephen Spender and William Wordsworth talk about the poet's problems. To what extent are these the problems of all writers?

William Wordsworth

Preface to second edition
of Lyrical Ballads

What is a Poet? To whom does he address himself? And what language is to be expected from him?—He is a man speaking to men: a man, it is true, endowed with more lively sensibility, more enthusiasm and tenderness, who has a greater knowledge of human nature, and a more comprehensive soul, than are supposed to be common among mankind; a man pleased with his own passions and volitions, and who rejoices more than other men in the spirit of life that is in him; delighting to contemplate similar volitions and passions as manifested in the goings-on of the Universe, and habitually impelled to create them where he does not find them. To these qualities he had added a disposition to be affected more than other men by absent things as if they were present; an ability of conjuring up in himself passions, which are indeed far from being the same as those produced by real events, yet (especially in those parts of the general sympathy which are pleasing and delightful) do more nearly resemble the passions produced by real events, than anything which, from the motions of their own minds merely, other men are accustomed to feel in themselves:—whence, and from practice, he has acquired a greater readiness and power in expressing what he thinks and feels, and especially those thoughts and feelings which, by his own choice, or from the structure of his own mind, arise in him without immediate external excitement. . . .

Not that I always began to write with a distinct purpose formally conceived; but habits of meditation have, I trust, so prompted and regulated my feelings, that my descriptions of such objects as strongly excite those feelings, will be found to carry along with them a *purpose*. If this opinion be erroneous, I can have little right to the name of a Poet. For all good poetry is the spontaneous overflow of powerful feelings: and though this be true, Poems to which any value can be attached were never produced on any variety of subjects but by a man who, being possessed of more than usual organic sensibility, had also thought long and deeply. For our continued influxes of feeling are modified and directed by our thoughts, which are indeed the representatives of all our past feelings: and as, by contemplating the relation of these general representatives to each other, we discover what is really important to men, so, by the repetition and continuance of this act, our feelings will be connected with important subjects, till at length, if we be originally possessed of much sensibility, such habits of mind will be produced, that, by obeying blindly and mechanically the impulses of those habits, we shall describe objects, and utter sentiments, of such a nature, and in such connection with each other, that the understanding of the reader must necessarily be in some degree enlightened, and his affections strengthened and purified. . . .

I have said that poetry is the spontaneous overflow of powerful feelings: it takes its origin from emotion recollected in tranquillity: the emotion is contemplated till, by a species of reaction, the tranquillity gradually disappears, and an emotion, kindred to that which was before the subject of contemplation, is gradually produced, and does itself actually exist in the mind. In this mood successful composition generally begins, and in a mood similar to this it is carried on. . . .

Stephen Spender

The Making of a Poem

Apology

It would be inexcusable to discuss my own way of writing poetry unless I were able to relate this to a wider view of the problems which poets attempt to solve when they sit down at a desk or table to write, or walk around composing their poems in their heads. There is a danger of my appearing to put across my own experiences as the general rule,

Reprinted from *The Making of a Poem* by Stephen Spender. By permission of W. W. Norton & Company, Inc. Copyright © 1962, 1965 by Stephen Spender.

when every poet's way of going about his work and his experience of being a poet are different, and when my own poetry may not be good enough to lend my example any authority.

Yet the writing of poetry is an activity which makes certain demands of attention on the poet and which requires that he should have certain qualifications of ear, vision, imagination, memory and so on. He should be able to think in images; he should have as great a mastery of language as a painter has over his palate, even if the range of his language be very limited. All this means that, in ordinary society, a poet has to adapt himself, more or less consciously, to the demands of his vocation, and hence the peculiarities of poets and the condition of inspiration which many people have said is near to madness. One poet's example is only his adaptation of his personality to the demands of poetry, but if it is clearly stated it may help us to understand other poets, and even something of poetry.

Today we lack very much a whole view of poetry, and have instead many one-sided views of certain aspects of poetry which have been advertised as the only aims which poets should attempt. Movements such as free verse, imagism, surrealism, expressionism, personalism and so on, tend to make people think that poetry is simply a matter of not writing in metre of rhyme, or of free association, or of thinking in images, or of a kind of drawing room madness (surrealism) which corresponds to drawing room communism. Here is a string of ideas: Night, dark, stars, immensity, blue, voluptuous, clinging, columns, clouds, moon, sickle, harvest, vast camp fire, hell. Is this poetry? A lot of strings of words almost as simple as this are set down on the backs of envelopes and posted off to editors or to poets by the vast army of amateurs who think that to be illogical is to be poetic, with that fond question. Thus I hope that this discussion of how poets work will imply a wider and completer view of poets.

Concentration

The problem of creative writing is essentially one of concentration, and the supposed eccentricities of poets are usually due to mechanical habits or rituals developed in order to concentrate. Concentration, of course, for the purpose of writing poetry, is different from the kind of concentration required for working out a sum. It is a focussing of the attention in a special way, so that the poet is aware of all the implications and possible developments of his idea, just as one might say that a plant was not concentrating on developing mechanically in one direction, but in many directions, towards the warmth and light with its leaves, and towards the water with its roots, all at the same time.

Schiller liked to have a smell of rotten apples, concealed beneath the lid of his desk, under his nose when he was composing poetry. Walter de la Mare has told me that he must smoke when writing. Auden drinks endless cups of tea. Coffee is my own addiction, besides smoking a great deal, which I hardly ever do except when I am writing. I notice also that as I attain a greater concentration, this tends to make me forget the taste of the cigarette in my mouth, and then I have a desire to smoke two or even three cigarettes at a time, in order that the sensation from the outside may penetrate through the wall of concentration which I have built round myself.

For goodness sake, though, do not think that rotten apples or cigarettes or tea have anything to do with the quality of the work of a Schiller, a de la Mare, or an Auden. They are a part of a concentration which has already been attained rather than the causes of concentration. De la Mare once said to me that he thought the desire to smoke when writing poetry arose from a need, not of a stimulus, but to canalize a distracting leak of his attention away from his writing towards the distraction which is always present in one's environment. Concentration may be disturbed by someone whistling in the street or the ticking of a clock. There is always a slight tendency of the body to sabotage the attention of the mind by providing some distraction. If this need for distraction can be directed into one channel—such as the odor of rotten apples or the taste of tobacco or tea—then other distractions outside oneself are put out of competition.

Another possible explanation is that the concentrated effort of writing poetry is a spiritual activity which makes one completely forget, for the time being, that one has a body. It is a disturbance of the balance of body and mind and for this reason one needs a kind of anchor of sensation with the physical world. Hence the craving for a scent or taste or even, sometimes, for sexual activity. Poets speak of the necessity of writing poetry rather than of a liking for doing it. It is spiritual compulsion, a straining of the mind to attain heights surrounded by abysses and it cannot be entirely happy, for in the most important sense, the only reward worth having is absolutely denied: for, however confident a poet may be, he is never quite sure that all his energy is not misdirected nor that what he is writing is great poetry. At the moment when art attains its highest attainment it reaches beyond its medium of words or paints or music, and the artist finds himself realizing that these instruments are inadequate to the spirit of what he is trying to say.

Different poets concentrate in different ways. In my own mind I make a sharp distinction between two types of concentration: one is immediate and complete, the other is plodding and only completed by stages. Some poets write immediately works which, when they are written, scarcely need revision. Others write their poems by stages, feeling their way from rough draft to rough draft, until finally, after many revisions, they have produced a result which may seem to have very little connection with their early sketches.

These two opposite processes are vividly illustrated in two examples drawn from music: Mozart and Beethoven. Mozart thought out symphonies, quartets, even scenes from operas, entirely in his head—often on a journey or perhaps while dealing with pressing problems—and then he transcribed them, in their completeness, onto paper. Beethoven wrote fragments of themes in note books which he kept beside him, working on and developing them over years. Often his first ideas were of a clumsiness which makes scholars marvel how he could, at the end, have developed from them such miraculous results.

Thus genius works in different ways to achieve its ends. But although the Mozartian type of genius is the more brilliant and dazzling, genius, unlike virtuosity, is judged by greatness of results, not by brilliance of performance. The result must be the fullest development in a created aesthetic form of an original moment of insight, and it does not matter whether genius devotes a lifetime to producing a small result if that result be immortal. The difference between two types of genius is that one type (the Mozartian) is able to plunge the greatest depths of his own experience by the tremendous effort of a moment, the other (the Beethovenian) must dig deeper and deeper into his consciousness, layer by layer. What counts in either case is the vision which sees and pursues and attains the end; the logic of the artistic purpose.

A poet may be divinely gifted with a lucid and intense and purposive intellect; he may be clumsy and slow; that does not matter, what matters is integrity of purpose and the ability to maintain the purpose without losing oneself. Myself, I am scarcely capable of immediate concentration in poetry. My mind is not clear, my will is weak, I suffer from an excess of ideas and a weak sense of form. For every poem that I begin to write, I think of at least ten which I do not write down at all. For every poem which I do write down, there are seven or eight which I never complete.

The method which I adopt therefore is to write down as many ideas as possible, in however rough a form, in note books (I have at least twenty of these, on a shelf beside my desk, going back over fifteen years). I then make use of some of the sketches and discard others.

An exercise . . .

Based on your own experience and on the selections in the preceding pages, make a list of personality traits that you would expect to favor creativity. You may want to write a short paper on the concept of creativity. (Granted, the material so far is very limited compared to what one might want to know.)

THE PSYCHOLOGISTS' LISTS

Berkeley's Institute of Personality Assessment and Research has investigated several kinds of creativity. In the next two selections, psychologist Frank Barron reports what the Berkeley studies found out about creativity in writers and scientists.

Frank Barron

The Needs for Order and for Disorder as Motives in Creative Activity

In Webster's dictionary the primary definition of "order" is given as "the regular disposition or methodical arrangement of things; harmonious relation between the parts of anything; the desirable condition consequent upon conformity with law; absence of confusion or disturbance." "Disorder" is defined as "the want of order or regular disposition; immethodical distribution; confusion; neglect of rule; irregularity." A secondary definition of "disorder" refers to "discomposure of the mind; turbulence of the passions." Among the synonyms listed are "irregularity," "disarrangement," "confusion," "tumult," "disease." For the verb, "to disorder," these synonyms are given: "to disarrange," "derange," "confuse," "discompose," "disturb," "ruffle."

These dictionary definitions reflect accurately the common usage of the terms "order" and "disorder." To consider an example from daily life, if an adult enters a room in which children have been playing, he is likely, upon thinking of the adult-arranged furniture before the children got there, to say that it is now in disorder. In abnormal psychology we are accustomed to think of a mind as disordered if there has occurred a substantial suspension of the laws or expected regularities which characterize the functioning of the mature ego. We consider a polity to be in disorder if the authority of the government is not respected by a great majority of the people and if civil anarchy replaces regulation by law.

In all these instances, the word "order" is used to communicate some sense of a norm which is desirable, and the word "disorder" implies an undesirable state of affairs from the point of view of mature social functioning. Considered outside such a normative context, however, it is apparent that the states of affairs indicated by the term "disorder" are themselves a form of order, the principles of organization of the given state being, however, not readily recognized or assimilable to the attributes of order which our intelligence in its function of adaptation to external reality has gradually evolved. The room which is in disorder is in perfect order if one considers furniture in terms of objects for disposition in the play of children; the disordered mind is in perfect order if one can discern the psychic forces which are "at play" when the governing function of the ego is put out of commission by an aberrant biochemical state or a psychic trauma; the disordered polity is in order if the historical and economic forces which generate revolution, that is to say, an overthrow from below of the hierarchy of authority, are understood. In one of the more common examples of psychological jargon current in hospitals for the mentally ill, it is often said of a patient that "his affect is inappropriate." What is meant is that the existing affect, which reflects one aspect of a highly ordered state of affairs, is not understood in its context. In brief, the term "disorder" is by almost universal agreement used to refer to a state of order whose principles of organization are not clearly articulated in the framework of the most commonly adopted perceptual schemata, with the implication that this absence of common regularity is highly undesirable.

When one turns from the conventional construction of the term "disorder," however, and asks how disorder is construed by individuals who turn out original work in science or art, a startling reversal of the usual understanding of and attitude toward apparent disorder may be observed. My own initial observation of this reversal under relatively controlled experimental conditions came with my research on preferences for varied sorts of abstract line drawings. The drawings I used were made in black ink on 3 × 5 inch white cards, and they were varied primarily in terms of the degree to which they were drawn according to a geometric principle educible at a glance. The simplest forms were the straight line, the circle, the square, and the triangle. Complex polygons presented a somewhat less obvious geometrical principle of construction, and complex arrangements of curves a still less obvious principle. At the other pole from the simple geometrical figures were drawings which appeared almost as childish scrawls or as totally disarranged configurations. When I asked subjects to describe these figures, they applied such words as "regular," "neat," "clean," "orderly," and "static" to the simple geometric figures, and such words as "irregular," "messy," "whimsical," "dynamic," "disorderly," and "chaotic" to figures at the other extreme.

I was enabled through my participation in a study of doctoral candidates in a number of teaching departments in the faculty of science at the University of California to elicit expressions of relative degrees of preferences for these figures from subjects who had been rated by faculty members in terms of the originality of their research and their formulation of problems in their field. A correlation emerged in that study, and has been confirmed in subsequent studies, between rated originality and preference for the less simply ordered figures, that is, for figures which are generally seen as disordered, irregular, or even chaotic. The same kind of preference is shown to a marked degree by artists, and even among active painters a significant relationship has been found to exist between judgments in open competition of the originality of their work and their degree of preference for the apparently disordered drawings. In other studies this kind of preference has been shown to relate to independence of judgment when one is under pressure to conform to a false group consensus. In summary, a higher degree of acceptance of what is not obviously in simple good order characterizes persons who are independent in judgment and original in their thinking. This is a weaker form of the statement which I shall later attempt to show is the more accurate appraisal of the facts: namely, that creative individuals have a positive liking for phenomenal fields which cannot be assimilated to principles of geometric order and which require the development or, better, the creation of new perceptual schemata which will re-establish in the observer a feeling that the phenomena are intelligible, which is to say ordered, harmonious, and capable of arousing the esthetic sentiment.

The Psychology of
the Creative Writer

I shall present some observations drawn from a study of fifty-six professional writers and ten students in a creative writing course. Of the professional writers, thirty were persons of high reputation as creators of literature, while the other twenty-six were successful commercial writers of lesser reputation. The groups differed not only in reputation, however, but probably also in intent; in general, though certainly there were exceptions, the members of the distinguished group were consciously seeking to create imaginative literature, while the members of the less distinguished group more frequently chose their themes and shaped their compositions for the market.

In this paper, I shall draw upon data primarily from the study of the thirty distinguished writers, most of whom participated in the research as subjects in so-called "living-in" assessments at the Institute of Personality Assessment and Research. Each assessment subject spent three days at the Institute, usually in company with four other writers.

Writers were chosen for study for several reasons. First of all, writing is probably the most prevalent and most widely understood form of communication of creative interpretations of experience. Then too, the social impact of writers in disseminating information, influencing public opinion, forming public taste, and advancing culture, is very great. Finally, language itself is so much an expression of culture that a study of its use in any particular society provides a unique field for observation of creative forces in the culture itself.

Creative writing was defined for the purpose of the study as the composition of phrases, essays, stories, poems, and plays which communicate a single individual's interpretation of experience in an original manner. The primary aim of the study was to characterize creative writers in terms of abilities and personality, in order to compare them with various other groups of creative individuals, as well as with less creative writers and with people in general. A secondary aim was to investigate the process of creation in writing, through careful study of an author's work, through intensive interviews with him about his work, and through tests calling for composition, or providing an opportunity for creative perception and expression. . . .

Let me begin by presenting a composite Q-sort description of the writers who were assessed. This composite was arrived at in the following fashion: each member of the assessment staff, without discussing the person with any other member of the staff, employed a 100-item set of sentences to describe each subject at the end of three days of assessment. The Q-sort deck was constructed especially to allow the expression of clinical inference. Sorting was on a 9-point scale with forced-normal distribution. Item placements were then averaged for the staff as a whole to arrive at a composite description of each subject, and these item placements were in turn averaged to arrive at a composite description of the group.

When this was done, the five items most characteristic of the group of 30 creative writers were these:

Appears to have a high degree of intellectual capacity.

Genuinely values intellectual and cognitive matters.

Values own independence and autonomy.

Is verbally fluent; can express ideas well.

Enjoys aesthetic impressions; is aesthetically reactive.

The next eight more characteristic items were:

Is productive; gets things done.

Is concerned with philosophical problems; e.g., religion, the meaning of life, etc.

Has a high aspiration level for self.

Has a wide range of interests.

Thinks and associates to ideas in unusual ways; has unconventional thought processes.

Is an interesting, arresting person.

Appears straightforward, candid in dealings with others.

Behaves in an ethically consistent manner; is consistent with own personal standards.

    The student writers, as perceived by the assessment staff, differed from these mature creative writers in several important respects. For them, the second most characteristic item was: "Concerned with own adequacy as a person, either at conscious or unconscious levels." Also, highly characteristic were these items: "Is basically anxious"; "has fluctuating moods"; "engages in personal fantasy and daydreams, fictional speculations." One might put this down simply to their youth and the problems of ego-identity with which they were grappling, but I am inclined to think that something more was involved. From subsequent observation of these student writers, I believe that for them writing was much more a form of self-therapy, or at least an attempt at working out their problems through displacement and substitution in a socially acceptable form of fantasy. They fit closely to the sort of picture Freud gives of the poet in his essay, *The Poet and Daydreaming*; the true artist, however, is of another breed, whatever troubles he may have. Of this I shall try to say more later.

✿   ✿   ✿   ✿   ✿

    One of the tests constructed especially for this study is the Symbol Equivalence Test, in which the subject is given a stimulus image (verbally) and asked to think up a symbolically equivalent image. "Leaves being blown in the wind," for example, might suggest "a civilian population fleeing chaotically before armed aggression" (i.e., powerless particles blown by the winds of war). Ten test images were presented, and three responses sought to each. The test was scored by typing each response on a separate card for each of the several hundred subjects who took part in the creativity studies, with the name of the respondent removed, and then having three raters independently rate all responses to a given item relative to one another on a 9-point scale on the variable "original-ity." This was an onerous procedure, requiring more than ten thousand judgments from each rater, but it served to ensure that the results would be free of bias, since neither the identity of the subject nor the sample of which he was a member would be known to the rater. In this test, creative writers proved significantly more original than any other group of creative individuals we studied.

✻   ✻   ✻   ✻   ✻

The really striking differences between writers and other groups, however, lies in the general area of fantasy and originality of perception. One of our interviews was devoted especially to the fantasy life, from daydreams and night dreams and hypnagogic experiences to transcendental experiences in full and acute consciousness. An unusually high percentage (40 percent, in fact) of creative writers claimed to have had experiences either of mystic communion with the universe or of feelings of utter desolation and horror. The prologues to these experiences were frequently described with considerable vividness in the interview, and this statistic does not represent a checking of "Yes" or "No" to a question such as, "Have you ever had a mystical experience?" Other experiences of an unusual sort were also described, such as being barraged by disconnected words as though one were caught in a hailstorm, with accompanying acute discomfort, or seeing the world suddenly take on a new brightness. A high frequency of dreaming was also reported, as well as a high frequency of dreaming in color, as compared with student groups we have studied.

Most impressive of all, however, was the extent to which motivation played a role, both in the writer's becoming a writer, and in the way in which creative writing served a more general philosophic purpose. Almost without exception, the successful creative writer had had to suffer considerable hardship in holding to his calling. The hardships included criticism from family and friends, periods of intense self-doubt, financial adversity, sacrifice sometimes of important personal relationships, and even public censure or ridicule. By the time the writer got to us, he was past many of these adversities, although poets, even internationally famous ones, were generally living in very modest circumstances, and there were some surprising, to us, instances of distinguished writers of fiction who still had to take other jobs occasionally to stay afloat. One of the poets in our sample, whose work was reviewed recently in the London *Times Literary Supplement* and was hailed as "the most remarkable body of poetry to come from America in the past decade," was earning his living working in a gymnasium and occasionally as a dock worker, while still another was typing term papers for undergraduates. At the other extreme, there were several novelists whose earnings were in the millions of dollars. Yet to all of them the economic question was of secondary importance; this is true of all of our groups of creative individuals. On the Economic value scale of the Allport-Vernon-Lindzey scale of values, creative individuals consistently earn their very lowest score. It is quite apparent that they are playing for other stakes. What then are the stakes, and if there are stakes, just what is the game?

The game, I believe, centers upon the nature of intellect itself and upon the meaning of human life. In reviewing the performance of creative writers on the Symbol Equivalence test, I was struck by the rapidity with which they moved from the commonplace stimulus image to the cosmic metaphor. Their concerns, as shown in projective tests like the Thematic Apperception Test and the Rorschach, are with mythical themes, with death, with great inanimate forces, with the symbolic rather than the literal meaning of shapes and colors. The freedom-determinism question arises again and again, both in their work and their fantasies. The nature of man in relation to the cosmos is the engaging problem.

Here again, however, a difference must be noted between the mature creative writers and the students, who, as I have indicated, I consider to have been using writing for another purpose. The most intolerable of all forms of banality is cosmic banality, and mooning around about death and the cosmos can be a cheap way of getting out of working. Sharpness of detail, validity of characterization, discipline of form, tireless rewriting and shaping up, a touch of the old shoemaker in finding pride in the craft and even in keeping trade secrets; these were among the characteristics of these creative writers, and when I say that their concern is with cosmic issues, I should add that the issues are brought to life in characterization and in language, so that to the reader is given an opportunity to experience through *his* own nature the reality that the writer perceives.

My own conclusion, then, is that creative writers are persons whose dedication is to nothing less than a quest for ultimate meanings. Or perhaps it is not so much that they are dedicated as that they understand themselves to have been elected and have accepted the office. What is enjoined upon them, then, is to listen to the voice within and to speak out. What they speak is to be truth, but it need not be everyone's truth, or even anyone else's. In these essentials, omitting writing as the specific form, I believe creative writers are no different from creative individuals in all walks of life, including those whose business it is to be silent.

We all know that all men are not born equal (though they may have equal rights). Psychologist David MacKinnon gives us some idea of the inborn advantages of creative people. His description is part of a comparison between creative, highly original people and others who are rated more highly in terms of personal stability and social conformity.

David MacKinnon

The Highly Effective
Individual

Life History of Creative Subjects

A quite different picture of the early life history appears when we examine the reports of highly original and creative persons. In one group of subjects, an item analysis of the questionnaire responses of those who scored higher on a composite index of originality revealed that they tended to answer "Yes" to the item, "As a child, my home life was not as happy as that of most others," and to say "No" to the statements, "My father was a good man," "I love my mother," "As a child I was able to go to my parents with my problems," "My home life was always happy."

A glance at the life history interview protocols for several of our samples of highly creative subjects reveals that certainly not all of them had the kind of happy family situation and favorable life circumstances so generally thought to be conducive to sound psychological development. Some endured the most brutal treatment at the hands of sadistic fathers. These, to be sure, constitute the minority, but they appear today no less creative than those whose fathers offered them quite satisfactory male figures with whom easy identification could be made. There is, however, some evidence that those who were harshly treated in childhood have not been so effective or so successful in their professions as those who were more gently treated; and there is more than a hint that these subjects have had some difficulty in assuming an aggressive professional role, because, through fear of their fathers, their feminine identifications were emphasized.

It must be stressed that we are here dependent upon the self-reports of our subjects. Those of superior emotional stability tend to report happy early life circumstances, while those outstanding in originality and creativity more often describe a less harmonious and happy atmosphere within the family circle. We know nothing with certainty about the true state of affairs for either group. In reality, the family situations of the two groups may have been indistinguishable. The differences may have resided only in their perceptions and memories of childhood experiences, and yet it is difficult to think that this alone explains the differences in self-report of the more emotionally stable and the more original and creative.

© *Teachers College Record*, 1960.

If, as there is some reason to believe, our more creative subjects have overcome adversities and in some instances even profited from them, what, we may ask, are some of the factors determining such favorable outcomes?

Briefcase Syndrome of Creativity

One of the most striking observations we have made is that the creative person seldom fits the layman's stereotype of him. In our experience, he is not the emotionally unstable, sloppy, loose-jointed Bohemian. More often, it is the unoriginal and uncreative person who appears to be artistic, clever, emotional, whereas we discover ourselves using such adjectives as deliberate, reserved, industrious, and thorough to describe truly original and creative persons. Among ourselves, we have jokingly described this cluster of traits characteristic of the creative person as "the briefcase syndrome of creativity"—closer, if you will, to the notion of professional responsibility than to the Greenwich Village Bohemian or the North Beach Beatnik.

The truly creative individual has an image of himself as a responsible person and a sense of destiny about himself as a human being. This includes a degree of resoluteness and almost inevitably a measure of egotism. But over and above these, there is a belief in the foregone certainty of the worth and validity of one's creative efforts. This is not to say that our creative subjects have been spared periods of frustration and depression when blocked in their creative striving, but only that overriding these moods has been an unquestioning commitment to their creative endeavor.

Some Qualities Related to Creativity

Closely related to the above observation is our finding that although both introverts and extraverts are to be found among creative persons, they tend as individuals to be self-assertive and dominant and possessed of a high level of energy. Whether persons recognized as highly creative would show such energetic assertion and dominance in all societies, we cannot say, but in mid-twentieth century in the United States, they do. If such assertiveness is not a prerequisite for their creativeness, it would appear to be at least necessary, if their creativity is to merit recognition and acclaim. But what is most important for their creative accomplishments is the persistent high level of energy with which they work. And this seems possible because their work is also their play. They do not need to retreat from work to be refreshed, but find refreshment and recreation for themselves in it.

Our creative subjects are in the main well above average in intelligence. Their brains have an unusual capacity to record and retain and have readily available the experiences of their life histories. The intelligent person is more discerning (more observant in a differentiated fashion), more alert (can concentrate attention readily and shift it appropriately), and more fluent in scanning thoughts and producing those which meet some problem-solving criterion. Such a person will generally have more information (in the most general sense of the term) at his command. Furthermore, items of information which he possesses may more readily enter into combinations among themselves, and the number of possible combinations is increased for such a person because of the greater information and the greater fluency of combination. Since true creativity is defined by the adaptiveness of a response as well as its unusualness, it is apparent that intelligence alone will tend to produce greater creativity. The more combinations that are formed, the more likely it is that some of them will be creative

But intelligence alone does not make for creativity, especially in the arts. Some of our most creative subjects score lower on measures of intelligence than do less creative ones. What seems to characterize the more artistically creative person is a relative absence of repression and suppression as mechanisms for the control of impulses and images. Repression operates against creativity regardless of how intelligent a person may be because it makes unavailable to the individual large aspects of his own experience, particularly the life of impulse and experience which gets assimilated to the symbols of aggression and sexuality. Dissociated items of experience cannot combine with one another; there are barriers to communication among different systems of experience. The creative person, who does not characteristically suppress or repress, but rather expresses, has his own unconscious more available to him and thus has fuller access to his own experience. Furthermore, because the unconscious operates more by symbols than by logic, the creative person is more open to the perception of complex equivalences in experience, facility in poetic metaphor being one consequence of the creative person's greater openness to his own depths.

We have discovered that our creative subjects have interests and hobbies in common with individuals in certain professions and quite unlike those of persons in other fields of endeavor (these being interests and hobbies unrelated to the field of work). For example, creative subjects in a wide range of fields share common interests with such professional people as architects, authors, journalists, and psychologists but have interests rather unlike those of office men, purchasing agents, and bankers, and, understandably enough, quite unlike those of policemen and morticians.

These patterns of interests and hobbies suggest that original and creative persons are less interested in small detail, in facts as such, and more concerned with their meanings and implications, possessed of greater cognitive flexibility, and characterized by verbal skills and interests in, as well as accuracy in, communication with others.

Invariably, we find our creative subjects entertaining both theoretical and aesthetic values, although for many people, perhaps most, there is some incompatibility and conflict between a cognitive and rational concern with truth and an emotional concern with form and beauty. When there is conflict, it would appear that the creative individual has the capacity to tolerate the tension created in him by strong opposing values, and in his life and work, he effects some reconciliation of them.

In the realm of sexual identifications and interests, our creative male subjects appear to give more expression to the feminine side of their nature than do less creative persons. On a number of tests of masculinity-femininity, they score relatively high on femininity, and this despite the fact that, as a group, they do not present an effeminate appearance or make frequent reference to homosexual interests or experiences in their life histories. In assessment, they appear to be quite masculine, though at the same time showing an openness to their own feelings and emotions, an understanding self-awareness, and wide-ranging interests including many which in our society are thought of as feminine.

If one were to cast this into Jungian terms, one would say that these creative persons are not so completely identified with their masculine *persona* roles as to blind themselves to or deny expression to the more feminine traits of the *anima*. For some, the balance between masculine and feminine traits, interests, and identifications is a precarious one, and for several, it would appear that their present reconciliation of these opposites of their nature has been barely achieved and only after considerable psychic stress and turmoil.

This openness to experience, this wide perceptiveness appears, however, to be more characteristic of those with artistic creativity than of those with scientific creativity. If—grossly oversimplifying psychological functioning—one were to say that whenever a person uses his mind for any purpose he performs either an act of perception (he becomes aware of something) or an act of judging (he comes to a conclusion about something), then we might interpret out findings as follows: our artistic creative subjects are predominantly perceptive, while our scientific creative subjects tend to be more evaluative and judgmental in their orientation to life.

In his perceptions, both of the outer world and of his inner experience, a person may tend to focus upon what is presented to his senses—the facts as they are—or he may focus upon their deeper meanings and possibilities. Now there is no doubt that we would expect creative persons not to be stimulus- and object-bound in their perceptions but ever alert to the as-yet-not-realized, and that is precisely what we find to be true of all our creative groups.

The Jungian distinction between introversion and extroversion is well known: the extravert's primary interests lie in the outer world of people and things, while the introvert's primary interests lie in the inner world of concepts and ideas.

It will come as no surprise, I believe, that the majority of our creative subjects are introverts: 80 percent of the female mathematicians, 68 percent of the architects, 65 percent of the writers, and 60 percent of the research scientists whom we have tested are introverts.

Two exercises and some questions . . .

1. From the reading selections make a list in your own terms of traits you would expect to find in a creative person.

2. In your own words explain how writers look at themselves.

3. What influences on your life have tended to make you original and creative? Which have moved you away from these qualities?

4. What forces in our society work for and against the development of creative individuals?

5. What aspects of language work for and against creativity and originality?

Two assignments . . .

1. Take a brief walk with a notebook. Jot down fifty random and concrete observations (a clogged gutter, a window painted white, etc.). Don't worry about what you record. Now, look at the list as if it were the data from a happening. Try to find some order in it (other than saying it is a campus or town).

2. Without talking about creativity in psychological terms, write a character study of a creative person. You might want to show him doing something. Try to *dramatize* many of the traits of a creative person.

FREEING IDEAS: FREE ASSOCIATION

Popular philosophy honors first impressions as the harbingers of truth and correctness; however, first impressions are often dictated by tradition and habit, rather than by individual circumstance, vision, and reason. First impressions too often do nothing more than identify what has been thought true in the past.

In looking for new solutions to problems and when trying to break out of old ways of seeing things, we are helped very little by first impressions. Psychologically, first impressions are what we call *dominant responses*. They are the responses we have learned to give in the past, so they come most easily.

What is your immediate response to each of the following words?

> red
>
> water
>
> black
>
> farm
>
> book
>
> plane

Each word elicits its own response, but these responses are usually similar for most people. In order to think about *water, farms,* or *planes* in new ways, we must go beyond *drink, animals,* and *fly.*

In talking about creativity and personality, researchers often speak of *fluency of idea* and *willingness to be nonconforming.* A creative person produces many ideas, and he is willing to let them be unusual, even grotesque or ridiculous (which is to say he is willing to fail, also). Of course, the ability to have unusual ideas is not limited to creative people. Even very inhibited and conventional people often have weird ideas when they release control—in drinking, taking drugs, dreaming, daydreaming, and going insane.

Creativity relies in part on irrationality. Old orders seem rational or logical because we are used to seeing one part follow the other. So new creations of order almost always seem illogical, at least in the traditional frame of reference. This apparent departure from logic blocks many people from creativity. They do not want to be irrational, even for a short period of time. They refuse by reflex. They use acceptable, well-known first impressions to cut off the flow of ideas about a subject. They hide unconventional ideas or condemn them before they can really examine them. Perhaps they have been taught to do this at home or even in school. Anyway, in these uncreative people, *judging* dominates seeing and imagining and developing at all levels of thought except the unconscious.

The drug experience may not prove much in the long run, but it has taught us that to be deranged is not necessarily to be useless.

Eric Burdon, *The Animals*

Unnatural, that's what the old idea of art was for most Americans. It's inevitable for us to create art which is natural to us.

Brian Wilson, *The Beach Boys*

Why should an Indonesian sect (Subud) attract so many dopers and musicians? Especially since the principles of the thing demand an undoped head. It may be the form. Or lack of form. Music at least has notes and scales and tones and even instruments. All the latihan has is someone saying "Begin" and someone saying "Finish" and anyoldthing inbetween. Sometimes it comes out like a Bach Chorale. Sometimes it sounds like a snake pit. Nobody has to do anything, or is forbidden anything.

Antonia Lamb, *Crawdaddy*

Writing, like other forms of creativity, relies in part on the irrational. In one form or another, most writers use something psychologists and psychiatrists call *free association*. Free association may be part of our stereotype of the psychiatrist's office, where we imagine the patient on the couch rambling on about anything that comes to his mind. For patient and doctor, this may be a process of discovery. That is what it may be for the writer, too. (Two recent novels, *Portnoy's Complaint* by Philip Roth and *Why Are We in Vietnam?* by Norman Mailer, have used the psychoanalytic free association monologue as a means of discovery.)

We know that the patient is not merely rambling. Thoughts do not usually just pop into the mind. One thought brings on another by association. And writers (if they are not being real patients) often set up loose limits by thinking only about things associated with their subjects. But within those limits the mind is free and often seems to jump irrationally from one idea to another. You can see that process in the following thoughts about water.

WATER

Drink
Thirst, as in hospital patient
Water comes and goes with life
Also comes and goes during life.
Rain comes on us.
Floods come and destroy us.
Nature has neither good nor bad water.
How nice it looks coming clear from a fountain—colored lights are man's vanity trying to outdo nature.
So does farming imply vanity. We think we can grow crops, but water does, and we can't control it. Not much anyhow.
We use it disdainfully sweeping streets, in urinals.
Hudson River is a gray sewer. A gray day for mankind.
We drink it, and our sin kills us. I am filled with gray water. Could I feel better if water were cleaner?
Body purifies water. We defile the body. Oh, my aching kidney.
Water in Hudson eddies like gray smoke.
Hooka water smoker, water purifies smoke. But it turns yellow like smoker's fingers.
We need water to cleanse all this, not only clothes.
Water is spiritual, if we make it that way.
Material now.

Sometimes the thoughts form patterns; sometimes they are seemingly unrelated.

What the writer is doing here is examining his language, feelings, and ideas about water. He may find that water has a particular and personal importance to him. It is not just the abstract "water" everyone talks about.

Free association exercises several facets of the creative personality.

First, it stimulates a fluency and abundance of ideas.

Second, it brings out new and therefore unconventional relationships.

Third, it requires a suspension of judgment, criticism, and labeling. The mind looks at a subject rather than categorizes it.

Fourth, it emphasizes the possibilities of something as much as, or more than, the immediate appearance.

Fifth, it encourages personalized responses.

Perhaps the most frequent block to free association and to good writing is the problem of *deferring judgment*. Too often a writer goes beyond the dominant response or first impression, then settles too quickly on his new idea. Or else his associations seem to get out of hand, too absurd, and he rejects them.

Judgment should start only after free association is finished. Perhaps there should even be a time lag for *incubation*. After all, the processes of free association and judgment require very different attitudes or moods.

Many people use free association without knowing it. A writer almost always uses it in some form. Understanding the reasons for its importance and its place in the writing process allows the writer to summon it at will. Like most things about writing, it can be practiced.

Assignment . . .

Produce a free association list about one or more of the following things:

1. A topic, specific or general, from one of your courses.

2. An abstraction: love, beauty, truth, patriotism, faith, communism.

3. An object: a pencil, lightbulb, pond, house, car.

4. A quality: red, smooth, dark, fast.

LOOKING BACK AT CREATIVITY

The words and phrases below come from the text and reading in this chapter. Give a clear and concrete illustration for each. What role does each of these things play in creative behavior?

a more comprehensive soul	wide range of interests
autonomy	extending possibilities
concentration	play
solitude	unconventional thought processes
integrity of purpose	deferred judgment

ease of motion between
    commonplace and cosmic

self-assertive

reserved

the briefcase syndrome of creativity

cognitive flexibility

incubation

consistent with personal standards

low economic values

absence of repression

toleration of the tension of
    opposing values

more expression to the feminine

predominantly perceptive

introversion

fluency

free association

DOCUMENTS

Langston Hughes

What Happens to a Dream Deferred?

Does it dry up
like a raisin in the sun?
Or fester like a sore—
And then run?
Does it stink like rotten meat?
Or crust and sugar over—
like a syrupy sweet?

Maybe it just sags
like a heavy load.

Or does it explode?

Billy Barnes, for the North Carolina Fund.

8

What things are an idea?

Here are some abstractions found in a single piece of writing: *voice of justice; a free people; works of death; a civilized nation; destroyed the lives of our people; altering fundamentally the forms of our government; absolute despotism; invasions on the rights of the people.* These abstract phrases could appear in a document authorized by either a modern socialist or capitalist system, by an American or a Yugoslavian government, by a revolutionary or by a conservative businessman. They have proved to have no absolute meaning in human society, yet we treasure the document in which they are found—the Declaration of Independence —and we encourage children to repeat its most famous abstractions, "life, liberty, and the pursuit of happiness." We feel that the authors were trying to communicate with people, not to deceive them, because we think we know the context to which those abstract terms referred when they were written.

Because an abstraction is like an easily moved net which can be placed over any number of circumstances, its meaning is constantly changed and stretched. Sometimes abstractions are deliberately manipulated, as they are in the phrase *law and order*. Sometimes merely the evolution of society changes the meaning of a word. Twenty years ago, female *beauty* was not what it is today.

By its very nature, an abstraction is subject to manipulation and change. This is both its strength and weakness. That an abstraction is subject to manipulation is its weakness; that it may change with a society is its strength. An abstraction can suddenly cover a new phenomenon and make it understandable. Or it can give new meaning to something familiar. The English historian D. W. Brogan noted this flexibility as a source of strength in the American Constitution. Its words, because they are abstract, remain applicable to new situations. Their capacity is not without trouble of course, and one of the major jobs of the Supreme Court is declaring to what concrete situations the words of the Constitution apply. It must do that, however, without manipulation.

A good writer is like the Court at its best—he is constantly renewing our sense of what abstractions mean. Many people have said that the best literature contains only a few themes: love, death, hatred, suffering, joy, fear. If this is true, then good writers are those who renew our sense of what words like *love* and *death* mean to us as human beings.

Every writer's job is to think two ways: from abstract to concrete and from concrete to abstract. In the following paragraph, a student simply records concrete detail and makes little of it.

I walked past the Museum of Natural History and turned into Central Park. I had heard that a woman had been attacked there, but it was daylight and I was not afraid. Central Park is a nice place to rest the eye in the big city. It took me half an hour to find my way out the west side of the park. From there I caught a ride with a cab driver who would not answer my questions about New York. Even riding in the cab made me tired. By the time I met Tommy at Lincoln Center my first day in New York had exhausted me.

The day apparently tired her out, but in this paragraph there is only the slightest sense of that tiredness as the sum of her day. Instead we find a list of details—often unrelated. In the paragraph below, another student has a different problem.

Being at the beach with Josie and away from parents was wonderful. We both felt real freedom for the first time in weeks. My mind could not see and hear enough. Neither could hers. We kept running from one thing to another, in between just soaking everything up. Only after three hours did I realize time was passing and taking our freedom with it.

Josie and the author probably did have some freedom and enjoy themselves, but we get only the vaguest idea of what the day *was*. We get only the author's feeling about the day. The rest is a do-it-yourself job for the reader. And what the reader does may be to make freedom mean something entirely different from the author's definition. Was freedom the experience of being

© Jerry Cooke.

lost in ten thousand people and hot dog stands or being alone on a clear and endless beach? If the author were a government official or planner, we would surely want to know that his ideas of freedom and ours mean similar things.

Of course almost everyone agrees that freedom does not mean being in prison. But that is reasonably obvious. (Or is it?) What is most interesting is to find out something new about freedom or about any abstraction: to expand our awareness of a word or to rediscover its significance.

Before we try this out, read the three selections which follow and use them to discuss the nature and psychology of abstraction.

Susanne K. Langer

Emotion and Abstraction

Abstract thinking, which is essential to any extensive course of reasoning, is traditionally treated as incompatible with emotional response. Cold reason and warm feeling (meaning emotion) are supposed to be antagonistic tendencies in the human mind, and people generally admire the one and trust its promptings, while they disparage and distrust the other. Religious mystics, many artists, and some philosophers in our own century, notably Bergson and his disciples, regard all abstract conception as an essential falsification of reality, and look to some inarticulate feeling, a product of instinct or intuition, to guide not only their practical behavior, but their knowledge of the nature of things. Scientists, educators, and analytic philosophers, perhaps also most men of affairs, take just the opposite stand, and hold abstract thought and cold reason—indeed, the colder the better—to be the safest guide to action and the arbiter of truth about a world of hard facts. They usually admit that their actions and even their beliefs are prone to follow the lures of feeling inspired by "the concrete situation" rather than the dictates of reason based on "abstract logic"; but that is because a certain amount of emotion inevitably interferes with one's logical thinking.

The antagonism between emotive responses and abstract ideation has become an accepted principle even among professional psychologists. Since reasoning—the prime use of such ideation—is regarded by most of them as an improved technique of getting food, safety, and sex partners, i.e., realizing the universal animal aims at a higher level, our spontaneous emotional reactions must be viewed as reversions to less suitable ways of dealing with the world and with each other; and they are, indeed, generally treated as disturbances of normal functions.[1] And even more than the behavioral psychologists, our rationally inclined epistemologists decry the influence of emotion on the working of other people's minds and on those people's resultant claims to knowledge. Such claims rest on "mere feeling," "wishful thinking," or what William James called "tender-mindedness," making concessions to sentiment; and, in the words of one of our contemporary analytic philosophers, they are "nothing more than the invisible shadows cast by emotive meaning."[2]

[1] D. O. Hebb, in *The Organization of Behavior* (New York, 1949), considers emotion as a disruption of cortical organization (p. 148).

[2] C. L. Stevenson, "The Nature of Ethical Disagreement," in *Readings in Philosophical Analysis*, ed. by H. Feigl and W. Sellars (New York, 1949), p. 593.

Those thinkers who, on the contrary, are deeply suspicious of the powers of reason, have to put something in its place as the cognitive and directive act of the mind. Their resort is usually to "instinct," which is supposed to be replaced at the human level by "intuition." As animal instincts express themselves in spontaneous "drives" to action, and produce great emotional symptoms if they are thwarted, so human intuition is experienced as an immediate feeling of certainty about the truth or falsehood of propositions, the rightness or wrongness of acts, and the nature of the unspoken thoughts and feelings of other people. Its chief theoretical virtue as a presumed mental faculty is its similarity to instinct, which makes it seem a little nearer than reason to most people's idea of "nature"; it is easier to imagine intuition as a higher form of instinct than to imagine the processes of generalization, deduction, and logical conclusion in that role. Actually, the shift from instinct to intuition is as hard to construe in terms of zoological development, i.e., evolution, as the shift from instinct to rationality. But the former seems simpler because it does not bring in the moot problem of abstraction. Intuitive knowledge of facts, like instinct, is bound to concrete situations; and to a great many minds "concrete" means "real," so that to them intuition seems "nearer to reality" than thought, which manipulates abstract concepts and applies its "spectral dance of bloodless categories" to the real world. The protagonists of intuitive knowledge and instinctive guidance, whose greatest spokesman in modern European philosophy was Bergson, hold as he did that abstraction is a precarious and essentially unnatural artifice invented for practical purposes, but at the price of truth and genuine vital experience.

This tenet raises a grave question of human evolution. If abstraction is not a natural function, how was it ever invented? How was an act so foreign to animal mentality ever performed for the first time? We have various devices, accidentally discovered or deliberately designed, for making very rarefied and strained abstractions, which empower us to construct our admirable mathematics and rather terrifying science. But an artificial device is always essentially a real or intended improvement on natural means to an end, or a substitute for such means where they themselves fail (that is, a prosthesis). It may accidentally have an unforeseen effect which sets up a new purpose, as the invention of gunpowder was incidental to an alchemist's attempts to make gold, but once invented, production of gunpowder became the primary purpose of countless industrial artifices and techniques. These could never have been found, however, before the idea of an explosive substance had occurred to anyone; and if there had never been an explosion of any sort in human experience (e.g., in the course of a conflagration or volcanic upheaval), surely no one could have imagined such an event clearly enough to think of what we call "explosives," let alone seek or invent them. Similarly, the trick of abstract conception could never have been adopted for the sake of its practical advantages if it had not somehow occurred naturally in prehuman brains. It could only be put to practical use after it had evolved in the course of that cerebral specialization which made one primate genus become Man.

The question that invites our speculation (corroboration by factual findings being a sanguine hope at this stage) is, how the tendency to single out the salient features of experience that recur on different occasions or occurs simultaneously in multiple instances, and to remember those features and recognize them as the same in each case, could have originated in a being that presumably was a pure animal when the process began. The use of concepts is the mark of human mentality; the earliest production of something like a concept must have resulted from the progressive development of activities that were natural and habitual to a high animal.

One of our besetting difficulties in forming hypotheses about the evolution of human traits is, I think, that we look for their origins in functions which served most nearly the same purposes. That is, however, to ignore a cardinal principle of biological advance, the shift of functions from one mechanism to another as the new one arises, and with that shift some entirely new goals to be attained.[3] Very often, moreover, an important purpose, such as for instance the balancing of the body, is served by several organic complexes, working on different principles[4]—older and newer structures sometimes coexisting, and able to stand in for each other under some, though seldom all, circumstances.[5] A new one becomes dominant because it has the greatest scope for elaboration. Had it not, we might never notice its existence, and there would be no radical shift from old ways of life to a new pattern.

Very high functions are usually composite in origin and await the development of necessary conditions, some of which, at a later stage, seem unessential or even inimical to them. Others, of course, are clearly recognizable in retrospect, and apt to be taken for "the cause." In the case of abstract conception, the role of sensory specialization and of the consequent selection of stimuli by the highly specialized organs has long been recognized, since it resembles that of the selection or "taking out" of features from the welter of experience, which abstraction is

---

[3]This principle has been recognized and largely explored by Arnold Gehlen in his valuable book *Der Mensch, seine Natur und seine Stellung in der Welt* (4th ed.; Bonn, 1950).

[4]Henri Piéron, in a paper entitled "Relations des receptions visuelles et labyrinthiques dans les réactions spatiales," *L'année psychol.*, LI (1949), 161–172, lists four different mechanisms of equilibration found in most mammals and some other animals, but of varying importance from species to species, and also, within each species and individual, from one situation to another.

[5]See, for example, J. G. Dusser de Barenne, "Corticalization of Function and Functional Localization in the Cerebral Cortex," *Arch. Neurol. & Psychiat.*, XXX (1930), 884–901; see also K. S. Lashley, "The Problem of Cerebral Organization in Vision," in *Visual Mechanisms* (Lancaster, Pa., 1942), pp. 301–22.

supposed to be. In effect, of course, such a "taking out" does occur in fully developed conceptual abstraction; but it may have a different origin from that of what one might call "sensory abstraction," which has been seriously studied since the development of computing machines suggested some hypotheses that really seem to be fertile. The growing literature concerned with the mechanisms of abstractive vision and hearing is scattered over the fields of psychology, mathematics, small-current engineering, physiology, and neurology, but the ideas developed in these diverse fields are convergent. There is a good deal of evidence for the theory that the visual organ (which is easier to study than the auditory or tactual) has a function much like the "scanning" process of television instruments and some electron microscopes. According to Norbert Wiener, we can use and interpret line drawings because "somewhere in the visual process, outlines are emphasized and some other aspects of an image are minimized in importance. The beginning of the processes is in the eye itself."[6] For very plausible mechanical reasons, "the eye receives its most intense impression at boundaries, and . . . every visual image in fact has something of the nature of a line drawing."[7]

The emphasis on the outline here is produced by elimination of the "redundant" portions of the image, or "abstraction" in the purest classical sense; the process is automatically determined by the structure of the organ (not only the eye, but the whole optic tract, including the visual cortex), and the abstraction is performed unknown to its performer. On this hypothetical basis, Pitts and McCulloch have worked out a further theory of intellectual abstraction briefly presented in an article entitled, "How We Know Universals."[8] It is most reasonable, of course, on finding an abstractive function of eye and ear, to explore the possibilities of analogous processes in other highly developed parts of the central nervous system, which might furnish a theory of further cognitive mechanisms. Yet the account in the above-mentioned paper somehow does not fulfill the promise in the title, although the explanation rings true enough as far as it goes. It seems not to go far enough, but to stop somewhere short of explaining the genesis of human conception. One is left with the question: What is missing?

What is missing is the recognition of a difference between the way we form "universals" and the way we know them. The analogy between the hypothetical processes in the sensory mechanisms and the more

[6] *Cybernetics, or Control and Communication in the Animal and the Machine* (New York, 1948), p. 159.
[7] *Ibid.*, p. 159.
[8] Walter Pitts and W. S. McCulloch, "How We Know Universals: The Perception of Auditory and Visual Forms," *Bull. Math. Biophys.*, IX (1947), 127–47. See also W. S. McCulloch and W. Pitts, "The Statistical Organization of Nervous Activity," *Biometrics*, IV (1948), 91–99.

elaborate and variable ones in the "interpretive cortex" serves to explain the element of pattern recognition that is evinced in the behavior of animals. As Russell Brain said, it is essential to their survival that they should recognize not only a specific thing or creature again, but any other of the same sort; and, indeed, "what the animal reacts to is not a mosaic of all the individual features of the object perceived, but a pattern which constitutes an abstraction from any particular individual, but for that reason is common to all individuals of the group."[9] This sort of abstraction, however, is still what Bouissou has called "abstraction implicite";[10] it is a selective response on the organic level, but not on a conceptual one. And Sir Russell makes a very precise statement when he says, "Pitts and McCulloch have attempted to describe in mathematical terms the physiological processes in virtue of which the brain renders possible the recognition of universals."[11]

These processes—be they like scanning and "seeking" techniques in our machines, or not—are undoubtedly necessary for the making of abstract concepts, but not sufficient. They may, indeed, make conception possible, yet to make it actual requires something more. That further element, I maintain, is emotional.

The only functions which can be granted to emotion in a computer animal are those of sustaining attention and acting as an "overdrive" to action in emergency. If our mental superiority to the Metazoa were a direct and simple result of more and more formalized responses to more and more filtered, fused, and automatically generalized perceptual stimuli, then the strength of our emotions, which far exceeds the requirements of those functions, would certainly not exemplify the principles of economy that the organism (apparently devising itself with more forethought than it will ever have again) is supposed to observe in its designs.[12] Were our rationality purely an increase of automatic processes instead of a new development supervening on such an increase, emotions would really be the sheer disturbances they are often taken to be, atavistic responses disrupting practical behavior, and the continued toleration of such monkey wrenches in an exemplary self-preservation machine would be an evolutionary curiosity. Animals, living as they do from one emergency to another, need terror to put speed into their escapes or to "freeze" them into invisibility for motion-seeking eyes,

[9]"The Cerebral Basis of Consciousness," *Brain*, LXXIII (1950), 465–79; see esp. p. 471.
[10]René Bouissou, *Essai sur l'abstraction et son rôle dans la connaissance* (1942), p. 55.
[11]*Op. cit.*, p. 472.
[12]Cf. Wiener, *op. cit.*, p. 155: "There should be some parts of the apparatus . . . which will search for free components and connectors of the various sorts of combinations and allot them as they are needed. This will eliminate . . . expense which is due to having a great number of unused elements, which cannot be used unless their entire large assembly is used." And below: "The blood leaving the brain is a fraction of a degree warmer than that entering it. No other computing machine approaches the economy of energy of the brain."

because they cannot figure out strategies or gauge the best goal for a retreat. They need the intense excitement of the hunt to keep them on the trail past momentary discouragements by obstacles or disappearance of the quarry.[13] Men can organize a hunt long in advance, and gather for it with or without enthusiasm, if it is necessary to fill the larder while the game is running or while other affairs permit. Yet most animals seem to be indifferent when no exciting situation evokes their emotions, while human beings generally exhibit some degree of elation or gloom, readiness to be touched in one way or another by everything around them; and the waves of feeling elicited by trivial events are greater than any practical response requires, especially where the most appropriate behavior is to desist from any overt action.

The rise of human mentality from animal mentality rests, I think, on one of those shifts of functions from old to new mechanisms which occur as the old ones develop to their limit of complexity and refinement, the point of physiological overelaboration and overresponsiveness. In the human brain, the cortical structures which we currently hold responsible for the automatic abstraction of formal features from experience are certainly developed far beyond those in any other brains. Professor Wiener, in fact, proposed that the human cortex has already exceeded its most serviceable degree of complication, and that its continued overgrowth must finally lead the human species to extinction.[14] If a phylogenetic tendency always continued to its own highest realization at the expense of the organism as a whole, this prediction would carry great weight. But unlimited phylogenetic progressions are rare. The armored saurians, the dodo, and a few other extinct creatures are supposed to have become unviable through their exaggerated specialties; usually, however, such excesses are not reached. When an organ becomes too elaborate, so that the minutiae of its performance begin to cancel or block each other, these detailed acts may be replaced by a simpler function of some new mechanism, or else fall under the influence of another, separately developed organ, so that the joint operation constitutes a higher function serving the same vital ends. If human brains continued to work as animal brains, only with ever-widening generality of perception and ever-widening transfer of responses, we might really be outdoing ourselves in filtering out details, and ignore too many cues for quick extempore response. But human beings do not depend to a very great extent on short-range direct responses, because their chief stock in trade is a tremendous store of symbols—images, words, and fragmentary presentations without clear identity, but with

[13]Hans Jonas has developed this idea in "Motility and Emotion: An Essay in Philosophical Biology," *Proceedings of the Eleventh International Congress of Philosophy* (1953), Vol. VII, pp. 117–22.
[14]*Op. cit.*, p. 180.

meaning—which can be manipulated independently of current stimuli from the environment. At an advanced stage of symbolic activity such manipulation goes on almost all the time, either as reflective judging, predicting, and planning, or a free imagination, fiction, dramatic fancy, and—most effectively—new abstract formulation of facts, i.e., interpretation. This sort of thing does not result from filtering and scanning, or consist in making response combinations appropriate to a stimulus situation. Symbolic activity arises mainly from within the organism, especially from within the brain itself.

The cortical functions indubitably are not the only ones which have undergone great elaboration in the course of our rise from animal to human estate; all parts of the brain have changed, and their massive responses have split up into distinct and separately evocable acts. Emotions, too, have become articulated, and each impulse spends itself somewhere in the system. While formerly a strong perceptual stimulus would always throw the whole creature into overt action and a simple emotive state, our many percepts instantly touch off several different cerebral acts, which no longer summate to produce one total behavioral response, but terminate each in a moment of emotion which meets and cathects the act of perception, recall, expectation, or whatever else that induced it. Since the expression of one emotion is often incompatible with that of another, and yet the kaleidoscopic passage of events around and within us stirs feelings of every sort all the time, most of these emotive processes are cut off from overt expression and have to spend themselves within the brain. We do not know just how their tiny courses run, any more than we know the whole career of a perceptual act; but the centrally based emotion seems to be carried along with the perception that stated it, and is shaped in its progress by the forms which automatic sensory abstraction has already prepared. This gives the "emotional charge" to forms which may recur, and since these forms may recur in events which are otherwise new, the cathexis, too slight to be called anything more than "interest" or even "notice," belongs to some common formal features of various percepts, memories, and even expectations, and lends them a different sort of emphasis from that which the perceptual apparatus itself provided.

The abstraction inherent in perception as such results (if our current theories are right) from the elimination of countless possible stimuli; so the simplification is effected as in a lithograph, by eliminating everything but the features that will be left to function. It is not a process of emphasizing anything, but essentially of simplifying, lightening the load before its impact on the nervous system has gone very far. This process is not usually felt. The emotive act, on the other hand, is really an act of emphasizing the exciting features, and is an act that is felt, even if only as awareness of them; it may enhance the original simplification or make a new one, even several new ones by turns, and yield the well-known phenomena of changing gestalt. In this process the irrelevant material is not filtered out, but eclipsed by the intensification of the great lines.[15] Consequently the form seems to emerge from a rich background of vaguer details that may attain varying degrees of importance, and it may be their fluctuation which makes the stable lines strong by contrast.

When forms of perception coincide with forms of emotion, percepts themselves become emotive symbols. That is, of course, a large and mainly speculative subject beyond consideration here. The attainment of symbolic value apparently antedates the final stage of real conceptual thought, which grows up only with language; so there is a phase of formal intuition and implicit meaning in the evolution of symbolism that may go further back in history than the phase I would call explicit abstraction, the basis of genuine conceptual thinking.[16] It is only in the phase of explicit abstraction that thought becomes a self-contained systematic process, by which attention is focused on highly refined forms extrapolated from experience, by virtue of a symbolism which has so little emotional value of its own that the form it exemplifies is its only possible point of interest. Specially restricted words, or marks on paper, are the most convenient symbols for long trains of reasoning; all richer exemplifications of concepts present irrelevant aspects which may receive extraneous emotional emphasis and confuse the abstracted concept.

Such undesired emphasis comes from the fact that in human life practically every detail of memory or current impression has its own emotional charge: that is to say, our emotive responses are as capable of differentiation as our perceptive ones. Experiments have shown the degree to which our cortical processes are individually cathected, and either facilitated or obstructed (though often as briefly as 0.01 sec.) by their particular cathexis.[17] There is, then, a play of felt processes arising from the deeper structures of the central nervous system, as well as a

[15]This may be what Anton Ehrenzweig, in *The Psychoanalysis of Artistic Vision and Hearing* (London, 1953), p. 15, calls "Structural Repression." If so, "repression" is not a good designation; "neglect" would be better. But I am not at all sure that we conceive the process in the same way, or even refer to the same phenomenon.

[16]Implicit abstraction and implicit meaning reach a high development in art, where they are recognized by artistic intuition, so-called "artistic sensibility," or not at all. The subject is too great to be treated in passing, but is touched on in "The Cultural Importance of Art" (No. 5), and discussed more fully in three essays: "Expressiveness," "Living Form," and "Abstraction in Science and Abstraction in Art," in *Problems of Art* (New York, 1956), as well as in the early chapters of *Feeling and Form* (New York, 1953).

[17]There is a growing literature in this field, of which I mention only an obvious example, the work of Jerome Bruner with various collaborators: J. S. Bruner and C. C. Goodman, "Need and Value as Organizing Factors in Perception," *J. Abnormal & Social Psychol.*, XLII (1947), 33–44; L. Postman, J. S. Bruner, and E. McGinnies, "Personal Values as Selective Factors in Perception," *J. Abnormal & Social Psychol.*, XLIII (1948), 142–54; J. S. Bruner and L. Postman, "Tension and Tension-Release as Organizing Factors in Perception," *J. Personality*, XV (1947), 300–308.

play of impressions; and the production of images, explicit memories, and conceptual elements probably takes place when the automatic formulations made by the sense organs and cortical neurone assemblies are utilized as channels for discharge of the rapid emotive responses made to those sensory and cortical acts themselves.

With the growth of perceptual and so-called "associational" activity in the human brain, events in psychical phase may well have become so numerous that behavior was confused by the welter of great and small feelings and lures to attention; and we should perhaps have already succumbed to the overdevelopment and overcomplication which Professor Wiener foresees as our fate, were it not for the fact that the new faculty of formal abstraction, and a still further one of symbolic thinking, have furnished means of completing countless induced processes very quickly, in a purely intracerebral way. At the same time, these new mechanisms which relieve the excessive pressures of conflicting emotions have greatly reduced the importance of those animal actions for which the brain is becoming uneconomically complex, because they perform equivalent actions on quite different principles. With the advent of abstract conception and conceptual thinking there has been a shift of functions all along the line, from intelligent behavior to intellect, from universal responses[18] to knowledge of universals, from animal mentality to the human mind.

If it is true that explicit abstraction is made by the joint functions of perceptual and emotional mechanisms, when these both reach the point where their differentiations become so fine that noticeable effects usually require summation of impulses, we are faced with the paradoxical finding that only a highly emotional creature could have developed the talent of abstract thought. At some period in our prehuman history the pressure of central excitements must have become so great that if the countless impulses started by the increasing cortical action had continued to commingle and break through to massive overt expression, the animal's behavior would have become disrupted. The only internal adaption to the overgrowing sensory mechanisms and their dependencies was to spend the emotional impulses aroused by their individuated acts in equally piecemeal fashion; and as it often happens, the very changes that caused the crisis offered the means of surviving it. The separate intellectual processes took up the separate central impulses they evoked, and the extra charge this gave them raised their automatically simplified main forms, and these only, to the psychical level. The conscious processes that resulted—images, gestures, explicit memories, and other mental

---

[18]I here use the term "universal" because McCulloch, Pitts, and other scientists use it to mean what logicians would call "general" (subsuming "universal" and "particular"), and sometimes to mean what is more strictly called "abstract," i.e., purely formal.

phenomena—provided the material for the final humanizing function, the use of symbols.

It is not impossible that mankind has passed through a much more emotional phase than it exhibits at present, a time when survival really hung in the balance. The function of symbolization, which is so deeply rooted in our brains that it begins spontaneously in infant experience and in dream, spends much of our central response. The most primitive symbols—the "archetypes," as Dr. Jung called them—still show a sur-charge of emotion that may have belonged to all symbols, before they so proliferated that the whole mental life was somewhat intellectualized and the pressure for purely self-expressive overt action was reduced. It is interesting to note that the animals nearest to man in the evolutionary scale, the great apes, are much more easily frenzied or reduced to cateleptic collapse by emotional stimuli than human beings. Are they at the end of their tether in the realm of animal mentation? There are indications in their behavior that they may be near the threshold of fantasy, the preparation for thought. But this thought may be too close to fantasy itself; so perhaps it had better be left alone.

Richard R. Lingeman

The Greeks Had a Word for It
— but What Does It Mean?

"*Beauty, wealth, birth—where could you find a better summary of what gives the Kennedys (and Rockefeller, too?) their charisma?*"—MAX LERNER, The New York Post, June 28, 1968.

"*Although he lacks [Moshe] Dayan's savior-of-the-nation charisma, he is a man to be reckoned with.*"—TIME, June 28, 1968.

"*Continues Hartley: a 'charismatic, quasi-religious style of leadership, the communion between the masses and a revered father figure, the irrational appeal that moves nations . . . '—all of this is a far cry from freedom and democracy . . . *"—TIME, June 28, 1968.

"*In Boston there was an interview with Elma Lewis, a vitally charismatic woman who teaches young people . . .*" —GEORGE GENT, The New York Times, June 27, 1968.

"*'I seem to have izyuminka, what you call 'charisma,' abnormal drive, nervosity, which are accepted on stage but in real life are rejected. People react very violently to that—or they reach out for it, they grab it, or they reject it and tear you to pieces.'*"—RUDOLF NUREYEV, quoted in Esquire, July, 1968.

"*Revealing and erotic poems offering insight into this

charismatic TV personality [Alan Burke]. Women will love it . . .*"—ADVERTISEMENT, The New York Times Book Review, June 30, 1968.

You can't hold a good look down, not when it's got the real charisma that classic tennis clothes do."—GLAMOUR, February, 1967.

What do the Kennedys, Rockefeller, Moshe Dayan, Mao Tse-tung, Elma Lewis, Rudolf Nureyev, Alan Burke and a tennis dress have in common? The answer, as the careful reader has discerned, is charisma. These quotes about charismatic people (and dress) were culled during a week's casual reading (except for one ringer) of newspapers and magazines by a dedicated Manhattan charisma-watcher. I have been

Richard R. Lingeman, "The Greeks Had a Word for It—but What Does It Mean?" *The New York Times Book Review.*

a charisma-watcher for several years now, having given up ornithology for want of birds. Charismology, is better adapted to city life anyhow, being a sedentary sport which requires nothing more than your favorite pundit and a pair of reading glasses by way of equipment. And you don't have to get up early in the morning to do it.

The rewards a charisma-watcher gets from his hobby are rather similar to the bird-watcher's—minus the fresh air: identifying new species, new plumages and colorations, spotting unusual habitats and mourning species that become extinct. The foregoing quotes will serve to illustrate.

The first Time quote (in an article about Deputy Premier Yigal Allon of Israel) is your ordinary backyard-birdfeeder journalese charisma. The only interesting thing about the word is that the writer brings it in in order to say that Allon does not have it. Dayan, on the other hand, has charisma—that old stand-by "savior-of-the-nation" charisma. Scratch any nation-savior and you're bound to find some charisma.

The second Time quote, from a scholar, is directed primarily at Mao Tse-tung and evokes a darker kind of charisma—totalitarian father-figure charisma, a predatory bird which devours its young in cultural revolutions.

Columnist Max Lerner's charisma is, in sharp contrast, more *haimische*, a warm happy kind of charisma that is not antidemocratic. The quotation occurs in a column about Prime Minister Pierre Elliott Trudeau of Canada and the need of the people for a "swinger" politician. Television critic George Gent, however, takes charisma out of the political arena and puts it into the classroom. The "vitally charismatic" schoolteacher obviously had a dynamic, inspirational personality. Rudolf Nureyev's self-ascribed charisma is of the artist-genius species, a sort of highbrow Beatlemania, seething with a volatile mixture of adoration and latent frustration-agression. This kind goes back at least to Orpheus, who, it will be recalled, was torn to pieces by the women of Thrace because he refused to give autographs.

The nature of television interviewer Alan Burke's charisma is not specified in the ad for his book of "revealing and erotic poetry." As one who has viewed Mr. Burke's program, I also find it unspecifiable. Glamour's charismatic tennis dress is the first such dress reported. Whether an article of clothing can have charisma is still being debated among charismologists. The possibility that a dress might undergo the rough handling accorded to charismatic people like Nureyev raises serious legal problems—primarily, rape.

Attributions of charisma in the public prints are so abundant that the charismologist is hard-pressed to keep track of them all. The following list will serve as a starter (noncharismatic figures in the same line of work are also given):

CHARISMATIC	NONCHARISMATIC
Charles de Gaulle	Georges Pompidou
The Kennedys	The Nixons
Martin Luther King	Ralph Abernathy
Rap Brown	Roy Wilkins
George Wallace	Lester Maddox
Fidel Castro (early)	Raul Castro
Che Guevara	Fidel Castro (late)
William F. Buckley	James Burnham
Ronald Reagan	Shirley Temple Black
Jomo Kenyatta	William Tubman
Gamal Nasser	King Faisal
John Lindsay	(any N.Y. Democrat)
Lenin, Stalin	Malenkov, Brezhnev
Khrushchev	Kosygin
Mao Tse-tung	Confucius

Having thoroughly mastered the identification of specific charismatic individuals, we are now in a position to lay down some general principles of charisma—notes on charisma we'll modestly call them.

(1) Charisma is theoretically transferable by heredity or otherwise, but in practice this rarely occurs. Jawaharlah Nehru's charismatic appeal to the Indian people was not inherited by his daughter Indira Gandhi; yet Nehru successfully inherited the worship accorded to his mentor, Mohandas Ghandi. Raul Castro does not, and probably never will, have Fidel's charisma; yet, Che Guevara seemed a logical candidate to assume it. The American politician most frequently called charismatic was Robert Kennedy ("Beyond a doubt he has charisma, an almost magical drawing power," etc.—Dick Schaap, "R.F.K."; "Though the face-lifting operation enhanced the candidate's charisma among Bobby-soxers as well as those who wish to be young again," etc.—"Bobby," from the "Images of Our Time" series of paperbound books), whose image was a palimpsest of his own personality and the memories of his martyred brother that he evoked. Yet, in life, John Kennedy was not considered a charismatic politician, except by Norman Mailer.

Another example of the nontransferability of charisma is the case of the Rev. Ralph Abernathy, who does not arouse quite the intense loyalty that Martin Luther King did among his followers.

(2) Just as there are antiheroes there are anticharismatic leaders. People perhaps tire of charisma; Khrushchev gives way to good gray Brezhnev and Kosygin, Sukarno to a colorless military junta.

(3) On the other hand, certain nations and political movements are starving for charisma. Nehru left a void which Indira Gandhi cannot fill. (But perhaps the dialogue from Bertolt Brecht can be paraphrased: "I pity the nation without charismatic leaders." "I pity the nation that needs charismatic leaders.") The German neo-Nazi move-

ment obviously needs another Hitler, but has to make do with "Bubi" von Thadden. People called "Bubi" just aren't charismatic.

(4) Then there is pseudocharisma, which is frequently the product of exaggerated publicity. Examples would be Timothy Leary and Maharishi Mahesh Yogi. Leary's charisma centered more around a drug than his teachings. The drug was made illegal; end of charisma. The Maharishi's was a reflection of his famous disciples; his downfall came when the disciples didn't like the food at his pad.

One could go on playing this game indefinitely, but perhaps the reader is wondering by now if a word which can be applied to such diverse phenomena as Mao Tse-tung's leadership and a tennis dress has any clear meaning at all. Actually, it is easier to apply the word than to define it—which may be the cause of all the trouble. The word is related to the Greek *charites*, denoting the three Graces of mythology, Aglaia, Thalia, Euphrosyne (sometimes a fourth, Charis, is given), who epitomized beauty, charm and grace. *Charisma*, a spin-off from the verb *charizomai*, to show favor, came to mean a gift or talent with which one has been naturally endowed.

In the early Greek versions of the New Testament charisma acquired a religious sense that was a basic tenet of early Christianity. It first appears in I Corinthians, xii 1, where Paul writes: "Now concerning spiritual *gifts*, brethren, I would not have you ignorant." Paul proceeded to enumerate these gifts, which range from prophecy to healing and speaking in tongues and which, of course, were of divine origin. In the 19th century the church historian Rudolf Sohm employed the term to explain the springs of church authority. Sohm wrote: ". . . the organization of Christianity is *not legal but charismatic*. Christianity is organized by the distribution of *gifts of grace* (charismata) which at the same time enable and call the individual Christians to different activities in Christianity. The charisma is from God. . . ."

From Sohm the term was borrowed and expanded beyond the religious sphere by the German sociologist Max Weber. Weber noted the phenomenon of charismatic leadership throughout history and applied the term, without any value content, to a diverse collection of persons, including Arab berserkers, Byzantine blond beasts, shamans, religious leaders such as Jesus and Mohammed, great warriors from Alexander the Great to Napoleon, demagogues such as Kurt Eisner, a German Communist leader, and hereditary, divine-right rulers such as the Emperors of China and Japan or the Dalai Lama.

Charisma was but one part of the Weberian theoretical superstructure; he saw three types of authority in society—the patriarchal or traditional, the bureaucratic-legal and the charismatic. The charismatic leader is always in opposition to the other two, and arises in times of social upheaval, when people seek emotional and spiritual allegiances not expressible through the bureaucratic or traditional institutions in power. The charismatic leader claims special gifts, whether divine, magical, superhuman or spurious. His followers are attracted to him because they believe unquestioningly in his claims, which he evidences (and must continue to evidence in order to hold their allegiance) through miracles, conquests or continuing good fortune. The charismatic leader is a revolutionary who sets the superiority of his *personal* revelations or capacities in direct conflict with the established order.

Weber's writings did not appear in full English translations until the early forties when two separate collections of his works, one by A. M. Henderson and Talcott Parsons and the other by C. Wright Mills and H. H. Gerth, were published. The word quickly spread from the halls of academe into the journalistic market place. In fact, it is possible to identify the precise moment when charisma first entered journalistic letters. In an article in The American Scholar, Columbia sociology professor Daniel Bell, discussing charisma, relates an anecdote about a writer for Fortune who in 1947 first used the word in an article about John L. Lewis. His editor promptly blue-penciled the word on grounds of obscurity, but the writer was able to insert "charismatic," in a picture caption at the last moment because an 11-letter word was needed to fill out the line. The incident was told in such vivid detail that it only required a little guesswork, plus the knowledge that Professor Bell was a Fortune staff man in 1947, to deduce that he was the anonymous Fortune staff writer who may be considered the father of journalistic charisma. Professor Bell confirmed this hunch in a recent letter to the author.

"I plead guilty to the charge of having introduced 'charisma' into American journalism. I was always being chided on Fortune for being an intellectual, and this was my effort at revenge. The story is quite true: Bill Furth, the executive editor, a man who liked plain talk, was ruffled by his inability to understand the word and threw it out of the article on John L. Lewis. But, my revenge came when I introduced the word in a caption. . . . I also did use the word in the body of the article and defended to the teeth its inclusion at that time. The great scavenger, of course, is Time magazine. Nobody there knew the meaning of the word, but one of their editors spotted it in Fortune and since Time, at that time, had a guidebook rule that one esoteric word a week had to be introduced into the magazine to annoy the reader, they chose charisma and rode it to a fare-thee-well."

And so from such colorful origins charisma has achieved its present pinnacle as one of the most indispensable words of political punditry and is applied to just about any leader whose appearance in the flesh stirs up crowd hysteria and who possesses some kind of extraordinary personal magnetism. Even though it is used so indiscriminately today that it may have lost most of whatever validity it once had, the word persists—perhaps because it reflects some deep-rooted need we have to believe in the magic of personality—in the Kennedys and the Rockefellers and the Beatles and Mao Tse-tung and Che Guevara—and in the possibility of men who promise a cause more righteous than the established order.

Be that as it may, it seems likely that true or pure charismatic appeal is not a major factor in American politics. A study of voter opinion during the 1952 election by the University of Michigan's Survey Research Center concluded that, out of 1,799 adults interviewed, "only 32 cases in which three judges agreed unanimously that charisma was predominant in the candidate perceptions" were uncovered (all among Eisenhower supporters). Nevertheless, I suspect that not a few national candidates, were Satan to appear in their studies in the black of night offering them a single political talent, would choose charisma.

As for the usage of the word, perhaps the last word should go to Professor Bell, whose recommendations regarding it are succinct: "Drop it." He explained, "People don't know what it means. Sociologists don't know what it means. Even the Greeks don't use it any more; and it was their word."

Professor Bell considers the only modern-day political figure who might conceivably be termed charismatic, in the correct sense, to be Charles de Gaulle, whose book *"Fil de l'Epée"* expressed a philosophy of charismatic leadership de Gaulle was later to employ: the towering, remote, godlike figure, who resorts to occasional plebiscites to reaffirm his authority. But de Gaulle emphasized, in Bell's words, "that the leader must maintain a sense of distance from the crowd in order to enhance his own seeming magical powers. What public figure today, especially in America, can be a 'mystery' to the crowd and create a sense of 'awe' —which is what charisma after all was about—the claim to some magical or divine authority superseding institutional authority?" Bell points out that the political leader in America who most closely fits that description is—Lyndon Johnson.

It is possible that the recent revivals of charismatic Christianity among American Christians, which seek to employ some of the gifts first described by Paul (including speaking in tongues or glossolalia, a practice on which Paul was not so keen, though he did not forbid it) will restore the word to its original religious meaning. If so, it would be a case, I suppose, of putting the Christ back in charisma.

I think I have some rights, too

THE right to walk the streets of my home town in safety. But courts and parole boards have so pampered criminals and hampered police that crime is skyrocketing into anarchy.

I have the right to expect my taxes to be prudently used for my country—not squandered on buying votes of pressure groups nor perpetuating useless bureaus.

I have the right to save my own money by doing without — save for a secure future; not to have it stolen by inflation created by wasteful government.

I have the right to start my own legitimate business and if I have ability, see it prosper; not succumb to greedy union bosses who, for their own power and profit, can close me out with an unreasonable, even illegal, strike.

I have the right and desire as a decent American to be sure no honest man goes hungry, but I also have the right to insist he do everything he can to earn his own living.

This nation was founded by men who rose up in anger against the bossism of Taxation without Representation, and established a country where the majority rules (not pressure groups) — the majority of law-abiding, hardworking, tax-paying citizens.

This great nation has come dangerously close to *mob* rule supplanting majority rule. Any official who supports or tolerates it is untrue to his country and should be treated accordingly.

THE WRITER AND ABSTRACTION

Abstraction and concrete detail can work together, but they need not come together as a list of details followed by a sentence like "Thus, we see in these things a great beauty." A good writer creates a strong alloy or at least a harmony. Read the two passages which follow. When you have finished:

1. List some important concrete details in each.
2. Ask yourself if there is an underlying abstraction for both the parts and the whole.

James Agee and Walker Evans

Let Us Now Praise
Famous Men

It stands just sufficiently short of vertical that every leaf of shingle, at its edges, and every edge of horizontal plank (blocked, at each center, with squared verticals) is a most black and cutting ink: and every surface struck by light is thus: such an intensity and splendor of silver in the silver light, it seems to burn, and burns and blinds into the eyes almost as snow; yet in none of that burnishment or blazing whereby detail is lost: each texture in the wood, like those of bone, is distinct in the eye as a razor: each nail-head is distinct: each seam and split; and each slight warping; each random knot and knothole: and in each board, as lovely a music as a contour map and unique as a thumbprint, its grain, which was its living strength, and these wild creeks cut stiff across by saws; and moving nearer the close-laid arcs and shadows even of those tearing wheels: and this, more poor and plain than bone, more naked and noble than sternest Doric, more rich and more valiant than watered silk, is the fabric and the stature of a house.

It is put together out of the cheapest available pine lumber, and the least of this is used which shall stretch a skin of one thickness alone against the earth and air; and this is all done according to one of the three or four simplest, stingiest, and thus most classical plans contrivable, which are all traditional to that country: and the work is done by half-skilled, half-paid men under no need to do well, who therefore take such vengeance on the world as they may in a cynical and part willful apathy; and this is what comes of it: Most naïve, most massive symmetry and simpleness. Enough lines, enough off-true, that this symmetry is strongly yet most subtly sprained against its centers, into something more powerful than either full symmetry or deliberate breaking and balancing of 'monotonies' can hope to be. A look of being most earnestly hand-made, as a child's drawing, a thing created out of need, love, patience, and strained skill in the innocence of a race. Nowhere one ounce or inch spent with ornament, not one trace of relief or of disguise: a matchless monotony, and in it a matchless variety and this again throughout restrained, held rigid: and all of this, nothing which is not

intrinsic between the materials of structure, the earth, and the open
heaven. The major lines of structure, each horizontal of each board,
and edge of shingle, the strictness yet subtle dishevelment of the
shingles, the nail-heads, which are driven according to geometric need,
yet are not in perfect order, the grain, differing in each foot of each
board and in each board from any other, the many knots in this cheap
lumber: all these fluencies and irregularities, all these shadows of pattern upon each piece of wood, all these in rectilinear ribbons caught
into one squared, angled, and curled music, compounding a chord of
four chambers upon a soul and center of clean air: and upon all these
masses and edges and chances and flowerings of grain, the changes of
colorings of all weathers, and the slow complexions and marchings of
pure light.

John Updike
Rabbit, Run

   Boys are playing basketball around a telephone pole with a backboard bolted to it. Legs, shouts. The scrape and snap of Keds on loose
alley pebbles seems to catapult their voices high into the moist March
air blue above the wires. Rabbit Angstrom, coming up the alley in a
business suit, stops and watches, though he's twenty-six and six three.
So tall, he seems an unlikely rabbit, but the breadth of white face, the
pallor of his blue irises, and a nervous flutter under his brief nose as
he stabs a cigarette into his mouth partially explain the nickname, which
was given to him when he too was a boy. He stands there thinking, the
kids keep coming, they keep crowding you up.
   His standing there makes the real boys feel strange. Eyeballs slide.
They're doing this for their own pleasure, not as a demonstration for
some adult walking around town in a double-breasted cocoa suit. It
seems funny to them, an adult walking up the alley at all. Where's his
car? The cigarette makes it more sinister still. Is this one of those going

to offer them cigarettes or money to go out in back of the ice plant with him? They've heard of such things but are not too frightened; there are six of them and one of him.

The ball, rocketing off the crotch of the rim, leaps over the heads of the six and lands at the feet of the one. He catches it on the short bounce with a quickness that startles them. As they stare hushed he sights squinting through blue clouds of weed smoke, a suddenly dark silhouette like a smokestack in the afternoon spring sky, setting his feet with care, wiggling the ball with nervousness in front of his chest, one widespread pale hand on top of the ball and the other underneath, jiggling it patiently to get some adjustment in air itself. The moons on his fingernails are big. Then the ball seems to ride up the right lapel of his coat and comes off his shoulder as his knees dip down, and it appears the ball is not going toward the backboard. It was not aimed there. It drops into the circle of the rim, whipping the net with a lady-like whisper. "Hey!" he shouts in pride.

"Luck," one of the kids says.

"Skill," he answers, and asks, "Hey. O.K. if I play?"

There is no response, just puzzled silly looks swapped. Rabbit takes off his coat, folds it nicely, and rests it on a clean ashcan lid. Behind him the dungarees begin to scuffle again. He goes into the scrimmaging thick of them for the ball, flips it from two weak white hands, has it in his own. That old stretched-leather feeling makes his whole body go taut, gives his arms wings. It feels like he's reaching down through years to touch his tautness. His arms lift of their own and the rubber ball floats toward the basket from the top of his head. It feels so right he blinks when the ball drops short, and for a second wonders if it went through the hoop without riffling the net. He asks, "Hey whose side am I on?"

THE EXISTENTIAL SENTENCE

Abstractions exist in our heads. We create them out of concrete things. Then we move them around. One way of examining the value of our abstractions is to reunite them with particular concrete details. The easiest way to do this for practice is the existential sentence. Start with an abstraction. Add some form of the verb *to be* and then a concrete predicate.

Glory is the winning touchdown in a tie game.

Of course we all know about that kind of glory. If we did a list of associations about glory the touchdown example might come to mind very early. What else is glory?

Glory is a shark in a school of minnows.

Glory is the ugly duckling learning he is handsome.

Glory is a moon rocket disappearing into space.

Glory is a river meeting the ocean.

Glory is raking in a big stack of poker chips.

Glory is a fat man dancing the Frug with Vanessa Redgrave.

You may not know these combinations, but at least you know very clearly what glory was for the author of each sentence. The existential sentence gives concrete existence to an abstraction. It gives ideas substance and life.

Which of these pictures give you an expanded sense of their subjects? Which call up only stock responses? What particular details work for these effects?

Misery is when your own mother won't let you play your new banjo in front of the other race.

Reprinted from the book *Black Misery* by Langston Hughes.
Published by Paul S. Eriksson, Inc.

Billy Barnes, for The North Carolina Fund.

269

Photos by Billy Barnes, for the North Carolina Fund.

Private collection.

Holly Hobbies, courtesy American Greeting Corporation.

Try making existential sentences out of these pictures. (We are not saying that the artist or photographer conceived the picture this way, but something about the way art works is revealed by comparing it to an existential sentence.) Like pictures, existential sentences give substance to abstractions, to personal attitudes. They may be humorous:

Boldness is walking backwards against Los Angeles Freeway Traffic.

Anxiety is a girl snowbound with a blind date.

Absentmindedness is a boy sitting down in a beauty parlor and asking for a haircut.

They may be sensuous:

Fear is the wrinkled snout and white teeth of a snarling dog.

Self-control is walking slowly toward the water even though the sand is burning your feet.

They may be suggestive:

Hope is a white flag waving during an atomic war.

Hope is owning two mailboxes.

They may be personal:

Boldness is telling my father he is a bore.

Some existential sentences seem very familiar, but they do not flash a clear picture. They are too conventional, too automatic, too much like an echo.

Glory is the winners' circle.

Freedom is a soaring bird.

Patriotism is dying for your country.

Innocence is a newborn baby.

Some existential sentences use scenes and objects so familiar and symbolic that they have almost become abstractions. No one really pays attention to the details.

Sacrifice is the tomb of the Unknown Soldier.

Power is the mushroom cloud of an atom bomb.

Freedom is the Statue of Liberty.

What about these:

Forgiveness is turning the other cheek.

Love is thinking about a person blissfully twenty-four hours a day.
Patriotism is the flag flying in a strong breeze.
Honor is turning yourself in for cheating.
Fear is the telegram brought to a soldier's mother.

What about Carl Sandburg's poem?

Carl Sandburg
The People, Yes

Hope is a tattered flag and a dream out of time.
Hope is a heartspun word, the rainbow, the shadblow in white,
The evening star inviolable over the coal mines,
The shimmer of northern lights across a bitter winter night,
The blue hills beyond the smoke of the steel works,
The birds who go on singing to their mates in peace, war, peace,
The ten-cent crocus bulb blooming in a used-car salesroom,
The horseshoe over the door, the luckpiece in the pocket,
The kiss and the comforting laugh and resolve—
Hope is an echo, hope ties itself yonder, yonder.

The spring grass showing itself where least expected,
The rolling fluff of white clouds on a changeable sky,
The broadcast of strings from Japan, bells from Moscow,
Of the voice of the prime minister of Sweden carried
Across the sea in behalf of a world family of nations
And children singing chorals of the Christ child
And Bach being broadcast from Bethlehem, Pennsylvania
And tall skyscrapers practically empty of tenants
And the hands of strong men groping for handholds
And the Salvation Army singing God loves us. . . .

Three assignments . . .

1. Write existential sentences about five of these words: love, beauty, pride, freedom, boldness, sorrow, danger, deceit, shyness, fear.

2. Take any cliché which strikes you as colorful: lonely as the long distance runner, happy as a clam, mad as a wet hen.

Sit back and think about the sense experience behind the cliché—what it feels or sounds like to run or to be a wet hen or to be a happy clam.

Rephrase the cliché in a new and meaningful way: loneliness is hearing your feet on a cinder track, feeling your heavy breathing, seeing a bird in flight and knowing that you are in last place and can't go any faster.

3. Read the following review and then make some sentences about intelligence and stupidity. What are some of the things people mean when they use the word *intelligence* or the abbreviation IQ?

Wallace Roberts
Believing Is Seeing

Self-fulfilling prophecies based on the assumption of innate intellectual inequality are not just rhetoric, according to the evidence presented in a new book, *Pygmalion in the Classroom* (Holt, Rinehart and Winston, Inc., 182 pp., $3.95 paper, $4.95 cloth) by a Harvard psychologist, Robert Rosenthal, and a school principal, Lenore F. Jacobsen. The book reports the statistical findings of an experiment which show that, in most cases, if a teacher expects a child to be intelligent, he will actually demonstrate greater intellectual capacity.

The authors conducted the experiment in a public elementary school in the South San Francisco Unified School District in a lower-class community. About one-sixth of the 650 children enrolled in the school's six grades were Mexican-Americans. In September 1964, the school's teachers were told that on the basis of intelligence tests conducted the previous spring, about 20 per cent of the students could be expected to show significant increases in intellectual ability during the year, and each teacher was given the names of the potential "spurters" in her class. In fact, the names had been chosen at random, so that, as the authors put it, "The difference between the special children and the ordinary children was only in the mind of the teacher."

Four months later and again the following May, the students were given the same intelligence test they had been given the previous spring. Children in both groups scored higher, but the first- and second-grade children in the experimental group—the ones the teachers were told were the potential "spurters"—scored significantly higher than the children in the control group. About 21 per cent of the children in the experimental group increased their IQ scores by thirty points, but only 5 per cent of the children in the control group had a gain that large. Almost half of the experimental group children gained at least twenty points, but only 19 per cent of the control group showed a similar gain. Finally, nearly 80 per cent of the experimental group had a gain of ten points, but only half of the control group showed a corresponding increase. Changes for children in other grades were not as dramatic but still tended to confirm the basic theory.

The possible explanations for these results are briefly explored by the authors and contain some serious implications for teachers and principals, as well as teacher-training programs. For instance, one aspect of the experiment compared the IQ gains of the Mexican-American children with teacher attitudes towards the "Mexican-ness" of the children's appearance. The result: Boys who looked "more Mexican" benefitted more from their teacher's positive prophecies. The apparent reason is that "teachers' pre-experimental expectancies for these boys' intellectual performance were probably lowest of all. Their turning up on a list of probable bloomers must have surprised their teachers. Interest may have followed surprise, and, in some way, watching for signs of increased brightness may have led to increased brightness."

"To summarize our speculations," the authors assert later on, "we may say that by what she said, by how and when she said it, by her facial expression, postures and perhaps by her touch, the teacher may have communicated to the children of the experimental group that she expected improved intellectual performance. Such communications, together with possible changes in teaching techniques, may have helped the child learn by changing his self-concept, his expectations of his own behavior, and his motivations, as well as his cognitive style and skills."

DOCUMENTS

Photos by Billy Barnes, for the North Carolina Fund.

9

From whom, where, what mind?

Point of view is a term often used in discussing fiction: first person, third person, omniscient. But point of view says more than whose eyes see something. In its most important sense, point of view means not just *who* but from *where*, from *when*, from *what kind of mind*. A good author recognizes that all things are seen from a certain perspective because no one can have perfectly complete insight or complete observation.

Point of view is evidence of the author's existence. A point of view which unnecessarily comes and goes or constantly switches reveals weakness in an author. The ability to control and utilize point of view to achieve clear new perspective is a valuable talent. Much of the grandeur and complexity of Tolstoy's fiction lies in his ability to use point of view. Here are three passages from the beginning of *Anna Karenina* in which a character is seen by himself and his beloved and his beloved's mother.

279

Leo Tolstoy

Anna Karenina

The mysterious, delightful Kitty herself could never love such a plain fellow as he thought himself, especially one so simple and undistinguished. Aside from that his former relationship to Kitty—the relationship of an adult to a child, because of his friendship with her brother—seemed still another obstacle to love. A plain, goodhearted fellow, such as he considered himself, might be loved as a friend, he thought, but to be loved the way he loved Kitty a man had to be handsome, and above all—someone special.

* * * * *

Levin's appearance at the beginning of the winter, his frequent visits, and his obvious love for Kitty, gave rise to the first serious conversations and arguments between her parents about her future.

The Prince was on Levin's side; he said he wished nothing better for Kitty. But the Princess, with the characteristic feminine habit of circling round a question, said that Kitty was too young, that Levin had not indicated in any way that his intentions were serious, that Kitty was not attached to him, and so on; but she didn't mention the chief things—that she was expecting a better match for her daughter and that she didn't like Levin or understand him. When Levin went off so abruptly the Princess was delighted; she said to her husband triumphantly: "You see, I was right!" And when Vronsky appeared she was still more pleased; it fortified her opinion that Kitty ought to make not simply a good match but a brilliant one.

For the mother there could be no comparison at all between Vronsky and Levin. The mother disliked both Levin's strange and bitter judgments and his awkwardness in society, which she thought based on pride, as well as the peculiar life, from her point of view, that he led in the country, busy with cattle and peasants; she also disliked particularly his coming to the house for six weeks in a row while in love with her daughter, when he seemed to be waiting for something and kept looking around as though afraid he would be doing them too great an honor if he proposed, not understanding that when he frequented a house with an unmarried girl in it he had to explain himself. Then suddenly, without declaring himself, he had left. It's a good thing that he's so unattractive, and that Kitty didn't fall in love with him, her mother thought.

From Leo Tolstoy, *Anna Karenina*, trans. Joel Carmichael. Copyright © 1960 by Bantam Books, Inc.

＊　＊　＊　＊　＊

After dinner, and before the evening party began, Kitty experienced a feeling like that of a young man going into combat. Her heart was pounding heavily, and her thoughts could not settle on anything.

She felt that this evening, when both men were going to meet for the first time, was bound to decide her future. She kept imagining them to herself over and over again, sometimes separately and sometimes together. When she thought of the past she dwelt with contentment and tenderness on the memories of her relations with Levin. The recollections of her childhood, and the recollections of Levin's friendship with her dead brother, lent a special, poetic charm to her relations with him. His love for her, which she was sure of, flattered her and made her happy; it was easy for her to think about Levin.

Few writers, if any, are as good as Tolstoy, but such extreme mastery over point of view is not prerequisite to its effective use. In fact, the problem with many writers is simply that they do not consciously make use of point of view. They do not develop its possibilities, or else they shift point of view at an awkward time. Consider this scene by a student.

Four of us were standing on the corner in a crowd of people waiting for the bus. I saw it coming and thought it odd that it approached so fast, but not until it was almost on top of us did we realize its brakes had failed. Fortunately, everyone jumped back to safety and a streetlight stopped the bus.

This writer was in a very interesting position, both psychologically and spatially, yet he does not use his point of view to convey the intensity of the actual experience. We do not see the bus head on; we do not feel the motion of the crowd; we do not know what doubts the author might have had. Of course these details should not be overplayed, but neither should all the work be left to the reader who has not been in that point of view.

An exercise . . .

To see how point of view matters, sketch the student's paragraph above from one or more of the following points of view: the driver, a man in a fiftieth-floor window, the original author's mother back home.

Point of view does not apply only to physical action. You can have a point of view on a philosophical question, on a historical essay, or even an engineering problem. Some buses and buildings are engineered for comfort, some for utility. History may be seen in panorama or in days or weeks; from East or West; from present, past, or future, from an economic or religious context. An ethical problem may be seen from a determinist's position, a pragmatist's position, or a hedonist's position. And anything can be seen from a personal or individual position.

A SENTENCE CAN CONTAIN A POINT OF VIEW

In the last chapter we used the existential sentence to give abstractions a sense of relationship to the concrete world (and vice versa perhaps). Here we ask you to do that again, only this time add a point of view. Here are some samples.

Point of view influenced by place:

BEACH   Glory is the moment when, running head on into the surf, you meet a cresting wave.

SCHOOL   Glory is being invited to read your exam paper to another class.

POOL   Glory is straightening out after the perfect double flip and seeing everybody watching you.

Point of view influenced by time:

EASTER   Ignorance is believing the Easter Bunny lays styrofoam eggs.

MORNING   Ignorance is waking up and momentarily not knowing who you are and where you are.

LUNCH   Ignorance is eating in the same bad cafeteria all semester.

Point of view influenced by a specific person:

GARBAGE MAN   Junk is good furniture and clothes people can't stand to look at.

HOMEOWNER   Junk is anything advertised by a discount house and mailed to "Patron."

MOTHER   Junk is anything in a kid's room except a bed, a chest of drawers, and a table.

If you think existential sentences are just a game, here are two that Robert Frost made famous in his "Death of the Hired Man."*

> Home is the place where, when you have to go there,
> They have to take you in.

>   I should have called it
> Something you somehow haven't to deserve.

*From *Complete Poems of Robert Frost.* Copyright 1930, 1939, 1947 by Holt, Rinehart and Winston, Inc. Copyright 1936 © 1958 by Robert Frost. Copyright © 1964, 1967 by Lesley Frost Ballantine. Reprinted by permission of Holt, Rinehart and Winston, Inc.

Another exercise . . .

Write existential sentences for boldness, pride, glory, patriotism, fear (or any abstractions of your choosing) from the following points of view:

TIME 4 A.M., breakfast, Thanksgiving, a season, the half-hour before supper.

PLACE Dormitory room, attic, the ball park, the gym, the supermarket, the car, the theater, the library.

PERSON Attitudes: sympathetic, gullible, skeptical, gushing, businesslike, filthy rich, practical. Role: employer, teacher, general, private, farmer, father, little sister, fraternity man, school principal.

This exercise is more difficult than the one that called for existential sentences in the last chapter. Point of view demands appropriateness. Remember, back in Chapter 3, we quoted the student's essay about the ocean—he was "tossed onto the beach out of the moving bowels of the ocean." If his point of view was relatively normal, then his figure of speech could be criticized on the basis of appropriateness: something more appropriate to his point of view would have been much more revealing.

Let us look at some points of view and consider two questions.

Edmund Rostand

from Cyrano de Bergerac

VALVERT   Observe. I myself will proceed
To put him in his place.
(He walks up to Cyrano, who has been watching him, and stands there, looking him over with an affected air.)
Ah . . . your nose . . . hem! . . .
Your nose is . . . rather large!

CYRANO	(gravely). Rather.
VALVERT	(simpering). Oh well—
CYRANO	(cooly). Is that all?
VALVERT	(turns away with a shrug). Well, of course—
CYRANO	Ah no, young sir!

You are too simple. Why, you might have said—
Oh, a great many things! Mon dieu, why waste
Your opportunity? For example, thus:—
AGGRESSIVE: I, sir, if that nose were mine,
I'd have it amputated on the spot!
FRIENDLY: How do you drink with such a nose?
You ought to have a cup made specially.
DESCRIPTIVE: 'Tis a rock—a crag—a cape—
A cape? say rather, a peninsula!
INQUISITIVE: What is that receptacle—
A razor-case or a portfolio?
KINDLY: Ah, do you love the little birds
So much that when they come and sing to you,
You give them this to perch on? INSOLENT:
Sir, when you smoke, the neighbors must suppose
Your chimney is on fire. CAUTIOUS: Take care—
A weight like that might make you topheavy.
THOUGHTFUL: Somebody fetch my parasol—
These delicate colors fade so in the sun!
PEDANTIC: Does not Aristophanes
Mention a mythologic monster called
Hippocampelephantocamelos?
Surely we have here the original!
FAMILIAR: Well old torchlight! Hang your hat
Over that chandelier—it hurts my eyes.
ELOQUENT: When it blows, the typhoon howls.
And the clouds darken. DRAMATIC: When it bleeds—
The Red Sea! ENTERPRISING: What a sigh
For some perfumer! LYRIC: Hark—the horn
Of Roland calls to summon Charlemagne!—
SIMPLE: When do they unveil the monument?
RESPECTFUL: Sir, I recognize in you
A man of parts, a man of prominence—
RUSTIC: Hey? What? Call that a nose? Na, na—
That there's a blue cucumber! MILITARY:
Point against cavalry! PRACTICAL: Why not
A lottery with this for the grand prize?
Or—parodying Faustus in the play—
"Was this the nose that launched a thousand ships
And burned the topless towers of Ilium?"

These, my dear sir, are things you might have said
Had you some tinge of letters, or of wit
To color your discourse. But wit,—not so,
You never had an atom—and of letters
You need but three to write you down—an Ass.
Moreover,—if you had the invention, here
Before these folk to make a jest of me—
Be sure you would not then articulate
The twentieth part of half a syllable
Of the beginning! For I say these things
Lightly enough myself, about myself,
But I allow none else to utter them.

Two questions . . .

1. Cyrano is touchy about his nose. What point of view of his adversary allows him to be so flippant?

2. Most of the points of view Cyrano suggests are figures of speech—concrete images. Are there any other aspects of his suggestions which contribute to the particularity of the point of view?

Tom McAfee
This Is My Living Room

My Living Room

it ain't big but big enough for me and my family—my wife Rosie setting over there reading recipes in the Birmingham *News* and my two girls Ellen Jean and Martha Kay watching the TV. I am setting here holding *Life* magazine in my lap. I get *Life*, the *News*, and *Christian Living*. I read a lots, the newspaper everyday from cover to cover. I don't just look at the pictures in *Life*. I read what's under them and the stories. I consider myself a smart man and I ain't bragging. A man can

Thomas McAfee, "This Is My Living Room," *Poems and Stories* © 1960 by the Curators of the Missouri Press. Reprinted by permission.

learn a lots from just watching the TV, if he knows what to watch for and if he listens close. I do. There ain't many that can say that and be truthful. Maybe nobody else in this whole town, which is Pine Springs.

Yonder in the corner, to the other side of the Coca-Cola calendar, is my 12 gauge. When I go in to bed, I take it with me, set it against the wall, loaded, ready to use, so I can use it if I need to. I've used it before and maybe will again. The only one to protect you is yourself and if you don't you're a fool. I got me a pistol and a .22 locked up in the back room. I could use them too.

Rosie can shoot, I taught her how, but she's afraid. The noise scares her. She said, Don't make me shoot that thing one more time. We was in the forest. The girls was waiting for us in the car. Don't make me shoot that thing again, she said, and started to cry. I slapped her face and told her to shoot the rifle. She did. Then I took it and told her to go back to the car with the girls. She started to cry again, but I stayed a long time—till it was dark—and shot the rifle and pistol and shotgun.

You can't tell what people are going to do in a town like this. They want your money and they're jealous of you. They talk about you in front of the courthouse and plan up schemes. You can't trust the police or sheriff. You got to watch out for yourself.

My Two Girls

are fourteen and sixteen year old. Both of them want to go on dates but I won't let them. I know what the boys will do, what they want to get out of a girl.

Ellen Jean, the oldest, is a right good-looking girl but sassy and you can't hardly do anything with her. She started to paint her face at school, so I took her out. I've got her working at my store.

I seen her passing notes to Elbert. I seen her get out of his car one night. She said she was going to the picture show by herself. She's a born liar and sassy. Like as not he's had her. Like as not she's got a baby starting in her belly right now. She's a sassy bitch-girl and don't take after her ma or me. Sometimes I wonder if she's mine.

Martha Kay is like her ma. She cries all the time, minds good. I let her stay in high school and will keep on letting her as long as she can act right. The first time I see lipstick, out she comes. She can work at the store too. I could use her to dust and sweep up. You can always use somebody to keep things clean.

I ask Martha Kay, Why're you late gettin' in from school? Where you been? Off in the woods with some boy? She starts to cry. She's like her ma.

Martha Kay helps at the store on Saturdays but can't add up figures good.

Ellen Jean is watching that man on TV make a fool of hisself and she's laughing. She'll end up a Birmingham whore. Her sister is laughing too and they look like a bunch of fools.

People

in this town are like they are in any other town on earth. I was in the World War I and seen a good many places. Since then I've stayed here most of the time. What's the good of moving? People are as mean one place as they are another and they're always out to get you. They won't get me because I won't let them.

Take Sam Coates who owed me twenty dollars for that fencing. Sam wouldn't pay. I said to him pay up by first of the month or I'll make you pay. He says how will I make him. Sue him for twenty dollars? Won't no lawyer in town take it anyway, he says, because they're all looking out for election. You pay, I told him.

When first of the month come I got in my car and rode out in the country to his front door. Where is your husband? I said to his wife. Milking, she said, and I went around to the barn with my .22, stuck it in his face, and told him to pay me or I'd blow the hell out of him. Sam turned as white as that bucket of milk. Him and his wife counted me out the money.

There ain't a one on earth that wouldn't try to cheat you if they could.

I use to think that women was worse than men but now I think just the opposite. Women are easier to handle. About the worst they can do is talk and what does that matter?

Niggers are better than anybody because you can handle them. They don't hardly ever give you any trouble. Except that one time with Ezmo. I didn't have no trouble handling him.

My Store

is about the best thing I know of. It seems like a human being sometimes except a lots better because you can trust it.

I've got as much business as I need and make more profit than some people I know of. Maybe they've got better houses and ride in finer cars, but maybe they didn't make all their money like I did. Honest. I ain't earned a cent crooked. I didn't inherit my money. I worked for it.

Country folks and niggers is my customers. Saturday is my big day. Ellen Jean helps me all through the week and Martha Kay helps out on Saturday. They're not much help. Don't take the right kind of interest.

I like the smell of my store from the time I open it up at 7 in the morning till the time Ellen Jean throws oil sand on the floor when it's time to sweep up. I like everything about that store.

I sell canned goods, fresh meat, bread and crackers, flour, fencing, nails, hammers, guns. I sell all the things a body could need.

Not like at Admore's where it's just women's hats and dresses, or Taylor's where it's just for younguns.

I want to know what the world is coming to.

If Rosie ever dies and the girls go off I'll sell this house and sleep in my store. I'll put up a cot, take my guns and my clothes and that's all. Maybe the TV.

What do I care about this house?

This Living Room

ain't no part of my body or my mind. The lace on the mantelpiece, what's it for? That nigger youngun setting on a commode with Mobile wrote on it, what's it for? Them pictures of movie stars in silver frames. This light-colored linoleum you can't step on without it leaving a mark from your heel. Them silky-lace curtains.

One time I took my hand across the mantel and knocked off Rosie's big clock and a vase full of flowers. Rosie set in here and cried half the night—till I got up and told her to get in bed with her husband where she belonged.

People

your own flesh and blood, will try to run over you, stomp you, steal from you, kill you if they can.

Take the law. A body would think—if he wasn't very smart—that a man of law was a good man. It ain't so. Ninety per cent of the time it ain't so. A body says then, if the law ain't good, who is? Nobody.

Sheriff Claine is a good example. He used to be always poking around my store, making hints. Standing outside the front window part of the time. One evening late I got in my car and followed Sheriff Claine down the highway towards Brushwood, then off down the country road towards Glory Church, and then he stopped. I stopped a good piece behind him and followed him through a pine thicket to a liquor still. A whole big wildcat setup. Sheriff Claine was the ringleader of the bunch.

Next time he come to my store, I said, Sheriff, finding much wildcat whisky? He grunted and pulled up his belt and let on like business was slow. Somebody said, and I eased it to him, they's a big still down towards Glory Church, off in a pine thicket.

Sheriff Claine couldn't talk for a minute and squinted his eyes. I'll have a look, he said.

Oh, probably ain't nothing to it, I told him. I ain't gonna mention it to nobody, nosir, not to a soul.

The police is just like him. They hide out at night and sleep when they're suppose to be patrolling. I've caught them at it.

Sheriff Claine didn't give me no trouble about Ezmo. He listened to what I said here at the house and that was that.

Old Ezmo

was what you'd call a low class of nigger. He'd come into the store and say, Give me a pound of sugar and I'll pay you Saturday evening. I wouldn't do it. I'd say, You give me the money. I give you the best prices in town. You give me the money.

One time Ellen Jean let him have a loaf of bread on credit. I smacked her for it and told her she was a fool, which she is. On Saturday Ezmo come in and wanted some side meat for cooking greens. Pay me off, I told him, for that loaf of bread. What loaf? he wanted to know.

Ellen Jean, didn't you charge this nigger a loaf of bread? She said yes and he said she didn't. You ain't calling my girl a liar, are you? Naw, he said, but he didn't get no loaf of bread. Somebody's a liar, I told him, and it ain't my girl.

He said he wouldn't pay me. You're a crooked, low-down nigger, I told him, and they ain't nothing much worse than that. You ain't fit for making side meat out of. I told him if he had any younguns he better watch out. I didn't wants lots of black bastards like him growing up in my town. You get out of here right now.

That night I was setting in this chair where I am right now—this same chair. The girls was watching TV. Rosie was shelling peas.

I heard somebody outdoors and I knew right off who it was. I got better ears than most people. Any time somebody sets foot in this yard, I know it. Even if I'm asleep.

That's Ezmo, I said to myself. I got up, picked up my 12 gauge over in the corner and said I was gonna clean it, went through the house without turning any lights on, then eased out the back door.

There wasn't much moon but I spotted Ezmo right off, standing behind some hedge bushes over by my bedroom window. I got just this side of him without him hearing. EZMO! I hollered, and up he come with a knife about eight inches long. I was ready for him. I triggered my 12 gauge and got him square in the face.

Rosie and the girls come running to the back door. Get me a flashlight, I told them. I never seen such a blowed-up face. The girls started getting sick and Rosie started crying. I want you to take a good look, I told Rosie, and see what this world is coming to. You see that knife he had. I held Rosie's arm and made her stand there till Ellen Jean could get Sheriff Claine.

Rosie

ain't exactly good-looking. She's got to be dried-up but once was on the fat side. She makes a good wife. I've been married to her for going on thirty years. Sometimes I get fed up with her and go to my woman in South Town. I take her a couple of cans of beans and some hose or a pair of bloomers. There ain't nothing much a woman won't do for food or clothes.

Rosie knows about her, all about her. I talk about it sometimes when we're in bed. I wouldn't trade Rosie for her but Rosie don't know that.

Tomorrow's Saturday and I got to get some sleep.

"Turn off the TV, girls. Get in yonder to bed. Tomorrow's Saturday."

I stand in front of Rosie. "Go in yonder and get in bed." She starts to cry and that's all right. It wouldn't be a bit like her if she didn't.

Three questions . . .

1. The point of view is obvious, but how did it develop? What gave this man his particular point of view on his world?

    2. Is anything here inappropriate to the point of view?

3. Is there an author's point of view present at all? If so, where? If not, why is this character interesting for so long when in real life we would probably find him intolerable?

Two assignments . . .

1. Choose a scene or an object and describe it from two very different or even opposed points of view. Remember that point of view is established by many different techniques. Try to choose something to which you really believe there are two important points of view.

    2. Find several newspaper articles or a combination of newspaper and magazine articles about the same topic. Discuss the differences in point of view. What are the specific devices that establish point of view in each case?

Guillaume Apollinaire

Annie

Between Mobile and Galveston
On the seacoast of Texas
There's a big garden full of rosebushes
And a house like a big rose

Often there is a woman
Walking alone in the garden
And when I pass along the lime-bordered highway
We look at one another

She is a Mennonite this woman
And her rosebushes and clothes are buttonless
I see that two buttons are missing from my jacket
The lady and I observe almost the same rite

Steve Baer

from The Dome Cookbook

Today you hear people who are said to be ahead of their time say "the world is a huge space ship!" I suppose that it is sometimes useful to think of the planet this way—the trouble is that space ships are built by men but this planet was not built by men—man evolved on and from this planet. There seems to be a huge urge to take over and completely control every variable of our environment—to in fact reform our planet into a giant space ship—living machine. I see this as the work of small time ingrates. Why not leave this place alone? Carry on these progressively more deadly adventures on a dead planet in some other solar system."

"Annie" trans. from the French by William Meredith.
The Dome Cookbook, published by the cookbook fund, the Lama Foundation, Corrales, N. M. Copyright by Steve Baer.

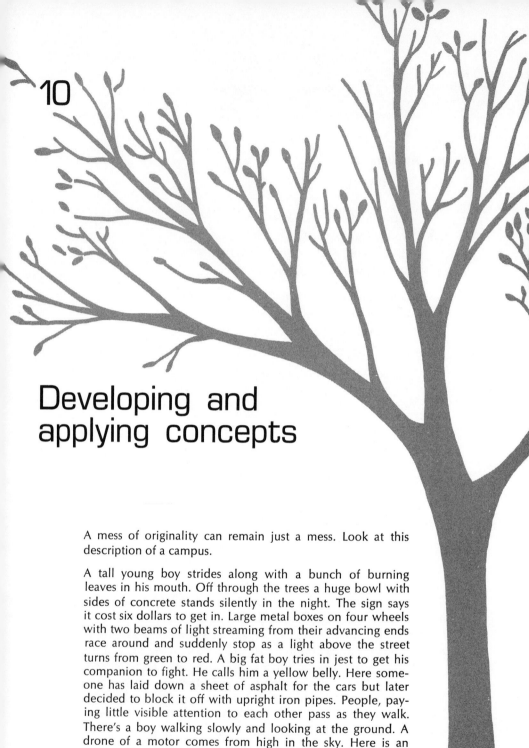

10

Developing and applying concepts

A mess of originality can remain just a mess. Look at this description of a campus.

A tall young boy strides along with a bunch of burning leaves in his mouth. Off through the trees a huge bowl with sides of concrete stands silently in the night. The sign says it cost six dollars to get in. Large metal boxes on four wheels with two beams of light streaming from their advancing ends race around and suddenly stop as a light above the street turns from green to red. A big fat boy tries in jest to get his companion to fight. He calls him a yellow belly. Here someone has laid down a sheet of asphalt for the cars but later decided to block it off with upright iron pipes. People, paying little visible attention to each other pass as they walk. There's a boy walking slowly and looking at the ground. A drone of a motor comes from high in the sky. Here is an improperly parked car with a note on it. It says:

THIS CAR WILL BE TOWED AWAY NEXT TIME.

The Police

There go six boys whose skin is black walking together. And as I walk into the dorm I see a welcome sign announcing free tutoring in English.

Bill Griffin

The writer has seen familiar events and images in his own original way. Basically he has stripped away traditional labels like *smoking* or *traffic signal* and tried to see each thing as naïvely as possible.

What the description lacks is some form of unity. It is really a list of details recorded in the order that Griffin originally saw them as he turned his head first one way, then another. If we could make nothing else of the world but a list of unusual and disconnected details, it would be a frightening place.

When talking about the happening in Chapter 6, however, we noted that most men instinctively crave order. Whether they make their own or accept someone else's, that order is the result of creating a concept. Here is the psychologist's definition once again:

. . . a concept exists whenever two or more distinguishable objects or events have been grouped or classified together and set apart from other objects on the basis of some common feature or property characteristic of each.

Look at Griffin's description again. Can we derive any concepts from it? Do any of the observations have common characteristics? The writer, in talking about his paper, at first said he could not find any. Later he agreed that many of these things involved motion or expenditure of energy. If he were an amateur or professional physicist, he might well have unified his details of the campus by concentrating on kinds of motion, their interrelationship, and what they reveal about energy. In fact, the Johnstown campus of the University of Pennsylvania got a new heating system because someone realized that buildings and people on campus were throwing off heat energy that could be collected. So engineers experimented with the concept and developed devices to collect the heat and use it.

New concepts may not always be as useful as the one that led to a heating system. (Creative people are not afraid to fail.) Nor must all concepts be radically new or different. Yet, if a concept is to represent an individual writer's point of view, the concept, too, will be individual, or else the writer might better spend his time paraphrasing or quoting, rather than composing. *Original or personal composition means making or finding a personally relevant concept which will draw together, in a new way, experience and information.* This discovery usually takes place before the writer completes a first draft of his work. It accounts for the need to spend as much time in preparation for writing as in the actual writing.

The hard thing is not always knowing the direction—it is knowing that one knows. The hard thing is not having experience, it is recognizing it. William J.J. Gordon wrote that creativity begins with making the strange familiar and making the familiar strange (see Chapter 6). In the student paper that Bill Griffin wrote, he had no trouble developing his awareness and data-collecting senses to the point where incoming material and remembered material could be made strange by avoiding preconceptions and old labels.

His second job was to develop his own concept, his own west for sailing. He had to solve the problem of how to understand or how to get along with or how to use the data in a new way. This, too, is a matter of making the familiar strange or making the strange familiar. If Griffin had worked out his energy expenditure idea, he would have been developing the strangeness. If he had decided that what he was looking at simply resembled something as familiar as a campus, say a dance, he would have been making the strange familiar again, but in a different way. While this second approach might not have led to a new invention, it could have led to a fresh awareness of what the campus was like.

Both are ways of forming new concepts.

Maria Montessori, one of the greatest innovators in childhood education, created many new concepts about teaching, and she developed them into classroom methods. Here she describes how she arrived at, and worked on, a new method of teaching beginning writing.

Maria Montessori

Teaching Reading and Writing

Let us observe mediocre men; they pompously assume erudition and disdain simple things. Let us study the clear thought of those whom we consider men of genius. Newton is seated tranquilly in the open air; an apple falls from the tree, he observes it and asks, "Why?" Phenomena are never insignificant; the fruit which falls and universal gravitation may rest side by side in the mind of a genius.

If Newton had been a teacher of children he would have led the child to look upon the worlds on a starry night, but an erudite person might have felt it necessary first to prepare the child to understand the sublime calculus which is the key to astronomy—Galileo Galilei observed the oscillation of a lamp swung on high, and discovered the laws of the pendulum.

In the intellectual life *simplicity* consists in divesting one's mind of every preconception, and this leads to the discovery of new things, as,

From Maria Montessori, *The Montessori Method*, trans. by Anne E. George (Cambridge, Mass.: Robert Bentley, Inc.), pp. 255–70.

in the moral life, humility and material poverty guide us toward high spiritual conquests.

* * * * *

Let us for a moment cast aside every dogma in this [learning to write] connection. Let us take no note of culture, or custom. We are not, here, interested in knowing how humanity began to write, nor what may have been the origin of writing itself. Let us put away the conviction, that long usage has given us, of the necessity of beginning writing by making vertical strokes; and let us try to be as clear and unprejudiced in spirit as the truth which we are seeking.

"Let us observe an individual who is writing, and let us seek to analyse the acts he performs in writing," that is, the mechanical operations which enter into the execution of writing. This would be undertaking the *philosophical study of writing*, and it goes without saying that we should examine the individual who writes, not the *writing*; the *subject*, not the *object*. Many have begun with the object, examining the writing, and in this way many methods have been constructed.

But a method starting from the individual would be decidedly original—very different from other methods which preceded it. It would indeed signify a new era in writing, *based upon anthropology.*

In fact, when I undertook my experiments with normal children, if I had thought of giving a name to this new method of writing, I should have called it without knowing what the results would be, the *anthropological method.* Certainly, my studies in anthropology inspired the method, but experience has given me, as a surprise, another title which seems to me the natural one, "the method of *spontaneous* writing."

While teaching deficient children I happened to observe the following fact: An idiot girl of eleven years, who was possessed of normal strength and motor power in her hands, could not learn to sew, or even to take the first step, darning, which consists in passing the needle first over, then under the woof, now taking up, now leaving, a number of threads.

I set the child to weaving with the Froebel mats, in which a strip of paper is threaded transversely in and out among vertical strips of paper held fixed at top and bottom. I thus came to think of the analogy between the two exercises, and became much interested in my observation of the girl. When she had become skilled in the Froebel weaving, I led her back again to the sewing, and saw with pleasure that she was now able to follow the darning. From that time on, our sewing classes began with a regular course in the Froebel weaving.

I saw that the necessary movements of the hand in sewing *had been prepared without having the child sew,* and that we should really find the way to *teach* the child *how,* before *making him execute* a task. I saw especially that preparatory movements could be carried on, and reduced to a mechanism, by means of repeated exercises not in the work itself but in that which prepares for it. Pupils could then come to the real work, able to perform it without ever having directly set their hands to it before.

I thought that I might in this way prepare for writing, and the idea interested me tremendously. I marvelled at its simplicity, and was annoyed that *I had not thought before* of the method which was suggested to me by my observation of the girl who could not sew.

In fact, seeing that I had already taught the children to touch the contours of the plane geometric insets, I had now only to teach them to touch with their fingers the *forms of the letters of the alphabet.*

I had a beautiful alphabet manufactured, the letters being in flowing script, the low letters 8 centimetres high, and the taller ones in proportion. These letters were in wood, ½ centimetre in thickness, and were painted, the consonants in blue enamel, the vowels in red. The under side of these letter-forms, instead of being painted, were covered with bronze that they might be more durable. We had only one copy of this wooden alphabet; but there were a number of cards upon which the letters were painted in the same colours and dimensions as the wooden ones. These painted letters were arranged upon the cards in groups, according to contrast, or analogy of form.

Corresponding to each letter of the alphabet, we had a picture representing some object the name of which began with the letter. Above this, the letter was painted in large script, and near it, the same letter, much smaller and in its printed form. These pictures served to fix the memory of the sound of the letter, and the small printed letter united to the one in script, was to form the passage to the reading of books. These pictures do not, indeed, represent a new idea, but they completed an arrangement which did not exist before. Such an alphabet was undoubtedly most expensive and when made by hand the cost was fifty dollars.

The interesting part of my experiment was, that after I had shown the children how to place the movable wooden letters upon those painted in groups upon the cards, I had them *touch them repeatedly in the fashion of flowing writing.*

I multiplied these exercises in various ways, and the children thus learned to make *the movements necessary to reproduce the form of the graphic signs without writing.*

I was struck by an idea which had never before entered my mind— that in writing we make *two diverse* forms of movement, for, besides the movement by which the form is reproduced, there is also that of *manipulating the instrument of writing.* And, indeed, when the deficient children had become expert in touching all the letters according to form, *they did not yet know how to hold a pencil.* To hold and to manipulate a little stick securely, corresponds to the *acquisition of a special muscular mechanism which is independent of the writing movement*; it must in fact go along with the motions necessary to produce all of the various letter forms. It is, then, *a distinct mechanism*, which must exist together with the motor memory of the single graphic signs. When I provoked in the deficients the movements characteristic of writing by having them touch the letters with their fingers, I exercised mechanically the psychomotor paths, and fixed the muscular memory of each letter. There remained the preparation of the muscular mechanism necessary in holding and managing the instrument of writing, and this I provoked by adding two periods to the one already described. In the second period, the child touched the letter, not only with the index finger of his right hand, but with two, the index and the middle finger. In the third period, he touched the letters with a little wooden stick, held as a pen in writing. In substance I was making him repeat the same movements, now with, and now without, holding the instrument.

I have said that the child was to follow the *visual* image of the outlined letter. It is true that his finger had already been trained through touching the contours of the geometric figures, but this was not always a sufficient preparation. Indeed, even we grown people, when we trace a design through glass or tissue paper, cannot follow perfectly the line which we see and along which we should draw our pencil. The design should furnish some sort of control, some mechanical guide, for the pencil, in order to follow with *exactness* the trace, *sensible in reality only to the eye.*

The deficients, therefore, did not always follow the design exactly with either the finger or the stick. The didactic material did not offer *any control* in the work, or rather it offered only the uncertain control of the child's glance, which could, to be sure, see if the finger continued upon the sign, or not. I now thought that in order to have the pupil follow the movements more exactly, and to guide the execution more directly, I should need to prepare letter forms so indented, as to represent a *furrow* within which the wooden stick might run. I made the designs for this material, but the work being too expensive I was not able to carry out my plan.

A question . . .

Maria Montessori noted that she was struck by the likeness between darning and weaving with paper. She went on to say that she had also discovered something about how to teach writing while she was learning how to teach darning. In what ways does writing correspond with darning or weaving?

And an answer . . .

Maria Montessori wrote about forming a new concept. Perhaps the easiest way to form a new concept is to ask, "What is my subject like?" or "What does it remind me of?" Here we are concerned with analogy, the process of recognizing similarities between two things. Making analogies seems to be one of man's favorite linguistic devices. Some good analogies have become clichés because they so clearly present a concept: *a man's home is his castle; she's an old battle-ax; this car purrs like a kitten.* Making an analogy is a simple way of finding new concepts. (Again, don't expect *all* new concepts to be useful or better than old ones.)

An exercise . . .

In order to see how analogy can work to create new concepts for you, make a list parallel to the activities here. Do not include activities from list 1. Now take an activity from one list and create phrases which present the activity in terms of an activity from the other list. For example, whirlpool of assignments (swimming and studying), an end run around the Internal Revenue Service (football and paying taxes). Avoid clichés and pat phrases like "shot down by my date" and "three shots and you're out." Also, do not write similes (x is like y). They too easily unite different things without actually creating new insight.

List 1	*Your list*	*Phrases*
Studying	_____	_____
		_____
		_____
Walking	_____	_____
		_____
		_____
Writing	_____	_____
		_____

Bathing   _____   _____

                                         _____

                                         _____

Golfing   _____   _____

                                         _____

                                         _____

Playing football _____   _____

                                         _____

                                         _____

Breathing   _____   _____

                                         _____

                                         _____

Sculpting   _____   _____

                                         _____

                                         _____

Reading   _____   _____

                                         _____

                                         _____

Humming   _____   _____

                                         _____

                                         _____

TWO WRITERS, TWO WAYS

Samuel Taylor Coleridge and William Wordsworth jointly wrote the volume *Lyrical Ballads*. They were conscious of presenting it as a clear break with the old forms and content of eighteenth-century poetry. In order to revive poetic imagination, they carefully planned the job each would undertake. Here is Coleridge's account.

Samuel Taylor Coleridge

from Biographia Literaria

During the first year that Mr. Wordsworth and I were neighbours, our conversations turned frequently on the two cardinal points of poetry, the power of exciting the sympathy of the reader by a faithful adherence to the truth of nature, and the power of giving the interest of novelty by the modifying colors of imagination. The sudden charm, which accidents of light and shade, which moon-light or sun-set diffused over a known and familiar landscape, appeared to represent the practicability of combining both. These are the poetry of nature. The thought suggested itself (to which of us I do not recollect) that a series of poems might be composed of two sorts. In the one, the incidents and agents were to be, in part at least, supernatural; and the excellence aimed at was to consist in the interesting of the affections by the dramatic truth of such emotions, as would naturally accompany such situations, supposing them real. And real in *this* sense they have been to every human being who, from whatever source of delusion, has at any time believed himself under supernatural agency. For the second class, subjects were to be chosen from ordinary life; the characters and incidents were to be such, as will be found in every village and its vicinity, where there is a meditative and feeling mind to seek after them, or to notice them, when they present themselves.

In this idea originated the plan of the "Lyrical Ballads"; in which it was agreed, that my endeavors should be directed to persons and characters supernatural, or at least romantic; yet so as to transfer from our inward nature a human interest and a semblance of truth sufficient to procure for these shadows of imagination that willing supsension of disbelief for the moment, which constitutes poetic faith. Mr. Wordsworth, on the other hand, was to propose to himself as his object, to give the charm of novelty to things of every day, and to excite a feeling analogous to the supernatural, by awakening the mind's attention from the lethargy of custom, and directing it to the loveliness and the wonders of the world before us; an inexhaustible treasure, but for which, in consequence of the film of familiarity and selfish solicitude we have eyes, yet see not, ears that hear not, and hearts that neither feel nor understand.

❀   ❀   ❀   ❀   ❀

[About Wordsworth's poetry]

It was the union of deep feeling with profound thought; the fine balance of truth in observing, with the imaginative faculty in modifying the objects observed; and above all the original gift of spreading the tone, the *atmosphere*, and with it the depth and height of the ideal world around forms, incidents, and situations, of which, for the common view, custom had bedimmed all the lustre, had dried up the sparkle and the dew drops. "To find no contradiction in the union of old and new; to contemplate the ANCIENT of days and all his works with feelings as fresh, as if all had then sprang forth at the first creative fiat; characterizes the mind that feels the riddle of the world, and may help to unravel it. To carry on the feelings of childhood into the powers of manhood; to combine the child's sense of wonder and novelty with the appearances, which every day for perhaps forty years had rendered familiar;

> 'With sun and moon and stars throughout the year,
> And man and woman;'

this is the character and privilege of genius, and one of the marks which distinguish genius from talents. And therefore is it the prime merit of genius and its most unequivocal mode of manifestation, so to represent familiar objects as to awaken in the minds of others a kindred feeling concerning them and that freshness of sensation which is the constant accompaniment of mental, no less than of bodily, convalescence. Who has not a thousand times seen snow fall on water? Who has not watched it with a new feeling, from the time that he has read Burns' comparison of sensual pleasure

> 'To snow that falls upon a river
> A moment white—then gone for ever!'

In poems, equally as in philosophic disquisitions, genius produces the strongest impressions of novelty, while it rescues the most admitted truths from the impotence caused by the very circumstance of their universal admission. Truths of all others the most awful and mysterious, yet being at the same time of universal interest, are too often considered as *so* true, that they lose all the life and efficiency of truth, and lie bed-ridden in the dormitory of the soul, side by side with the most despised and exploded errors."—THE FRIEND, p. 76, No. 5.

Exercise . . .

For the writer, words are just possibilities until fitted to the purpose at hand. Read Stephen Spender's poem. Note what he says about language and the writer.

Stephen Spender

Word

The word bites like a fish.
Shall I throw it back free
Arrowing to that sea
Where thoughts lash tail and fin?
Or shall I pull it in
To rhyme upon a dish?

1. In what ways is the word–fish analogy an appropriate one?
2. Could we compare the dish to a concept?

A group of psychologists invited Richard Wilbur to talk to them about how he created poems, and he spoke to them extemporally. In his account of one particular poem, he very clearly revealed how analogy aided him in realizing and communicating something new about an ordinary scene.

Richard Wilbur

The Problem of Creative
Thinking in Poetry

This is going to be very informal in the strict sense; that is, it's going to be shapeless. I scribbled some remarks down before lunch, and as I look at them now they seem pretty dreadful, but I'll talk them to you anyway. I'm not going to defend modern poetry. Perhaps I'll be given a chance to later on. What this amounts to is a series of footnotes to the two talks which you've already heard. I'm not a theorist about the arts; I'm not equipped to compare creativity in science with creativity in art; but perhaps I can give some naive testimony for you to interpret. To be theoretical a moment, I do suspect that there is no great gulf between scientific and artistic creativeness. Pascal invented the adding machine; he also invented a new literary style. Edgar Allan Poe, in his early writings, felt an antagonism between the scientific and the poetic minds, but toward the end of his career he was very much impressed by learning of Kepler's testimony that he'd made his discoveries as a result of hunches and guesses. Poe came at last to feel that the two kinds of intellect were equally poetic. It's not in their processes but in their final criteria for truth that the poetic and scientific minds seem to differ. We judge a poem by its shapeliness, its adequacy to the data considered, and its inclusiveness. By inclusiveness I mean what Coleridge meant when he said that poetry brings the whole soul of man into activity, accounting for all the scope and self-contradiction of mental experience. These criteria aren't of course foreign to science. Surely there is some resemblance between the shapeliness of a poem and the elegance of a mathematical demonstration, and I wonder if in modern descriptive physics there isn't some such criterion as "adequacy" operating. Poetry and science do differ sharply in regard to demonstrability. An adding machine is demonstrably right or wrong. A poem is not demonstrably right or wrong, good or bad, whatever our "scientific" literary critics may suppose. To repeat what I've said before, I suspect that scientists and poets differ far less in their creative processes than in their final criteria for truth, and I would guess that the optimum conditions for poetic creation are also the optimum conditions for scientific creation.

Now, to give a little of this naïve testimony about the poetic process as I experience it. Mr. Olsen kindly sent me, several days ago, a copy of a speech on the subject of invention which he delivered last year. In that speech he borrows from Mr. Graham Wallas four steps in the inventive process. These are called preparation, incubation, illumination and verification. I'll see if I can say what these four steps might be in my experience. Like the scientist, the poet is out to control the world though in a different way. The poet tries to do this first by naming things; that's the primitive poetic act—you're a chair, you're a table, you're a tree. To apply words to objects is to redeem them from namelessness and get them under your verbal control, your symbolic control. Francis Ponge, the French poet, said a while ago that man clings to language as the oyster clings to his shell. Language is a defensive thing. The poet assigns values to things: that tree is good, etc., and he relates things in terms of these values, making them into patterns. He knits together a version of the world. All the poet's constructions of course are provisional. Even such a tight and inclusive construction as Dante's *Divine Comedy* was only provisional. You have to write another poem after any poem you may write. The poet is involved in a constant struggle to reduce the world to imaginative order, an imaginative order that will stay there for a few minutes. The need to write a poem arises, I think, from the feeling that the world is getting out of hand, that it's shaking itself free from the names and values and patterns that the poet has previously imposed on it. This may happen five minutes after you've written a poem. In other words, the mother of invention for the poet is an inner necessity to reassert his imaginative control over the world. A poem begins with a feeling of inadequacy. That's the preparation stage, or part of it, anyway. The preparation for a poem may also include the development of some very slight notion as to what elements the coming poem may contain. But at this point, these elements will be completely awash and unrelated in the mind. It's important that they be unrelated. The incubation period of a poem may be short or long, but for me it involves first a retreat from language, the cultivation of a state of apparent stupidity. During this time the mind retreats as far as possible into a preverbal condition, and moves around among its fundamental images: brightness, darkness, falling, rising, that kind of thing. I suppose the condition is one which your mind deliberately refuses to relate the potential elements of a poem in any final or fully conscious way. They shake around at the bottom of the mind as bits of color in a kaleidoscope, and you consciously avoid any decision as to what patterns they might take. All the while, of course, the less conscious portion of the mind is making fluid experiments in pattern, trying on this and that, though you don't know it. At this stage in the coming of a poem I haven't any idea as to what the paraphrasable content of the poem is going to be when it comes—its prose meaning. I don't know what the poem is going to "say." At most I'll have some idea as to the mood of the poem, its probable size, its probable scope, the extent to which it's going to ramify. The poem doesn't begin with a meaning, it works towards meaning—it finds out what it's about. Only when you write the poem do you find out what it has to say. After all, this isn't disreputable. A poem is, as one of the previous speakers said, more than it means, more than the sum of its parts. It is the total pattern of the poem, the presentation of a state of psychic harmony, the whole soul in action, to which we respond.

The stage of creation called illumination seems to come at various points and in various ways. For William Butler Yeats, the poem began to create itself by appearing in his mind as a persistent musical phrase, a set of rhythms and sounds demanding words. For me, the poem is likely to start with the recognition of some resemblance between things which by implication points out a resemblance between ideas or fields of experience. Let's take one of the most hackneyed resemblances in poetry, that between the Fall of the year and the leaves, and the close of a human life. A poem for me is likely to begin with the irruption into consciousness of a few good fresh words which convey such a resemblance. That of course is only the beginning. At this point in the creation of a poem, which is the beginning of the stage called verification, you have a sense that the whole pattern of it exists potentially but still somewhat fluidly in the unconscious. You don't know where you're going, but you do know that you're going somewhere. In other words, you have an overriding premonition that the poem is going to take shape. The writing of the poem is a matter of making moment-by-moment choices among possibilities proposed by the unconscious. As Baudelaire said, in the process of writing a poem the poet must be hypnotist and subject at once. This is a very ticklish business. You have to give the unconscious free play, and at the same time shape the proposals of the unconscious into something that makes daylight sense. You have to be serious and logical with part of your being but playful and spontaneous with another part of your being. One great means, by the way, to a happy relationship between conscious and unconscious in poetry, is the use of rhyme. Victor Hugo said, "Between two words which rhyme there operates a kind of obligation to produce metaphor." This is very true, as you can prove at any moment by trying it on yourself, if you say to yourself any two rhyme words—for instance, dog, log . . . Of course, those are too close together, aren't they? But given any two rhyme words, your mind would start right off struggling to form some kind of phrase or visual image which would combine the two. Take lake and rake, for instance. By what imaginative means might you reconcile these words lake and rake? You might reconcile them first by means of a visual image. Looking out of a window over a hotel lawn, seeing the gardener raking the lawn and a glimpse of a lake in the distance. That's a sort of low-order way of reconciling these two rhyme words. Another more poetic person might recall that the wind, as it sweeps over the surface of a lake, very often furrows the water, as a rake might. Another more verbal imagination, a James Joyce kind of imagination, might recall that Lance-lot of the Lake in his dealings with Guinevere was something of a rake. So rhyme, as you see, is one of the many techniques by which the poet extorts suggestions from his unconscious mind. If the poem is going to be good, the poet must choose very carefully from these suggestions.

I hope the discussion period will give me a chance to be clearer and fuller. I'd like before we're through to read a poem and see if I can point out one or two of the things which I think made it jell—made it decide to take the shape it did. I want in closing very quickly to deduce one or two things about ideal conditions for creation from what I've said about the creative process. The incubation period, as I said, has to be a period of stupidity and apparent aimlessness, and it may go on for many days or weeks. Therefore, I think the situation of the creative person should be either one of solitary grandeur—with the door always open, of course, into the world—or one of solitary confinement. We mustn't be exposed to the ordinary tempo and pressures of daily life, at any rate not all the time. Yeats, the Irish poet to whom I've just referred, lived in a tower; and the Marquis de Sade, another great though little known poet, spent most of his time in prison. You can't be creative if someone is standing at your elbow urging you to produce; nor can you think creative think-ing in an office full of signs reading "Think."

This is done, I assure you, on the spur of the moment. It's going to be handsomely confused. But I thought it might be fun to read you a poem and then to distinguish some of the various kinds of adhesive there are in it, and try to guess—and it will be purely guesswork for me—where it began. The poem is about the experience of crossing the Pepperpot Bridge in Boston on the subway. The subway crosses the Charles River, as you know, into Boston over the Pepperpot Bridge, and for a moment you get a glimpse up and down the river. This happened, oh, I suppose, about March 20 or so, whenever the ice begins to break up on the Charles. It's probably pretty relevant that this is a Spring poem. Spring and poetry are always related, and I think rightly so. You do have to write a poem in Spring explaining that you're on the side of life and against death. It's a terrible demand, but it's laid upon you. I understand that the suicide rate is always highest in the Spring, and this is because, I suppose, people can't measure up to the emotional demands which the season makes; and I believe the suicide rate is highest of all in Norway, because the season comes most suddenly and violently there, after a long and deep winter. So, one of the fundamental things in this poem is that it's declaring for life. It's called "A Glance From The Bridge."

A Glance from the Bridge

Letting the eye descend from reeking stack
And black facade to where the river goes,
You see the freeze has started in to crack
(As if the city squeezed it in a vice)
And here and there the limbering water shows,
And gulls colonial on the sullied ice.
Some rise and braid their glidings, white and spare,
Or sweep the hemmed-in river up and down,
Making a litheness in the barriered air,
And through the town the freshening water swirls
As if an ancient whore undid her gown,
And showed a body almost like a girl's.

I'll read that once more, so that you can get the thing in mind. (He reads it again). Here, I think, there is a pretty good example of what I believe Mr. Thurstone was speaking of: subject matter as a means to the poem, not as the poem in itself. You have in the first place, here, a description of the scene itself, with all the necessary items for getting some kind of a visual image of it; black buildings and stacks on either side of the river, and cracking ice in the center, and gulls on the ice floes, and water perceived here and there through the cracks in the ice. There's some pleasure to be got from simple description, and poetry rides a great deal on that, but you can't make a whole poem of it. Another thing this poem does, on a higher poetic level, is to displace the obvious contrast between black banks and bright river, in the direction of certain ideas. Black buildings, white river are made to correspond to youth and age. The water is limber, the black banks are by implication aged, or dead. I'm for the water. That's why this is a poem about life. Again, freshness and fertility are suggested by the water; city filth and deadness are contrasted to these things. Innocence and vice are suggested by this word "vice" in the fourth line, which has an obvious double play and is picked up by the prostitute business at the end. Innocence is attributed to the white river, vice to the city, as is only right. The word colonial also displaces the meaning a little. There's one line in the poem which describes the gulls in groups on floes of ice as "gulls colonial on the sullied ice." This is a poem laid in New England: one thinks of colonial New England, then, and compares that time with the present degraded state of the region. So, this original description with its built-in visual contrast, ramified in a lot of ideal ways as well, has a whole set of parallel attitudes reconciled through the overtones of words. By this means the single scene is made to reflect and unify a number of attitudes. And this is reinforced by the underlying visual similarity of the two main images in the poem: the black banks on either side, the white river in between; the gown—the black gown of the woman—and the white body in between. Here I think we approach the abstract shapeliness of the poem towards which all the rest is a means, or to which all the rest is subsidiary. I strongly suspect that this poem began when these two visual patterns the woman in her gown, the black banks and the white ice, combined in my mind; that this begot the poem, and not any of the ideas which subsequently grew out of the banks—and—river image. Now, of course, finally, the total experience of the poem—and the most abstract experience of the poem—is the experience of the resonance of this combination of paralleled ideas, their unity through the prevailing image: the resonance, also, of the technical tricks employed in the poem, the returns, the rhymes, the meter itself. The main experience of a poem is something given off by the technique of the poem as a whole but as it interprets a state of balanced sensibility. Well, I think working off the top of my head I've wrung all I can out of this. Maybe I'll just try your patience by giving this poem a last reading. (He reads it again.)

The approach to writing in this book is relatively new. So why shouldn't an analogy be used to make it clearer? Much of our approach was first tried by Gordon Rohman and Albert Wlecke. Here is their view of writing as developed by analogy.

Gordon Rohman and Albert Wlecke
Strategy and Tactics in Writing

Military men divide the art of war into strategy and tactics. Generals take care of the former; sergeants the latter. Strategy involves the whole field of operations; tactics the specific field of the foxhole and the soldier. Strategy disposes of armies; tactics of squads. Strategy wins wars; tactics win battles.

The art of writing is analogous. Strategy here involves the large-scale planning and directing to insure that the idea gets stated, developed, compared and contrasted with skill; the intelligence to adjust the means to the ends of the composition desired and the audience imagined; the maneuvering of large bodies of proof and demonstration to support the offensive drive of the major idea; the mopping up of all possible objections to the idea in summation; and, finally, the setting of peace terms in conclusion. Strategy in writing means, in other words, defining a subject and assembling materials in relation to it. Defining a subject is not simply saying, "I think I'll write about American politics," or "I think I'll write about nature," anymore than a general can simply yell "Charge!" The strategy of wars (Hannibal crossing the Alps, Eisenhower crossing the Channel), and the strategy of composition ("Roosevelt Packs the Supreme Court," *Walden*) need specific ends. From the vague and generalized aspiration, the good general and the good writer move to the precisely defined and limited objective. Failing in the specialization, neither can assemble forces to get the war won, the composition written: Hannibal needed elephants, Eisenhower landing craft. In addition, the general or the writer, to be strategically effective, must single-mindedly fix his attention upon the object of his campaign. Neither Hannibal nor Eisenhower could have triumphed without singleness of purpose. The subject, when finally defined, is really the subject as seen by a writer's particular way of regarding it; the war, when finally understood, is really the enemy as held by the general's particular way of engaging him.

Strategy concerns planning, tactics concern procedure within the broad decisions laid down by the general staff. Tactics in writing include such things as what to begin with, what to end with, what level of usage to employ, what sorts of proof to marshall, what kind of wit to employ, and, of course, what degree of "correctness" to insist on. Tactics in military maneuver are full of short charges and withdrawals, digging in, enveloping a position, flank attack, hurrying up and waiting, boldness and caution, planning and guessing. The tactics of writing also involve drafting and redrafting, writing and erasing, checking and rechecking, hurrying through an inspired insight, and waiting for the cool detachment of criticism, witty maneuvers of metaphor, bold envelopment of analogies, and a good deal of plain marching of sentences in good order.

We contend that good writing is good strategy first and foremost. The wholeness of the whole composition we must first secure or all is lost; poor strategy loses wars, poor tactics only battles. Too often we are concerned only with the tactics of "correct" grammar, too seldom for the strategy of good design in writing. While we fuss with formalities, we lose the war. Sentences in Class A uniforms, Fowlered, Perrined, and Webstered, gallop off to annihilation like Tennyson's Six Hundred. The art of war is strategy first, tactics second. The art of writing cannot improve on this wisdom.

Analogies need not be very obvious. In May Sarton's poem, a human face and a mountain are the things brought together, but underlying them is a further analogy involving geometry.

May Sarton
Colorado Mountains

Plain grandeur escapes definition. You
Cannot speak about the mountains well.
About the clear plane, the sharp shadow
You cannot tell.

Mountains define you. You cannot define
Them. And all your looking serves to set
What you have learned of the stern line
Against the absolute.

The frail taut structure of a human face
Beside the sheer cliff drawn, all that you loved,
All that can stand in such a bare clear place
Is to be proved.

And love that is a landscape in the past
Becomes, like mountains, changeless. It is there.
It is standing against its own image at last
In a high air.

"Colorado Mountains" reprinted from *Cloud, Stone, Sun, Vine: Poems, Selected and New* by May Sarton. By permission of W. W. Norton & Company, Inc. Copyright © 1961 by May Sarton.

Analogy also operates in the following excerpt from a short story, "The Hollow." A college student and his girlfriend are parked in the woods, when they hear a call for help from down in a hollow. They cannot see, so the boy starts down to investigate. The ordinary actions are given more depth by the use of a somewhat hidden analogy.

Wallace Kaufman

from The Hollow

"*Help!*" Again only the one word. And so strong. She watched Bart as he listened for some noise to locate the voice. If help were needed, they were not giving it, but who would want help out here, miles from the nearest house or road? "Ask what's wrong," she whispered to Bart.

Without turning, he raised a hand and motioned her to be quiet. "*I'm coming down,*" he shouted, beginning to descend quietly among the rocks.

"HELP!"

"Okay," Bart answered. He stopped and looked back. "Wait in the car," he said and began to descend faster.

She looked back at the car but could not go and sit there and close the door and wait, all closed in. Standing on a rock she followed with her eyes as far as she could, glad that he moved easily over the rocks and that he was strong. Even glad that he had not waited any longer. He was out of sight quickly and soon out of hearing though she guessed he had gone down and to her left. She still strained for sight and sound but received none as if trying to follow a diver under water. For a moment she even had the feeling that a long delay would indicate something as bad as drowning. She was as much alone as if he had never called for her this afternoon. If she were his wife, he might have taken her along. No, that was stupid. She should have gone, not waited to be asked.

Her own name startled her. It came up out of the hollow louder than she had ever heard it. In her first fright her mind translated her own echoing name into the word she waited for—help. Then she wished she had heard it right. "Vanity," she said to herself at the very moment Bart called again.

"*Here,*" she yelled back, her voice ringing like a shrill pipe in contrast to his.

"*Can you find your way down?*"

"*Yes. I think so.*" She should have said just yes. Any motion was better than waiting in the empty dusk-filled woods for someone she could not see.

She started down carefully, testing each of the smaller rocks she had to step on. When it came to climbing she was a stringbean. Too bad they didn't teach you dancing right out in the woods instead of in gym. She was glad Bart could not see her. Finding the slope easier than she had expected and the hollow not as dark as it seemed, she hurried her descent. She twisted her ankle once but only enough to restore her caution. Halfway down she stopped to listen. Before, she had thought of Bart as a diver, now the silence made her a diver also, moving with only faith toward a guessed location. "Bart?" she called.

THREE POEMS

Samuel Taylor Coleridge

from The Rime of the Ancient Mariner

PART IV

The Wedding-Guest feareth that a Spirit is talking to him;	'I fear thee, ancient Mariner! I fear thy skinny hand! And thou art long, and lank, and brown, As is the ribbed sea-sand.[1]

---

[1]For the last two lines of this stanza, I am indebted to Mr. WORDSWORTH. It was on a delightful walk from Nether Stowey to Dulverton, with him and his sister, in the Autumn of 1797, that this Poem was planned, and in part composed.

I fear thee and thy glittering eye,
And thy skinny hand, so brown.'—

*But the
ancient Ma-
riner assureth
him of his
bodily life, and
proceedeth to
relate his hor-
rible penance.*

Fear not, fear not, thou Wedding-Guest!
This body dropt not down.

Alone, alone, all, all alone,
Alone on a wide wide sea!
And never a saint took pity on
My soul in agony.

*He despiseth
the creatures
of the calm,*

The many men, so beautiful!
And they all dead did lie:
And a thousand thousand slimy things
Lived on; and so did I.

*And envieth
that* they
*should live,
and so many
lie dead.*

I looked upon the rotting sea,
And drew my eyes away;
I looked upon the rotting deck,
And there the dead men lay.

I looked to heaven, and tried to pray;
But or ever a prayer had gusht,
A wicked whisper came, and made
My heart as dry as dust.

I closed my lids, and kept them close,
And the balls like pulses beat;
For the sky and the sea, and the sea and the sky
Lay like a load on my weary eye,
And the dead were at my feet.

*But the curse
liveth for him
in the eye of
the dead men.*

The cold sweat melted from their limbs,
Nor rot nor reek did they:
The look with which they looked on me
Had never passed away.

An orphan's curse would drag to hell
A spirit from on high;
But oh! more horrible than that
Is the curse in a dead man's eye!
Seven days, seven nights, I saw that curse,
And yet I could not die.

The moving Moon went up the sky,
In his lone-
liness and   And a star or two beside—
fixedness he   Softly she was going up,
yearneth to-
wards the   And a star or two beside—
journeying
Moon, and the   Her beams bemocked the sultry main,
stars that still
sojourn, yet   Like April hoar-frost spread;
still move   But where the ship's huge shadow lay,
onward; and
every where   The charméd water burnt alway
the blue sky   A still and awful red.
belongs to

them, and is their appointed rest, and their native country and their own natural
homes, which they enter unannounced, as lords that are certainly expected and yet
there is a silent joy at their arrival.

By the light   Beyond the shadow of the ship,
of the Moon he
beholdeth   I watched the water-snakes:
God's crea-   They moved in tracks of shining white,
tures of the
great calm.   And when they reared, the elfish light
Fell off in hoary flakes.

Within the shadow of the ship
I watched their rich attire:
Blue, glossy green, and velvet black,
They coiled and swam; and every track
Was a flash of golden fire.

Their beauty   O happy living things! no tongue
and their
happiness.   Their beauty might declare:
A spring of love gushed from my heart,

He blesseth   And I blessed them unaware:
them in his
heart.   Sure my kind saint took pity on me,
And I blessed them unaware.

The spell   The self-same moment I could pray;
begins to
break.   And from my neck so free
The Albatross fell off, and sank
Like lead into the sea.

William Wordsworth
Stepping Westward

While my Fellow-traveller and I were walking by the side of Loch Ketterine, one fine evening after sunset, in our road to a Hut where, in the course of our Tour, we had been hospitably entertained some weeks before, we met, in one of the loneliest parts of that solitary region, two well-dressed Women, one of whom said to us, by way of greeting, "What, you are stepping westward?"

"WHAT, you are stepping westward?"—"Yea."
—'Twould be a *wildish* destiny,
If we, who thus together roam
In a strange Land, and far from home,
Were in this place the guests of Chance:
Yet who would stop, or fear to advance,
Though home or shelter he had none,
With such a sky to lead him on?

The dewy ground was dark and cold;
Behind, all gloomy to behold;
And stepping westward seemed to be
A kind of *heavenly* destiny:
I liked the greeting; 'twas a sound
Of something without place or bound;
And seemed to give me spiritual right
To travel through that region bright.

The voice was soft, and she who spake
Was walking by her native lake:
The salutation had to me
The very sound of courtesy:
Its power was felt; and while my eye
Was fixed upon the glowing Sky,
The echo of the voice enwrought
A human sweetness with the thought
Of travelling through the world that lay
Before me in my endless way.

The Solitary Reaper

Behold her, single in the field,
Yon solitary Highland Lass!
Reaping and singing by herself;
Stop here, or gently pass!
Alone she cuts and binds the grain,
And sings a melancholy strain;
O listen! for the Vale profound
Is overflowing with the sound.

No Nightingale did ever chaunt
More welcome notes to weary bands
Of travellers in some shady haunt,
Among Arabian sands:
A voice so thrilling ne'er was heard
In spring-time from the Cuckoo-bird,
Breaking the silence of the seas
Among the farthest Hebrides.

Will no one tell me what she sings?—
Perhaps the plaintive numbers flow
For old, unhappy, far-off things,
And battles long ago:
Or is it some more humble lay,
Familiar matter of to-day?
Some natural sorrow, loss, or pain,
That has been, and may be again?

Whate'er the theme, the Maiden sang
As if her song could have no ending;
I saw her singing at her work,
And o'er the sickle bending;—
I listened, motionless and still;
And, as I mounted up the hill,
The music in my heart I bore,
Long after it was heard no more.

Seven questions . . .

1. In the selection from "The Rime of the Ancient Mariner," does Coleridge succeed in making the strange seem familiar? Conversely, does either Wordsworth poem make the familiar seem strange?

   2. In what ways do you find analogy present in these poems by Wordsworth and Coleridge?

3. Looking back at the chapter, can you think of any other analogies which Richard Wilbur might have used for his scene? Does his analogy suit you or would you want something different?

   4. How does analogy determine Wilbur's techniques?

5. In Rohman and Wlecke's essay, could they have used a third part of the analogy called logistics? Did they give writing a warlike tone?

   6. What words in May Sarton's poem remind you of geometry? Does geometry separate or unite the face and the landscape?

7. What words in the excerpt from "The Hollow" are related to the diving analogy? How does the analogy reveal something of the relationship between the two lovers?

Assignment . . .

Choose a topic of interest to you and ask yourself what else it resembles. Make a free association list of analogies. Now choose the most interesting one and write a short essay that develops your subject in terms of that analogy. Do not get so carried away by the analogy that your subject is obscured.

DOCUMENTS

Carl Sandburg

The People, Yes

"So you want to divide all the money there is
 and give every man his share?"
"That's it. Put it all in one big pile and split
 it even for everybody."
"And the land, the gold, silver, oil, copper, you want
 that divided up?"
"Sure—an even whack for all of us."
"Do you mean that to go for horses and cows?"
"Sure—why not?"
"And how about pigs?"
"Oh to hell with you—you know I got a couple of
 pigs."

Frank Lloyd Wright

The Natural House

Every house worth considering as a work of art must have a grammar of its own. "Grammar," in this sense, means the same thing in any construction—whether it be of words or of stone or wood. It is the shape-relationship between the various elements that enter into the constitution of the thing. The "grammar" of the house is its manifest articulation of all its parts. This will be the "speech" it uses. To be achieved, construction must be grammatical.

Your limitations of feeling about what you are doing, your choice of materials for the doing (and your budget of course) determine largely what grammar your building will use. It is largely inhibited (or expanded) by the amount of money you have to spend, a feature only of the latitude you have. When the chosen grammar is finally adopted (you go almost indefinitely with it into everything you do) walls, ceilings, furniture, etc., become inspired by it. Everything has a related articulation in relation to the whole and all belongs together; looks well together because all together are speaking the same language. If one part of your house spoke Choctaw, another French, another English, and another some sort of gibberish, you would have what you mostly have now—not a very beautiful result. Thus, when you do adopt the "grammar" of your house—it will be the way the house is to be "spoken," "uttered." You must be consistently grammatical for it to be understood as a work of Art.

Consistency in grammar is therefore the property—solely—of a well-developed artist-architect. Without that property of the artist-architect not much can be done about your abode as a work of Art. Grammar is no property for the usual owner of the occupant of the house. But the man who designs the house must, inevitably, speak a consistent thought-language in his design. It properly may be and should be a language of his own if appropriate. If he has no language, so no grammar, of his own, he must adopt one; he will speak some language or other whether he so chooses or not. It will usually be some kind of argot.

Hedrich-Blessing.

11

The whole thing
~ from pre-writing
into writing

We have written about language and what it is and why we
use it. We have emphasized originality and individuality and
provided some checks and some tools for achieving these.
Now all of that must relate to actual writing. How do you
get from existential sentences and free association and analogy to a whole piece of original writing?

Our answer is that you take that step by recognizing
it as a step. In pre-writing you were asked for bits and
pieces—sentences, phrases, and paragraphs in which you
could begin to come to terms with your own experience
and belief. In writing, you are asked to take hold of your
experience and belief, and to make it known in a formal
way. Writing a longer work is obviously more difficult than
jotting down feelings, yet with the long piece as with the
short one, the form depends on you. You are not simply
choosing among other people's forms.

Even if you eventually arrive at agreement with an already established way of thinking, the agreement must be personal. Stephen Spender, a poet who briefly joined the Communist Party in the Thirties, says that even such great political choices must be made within the individual.

Today, we are constantly told that we must choose between the West and the East. Confronted by such a choice, I can only say that first and foremost, I am for neither West nor East, but for my self considered as a self—one of the millions who inhabit the earth. The conflict between East and West does not in itself involve a moral choice, if it is a choice within myself: that is to say, if having chosen my own self, my humanity, my conscience, I can then judge the rival claims of both sides. I do not *choose* America or Russia: I judge between them. If it seems absurd that an individual should set up as a judge between these vast powers, armed with their super human instruments of destruction, I can reply that the very immensity of the means to destroy proves that judging and being judged does not lie in these forces. For supposing that they achieved their utmost and destroyed our civilization, whoever survived would judge them by a few statements, a few poems, a few *temoignages*, surviving from all the ruins, a few words of those men who saw outside and beyond the means which were used and all the arguments which were marshalled in the service of those means.

Thus I could not escape from myself into some social situation of which my existence was a mere product, and my witnessing a wilfully distorting instrument. I had to be myself, choose and not be chosen.*

Pre-writing is a way of making a choice within yourself, of choosing your self in relation to your subject. In pre-writing, the writer takes an inert subject and finds a personal perspective. From there he can go on to make his choices or take his position. A good perspective will urge him to say more, to develop new ideas. It will suggest organization and purpose, and it will carry him into the formal assignment.

You can look at pre-writing as preparation and at the finished work as something which grows out of pre-writing when you have reached the point where you know you have something interesting to say and feel the need to say it. Or you might see pre-writing as soil, and the writing as a plant. Soil is of little use unless it grows something.

If you see writing in this way, then you will understand what makes the form and style of a composition important. The rules or modes or rhetoric by themselves do not make the act of writing important. It is the writer's perspective, his conceptualization, that makes modes and rhetorical forms important.

Following the plant analogy, we could say that a good essay is an organic one, one that grows naturally from its soil and is of one piece, rather than of bits and pieces bolted together. Meyer Abrams has formalized the plant analogy in his book *The Mirror and The Lamp.*

Meyer H. Abrams

The Mirror and the Lamp

What, then, are the characteristic properties of a plant, or of any living organism?

(1) The plant originates in a seed. To Coleridge, this indicates that the elementaristic principle is to be stood on its head; that the whole is primary and the parts secondary and derived.

"In the world we see every where evidences of a Unity, which the component parts are so far from explaining, that they necessarily pre-suppose it as the cause and condition of their existing *as* those parts; or even of their existing at all. . . . That the root, stem, leaves, petals, &c. [of this crocus] cohere to one plant, is owing to an antecedent Power or Principle in the Seed, which existed before a single particle of the matters that constitute the *size* and visibility of the crocus, had been attracted from the surrounding soil, air, and moisture."

'The difference between an inorganic and organic body,' he said elsewhere, 'lies in this: In the first . . . the whole is nothing more than a collection of the individual parts or phenomena,' while in the second, 'the whole is everything, and the parts are nothing.' And Coleridge extends the same principle to non-biological phenomena: 'Depend on it, whatever is grand, whatever is truly organic and living, the whole is prior to the parts.'

(2) The plant *grows*. 'Productivity or Growth,' Coleridge said, is 'the first power' of all living things, and it exhibits itself as 'evolution and extension in the Plant.' No less is this a power of the greatest poets. In Shakespeare, for example, we find '*Growth* as in a plant.' 'All is growth, evolution, *genesis*—each line, each word almost, begets the following. . . .' Partial and passing comparisons of a completed discourse or poem to an animal body are to be found as early as Plato and Aristotle, but a highly developed organismic theory, such as Coleridge's differs from such precedents in the extent to which all aspects of the analogy are exploited, and above all in the extraordinary stress laid on this attribute of growth. Coleridge's interest is persistently genetic—in the process as well as in the product; in becoming no less than in being. That is why Coleridge rarely discusses a finished poem without looking toward

From M. H. Abrams, *The Mirror and the Lamp* (New York: Oxford University Press, 1953), pp. 171–73.

323

the mental process which evolved it; this is what makes all his criticism so characteristically psychological.

(3) Growing, the plant assimilates to its own substance the alien and diverse elements of earth, air, light, and water. 'Lo!' cries Coleridge eloquently, on this congenial subject:

"Lo!—with the rising sun it commences its outward life and enters into open communion with all the elements, at once assimilating them to itself and to each other. . . Lo!—at the touch of light how it returns an air akin to light, and yet with the same pulse effectuates its own secret growth, still contracting to fix what expanding it had refined."

Extended from plant to mind, this property effects another revolution in associationist theory. In the elementarist scheme, all products of invention had consisted of recombinations of the unit images of sense. In Coleridge's organic theory, images of sense become merely materials on which the mind feeds—materials which quite lose their identity in being assimilated to a new whole. 'From the first, or initiative Idea, as from a seed, successive Ideas germinate.'

"Events and images, the lively and spirit-stirring machinery of the external world, are like light, and air, and moisture, to the seed of the Mind, which would else rot and perish. In all processes of mental evolution the objects of the senses must stimulate the hand and the Mind must in turn assimilate and digest the food which it thus receives from without."

At the same time the 'ideas,' which in the earlier theory had been fainter replicas of sensation, are metamorphosed into seeds that grow in the soil of sensation. By his 'abuse of the word "idea," ' Locke seems to say 'that the sun, the rain, the manure, and so on had made the wheat, had made the barley. . . . If for this you substitute the assertion that a grain of wheat might remain for ever and be perfectly useless and to all purposes nonapparent, had it not been that the congenial sunshine and proper soil called it forth—everything in Locke would be perfectly rational.' To Coleridge, the ideas of reason, and those in the imagination of the artist, are 'living and life-producing ideas, which . . . are essentially one with the germinal causes in nature. . . .'

(4) The plant evolves spontaneously from an internal source of energy—'effectuates,' as Coleridge put it, 'its own secret growth'—and organizes itself into its proper form. An artefact needs to be made, but a plant makes itself. According to one of Coleridge's favorite modes of stating this difference, in life 'the unity . . . is produced *ab intra*,' but in mechanism, '*ab extra*.' 'Indeed, evolution as contra-distinguished from apposition, or superinduction *ab aliunde*, is implied in the conception of life. . . .' In the realm of mind, this is precisely the difference between a 'free and rival originality' and that 'lifeless mechanism' which by servile

imitation imposes an alien form on inorganic materials. As he says, echoing A. W. Schlegel:

"The form is mechanic when on any given material we impress a predetermined form . . . as when to a mass of wet clay we give whatever shape we wish it to retain when hardened. The organic form, on the other hand, is innate; it shapes as it develops itself from within, and the fullness of its development is one and the same with the perfection of its outward form."

The plant analogy of course is only a way of thinking about writing. We use it to demonstrate the relationship between writer and writing. The plant analogy is a concrete image that we use to communicate the central idea of this book. However, you can use the plant analogy also to plan or outline your own writing. The analogy is more detailed than the notes you will usually make, but try it a few times to see if you get a clearer sense of organization and plan. Here are one student's notes following the plant analogy.

TOPIC—Barber Shop

SEED IDEA—The barber shop can form a kind of intellectual center.

GROWTH—A barber talks all day

He talks to a diversity of customers

Sample conversations

Barber as moderator between customers

Shops differ

Suppose these centers were deliberately taken over by idea men? or propagandists?

Perhaps the nature of the shops as they are now is valuable and a good example of unacknowledged public forum

Peaceful compared to most forums today.

ASSIMILATION—Diverse and foreign elements include propaganda agents, customers' occupations, democracy. None of these usually seem relevant to barber shops.

INNER ENERGY—Seeing the shop as an intellectual center, I wanted to talk of intellectuals or intellect, of conversations. Since American barber shops have a unique character, I wanted to talk about the country they are in. This is the development of what psychologists call the hedonic response—the feeling of pleasurable rightness in a concept.

ACHIEVED STRUCTURE—I am working outward from individuals, from individual shops to a generalization and finally a national setting. Sort of an upside down triangle, surrounded by a circle.

Any of these steps might have been different, but then the whole essay would have shifted in content or meaning. The main point is that the writer seems to have found a natural development of ideas, and this development unfolds from his seed idea.

READINGS AND EXERCISE

Let's assume that the process of writing each of the following selections could be described by the plant analogy. In each piece analyze the steps in writing beginning with the seed idea, the subject plus perspective.

Vachel Lindsay

Factory Windows
Are Always Broken

Factory windows are always broken.
Somebody's always throwing bricks,
Somebody's always heaving cinders,
Playing ugly Yahoo tricks.

Factory windows are always broken.
Other windows are let alone.
No one throws through the chapel-window
The bitter, snarling derisive stone.

Factory windows are always broken.
Something or other is going wrong,
Something is rotten—I think, in Denmark.
End of the factory-window song.

William Wordsworth

Composed Upon Westminster Bridge, Sept. 3, 1802

Earth has not anything to show more fair:
Dull would he be of soul who could pass by
A sight so touching in its majesty:
This city now dowth, like a garment, wear
The beauty of the morning: silent, bare,
Ships, towers, domes, theaters, and temples lie
open unto the fields, and to the sky;
All bright and glittering in the smokeless air.
Never did sun more beautifully steep
In his first splendor, valley, rock or hill;
Ne'er saw I, never felt, a calm so deep:
The river glideth at his own sweet will:
Dear God: the very houses seem asleep;
And all that mighty heart is lying still.

Four questions about the selections from Lindsay and Wordsworth . . .

1. Lindsay's poem is from a time when labor-management relations were often violent. Which point of view does Lindsay take?

2. How does the allusion to *Hamlet* get into Lindsay's poem?

3. Wordsworth is best known for rural poetry. What went through his mind in seeing London that early morning?

4. What underlying analogy does Wordsworth use in making his feeling concrete?

Francis Bacon

Of Studies

Studies serve for delight, for ornament, and for ability. Their chief use for delight is in privateness and retiring; for ornament, is in discourse; and for ability, is in the judgment and disposition of business; for expert men can execute, and perhaps judge of particulars, one by one; but the general counsels, and the plots and marshaling of the affairs come best from those that are learned. To spend too much time in studies is sloth; to use them too much for ornament is affectation; to make judgment wholly by their rules is the humor of a scholar. They perfect nature, and are perfected by experience; for natural abilities are like natural plants, that need pruning by study; and studies themselves do give forth directions too much at large, except they be bounded in my experience. Crafty men contemn studies, simple men admire them, and wise men use them; for they teach not their own use; but that is a wisdom without them and above them, won by observation. Read not to contradict and confute, nor to believe and take for granted, nor to find talk and discourse, but to weigh and consider. Some books are to be tasted, others to be swallowed, and some few to be chewed and digested; that is, some books are to be read only in parts; others to be read but not curiously, and some few to be read wholly, and with diligence and attention. Some books also may be read by deputy, and extracts made of them by others; but that would be only in the less important arguments and the meaner sort of books; else distilled books are, like common distilled waters, flashy things. Reading maketh a full man; conference a ready man; and writing an exact man. And, therefore, if a man write little, he had need have a great memory; if he confer little he had need have a present wit; and if he read little, he had need have much cunning, to seem to know that he doth not. Histories make men wise; poets, and rhetoric, able to contend. *Abeunt studia in mores* (studies develop into habits— Ovid). Nay, there is no stand or impediment in the wit but may be wrought out by fit studies; like as diseases of the body may have appropriate exercises. Bowling is good for stone and kidneys, shooting for the lungs and breast, gentle walking for the stomach, riding for the head, and the like. So if a man's wit be wandering, let him study the mathematics; for in demonstrations, if his wit be called away never so little, he must begin again. If his wit be not apt to distinguish or find differences, let him study the schoolman; for they are hair-splitters! If he be not apt to beat over matters, and to call up one thing to prove and illustrate another, let him study the lawyers' cases. So every defect of the mind may have a special receipt.

Two questions on the selection from Bacon . . .

1. In two words from the first sentence, give a possible statement of the seed idea.

   2. If you had to divide this into paragraphs or important transitions in thought, where would you make your divisions?

E. B. White

Once More to the Lake — August 1941

One summer, along about 1904, my father rented a camp on a lake in Maine and took us all there for the month of August. We all got ringworm from some kittens and had to rub Pond's Extract on our arms and legs night and morning, and my father rolled over in a canoe with all his clothes on; but outside of that the vacation was a success and from then on none of us ever thought there was any place in the world like that lake in Maine. We returned summer after summer—always on August 1st for one month. I have since become a salt-water man, but sometimes in summer there are days when the restlessness of the tides and the fearful cold of the sea water and the incessant wind that blows across the afternoon and into the evening make me wish for the placidity of a lake in the woods. A few weeks ago this feeling got so strong I bought myself a couple of bass hooks and a spinner and returned to the lake where we used to go, for a week's fishing and to revisit old haunts.

I took along my son, who had never had any fresh water up his nose and who had seen lily pads only from train windows. On the journey over to the lake I began to wonder what it would be like. I wondered how time would have marred this unique, this holy spot—the coves and streams, the hills that the sun set behind, the camps and the paths behind the camps. I was sure that the tarred road would have found it out and I wondered in what other ways it would be desolated. It is strange how much you can remember about places like that once you allow your mind to return into the grooves that lead back. You remember one thing, and that suddenly reminds you of another thing. I guess I remembered clearest of all the early mornings, when the lake was cool and motionless, remembered how the bedroom smelled of the lumber it was made of and of the wet woods whose scent entered through the screen. The partitions in the camp were thin and did not extend clear to the top of the rooms, and as I was always the first up I would dress softly so as not to wake the others, and sneak out into the sweet outdoors and start out in the canoe, keeping close along the shore in the long shadows of the pines. I remembered being very careful never to rub my paddle against the gunwale for fear of disturbing the stillness of the cathedral.

The lake had never been what you would call a wild lake. There were cottages sprinkled around the shores, and it was in farming country although the shores of the lake were quite heavily wooded. Some of the cottages were owned by nearby farmers, and you would live at the shore and eat your meals at the farmhouse. That's what our family did. But although it wasn't wild, it was a fairly large and undisturbed lake and there were places in it which, to a child at least, seemed infinitely remote and primeval.

I was right about the tar: it led to within half a mile of the shore. But when I got back there, with my boy, and we settled into a camp near a farmhouse and into the kind of summertime I had known, I could tell that it was going to be pretty much the same as it had been before— I knew it, lying in bed the first morning, smelling the bedroom, and hearing the boy sneak quietly out and go off along the shore in a boat. I began to sustain the illusion that he was I, and therefore, by simple transposition, that I was my father. This sensation persisted, kept cropping up all the time we were there. It was not an entirely new feeling, but in this setting it grew much stronger. I seemed to be living a dual existence. I would be in the middle of some simple act, I would be picking up a bait box or laying down a table fork, or I would be saying something, and suddenly it would be not I but my father who was saying the words or making the gesture. It gave me a creepy sensation.

We went fishing the first morning. I felt the same damp moss covering the worms in the bait can, and saw the dragonfly alight on the tip of my rod as it hovered a few inches from the surface of the water. It was the arrival of this fly that convinced me beyond any doubt that everything was as it always had been, that the years were a mirage and there had been no years. The small waves were the same, chucking the rowboat under the chin as we fished at anchor, and the boat was the same boat, the same color green and the ribs broken in the same places, and under the floor-boards the same fresh-water leavings and débris—the dead helgramite, the wisps of moss, the rusty discarded fishhook, the dried blood from yesterday's catch. We stared silently at the tips of our rods, at the dragonflies that came and went. I lowered the tip of mine into the water, tentatively, pensively dislodging the fly, which darted two feet away, poised, darted two feet back, and came to rest again a little farther up the rod. There had been no years between the ducking of this dragonfly and the other one—the one that was part of memory. I looked at the boy, who was silently watching his fly, and it was my hands that held his rod, my eyes watching. I felt dizzy and didn't know which rod I was at the end of.

We caught two bass, hauling them in briskly as though they were mackerel, pulling them over the side of the boat in a businesslike manner without any landing net, and stunning them with a blow on the back of the head. When we got back for a swim before lunch, the lake was exactly where we had left it, the same number of inches from the dock, and there was only the merest suggestion of a breeze. This seemed an utterly enchanted sea, this lake you could leave to its own devices for a few hours and come back to, and find that it had not stirred, this constant and trustworthy body of water. In the shallows, the dark, water-soaked sticks and twigs, smooth and old, were undulating in clusters on the bottom against the clean ribbed sand, and the track of the mussel was plain. A school of minnows swam by, each minnow with its small individual shadow, doubling the attendance, so clear and sharp in the sunlight. Some of the other campers were in swimming, along the shore, one of them with a cake of soap, and the water felt thin and clear and unsubstantial. Over the years there had been this person with the cake of soap, this cultist, and here he was. There had been no years.

Up to the farmhouse to dinner through the teeming, dusty field, the road under our sneakers was only a two-track road. The middle track was missing, the one with the marks of the hooves and splotches of dried, flaky manure. There had always been three tracks to choose from in choosing which track to walk in; now the choice was narrowed down to two. For a moment I missed terribly the middle alternative. But the way led past the tennis court, and something about the way it lay there in the sun reassured me; the tape had loosened along the backline, the alleys were green with plantains and other weeds, and the net (installed in June and removed in September) sagged in the dry noon, and the whole place steamed with midday heat and hunger and emptiness. There was a choice of pie for dessert, and one was blueberry and one was apple, and the waitresses were the same country girls, there having been no passage of time, only the illusion of it as in a dropped curtain—the waitresses were still fifteen; their hair had been washed, that was the only difference—they had been to the movies and seen the pretty girls with the clean hair.

Summertime, oh summertime, pattern of life indelible, the fadeproof lake, the woods unshatterable, the pasture with the sweetfern and the juniper forever and ever, summer without end; this was the background, and the life along the shore was the design, the cottagers with their innocent and tranquil design, their tiny docks with the flagpole and the American flag floating against the white clouds in the blue sky, the little paths over the roots of the trees leading from camp to camp and the paths leading back to the outhouses and the can of lime for sprinkling, and at the souvenir counters at the store the miniature birch-bark canoes and the post cards that showed things looking a little better than they looked. This was the American family at play, escaping the city heat, wondering whether the newcomers in the camp at the head of the cove were "common" or "nice," wondering whether it was true that the people who drove up for Sunday dinner at the farmhouse were turned away because there wasn't enough chicken.

It seemed to me, as I kept remembering all this, that those times and those summers had been infinitely precious and worth saving. There had been jollity and peace and goodness. The arriving (at the beginning of August) had been so big a business in itself, at the railway station the farm wagon drawn up, the first smell of the pine-laden air, the first glimpse of the smiling farmer, and the great importance of the trunks and your father's enormous authority in such matters, and the feel of the wagon under you for the long ten-mile haul, and at the top of the last long hill catching the first view of the lake after eleven months of not seeing this cherished body of water. The shouts and cries of the other campers when they saw you, and the trunks to be unpacked, to give up their rich burden. (Arriving was less exciting nowadays, when you sneaked up in your car and parked it under a tree near the camp and took out the bags and in five minutes it was all over, no fuss, no loud wonderful fuss about trunks.)

Peace and goodness and jollity. The only thing that was wrong now, really, was the sound of the place, an unfamiliar nervous sound of the outboard motors. This was the note that jarred, the one thing that would sometimes break the illusion and set the years moving. In those other summertimes all motors were inboard; and when they were at a little distance, the noise they made was a sedative, an ingredient of summer sleep. They were one-cylinder and two-cylinder engines, and some were make-and-break and some were jump-spark, but they all made a sleepy sound across the lake. The one-lungers throbbed and fluttered, and the twin-cylinder ones purred and purred, and that was a quiet sound too. But now the campers all had outboards. In the daytime, in the hot mornings, these motors made a petulant, irritable sound; at night, in the still evening when the afterglow lit the water, they whined about one's ears like mosquitoes. My boy loved our rented outboard, and his great desire was to achieve singlehanded mastery over it, and authority, and he soon learned the trick of choking it a little (but not too much), and the ad-

justment of the needle valve. Watching him I would remember the things
you could do with the old one-cylinder engine with the heavy flywheel,
how you could have it eating out of your hand if you got really close
to it spiritually. Motor boats in those days didn't have clutches, and you
would make a landing by shutting off the motor at the proper time and
coasting in with a dead rudder. But there was a way of reversing them,
if you learned the trick, by cutting the switch and putting it on again
exactly on the final dying revolution of the flywheel, so that it would
kick back against compression and begin reversing. Approaching a dock
in a strong following breeze, it was difficult to slow up sufficiently by the
ordinary coasting method, and if a boy felt he had complete mastery
over his motor, he was tempted to keep it running beyond its time and
then reverse it a few feet from the dock. It took a cool nerve, because
if you threw the switch a twentieth of a second too soon you would catch
the flywheel when it still had speed enough to go up past center, and
the boat would leap ahead, charging bull-fashion at the dock.

We had a good week at the camp. The bass were biting well and
the sun shone endlessly, day after day. We would be tired at night and
lie down in the accumulated heat of the little bedrooms after the long
hot day and the breeze would stir almost imperceptibly outside and the
smell of the swamp drift in through the rusty screens. Sleep would come
easily and in the morning the red squirrel would be on the roof, tapping
out his gay routine. I kept remembering everything, lying in bed in the
mornings—the small steamboat that had a long rounded stern like the
lip of a Ubangi, and how quietly she ran on the moonlight sails, when
the older boys played their mandolins and the girls sang and we ate
doughnuts dipped in sugar, and how sweet the music was on the water
in the shining night, and what it had felt like to think about girls then.
After breakfast we would go up to the store and the things were in the
same place—the minnows in a bottle, the plugs and spinners disarranged
and pawed over by the youngsters from the boys' camp, the fig newtons
and the Beeman's gum. Outside, the road was tarred and cars stood in
front of the store. Inside, all was just as it had always been, except there
was more Coca Cola and not so much Moxie and root beer and birch
beer and sarsaparilla. We would walk out with a bottle of pop apiece
and sometimes the pop would backfire up our noses and hurt. We explored the streams, quietly, where the turtles slid off the sunny logs and
dug their way into the soft bottom; and we lay on the town wharf and
fed worms to the tame bass. Everywhere we went I had trouble making
out which was I, the one walking at my side, the one walking in my
pants.

One afternoon while we were there at that lake a thunderstorm
came up. It was like the revival of an old melodrama that I had seen
long ago with childish awe. The second-act climax of the drama of the
electrical disturbance over a lake in America had not changed in any

important respect. This was the big scene, still the big scene. The whole thing was so familiar, the first feeling of oppression and heat and a general air around camp of not wanting to go very far away. In midafternoon (it was all the same) a curious darkening of the sky, and a lull in everything that had made life tick; and then the way the boats suddenly swung the other way at their moorings with the coming of a breeze out of the new quarter, and the premonitory rumble. Then the kettle drum, then the snare, then the bass drum and cymbals, then crackling light against the dark, and the gods grinning and licking their chops in the hills. Afterward the calm, the rain steadily rustling in the calm lake, the return of light and hope and spirits, and the campers running out in joy and relief to go swimming in the rain, their brights cries perpetuating the deathless joke about how they were getting simply drenched, and the children screaming with delight at the new sensation of bathing in the rain, and the joke about getting drenched linking the generations in a strong indestructible chain. And the comedian who waded in carrying an umbrella.

When the others went swimming my son said he was going in too. He pulled his dripping trunks from the line where they had hung all through the shower, and wrung them out. Languidly, and with no thought of going in, I watched him, his hard little body, skinny and bare, saw him wince slightly as he pulled up around his vitals the small, soggy, icy garment. As he buckled the swollen belt suddenly my groin felt the chill of death.

Four questions about the selection by E. B. White . . .

1. This essay ends abruptly with a telling about the feeling of death. Does anything in the first paragraph relate to feeling death in the last one?

     2. Why is it only his son who goes with White to the lake? In the old days, it seems to have been the whole family.

3. Can you characterize the changes at the lake as of one general sort?

     4. This essay is dated August, 1941. What might have been in the mind of an American in late summer or early fall, 1941?

Richard Bach

Stranger to the Ground

The wind tonight is from the west, down runway two eight. It pushes gently at my polka-dot scarf and makes the steel buckles of my parachute harness tinkle in the darkness. It is a cold wind, and because of it my takeoff roll will be shorter than usual and my airplane will climb more quickly than it usually does when it lifts into the sky.

Two ground crewmen work together to lift a heavy padlocked canvas bag of Top Secret documents into the nose of the airplane. It sags awkwardly into space normally occupied by contoured ammunition cans, above four oiled black machine guns, and forward of the bomb release computers. Tonight I am not a fighter pilot. I am a courier for 39 pounds of paper that is of sudden urgent interest to my wing commander, and though the weather this night over Europe is already freakish and violent, I have been asked to move these pounds of paper from England into the heart of France.

In the bright beam of my flashlight, the Form One, with its inked boxes and penciled initials, tells me that the airplane is ready, that it carries only minor shortcomings of which I already know: a dent in one drop tank, an inspection of the command radio antenna is due, the ATO system is disconnected. It is hard to turn the thin pages of the Form One with gloves on, but the cold wind helps me turn them.

Form signed, gun bay door locked over the mysterious canvas bag, I climb the narrow yellow ladder to my dark cockpit, like a high-booted mountain climber pulling himself to a peak from whose snows he can stand and look down upon the world. My peak is the small cockpit of a Republic F-84F *Thunderstreak*.

The safety belt of the yellow-handled ejection seat is wide nylon web, heavy and olive-drab; into its explosive buckle fits the nylon harness from over my shoulders and the amber steel link that automatically opens my parachute if I should have to bail out tonight. I surround myself with the universal quiet metallic noises of a pilot joining himself to his airplane. The two straps to the seat cushion survival kit, after their usual struggle, are captured and clink softly to my parachute harness. The green oxygen mask fits into its regulator hose with a muffled rubbery snap. The steel D-ring lanyard clanks as it fastens to the curved bar of the parachute ripcord handle. The red-streamered ejection seat safety pin scrapes out of its hole drilled in the trigger of the right armrest and rustles in the darkness into the small pocket on the leg of my tight-laced G-suit. The elastic leg strap of my scratched aluminum kneeboard cinches around my left thigh, latching itself with a hollow clank. My hard white fiberglass crash helmet, dark-visored, gold-lettered 1/LT. BACH, fits stiffly down to cover my head, its soft sponge-rubber earphones waiting a long cold moment before they begin to warm against my ears. The chamois chinstrap snaps at the left side, microphone cable connects with its own frosty click into the aircraft radio cord, and at last the wind-chilled green rubber oxygen mask snugs over my nose and mouth, fitting with a tight click-click of the smooth chromed fastener at the right side of the helmet. When the little family of noises is still, by tubes and wires and snaps and buckles, my body is attached to the larger, sleeping body of my airplane.

Outside, in the dark moving blanket of cold, a ghostly yellow auxiliary power unit roars into life, controlled by a man in a heavy issue parka who is hoping that I will be quick to start my engine and taxi away. Despite the parka, he is cold. The clatter and roar of the big gasoline engine under his hands settles a bit, and on its voltage dials, white needles spring into their green arcs.

From the engine of the power unit, through the spinning generator, through the black rubber snake into the cold silver wing of my airplane, through the marked wires of the DC electrical system, the power explodes in my dark cockpit as six brilliant red and yellow warning lights, and as quick tremblings of a few instrument pointers.

My leather gloves, stamped with the white wings and star of Air Force property, go through a familiar little act for the interested audience that watches from behind my eyes. From left to right around the cockpit they travel; checking left console circuit breakers in, gun heater switch *off*, engine screen switch *extend*, drop tank pressure switches *off*, speed break switch *extend*, throttle *off*, altimeter, drag chute handle, sight caging lever, radiocompass, TACAN, oxygen, generator, IFF, inverter selector. The gloves dance, the eyes watch. The right glove flourishes into the air at the end of its act and spins a little circle of information to the man waiting in the wind below: checks are finished, engine is starting in two seconds. Now it is throttle on, down with the glove, and starter switch to *start*.

There is no time to take a breath or blink the eye. There is one tiny tenth-second hiss before concussion shatters icy air. Suddenly, instantly, air and sparks and Jet Propellant Four. My airplane is designed to start its engine with an explosion. It can be started in no other way. But the sound is a keg of black powder under the match, a cannon firing, the burst of a hand grenade. The man outside blinks, painfully.

With the blast, as though with suddenly-opened eyes, my airplane is alive. Instantly awake. The thunderclap is gone as quickly as it came, replaced by a quiet rising whine that peaks quickly, very high, and slides back down the scale into nothingness. But before the whine is gone, deep inside the engine, combustion chambers have earned their name. The luminous white pointer of the gage marked *exhaust gas temperature* pivots upward, lifting as thermocouples taste a swirling flood of yellow fire that twists from fourteen stainless steel chambers. The fire spins a turbine. The turbine spins a compressor. The compressor crushes fuel and air for the fire. Weak yellow flames change to businesslike blue torches held in their separate round offices, and the ghostly power unit is needed no more.

Flourish with the right glove, finger pointing away; away the power, I'm on my own.

Tailpipe temperature is settled and at home with 450 degrees of centigrade, tachometer steadies to note that the engine is turning at 45 percent of its possible rpm. The rush of air to the insatiable steel engine is a constant rasping scream at the oval intake, a chained banshee shrieking in the icy black air and the searing blue fire.

Hydraulic pressure shows on a dial, under a pointer. Speed brake switch to *retract*, and the pressure pulls two great slabs of steel to disappear into the smooth sides of my airplane. Rainbow lights go dark as pressure rises in systems for fuel and oil. I have just been born, with the press of wind at my scarf. With the wind keening along the tall swept silver of my rudder. With the rush of wind to the torches of my engine.

There is one light left on, stubbornly glowing over a placard marked *canopy unlocked*. My left glove moves a steel handle aft. With the right I reach high overhead to grasp the frame of the counterbalanced section of double-walled plexiglass. A gentle pull downward, and the smooth-hinged canopy settles over my little world. I move the handle forward in my left glove, I hear a muffled sound of latches engaging, I see the light wink out. The wind at my scarf is gone.

I am held by my straps and my buckles and my wires in a deep pool of dim red light. In the pool is all that I must know about my airplane and my position and my altitude until I pull the throttle back to *off*, one hour and 29 minutes and 579 airway miles from Wethersfield Air Base, England.

This base means nothing to me. When I landed it was a long runway in the sunset, a tower operator giving taxi directions, a stranger waiting for me in Operations with a heavy padlocked canvas bag. I was in a hurry when I arrived, I am in a hurry to leave. Wethersfield, with its hedges and its oak trees that I assume are part of all English towns, with its stone houses and mossed roofs and its people who watched the Battle of Britain cross the sky with black smoke, is to me Half Way. The sooner I leave Wethersfield a smudge in the darkness behind, the sooner I can finish the letter to my wife and my daughter, the sooner I can settle into a lonely bed and mark another day gone from the calendar. The sooner I can take myself beyond the unknown that is the weather high over Europe.

On the heavy black throttle under my left glove there is a microphone button, and I press it with my thumb. "Wethersfield Tower," I say to the microphone buried in the snug green rubber of my oxygen mask. I hear my own voice in the earphones of my helmet, and know that in the high glass cube of the control tower the same voice and the same words are this moment speaking. "Air Force Jet Two Niner Four Zero Five; taxi information and standing by for ATC clearance."

It still sounds strange. Air Force Jet. Six months ago it was Air Guard Jet. It was one weekend a month, and fly when you have the spare time. It was the game of flying better than Air Force pilots and shooting straighter than Air Force pilots, with old airplanes and with a full-time civilian job. It was watching the clouds of tension mushroom over the world, and knowing for certain that if the country needed more firepower, my squadron would be a part of it. It was thirty-one pilots in the squadron knowing that fact, knowing that they could leave the squadron before the recall came; and it was the same thirty-one pilots, two months later, flying their worn airplanes without inflight refueling, across the Atlantic into France. Air Force Jet.

"Roger, Zero Five," comes a new voice in the earphones. "Taxi runway two eight; wind is two seven zero degrees at one five knots, altimeter is two niner niner five, tower time is two one two five, clearance is on request. Type aircraft, please."

I twist the small knurled knob near the altimeter to set 29.95 in a red-lit window. The hands of the altimeter move slightly. My gloved thumb is down again on the microphone button. "Roger, tower, Zero Five is a Fox Eight Four, courier: returning to Chaumont Air Base, France."

Forward goes the thick black throttle and in the quickening roar of startled, very hot thunder, my Republic F-84F, slightly dented, slightly old-fashioned, governed by my left glove, begins to move. A touch of boot on left brake and the airplane turns. Back with the throttle to keep from blasting the man and his power unit with a 600-degree hurricane from the tailpipe. Tactical Air Navigation selector to *transmit and receive.*

The sleeping silver silhouettes of the F-100's of Wethersfield Air Base sweep by in the dark as I taxi, and I am engulfed in comfort. The endless crackle of light static in my earphones, the intimate weight of my helmet, the tremble of my airplane, rocking and slowly pitching as it rolls on hard tires and oil-filled struts over the bumps and ridges of the taxiway. Like an animal. Like a trusted and trusting eager heavy swift animal of prey, the airplane that I control from its birth to its sleep trundles toward the two-mile runway lulled by the murmur of the cold wind.

The filtered voice of the tower operator shatters the serene static in the earphones. "Air Force Jet Two Niner Four Zero Five, clearance received. Ready to copy?"

My pencil springs from flight jacket sleeve to poise itself over the folded flight plan trapped in the jaws of the clipboard on my left leg. "Ready to copy."

"ATC clears; Air Force Jet Two Niner Four Zero Five to the Chaumont Airport . . ." I mark the words in scrawled shorthand. I have been cleared to fly the route I have planned. ". . . via direct Abbeville, direct Laon, direct Spangdahlem, direct Wiesbaden, direct Strasbourg, direct Chaumont." A route detoured before it begins; planned to avoid the mass of storms and severe weather that the forecaster has marked in red squares across the direct route to my home base. "Climb in radar control to flight level three three zero, contact Anglia control . . ." The clearance comes in through the earphones and out through the sharp point of the pencil; whom to contact and when and on which frequency, one hour and 29 minutes of flying pressed onto a four-inch square of penciled paper bathed in dim red light. I read the shorthand back to the tower operator, and tap the brakes to stop short of the runway.

"Roger, Zero Five, readback is correct. Cleared for takeoff; no reported traffic in the local area."

Throttle forward again and the airplane swings into takeoff position on runway two eight. The concrete is wide and long. The painted white stripe along its center is held at one end by my nosewheel, at the invisible other end by the tough nylon webbing of the overrun barrier. A twin row of white edge lights converges in the black distance ahead, pointing the way. The throttle moves now, under my left glove, all the way forward; until the radium-caked tachometer needle covers the line marked *100 percent*, until the tailpipe temperature is up by the short red arc on the dial that means 642 degrees centigrade, until each pointer on each dial of the red-soaked instrument panel agrees with what we are to do, until I say to myself, as I say every time, Here we go. I release the brakes.

There is no instant rush of speed, no head forced against the headrest. I feel only a gentle push at my back. The stripe of the runway unrolls, lazily at first, beneath the nosewheel. Crackling thunder twists and blasts and tumbles behind me, and, slowly, I see the runway lights begin to blur at the side of the concrete and the airspeed needle lifts to cover 50 knots, to cover 80 knots, to cover 120 knots (go-no-go speed checks OK) and between the two white rows of blur I see the barrier waiting in the darkness at the end of the runway and the control stick tilts easily back in my right glove and the airspeed needle is covering 160 knots and the nosewheel lifts from the concrete and the main wheels follow a half-second later and there is nothing in the world but me and an airplane alive and together and the cool wind lifts us to its heart and we are one with the wind and one with the dark sky and the stars ahead and the barrier is a forgotten dwindling blur behind and the wheels swing up to tuck themselves away in my seamless aluminum skin and the airspeed is up to one nine zero and flap lever forward and airspeed two two zero and I am in my element and I am flying. I am flying.

The voice that I hear in the soft earphones is unlike my own. It is the voice of a man concerned only with business; a man speaking while he has yet many things to do. Still it is my thumb down on the microphone button and my words screened through the receiver in the tower. "Wethersfield Tower, Air Force Jet Two Niner Four Zero Five departing on course, leaving your station and frequency."

My airplane climbs easily through the strange clear air over southern England, and my gloves, not content to accept idleness, move across the cockpit and complete the little tasks that have been assigned to them. The needles of my altimeter swing quickly through the 5,000-foot mark, and while my gloves work at the task of retracting the engine screens, pressurizing the drop tanks, loosing the D-ring lanyard from the ripcord, setting the pneumatic compressor into life, I notice suddenly that there is no moon. I had hoped for a moon.

My eyes, at the command of the audience behind them, check once again that all the small-dialed engine instruments have pointers properly under their arcs of green paint on the glass. The right glove, conscientious, pushes the oxygen lever from *100 percent* to *normal,* and sets the four white numbers of the departure control frequency in the four black windows of the command ultra-high frequency transmitter.

The strange voice that is mine speaks to the radar control center guiding my departure. The voice is capable of doing the necessary talking, the gloves are capable of moving throttle and control stick to guide the slanting climb of my airplane into the night. Ahead of me, through the heavy angled glass of the windscreen, through a shrinking wall of clear air, is the weather. I can see that it hugs the ground at first, low and thin, as if uncertain that it is over the land that it has been assigned to cover.

The three white hands of the altimeter swing through 10,000 feet, sending my right glove into another, shorter, series of menial tasks in the cockpit. It dials now the numbers 387 into the pie-slice of window on the radiocompass control panel. In the soft earphones are the faint Morse letters A-B: the Abbeville radiobeacon.

Abbeville. Twenty years ago the Abbeville Boys, flying Messerschmitt 109's with yellow-spiral spinners around their propeller-hub cannon were the best fighter pilots in the German Luftwaffe. Abbeville was the place to go when you were looking for a fight, and a place to avoid when you carried canvas sacks instead of machinegun bullets. Abbeville on one side of the Channel, Tangmere and Biggin Hill on the other. Messerschmitt on one side and Spitfire on the other. And a tangle of white contrails and lines of falling black smoke in the crystal air between.

The only distance that lies between me and a yellow-nosed ME-109 is a little bend of the river called time. The wash of waves on the sands of Calais. The hush of wind across chessboard Europe. The spinning of one hourhand. Same air, same sea, same hourhand, same river of time. But the Messerschmitts are gone. And the magnificent Spitfires. Could my airplane tonight carry me not along the river, but across the bend of it, the world would look exactly as it looks tonight. And in this same air before them, in another block of old air, the Breguets and the Latés and One Lonely Ryan, coming in from the west, into the glare of search-lights over Le Bourget. And back across the confluences of the river, a host of Nieuports and Pfalzes and Fokkers and Sopwiths, of Farmans and Bleriots, of Wright Flyers, of Santos-Dumont dirigibles, of Mont-golfiers, of hawks circling, circling. As men looked up from the ground. Into the sky just as it is tonight.

The eternal sky, the dreaming man.

The river flows.

The eternal sky, the striving man.

The river flows.

The eternal sky, the conquering man.

Tonight Tangmere and Biggin Hill are quiet lighted rectangles of concrete under the cloud that slips beneath my airplane, and the airport near Abbeville is dark. But there is still the crystal air and it whispers over my canopy and blasts into the gaping oval intake a gun's length ahead of my boots.

It is sad, to be suddenly a living part of what should belong to old memory and faded gun-camera films. My reason for being on the far shore of the Atlantic is to be always ready to mold new memories of the victory of Us against Them, and to squeeze the trigger that adds another few feet to history's reel of gun-camera film. I am here to become a part of a War That Could Be, and this is the only place I belong if it changes into a War That Is.

But rather than learning to hate, or even to be more uncaring about the enemy who threatens on the other side of the mythical iron curtain, I have learned in spite of myself that he might actually be a man, a human being. During my short months in Europe, I have lived with German pilots, with French pilots, Norwegian pilots, with pilots from Canada and from England. I have discovered, almost to my surprise, that Americans are not the only people in the world who fly airplanes for the sheer love of flying them. I have learned that airplane pilots speak the same language and understand the same unspoken words, whatever their country. They face the same headwinds and the same storms. And as the days pass without war, I find myself asking if a pilot, because of the political situation under which he lives, can possibly be a totally dif-ferent man from all the pilots living in all the political systems across the earth.

This man of mystery, this Russian pilot about whose life and thoughts I know so little, becomes in my mind a man not unlike myself, who is flying an airplane fitted with rockets and bombs and machine guns not because he loves destruction but because he loves his airplane, and the job of flying a capable, spirited airplane in any Air Force cannot be divorced from the job of killing when there is a war to be fought.

I am growing to like this probable pilot of the enemy, the more so because he is an unknown and forbidden man, with no one to bear witness of the good in him, and so many at hand to condemn his evils.

If war is declared here in Europe, I will never know the truth of the man who mounts the cockpit of a red-starred airplane. If war is declared, we are unleashed against each other, like starved wolves, to fight. A friend of mine, a true proven friend, neither imagined nor conjured out of possibilities, will fall to the guns of a Russian pilot. Somewhere an American will die under his bombs. In that instant I will be swallowed up in one of the thousand evils of war; I will have lost the host of unmet friends who are the Russian pilots. I will rejoice in their death, take pride in the destruction of their beautiful airplanes under my own rockets and my own guns. If I succumb to hate, I will myself become certainly and unavoidably a lesser man. In my pride I will be less worthy of pride. I will kill the enemy, and in so doing will bring my own death upon me. And I am sad.

But this night no war has been declared. It seems, in the quiet days, almost as if our nations might learn to live with each other, and this night the eastern pilot of my imagining, more real than the specter he would become in wartime, is flying his own solitary airplane into his own capricious weather.

My gloves are at work again, leveling the airplane at 33,000 feet. Throttle comes back under the left glove until the engine tachometer shows 94 percent rpm. The thumb of the right glove touches the trim button on the control stick once and again, quickly, forward. The eyes flick from instrument to instrument, and all is in order. Fuel flow is 2,500 pounds per hour. Mach needle is resting over .8, which means that my true airspeed is settling at 465 knots. The thin luminous needle of the radiocompass, over its many-numbered dial, pivots suddenly as the Abbeville radiobeacon passes beneath my airplane, under the black cloud. Eyes make a quick check of transmitter frequency, voice is ready with a position report to air traffic control, left thumb is down on the microphone button at 2200 hours, and the audience behind the eyes sees the first faint flash of lightning in the high opaque darkness ahead.

Four questions about the selection by Bach . . .

1. Early in the piece, Bach twice refers to joining or attaching himself to the airplane. How is this description important to the whole selection?

2. In what ways is the wholeness of this piece revealed in reference to time? To places? To persons?

3. Can you define the arrangement of this selection as chronological or spatial?

4. The Bach selection is a chapter from a book written more than twenty years after the White essay. What do the two pieces have in common?

Four questions about the selections from Bach and White . . .

1. Can you explain something about a feeling of wholeness as it characterizes each selection?

2. In what ways does that feeling of wholeness reveal itself in the parts of the selections—in references to time? To place? To person?

3. How does this sense of wholeness govern the way in which each piece is composed? Can you define the arrangements as chronological or as spatial?

4. To Bach and White, how important a tool is analogy?

Exercise . . .

1. Set up an organic outline for a proposed essay of your own. Choose a subject, get a perspective.

2. Work from that seed idea into your probable first steps of development. (You may want to write the first few topic sentences. In any case, clearly show the chain of development.)

3. List several foreign elements that would be assimilated.

4. What is the inner energy? Give a brief statement of how you chose the seed idea and why you think the idea "germinates" and "grows." What questions does it pose? What problems? What explanations does it call for?

5. Finally, try to visualize some shape that you might have achieved. You may even draw a picture. Is the essay like a chain, a funnel, a tree, a river? Is it like a trap? You may want a nonvisual shape. Was it like a game, a journey?

Walt Whitman

from Song of Myself

I am the poet of the Body and I am the poet of the Soul,
The pleasures of heaven are with me and the pains of hell are with me,
The first I graft and increase upon myself, the latter I translate into a
    new tongue.

I am the poet of the woman the same as the man,
And I say it is as great to be a woman as to be a man,
And I say there is nothing greater than the mother of men.

I chant the chant of dilation or pride,
We have had ducking and deprecating about enough,
I show that size is only development.

Have you outstript the rest? are you the President?
It is a trifle, they will more than arrive there every one, and still pass on.

I am he that walks with the tender and growing night,
I call to the earth and sea half-held by the night.

Press close bare-bosom'd night—press close magnetic nourishing night!
Night of south winds—night of the large few stars!
Still nodding night—mad naked summer night.

Smile O voluptuous cool-breath'd earth!
Earth of the slumbering and liquid trees!
Earth of departed sunset—earth of the mountains misty-topt!
Earth of the vitreous pour of the full moon just tinged with blue!
Earth of shine and dark mottling the tide of the river!
Earth of the limpid gray of clouds brighter and clearer for my sake!
Far-swooping elbow'd earth—rich apple-blossom'd earth!
Smile, for your lover comes.

Prodigal, you have give me love—therefore I to you give love!
O unspeakable passionate love.

Herman Melville
The Maldive Shark

About the Shark, phlegmatical one,
Pale sot of the Maldive sea,
The sleek little pilot-fish, azure and slim,
How alert in attendance be.
From his saw-pit of mouth, from his charnel of maw
They have nothing of harm to dread,
But liquidly glide on his ghastly flank
Or before his Gorgonian head;
Or lurk in the port of serrated teeth
In white triple tiers of glittering gates,
And there find a haven when peril's abroad,
An asylum in jaws of the Fates!
They are friends; and friendly they guide him to prey,
Yet never partake of the treat—
Eyes and brains to the dotard lethargic and dull,
Pale ravener of horrible meat.

Henry Wadsworth Longfellow
The Fire of Drift-Wood

We sat within the farm-house old,
    Whose windows, looking o'er the bay,
Gave to the sea-breeze damp and cold
    An easy entrance, night and day.

Not far away we saw the port,
    The strange, old-fashioned, silent town,
The lighthouse, the dismantled fort,
    The wooden houses, quaint and brown.

We sat and talked until the night,
  Descending, filled the little room;
Our faces faded from the sight,
  Our voices only broke the gloom.

We spake of many a vanished scene,
  Of what we once had thought and said,
Of what had been, and might have been,
  And who was changed, and who was dead;

And all that fills the hearts of friends,
  When first they feel, with secret pain,
Their lives thenceforth have separate ends,
  And never can be one again;

The first slight swerving of the heart,
  That words are powerless to express,
And leave it still unsaid in part,
  Or say it in too great excess.

The very tones in which we spake
  Had something strange, I could but mark;
The leaves of memory seemed to make
  A mournful rustling in the dark.

Oft died the words upon our lips,
  As suddenly, from out the fire
Built of the wreck of stranded ships,
  The flames would leap and then expire.

And, as their splendor flashed and failed,
  We thought of wrecks upon the main,
Of ships dismasted, that were hailed
  And sent no answer back again.

The windows, rattling in their frames,
  The ocean, roaring up the beach,
The gusty blast, the bickering flames,
  All mingled vaguely in our speech;

Until they made themselves a part
  Of fancies floating through the brain,
The long-lost ventures of the heart,
  That send no answers back again.

O flames that glowed! O hearts that yearned!
They were indeed too much akin,
The drift-wood fire without that burned,
The thoughts that burned and glowed within.

EMOTION AND THE WHOLE ESSAY

Too often emotions and composition mix as badly as alcohol and guns or cars. The writer rages on and on—he condemns, curses, extols, or slobbers, but he does not actually say very much. In fact, he may not be writing about his subject at all, only about the way he, the author, feels.

No individual is entirely rational, however, and no composition is purely objective. Emotion is usually what makes something valuable to us. How I feel about my neighborhood, my teacher, or my car is what makes those things meaningful. Many acts of composition intend to communicate not only facts but a personal sense of the subject. The problem is how to write about the subject instead of the feelings. How can the subject appear to the reader as it appears to the writer? How do you avoid displaying emotion at the expense of your subject?

Readers often respond positively to writing which is little more than display of feeling. This is especially true of writing that agrees with the reader's own feelings. In the following pairs of readings, allow yourself to respond freely at first. Then analyze your response.

I

Barnaby Barnes
Burn on, Sweet Fire

Burn on, sweet fire, for I live by that fuel
   Whose smoke is as an incense to my soul.
Each sigh prolongs my smart. Be fierce and cruel,
   My fair Parthenophe. Frown and control,
Vex, torture, scald, disgrace me. Do thy will!
   Stop up thine ears; with flint immure thine heart,
And kill me with thy looks, if they would kill.
   Thine eyes, those crystal phials which impart

The perfect balm to my dead-wounded breast;
   Thine eyes, the quivers whence those darts were drawn
Which me to thy love's bondage have addressed;
   Thy smile and frown, night-star and daylight's dawn,
Burn on, frown on, vex, stop thine ears, torment me!
   More, for thy beauty borne, would not repent me.

William Shakespeare
Sonnet 130

   My mistress' eyes are nothing like the sun;
   Coral is far more red than her lips' red;
   If snow be white, why then her breasts are dun;
   If hairs be wires, black wires grow on her head.
   I have seen roses damasked red and white,
   But no such roses see I in her cheeks;
   And in some perfumes is there more delight
   Than in the breath that from my mistress reeks.
   I love to hear her speak, yet well I know
   That music hath a far more pleasing sound;
   I grant I never saw a goddess go:
   My mistress, when she walks, treads on the ground.
      And yet, by heaven, I think my love as rare
      As any she belied with false compare.

II

George Barker

To My Mother

Most near, most dear, most loved and most far,
Under the window where I often found her
Sitting as huge as Asia, seismic with laughter,
Gin and chicken helpless in her Irish hand,
Irresistible as Rabelais, but most tender for
The lame dogs and hurt birds that surround her,—
She is a procession no one can follow after
But be like a little dog following a brass band.

She will not glance up at the bomber, or condescend
To drop her gin and scuttle to a cellar,
But lean on the mahogany table like a mountain
Whom only faith can move, and so I send
O all my faith, and all my love to tell her
That she will move from mourning into morning.

Mary Dow Brine

Somebody's Mother

The woman was old and ragged and gray
And bent with the chill of the Winter's day.

The street was wet with a recent snow
And the woman's feet were aged and slow.

She stood at the crossing and waited long,
Alone, uncared for, amid the throng

Of human beings who passed her by
Nor heed the glance of her anxious eye.

Down the street, with laughter and shout,
Glad in the freedom of "school let out,"

Came the boys like a flock of sheep,
Hailing the snow piled white and deep.

Past the woman so old and gray
Hastened the children on their way.

Nor offered a helping hand to her—
So meek, so timid, afraid to stir

Lest the carriage wheels or horses' feet
Should crowd her down in the slippery street.

At last came one of the merry troop,
The gayest laddie in all the group;

He paused beside her and whispered low,
"I'll help you cross, if you wish to go."

Her aged hand on his strong young arm
She placed, and so, without hurt or harm,

He guided the trembling feet along,
Proud that his own were firm and strong.

Then back again to his friends he went,
His young heart happy and well content.

"She's somebody's mother, boys, you know,
For all she's aged and poor and slow,

"And I hope some fellow will lend a hand
To help my mother, you understand,

"If ever she's poor and old and gray,
When her own dear boy is far away."

And "somebody's mother" bowed low her head
In her home that night, and the prayer she said

Was, "God be kind to the noble boy,
Who is somebody's son, and pride and joy!"

III

Emily Dickinson

To Hear an Oriole Sing

To hear an Oriole sing
May be a common thing—
Or only a divine.

It is not of the Bird
Who sings the same, unheard,
As unto Crows—

The Fashion of the Ear
Attireth that it hear
In Dun, or fair—

So whether it be Rune,
Or whether it be none
Is of within.

The "Tune is in the Tree—"
The Skeptic—showeth me—
"No Sir! In Thee!"

Emily Dickinson, "To Hear an Oriole Sing," *The Complete Poems of Emily Dickinson*, ed. by Thomas H. Johnson (Boston: Little, Brown and Company).

Anonymous

Nestlings

O little bird! sing sweet among the leaves,
Safe hid from sight, beside thy downy nest;
The rain falls, murmuring to the drooping eaves
A low refrain, that suits thy music best.

Sing sweet, O bird! thy recompense draws nigh,—
Four callow nestlings 'neath the mother's wing.
So many flashing wings that by and by
Will cleave the sunny air. Oh, sing, bird, sing!

Sing, O my heart! Thy callow nestlings sleep,
Safe hidden 'neath a gracious folding wing,
Until the time when from their slumbers deep
They wake, and soar in beauty. Sing, heart, sing!

IV

Morton Marcus

Confession

How do I say
that I'm a murderer?

I drag my shadow
as if it were a sack
full of discarded bodies.

"Nestlings" is from a nineteenth-century newspaper.
Morton Marcus, "Confession," in *Where Is Vietnam* by Walter Lowenfels, © 1967
by Doubleday & Co., Inc. Reprinted by permission.

My victims are inside me.
Now *they* are murderers.
The bloody wafer
fountains in my stomach.
They wash their hands in it,
dance around it,
singing hymns
to all my hemorrhagings
before they invade my mouth
with a bad taste.

My count is indefinite
but probably includes
the 8 mothers
who run through the caves
of my colon
with burning hair;
the baby
shaped like a scream;
the two girls
with hands and wombs
of flaming water;
and, on my spinal road,
the boy who crawls
farther and farther
from his legs.

They face me, fire
chewing their hair.
These are the ones
I have allowed
to move inside me,
but they didn't wait
for my invitation.

Wilfred Owen

Dulce et Decorum Est

Bent double, like old beggars under sacks,
Knock-kneed, coughing like hags, we cursed through sludge,
Till on the haunting flares we turned our backs,
And towards our distant rest began to trudge.
Men marched asleep. Many had lost their boots,
But limped on, blood-shod. All went lame, all blind;
Drunk with fatigue; deaf even to the hoots
Of gas-shells dropping softly behind.

Gas! Gas! Quick, boys!—An ecstasy of fumbling,
Fitting the clumsy helmets just in time,
But someone still was yelling out and stumbling
And floundering like a man in fire or lime.—
Dim through the misty panes and thick green light,
As under a green sea, I saw him drowning.

In all my dreams before my helpless sight
He plunges at me, guttering, choking, drowning.

If in some smothering dreams, you too could pace
Behind the wagon that we flung him in,
And watch the white eyes writhing in his face,
His hanging face, like a devil's sick of sin;
If you could hear, at every jolt, the blood
Come gargling from the froth-corrupted lungs,
Bitter as the cud
Of vile, incurable sores on innocent tongues,—
My friend, you would not tell with such high zest
To children ardent for some desperate glory,
The old Lie: Dulce et decorum est
Pro patria mori.

Parson Weems

from Life of Washington

Having at length attained the acme of all his wishes—having lived to see a general and efficient government adopted, and for eight years in successful operation, exalting his country from the brink of infamy and ruin to the highest ground of prosperity and honour, both at home and abroad—abroad, peace with Britain—with Spain—and, some slight heart burnings excepted, peace with France, and with all the world: at home, peace with the Indians—our shining ploughshares laying open the best treasures of the earth—our ships flying over every sea—distant nations feeding on our bread, and manufacturing our staples—our revenue rapidly increasing with our credit, religion, learning, arts, and whatever tends to national glory and happiness, he determined to lay down that load of public care which he had borne so long, and which, now in his 66th year, he found was growing too heavy for him. But feeling towards his countrymen the solicitude of a father for his children, over whom he had long watched, but whom he was about to leave to themselves; and fearing, on the one hand, that they might go astray and hoping, on the other, that from his long labor of love, he might be permitted to impart the counsel of his long experience, he drew up for them a farewell address, which the filial piety of the nation has since called "his Legacy."

As this little piece, about the length of an ordinary sermon, may do as much good to the people of America as any sermon ever preached, that Divine one on the mount excepted, I shall offer no apology for laying it before them; especially as I well know that they will all read it with the feelings of children reading the last letter of a once loved father now in his grave. And who knows but it may check for a while the fatal flame of discord which has destroyed all the once glorious republics of antiquity, and here now at length in the United States has caught upon the last republic that is left on the face of the earth.

The appearance of this address in the gazettes of the United States, struck every where a damp on the spirits of the people. To be thus bidden farewell by one to whom, in every time of danger, they had so long and so fondly looked up, as, under God, their surest and safest friend, could not but prove to them a grievous shock. Indeed many could not refrain from tears, especially when they came to that part where he talked of being soon to be "consigned to the mansions of rest."

Charles Beard

from # The Rise of
American Civilization

At last, thoroughly alarmed by the peril of defeat, the administration resolved to bring all its influence to bear. Laying down his ledgers, Hamilton wrote a series of powerful papers which he published anonymously. With incisive rhetoric he stung indifferent Federalists to action, warning them that "the horrid principles of Jacobinism" were abroad in the land and that a war with England would throw the direction of affairs into the hands of men professing these terrible doctrines. "The consequences of this," he said, "even in imagination, are such as to make any virtuous man shudder." In the end, by dint of much maneuvering and the use of personal influence, Washington was able to wring from the Senate its approval of the treaty, in June, 1795.

The deed was done but the ill-will aroused by it was not allayed. To display its temper, the opposition in the House of Representatives called upon the President for papers pertaining to the negotiation of the treaty. When it was curtly rebuffed, its wrath deepened, and the populace upon which it relied for support was stirred to renewed opposition. By this time the Anti-Federalists, or Republicans, as they were fond of calling themselves, strengthened by recruits from many quarters, had grown into a fairly coherent party and were evidently resolved upon grasping the powers of the federal government at the coming national election.

This state of affairs confirmed Washington in his determination to retire at the end of his second term. He would then be sixty-five years of age and he was weary from his burdensome labors in field and forum. Since the opening of the Revolution, to say nothing of his provincial career, he had spent nearly fifteen years in public service and even while in retirement he had devoted irksome and anxious months to the movement that produced the Constitution. The glory of office had begun to pale. Once he had received respectful homage on all occasions; now near the close of his second administration he was shocked and grieved to find himself spattered with the mud of political criticism. Having definitely aligned himself with the Federalist group and having assumed responsibility for the policies of administration framed by that party, he had voluntarily incurred the risks of partisan attacks. Nevertheless he was distressed beyond measure to hear himself assailed, as he complained, "in such exaggerated and indecent terms as could scarcely be applied to a Nero, a notorious defaulter, or even to a common pickpocket."

These were the circumstances that led him to take advantage of the first opportunity to return to the peace of his Potomac estate. He had accepted reëlection in 1792 only on the urgent solicitation of both Hamilton and Jefferson, who had told him that he alone could save the new fabric of government. But another election was out of the question, not because he regarded the idea of a third term as improper or open to serious objections; he was simply through with the honors and turmoil of politics. Accordingly, in September, 1796, on the eve of the presidential election, he announced his decision in a Farewell Address that is now among the treasured state papers of the American nation.

In this note of affection and warning to his fellow citizens, Washington directed their attention especially to three subjects of vital interest. Having dimly sensed the conflict impending between the North and the South, he gravely cautioned them against sectional jealousies. Having suffered from the excesses of factional strife, he warned them against the extremes of partisanship, saying that in popular governments it is a spirit not to be encouraged. Having observed the turbulent influence of foreign affairs upon domestic politics, he put them on their guard against "permanent alliances with any portion of the foreign world," against artificial entanglements with the vicissitudes of European rivalries, against the insidious wiles of alien intrigues.

Then in simple words of reconciliation he expressed the hope that that his country would forgive the mistakes which he had committed during his forty-five years of public life and that he might enjoy, in the midst of his countrymen, "the benign influence of good laws under a free government—the ever favorite object of my heart, and the happy reward, as I trust, of our mutual cares, labors and dangers." Though many Anti-Federalists saw in the Address a veiled attack upon their partisanship and their affection for France, the more moderate elements in both parties regarded it as a message of sound advice from one whose motives were pure and whose devotion to the public good was beyond question.

Hearing that Washington was to retire, the opposition cast off every lingering qualm. Until that moment all save the most brutal critics had curbed somewhat the sweep of their passions, even in denouncing the worst rascals who took shelter behind the great President. At last he was to go from the capital forever and ordinary mortals were to hold the high office which he had filled with such superb decorum. That opened the flood gates. With a show of defiance, Anti-Federalists had branded the

Hamiltonians as monarchists and assumed for themselves the name Republican even if it savored of French excesses. Some of them now ventured to call themselves Democrats—a term as malodorous in the polite circles of Washington's day as Bolsheviki in the age of President Harding. Scorning the Puritan clergy who called Jefferson an atheist and anarchist, all the Anti-Federalists agreed that he was to be their leader and their candidate for President at the coming election.

This challenge the Federalists accepted by nominating a man of opposite opinions, John Adams of Massachusetts. His views on popular government were well known: he had openly declared that he feared the masses as much as he did any monarch and that he favored "government by an aristocracy of talents and wealth." On the main point, therefore, his theories were sound enough for any Federalist; but Adams, even so, was not a strong candidate for a boisterous campaign. While he had spoken contemptuously enough of the crowd, he had poured no libations at the feet of the aristocracy: in an elaborate work he had tried to prove that in every political society there is a perpetual conflict between the rich and the poor, each trying to despoil the other, and that the business of statesmanship is to set bounds for both the contending parties.

Besides being endowed with a somewhat reasoned suspicion of the high and the low, Adams was a student and unfitted for the hustings. He was not an orator or a skillful negotiator; his lightest word smelt of the lamp and his friendliest gesture betrayed a note of irritation. It, therefore, required a desperate campaign to get him into the presidency, with the narrow margin of three votes and, to make the dose more unpalatable, since Jefferson stood second in the poll, Adams found himself yoked for a four-year term with his most redoubtable foe as Vice-President.

Relieved of his burdens, Washington now hurried away from the capital to his haven at Mount Vernon, where praise and affection followed him, yet not without taunts from Republican champions who broke in upon the anthem of gratitude from time to time. In fact, one of the critical editors, a grandson of Benjamin Franklin, flung after the retiring President the burning words: "If ever there was a period for rejoicing, this is the moment—every heart, in unison with the freedom and happiness of the people ought to beat high with exultation that the name of Washington from this day ceases to give a currency to political iniquity and to legalize corruption." If such was the treatment accorded to the great hero of the Revolution, Adams must have been without hope of mercy. And he received none.

Three questions . . .

1. Were you conscious of a difference between the sense that you *should* respond to an emotion—mother love—and the sense of actually knowing something about that emotion as it had meaning for a writer?

   2. Which selection in each pair is more characterized by exclamations, by lists of adjectives, by numerous comparisons?

3. Instead of exclamations, lists of adjectives, and numerous comparisons, what qualities distinguish some of the selections?

Two exercises . . .

1. Write a brief statement using two of the selections to illustrate a difference between sentimentality and shared emotion.

   2. Rewrite one of the poems which you would characterize as sentimental. You may turn it into prose.

HONESTY AND EMOTION

There is a difference between emotion used to *see* a subject and a subject used to hide an emotion. An obvious example of subject hiding emotion or disguising it is the gossip who tells of someone's divorce, says how sad it is but obviously relishes the telling. Often the writer hides his real emotion in material which itself often carries a different tone. James Dickey and Robert Bly are both American poets. Read Dickey's poem, then Bly's essay about Dickey. Does one, both, or neither create a false front for a display of emotion?

James Dickey

The Firebombing

Denke daran, dass nach den grossen Zerstörungen
Jedermann beweisen wird, dass er unschuldig war.
> —*Günter Eich*

Or hast thou an arm like God?
> —*The Book of Job*

Homeowners unite.

All families lie together, though some are burned alive.
The others try to feel
For them. Some can, it is often said.

Starve and take off

Twenty years in the suburbs, and the palm trees willingly leap
Into the flashlights,
And there is beneath them also
A booted crackling of snailshells and coral sticks.
There are cowl flaps and the tilt cross of propellers,
The shovel-marked clouds' far sides against the moon,
The enemy filling up the hills
With ceremonial graves. At my somewhere among these,

Snap, a bulb is tricked on in the cockpit

And some technical-minded stranger with my hands
Is sitting in a glass treasure-hole of blue light,
Having potential fire under the undeodorized arms
Of his wings, on thin bomb-shackles,
The "tear-drop-shaped" 300-gallon drop-tanks
Filled with napalm and gasoline.

Thinking forward ten minutes
From that, there is also the burst straight out
Of the overcast into the moon; there is now
The moon-metal-shine of propellers, the quarter-
moonstone, aimed at the waves,
Stopped on the cumulus.

There is then this re-entry
Into cloud, for the engines to ponder their sound.
In white dark the aircraft shrinks; Japan

Dilates around it like a thought.
Coming out, the one who is here is over
Land, passing over the all-night grainfields,
In dark paint over
The woods with one silver side,
Rice-water calm at all levels
Of the terraced hill.

               Enemy rivers and trees

Sliding off me like snakeskin,
Strips of vapor spooled from the wingtips
Going   invisible   passing   over   on
Over   bridges   roads for nightwalkers
Sunday night in the enemy's country   absolute
Calm   the moon's face   coming   slowly
About

        the inland sea
Slants   is woven with wire thread
Levels out   holds together like a quilt
Off the starboard wing   cloud flickers
At my glassed-off forehead   the moon's now and again
Uninterrupted face going forward
Over the waves in a glide-path
Lost into land.
Going: going with it

Combat booze by my side in a cratered canteen,
Bourbon frighteningly mixed
With GI pineapple juice,
Dogs trembling under me for hundreds of miles, on many
Islands, sleep-smelling that ungodly mixture
Of napalm and high-octane fuel,
Good bourbon and GI juice.

Rivers circling behind me around
Come to the fore, and bring
A town with everyone darkened.
Five thousand people are sleeping off
An all-day American drone.

Twenty years in the suburbs have not shown me
Which ones were hit and which not.

Haul on the wheel   racking slowly
The aircraft blackly around
In a dark dream   that   that is
That is like flying inside someone's head

Think of this   think of this

I did not think of my house
But think of my house now

Where the lawn mower rests on its laurels
Where the diet exists
For my own good   where I try to drop
Twenty years, eating figs in the pantry
Blinded by each and all
Of the eye-catching cans that gladly have caught my wife's eye
Until I cannot say
Where the screwdriver is   where the children
Get off the bus   where the new
Scoutmaster lives   where the fly
Hones his front legs   where the hammock folds
Its erotic daydreams   where the Sunday
School text for the day has been put   where the fire
Wood is   where the payments
For everything under the sun
Pile peacefully up,

But in this half-paid-for pantry
Among the red lids that screw off
With an easy half-twist to the left
And the long drawers crammed with dim spoons,
I still have charge—secret charge—
Of the fire developed to cling
To everything: to golf carts and fingernail
Scissors as yet unborn   tennis shoes
Grocery baskets   toy fire engines
New Buicks stalled by the half-moon
Shining at midnight on crossroads   green paint
Of jolly garden tools   red Christmas ribbons:

Not atoms, these, but glue inspired
By love of country to burn,
The apotheosis of gelatin.

Behind me having risen the Southern Cross
Set up by chaplains in the Ryukyus—

Orion, Scorpio, the immortal silver
Like the myths of king-
insects at swarming time—
One mosquito, dead drunk
On altitude, drones on, far under the engines,
And bites between
The oxygen mask and the eye.
The enemy-colored skin of families
Determines to hold its color
In sleep, as my hand turns whiter
Than ever, clutching the toggle—
The ship shakes   bucks
Fire hangs   not yet fire
In the air above Beppu
For I am fulfilling

An "anti-morale" raid upon it.
All leashes of dogs
Break under the first bomb, around those
In bed, or late in the public baths: around those
Who inch forward on their hands
Into medicinal waters.
Their heads come up with a roar
Of Chicago fire:
Come up with the carp pond showing
The bathhouse upside down,
Standing stiller to show it more
As I sail artistically over
The resort town followed by farms,
Singing and twisting
All the handles in heaven   kicking
The small cattle off their feet
In a red costly blast
Flinging jelly over the walls

Too intense for war. Ah, under one's dark arms
Something strange-scented falls—when those on earth
Die, there is not even sound;
One is cool and enthralled in the cockpit,
Turned blue by the power of beauty,
In a pale treasure-hole of soft light

Deep in aesthetic contemplation,
Seeing the ponds catch fire
And cast it through ring after ring
Of land: O death in the middle
Of acres of inch-deep water!   Useless
Firing   small arms
Speckles   from the river
Bank   one ninety-millimeter
Misses   far down   wrong petals   gone

It is this detachment,
The honored aesthetic evil,
The greatest sense of power in one's life,
That must be shed in bars, or by whatever
Means, by starvation
Visions in well-stocked pantries:
The moment when the moon sails in between
The tail-booms   the rudders nod   I swing
Over   directly over the heart
The *heart* of the fire. A mosquito burns out on my cheek
With the cold of my face   there are the eyes
In blue light   bar light
All masked but them   the moon
Crossing from left to right   in the streams below
Oriental fish form quickly
In the chemical shine,
In their eyes one tiny seed

As in a chemical war-
fare field demonstration.
With fire of mine like a cat

Holding onto another man's walls,
My hat should crawl on my head
In streetcars, thinking of it,
The fat on my body should pale.

Gun down
The engines, the eight blades sighing
For the moment when the roofs will connect
Their flames, and make a town burning with all
American fire.

Reflections of houses catch;

Fire shuttles from pond to pond
In every direction, till hundreds flash with one death.
With this in the dark of the mind,
Death will not be what it should;
Will not, even now, even when
My exhaled face in the mirror
Of bars, dilates in a cloud like Japan.
The death of children is ponds
Shutter-flashing; responding mirrors; it climbs
The terraces of hills
Smaller and smaller, a mote of red dust
At a hundred feet; at a hundred and one it goes out.
That is what should have got in
To my eye

And shown the insides of houses, the low tables
Catch fire from the floor mats,
Blaze up in gas around their heads
Like a dream of suddenly growing
Of deranged, Old Testament light.

Letting go　　letting go
The plane rises gently　　dark forms
Glide off me　　long water　　pales
In safe zones　　a new cry enters
The voice box of chained family dogs

We buck　　leap over something
Not there　　settle back
Leave it　　leave it clinging and crying
It consumes them in a hot
Body-flash, old age or menopause
Of children, clings and burns

eating through

And when a reed mat catches fire
From me, it explodes through field after field
Bearing its sleeper　　another

Bomb finds a home
And clings to it like a child. And so

Goodbye to the grassy mountains
To cloud streaming from the night engines
Flags   pennons   curved silks
Of air   myself streaming also
My body covered
With flags, the air of flags
Between the engines.
Forever I do sleep in that position,
Forever in a turn
For home that breaks out streaming banners
From my wingtips,
Wholly in position to admire.

O then I knock it off
And turn for home over the black complex thread worked through
The silver night-sea,
Following the huge, moon-washed steppingstones
Of the Ryukyus south,
The nightgrass of mountains billowing softly
In my rising heat.

                          Turn and tread down

The yellow stones of the islands
To where Okinawa burns,
Pure gold, on the radar screen,
Beholding, beneath, the actual island form
In the vast water-silver poured just above solid ground,
An inch of water extending for thousands of miles
Above flat ploughland. Say "down," and it is done.

All this, and I am still hungry,
Still twenty years overweight, still unable
To get down there or see
What really happened.

                          But it may be that I could not,

If I tried, say to any
Who lived there, deep in my flames: say, in cold
Grinning sweat, as to another
As these homeowners who are always curving
Near me down the different-grassed street: say
As though to the neighbor

I borrowed the hedge-clippers from
On the darker-grassed side of the two,
Come in, my house is yours, come in
If you can, if you
Can pass this unfired door. It is that I can imagine
At the threshold nothing
With its ears crackling off

Like powdery leaves,
Nothing with children of ashes, nothing not
Amiable, gentle, well-meaning,
A little nervous for no
Reason   a little worried   a little too loud
Or too easygoing   nothing I haven't lived with
For twenty years, still nothing not as
American as I am, and proud of it.

Absolution? Sentence? No matter;
The thing itself is in that.

Robert Bly

"Buckdancer's Choice"

Buckdancer's Choice has received a lot of attention from reviewers, but curiously no one has talked about the content. I thought the content of the book repulsive. The subject of the poems is power, and the tone of the book is gloating—a gloating about power over others.

"Slave Quarters" is a perfect example. A true work of art is sometimes able to be a kind of atonement. It moves into deep and painful regions of the memory, to areas most people cannot visit without wincing, and so do not visit. No one needs works of art like that more than we do. All over the American brain, there are huge areas like cut-over forests, lobes made sterile by collective cruelty toward a race, by one egotistical murder after the other in order to keep a people in poverty as one keeps cows . . . the psyche, faced with 20th century ideals, goes groggy with guilt. An art work can pierce that mass of guilts, gradually loosen it, help it to fall apart. But in order to do this, the work of art must carry real grief; it has to carry a masculine and adult sorrow. That is what Turgenev's, Chekhov's, and Tolstoy's work expressed when they talked about Russian serfdom. They told the truth both about the masters and about the serfs. Mr. Dickey's poem, "Slave Quarters," however, brings with it no grief: it gives the old romantic lying picture of the slaves, and of the slave owner. It is pure kitch, a *Saturday Evening Post* cover, re-touched by the Marquis de Sade. Being sentimental, it does not help cure illness, but instead increases the illness. Far from expressing remorse, the poem conveys a childish longing for ultimate power, a desire to go back and simply do the things over again:

I look across low walls
Of slave quarters, and feel my imagining loins
Tense with the madness of owners
To take off the Master's white clothes
And slide all the way into moonlight
Two hundred years old with this moon.

The poet feels that the old South treated the Negro pretty much all right. He accepts in fact all the Southern prejudices, and by adding artistic decoration to them tries to make them charming. "Slave Quarters" pretends to be a poem about the moral issue of ownership, but instead lingers in the fantasies of ownership.

A child who belongs in no world   my hair in that boy
Turned black   my skin
Darkened by half   his, lightened
By that half exactly   the beasts of Africa reduced
To cave shadows flickering on his brow.

The poem becomes ugly as he sniffs the Negro women, and prepares to do his great deed in the slave huts. He feels the same thrill from his power over dogs as over people:

A child would rise from that place
with half my skin

In the yard where my dogs would smell
For once what I totally am
Flaming up in their brains as the Master

On the whole, I consider this poem one of the most repulsive poems ever written in American literature. The tone is not of race prejudice, but of some incredible smugness beyond race prejudice, a serene conviction that Negroes are objects. It is not great life-enhancing poetry as the critics burbled, but bad tasteless slurping verse. The language is dead and without feeling.

> and above
> A gull also crabs slowly,
> Tacks, jibes   then turning the corner
> Of wind, receives himself like a brother
> As he glides down upon his reflection:

The language after all can be no better than the quality of the imagination, which in this poem is paralytic. The poet is sure the Negro women would have welcomed his rape, and when he envisions his half-Negro son grown up, the well-worn pictures pop up in the shooting gallery: a heavyweight champion, a waiter in "epauletted coats," a parking lot attendant, a construction worker, etc. The poem is ugly in the numbness, and its indifference. If I were a Negro, I would read this poem with rage.

At the end the poet asks, thinking of his bastard Negro son, What would it be like, not to "acknowledge" a son, but to "own" him? This question is a gesture in the direction of the Northern liberals, showing he knows it is wrong to own people. The only *feeling* in the line however is curiosity.

The tone of "Firebombing" is like the tone of "Slave Quarters." As objects of sadism, the Negro women have been replaced by the civilian population of Asia. The sentence makes us shudder; we realize we are talking about the psyche of the United States. In these matters, Dickey balances on his shoulders an absolutely middle class head. He embraces the psychoses of the country, and asks us to wait until he dresses them up a bit with breathless words: then all the liberals will see those psychoses are really "lifegiving."

"Firebombing" makes no real criticism of the American habit of firebombing Asians. It starts off with some criticism of the pilot. We learn that the bomber pilot, twenty years after his fire raids on the Japanese, feels no remorse in his overstuffed kitchen, feels no guilt for having burned people to death, feels no anguish, feels nothing, and this is intended as a complaint. He has burned up families:

> The others try to feel
> For them. Some can, it is often said.

The poem soon drops this complaint, however, and concentrates on the excitement of re-living the bombing.

All leashes of dogs
Break under the first bombs, around those
In bed, or late in the public baths: around those
Who inch forward on their hands
Into medicinal waters.

We notice the same curious obsession with power over dogs and over cows:

Singing and twisting
All the handles in heaven   kicking
The small cattle off their feet
In a red costly blast

and people:

With fire of mine like a cat
Holding onto another man's walls

Everything, dogs, cats, cows, people, are objects to use power on. If this were a poem scarifying the American conscience for the napalm raids, it would be a noble poem. But this poem has no real anguish. If the anguish were real, we would feel terrible remorse as we read, we would stop what we were doing, we would break the television set with an axe, we would throw ourselves on the ground sobbing. We feel no such thing. The poem emphasizes the picturesque quality of firebombing instead, the lordly and attractive isolation of the pilot, the spectacular colors unfolding beneath, and describes the way the fire spreads. It reminds one of Count Ciano's lyrical descriptions of his bombs falling on the Ethiopians in 1938: "The bombs opened beneath like great red flowers, beautiful in the center, like roses." Mr. Dickey remarks that in the cockpit he is "deep in aesthetic contemplation." "He sails artistically over / The resort towns." Some kind of hideous indifference numbs us, after having already numbed the language:

The heads come up with a roar
Of Chicago fire:

How cozy the whole thing seems to him is shown by:

Dogs trembling beneath me for hundreds of miles, on many
Islands, sleep-smelling that ungodly mixture
Of Napalm and high-octane fuel,
Good bourbon and GI juice.

The poet feels so little anguish, he provides charming little puns:

Where (my) lawn mower rests on its laurels.

In its easy acceptance of brutality, the poem is deeply middleclass. Dickey in the poem appears to be embarrassing the military establishment for its Japanese air raids, but he is actually performing a function for the establishment. He is teaching us that our way of dealing with military brutality is right: do it, later talk about it, and take two teaspoonsful of remorse every seventh year. In short, if we read this poem right, we can go on living with napalm.

The third ugly poem is "The Fiend." "The Fiend" is a foggy, overwritten fantasy about another sort of power—this time the power the man who is utterly cold has over those who still feel human warmth and enthusiasm. It is about the power the Snow Queen has over the human children. The power is symbolized this time by a window-peeper, who is sexually not quite all there. The poem begins with some good descriptions of window-peeping, interiors of houses seen by a tree climber. The poem then tries to become "poetic" and talks about things Dickey used to make poetry out of—how the man interacts with the tree, how the tree itself perhaps is human too. The poem finally returns to its sadistic business at hand, the cold, excitable window-peeper and the curious malignance he feels toward defenseless people, toward stenographers and working girls:

and when she comes and takes down
Her pants, he will casually follow her in
like a door-to-door salesman
The godlike movement of trees stiffening
with him   the light
Of a hundred favored windows   gone wrong
somewhere in his glasses
Where his knocked-off Panama hat was   in
his painfully vanishing hair.

The question is: why does the poem abruptly end there? My guess is that when the peeper went into the house, he cut the girl up with a knife. The knife is mentioned early in the poem. Of course speculations about what doesn't happen in a work of art are futile, like asking what Fortinbras did after Hamlet's death, but here the abrupt end calls for some explanation, and an escalation of sadism seems the only possibility. We realize reading it that something sadistic has entered wholeheartedly into Dickey's fantasy. The poem breaks off where it did, in my opinion, because Mr. Dickey realized that if he described the next scene he would lose his *New Yorker* audience. He didn't quite have the courage of his own sadism.

"Slave Quarters," "Firebombing," and "The Fiend," the three long pieces in the book, have a similar content and fail artistically for the same reasons. The language is inflated, the rhythms manufactured. All three are obsessed with power, and driven by a childish longing for it, disguised only by the feeblest verbal veil. The humanistic mumblings at beginning or end hide the naked longing for power about as well as a Johnson white paper on foreign policy hides its own realities. The amazing thing is that none of the reviewers noticed what the poems were saying. Even reviewers as acute as David Ignatow, and as aware of American ambiguities, praised the pointless violence of these poems, and accepted the poems' explanations of themselves at face value.

We can only lay this blindness to one thing: a brainwashing of readers by the New Critics. Their academic jabber about "personae" has taken root. Instead of thinking about the content, they instantly say, "Oh, that isn't Dickey in the 'Firebombing' poem! That is a persona!" This is supposed to solve everything. Yeats did use persona at times, a beggar for example: yet as we read his beggar poems we are very conscious that Yeats is *not* the beggar. A great impersonal poem could be written on the old South and its slaves, shaped like "Slave Quarters." One could imagine an artist like Yeats in fact creating such a poem, yet all through the poem, we would be conscious that the poet was none of the characters, that he was outside of or beside the poem, his opinions made even more clear by their absence in the poem. But in "Slave Quarters" the umbilical cord has not been cut. Mr. Dickey is not standing outside the poem. On the contrary, the major characteristic of all these poems is their psychic blurriness. There are no personas. The new critical ideas do not apply at all. Readers go on applying them anyway, in fear of the content they might have to face if they faced the poem as they face a human being.

Not all the poems in the book are as bad as these three, though all are touched by the same inflation. The best poem I think is "Sled Burial." "The Escape," about buying a grave lot, is also touching. Reading these two poems, some of the old affection I have always felt for Dickey's good poems returns. But even in the poems that are not sadistic, even in the "innocent" poems, a curious alienation takes place. James Dickey reminds you of some 19th century flying enthusiast, whose deflated balloon is on the ground, and he is trying with tremendous will power and large lungs to blow it up himself. In "The Shark's Parlor," he succeeds. As he puffs, the genial poem grows larger and larger. But then an unexpected thing happens: the balloon leaves without him. The poem floats away, we and the poet are left behind, standing in the same place we were before all the effort started. Fundamentally, "Shark's Parlor" has no meaning. Rilke thought that when the poem had meaning, it carried the author to a new place. Frost too said that a true poem, like a piece of ice on a hot stove, moves on the stream of its own melting, and by its end, the true poem is far away from its starting place. Thinking of Dickey's poems in this way, it is clear they are worked up. As someone said recently, more and more Mr. Dickey takes his life and laminates poetry onto it.

When Mr. Dickey visits college campuses for readings, he makes clear his wholehearted support of the Vietnam war. This is his business, but we must note again the unity of the man and his work. Of course the pilot he describes feels no remorse. If the pilot he describes felt any remorse for the earlier firebombings, he would be against the firebombings now. As a poet and as a man, Mr. Dickey's attitudes are indistinguishable from standard middle-class attitudes. In an article about him recently, Mr. Dickey boasted that he had made $25,000 on poetry last year. Obviously his decision to make poetry a "career" like football or advertising is associated somehow with the abrupt decline in the quality of his work. In any event, his decline from "A Mountain Tent" in *Drowning With Others* to "Slave Quarters" is catastrophic, enough to make you weep. One cannot help but feel that his depressing collapse represents some obscure defeat for the United States also. He began writing about 1950, writing honest criticism and sensitive poetry, and suddenly at the age of forty-three, we have a huge blubbery poet, pulling out Southern language in long strings, like taffy, a toady to the government, supporting all movements toward Empire, a sort of Georgia cracker Kipling. Numerous American artists have collapsed over a period of years—John Dos Passos is an example—but in Dickey's case the process seems accelerated, as in a nightmare, or a movie someone is running too fast.

SHARED FEELING

Strong feeling often seems unnamable and essentially abstract or indescribable; yet as you have seen, it can be revealed in concrete substance and specific terms. The first problem is to know what the emotion is, what you really feel. Too often, what we think we feel is only what we want or are expected to feel. Going to Great Aunt Elizabeth's funeral and looking at the corpse, we may say to her next of kin, "I'm so sorry." Like as not, we are more fascinated, bored, relieved, inconvenienced, guilty, or uncomfortable in the smelly room full of old people. Getting away from expected or desired feelings is just the beginning of writing, but it is no easy matter. Hemingway said of his days as a reporter:

. . . . I was trying to write then and I found the greatest difficulty, aside from knowing truly what you really felt, rather than what you were supposed to feel, and had been taught to feel, was to put down what really happened in action; what the actual things were which produced the emotion that you experienced. In writing for a newspaper you told what happened and, with one trick and another, you communicated the emotion aided by the element of timeliness which gives a certain emotion to any account of something that has happened on that day; but the real thing, the sequence of motion and fact which made the emotion and which would be as valid in a year or in ten years or, with luck and if you stated it purely enough, always, was beyond me and I was working very hard to try to get it.*

To work toward and understand the kind of accurate writing Hemingway has in mind, we recommend the following exercise.

Exercise . . .

With each step, we give a sample response. (For brevity our samples are shorter than your own work should be.)

1. Choose a topic about which you have strong emotional feelings. [Trees.]

2. Using free association, make a list of your emotional responses to your subject. Get your emotions out on paper without stopping to judge. [Tree-terrific, graceful, powerful, monstrous, ancient, protective.]

3. Choose the response in step 2 which seems most honest or accurate. The one which *feels* closest to your reaction. Now use free association and think up analogies which illustrate this response. [Monstrous—like a bear, elephant, dinosaur, building, robot, spaceship, dragon, mountain.]

*Reprinted with the permission of Charles Scribner's Sons from *Death in the Afternoon*, page 2, by Ernest Hemingway. Copyright 1932 Charles Scribner's Sons; renewal copyright © 1960 Ernest Hemingway.

4. Choose the analogy which best illustrates your feeling. Now make two columns on a page. Column 1, label *analogy*. Column 2, label *subject*. In column 1, list aspects of your analogy (forget about the subject). When you have finished with the analogy, go to the subject column, and opposite each analogy item try to write something it suggests about your subject. Is there a parallel thing in your subject? Developing your analogy allows you to develop the emotion embodied in the analogy. Then the analogy suggests what parts of your subject might also embody the emotion. The analogy helps you select and edit your material.

Dinosaur	Trees
Extinct	Being cut down rapidly
Largest of animals	Largest of plants, giant of plants
Weight	Weight (how much? look up)
Need much food	Feed from earth and air and rain
Very old	Ancient origins, longest lived plant
Small brain	Magnificent without intelligence
Would be plentiful food	Bountiful supply, feed industry
Motion	Slow, powerful, liquid swaying

5. Make a list of words and phrases which might combine the insight of analogy with the subject. Venison of industry, ponderous prey of woodsman or weather, colossal breaths of transpiration, limbs, armored scales of bark.

Assignment . . .

Do the above exercise and then write an essay using what you have discovered. You may be obvious about your analogy, but be sure you do not let it overwhelm your subject. Look back in Chapter 10 for samples of analogy used explicitly and implicitly.

12

What about
writing?

The old "Uncle Sam Wants You" recruiting poster has been preserved by popular demand while hundreds of posters for politicians, hotels, county fairs and automobiles have been forgotten. Whether you like the recruiting poster or not, the pointing finger singles you out. It is recognition. Your reaction may be a sense of duty or a feeling of indignation. Either response testifies to the poster's effectiveness. Effective writing, like the pointing finger, is recognition.

In pre-writing, the writer recognizes a new perspective of his own—an idea, an argument, a definition, or a way of seeing. He wants the reader to share his recognition. But before that second recognition occurs, the writer must sit down and write.

In previous chapters, we have divided the creative process into separate operations. All these operations lead to forming a concept. The concept, if it is a good one, urges the writer to write. But writing is not simply the result of

I WANT YOU
FOR U.S. ARMY
NEAREST RECRUITING STATION

dictation by the inspiration of the mind. Writing is proving that a concept is applicable. Writing is verification of the usefulness of your concept. When you verify the concept for the reader, he, too, has a recognition. The finger points at him.

Although writing and rewriting are the last step in the creative process, this step is where the imaginative writer most often fails. The first difficulty for an active person is simply to sit in a chair for the length of time it takes to make a first draft and then the revisions. The second and most serious difficulty lies in the fact that writing and rewriting are acts of judgment.

In pre-writing, judgment is often withheld, or it is limited to establishing boundaries for freewheeling thought. In writing, the writer must judge his own idea as it appears before him in words. Then an audience will judge the idea. That judgment may assess the quality of the writer's mind. This is

why, in our first chapters, we emphasized the relationship between language and personality. Later we tried to define some elements of a creative personality. Writing is the first judgment by the writer, the creative personality, insofar as he is consciously able to judge.

Sometimes we may not want that personality to be judged. We may fear that our thought or feeling will not be understood when put into writing —and behind that fear may lie the deeper fear that we are not really feeling or thinking what we want to feel or think. We may not want to know ourselves.

Rather than know ourselves, we may borrow words and phrases or we may put on an act that is only a superficial representation of our true feelings. Perhaps last month a family in South Holland, Illinois, may have sold its home rather than accept a court judgment on whether the "American Way of Life" really meant what they had in mind when they tried to control who lived near them or who went to school with their children. And when politicians are vague about what they mean by phrases like "law and order," they are trying to avoid judgment on what they really think. Yet we can judge their vagueness.

To write what we see, feel, or think is to judge those things and to allow others to judge them.

Thus almost all finished works of writings have been judged and changed by their authors before being cast loose among readers. The writer who has the courage to judge himself honestly and the skill to judge critically must also have the energy to rewrite. Perhaps every writer who is depressed by the thought of rewriting ought to keep in mind Tolstoy who rewrote *Anna Karenina* many times.

Here are some well-known works as they were written in early form and in their final versions. Read them and ask yourself first how the kinds of changes reflect a double judgment, first that of the writer on his work and second that of the reader.

THE DECLARATION OF INDEPENDENCE

Thomas Jefferson was the author of the first draft of the Declaration of Independence. The final version, however, reflected changes not of his making. Our text is from the four-page manuscript in the Library of Congress.* The earliest wording is reprinted here. Italics indicate passages that were struck out, bracketed, erased, or written over. Changes in wording are given in the notes. Jefferson's marginal notes attributed alterations to John Adams [JA] and Benjamin Franklin [BF], and those changes that we can attribute to Congress [Cong] are also signaled. Other revisions in the text are presumably those of Jefferson himself. The title is derived from Jefferson's endorsement of the manuscript.

*Reprinted with footnotes from Robert Ginsberg, *Casebook on the Declaration of Independence*, pp. 260–65. Copyright © 1967 by Thomas Y. Crowell Company, Inc.

Original Rough Draught of the
Declaration of Independence

A Declaration of[1] the Representatives of the UNITED STATES OF AMERICA, in General Congress assembled.

When in the course of human events it becomes necessary for *a*[2] people to *advance from that subordination in which they have hitherto remained, & to*[3] assume among the powers of the earth the *equal & independant*[4] station to which the laws of nature & of nature's god entitle them, a decent respect to the opinions of mankind requires that they should declare the causes which impel them *to the change.*[5]

We hold these truths to be *sacred & undeniable;*[6] that all men are created equal & *independant*; that *from that equal creation they derive in rights*[7] *inherent &*[8] inalienable,[9] among *which*[10] are *the preservation of* life, *&* liberty, & the pursuit of happiness; that to secure these *ends,*[11] governments are instituted among men, deriving their just powers from the consent of the governed; that whenever any form of government *shall become*[12] destructive of these ends, it is the right of the people to alter or to abolish it, & to institute new government, laying it's foundation on such principles, & organising it's powers in such form, as to them shall seem most likely to effect their safety & happiness. prudence indeed will dictate that governments long established should not be changed for light & transient causes: and accordingly all experience hath shewn that mankind are more disposed to suffer while evils are sufferable, than to right themselves by abolishing the forms to which they are accustomed, but when a long train of abuses & usurpations, *begun at a distinguished period, &*[13] pursuing invariably the same object, evinces a design to *subject*[14] them *to arbitrary power,*[15] it is their right, it is their duty, to throw off such government & to provide new guards for their future security. such has been the patient sufferance of these colonies; & such is now

---

1"By."
2"One."
3"Dissolve the political bands which have connected them with another ["other" inserted and then rejected], and to."
4"Separate and equal."
5"*To separate.*" Then: "to the separation."
6"Self-evident."
7"They are endowed by their creator with *equal rights, some of which are.*"
8"Certain." [Cong]
9Inserted: "rights; that."
10"These."
11"Rights."
12"Becomes."
13Deleted by Congress.
14"Reduce."
15"*Under absolute power.*" Then: "under absolute Despotism." [BF]

the necessity which constrains them to *expunge*[16] their former systems of government. the history of *his present majesty,*[17] is a history of *unremitting*[18] injuries and usurpations, *among which no one fact stands single or solitary*[19] *to contradict the uniform tenor of the rest,*[20] *all of which have*[21] in direct object the establishment of an absolute tyranny over these states. to prove this, let facts be submitted to a candid world, *for the truth of which we pledge a faith yet unsullied by falsehood.*[22] [1]

he has refused his assent to laws the most wholesome and necessary for the public good:

he has forbidden his governors to pass laws of immediate & pressing importance, unless suspended in their operation till his assent should be obtained; and when so suspended, he has *neglected utterly*[23] to attend to them.

he has refused to pass other laws for the accomodation of large districts of people unless those people would relinquish the right of representation;[24] a right inestimable to them, & formidable to tyrants *alone:*[25]

[he] has dissolved Representative houses repeatedly *& continually*[26] for opposing [with] manly firmness his invasions on the rights of the people:

[*when*[27]] *dissolved*, he has refused for a long *space of time*[28] to cause others to be elected, whereby the legislative powers, incapable of annihilation, have returned to the people at large for their exercise, the state remaining in the mean time exposed to all the dangers of invasion from without, &, convulsions within:

he has endeavored to prevent the population of these states; for that purpose obstructing the laws for naturalization of foreigners; refusing to pass others to encourage their migrations hither; & raising the conditions of new appropriations of lands:

he has *suffered*[29] the administration of justice *totally to cease in some of these colonies,*[30] refusing his assent to laws for establishing judiciary powers:

[16]"Alter." [Cong]
[17]"The present King of Great Britain." [JA]
[18]"Repeated." [Cong]
[19]*"Among which appears no solitary fact."*
[20]"Among which . . . the rest" deleted by Congress.
[21]*"But all possess."* Then: "all having." [Cong]
[22]Deleted by Congress.
[23]"Utterly neglected." [Cong]
[24]Inserted: "in the legislature."
[25]"Only." ¶ inserted: "he has called together legislative bodies at places unusual, unco[mfortable, & distan]t from the depository of their public records, for the sole purpose of fatigui[ng them into compl]iance with his measures."
[26]Deleted by Congress.
[27]Possibly: *"he has."*
[28]Inserted: "after such Dissolutions." [JA]. Then "space of time" shortened to "time."
[29]"Obstructed." [Cong]
[30]*"States."* Then the entire phrase replaced by: "by." [Cong]

he has made *our*[31] judges dependant on his will alone, for the tenure of their offices, and *amount*[32] of their salaries:

he has erected a multitude of new offices *by a self-assumed power,*[33] & sent hither swarms of officers to harrass our people & eat out their substance:

he has kept among us in times of peace[34] standing armies *& ships of war*:[35]

he has affected to render the military, independent of & superior to the civil power:

he has combined with others to subject us to a jurisdiction foreign to our constitutions and unacknoleged by our laws; giving his assent to their *pretended acts of legislation,*[36] for quartering large bodies of armed troops among us;

for protecting them by a mock-trial from punishment for any murders[37] they should commit on the inhabitants of these states;

for cutting off our trade with all parts of the world;

for imposing taxes on us without our consent;

for depriving us[38] of the benefits of trial by jury;

for transporting us beyond seas to be tried for pretended offences:[39] [2]

for taking away our charters,[40] & altering fundamentally the forms of our governments;

for suspending our own legislatures & declaring themselves invested with power to legislate for us in all cases whatsoever:

he has abdicated government here, *withdrawing his governors, & declaring us out of his allegiance & protection*:[41]

he has plundered our seas, ravaged our coasts, burnt our towns & destroyed the lives of our people:

he is at this time transporting large armies of[42] foreign mercenaries to compleat the works of death, desolation & tyranny, already begun

[31]Deleted by Congress.
[32]"The amount & payment." [BF]
[33]Deleted by Congress.
[34]Inserted: *"without our consent."*
[35]Inserted: *"without our consent."* Then: "without the consent of our legislatures." "& ships of war" deleted by Congress.
[36]"Acts of pretended legislation."
[37]Inserted: "which."
[38]Inserted: "in many cases." [Cong]
[39]¶ inserted: "for abolishing the free system of English laws in a neighboring province, establishing therein an arbitrary government and enlarging its boundaries so as to render it at once an example & fit instrument for introducing the same absolute rule into these *colonies.*" The last word replaced by: *"states."* Then: "colonies." [Cong]
[40]Inserted: "abolishing our most *important* [then: "valuable"] Laws." [BF]
[41]"By declaring us out of his protection & waging war against us." [Cong]
[42]Inserted: "Scotch and other."

with circumstan[ces] of cruelty & perifidy[43] unworthy the head of a civilized nation:[44]

he has[45] endeavored to bring on the inhabitants of our frontiers the merciless Indian savages, whose known rule of warfare is an undistinguished destruction of all ages, sexes, & conditions *of existence*:[46]

he has incited treasonable insurrections of our fellow-subjects,[47] *with the allurements of forefeiture & confiscation of our property:*[48]

he has waged cruel war against human nature itself, violating it's most sacred rights of life & liberty in the persons of a distant people who never offended him, captivating & carrying them into slavery in another hemisphere, or to incur miserable death in their transportation thither. this piratical warfare, the opprobrium of infidel *powers, is the warfare of the* CHRISTIAN *king of Great Britain. determined to keep open a market where MEN should be bought & sold*[49] *he has prostituted his negative for suppressing every legislative attempt to prohibit or to restrain this execrable commerce:*[50] *and that this assemblage of horrors might want no fact of distinguished die, he is now exciting those very people to rise in arms among us, and to purchase that liberty of which he has deprived them, by murdering the people upon whom he also obtruded them; thus paying off former crimes committed against the* liberties *of one people, with* crimes *which he urges them to commit against the* lives *of another.*[51]

in every stage of these oppressions we have petitioned for redress in the most humble terms; our repeated petitions have been answered[52] by repeated *injury.*[53] a prince whose character is thus marked by every act which may define a tyrant, is unfit to be the ruler of a *people who mean to be free.*[54] *future ages will scarce believe that the hardiness*[55] *of one man, adventured within the short compass of 12*[56] *years only, on so many*

---

[43]Inserted: "scarcely paralleled in the most barbarous ages and totally." [Cong]
[44]Line inserted: "he has constrained cˢ." [Cong]
[45]Inserted: "excited domestic insurrections amongst us and has." [Cong]
[46]Deleted by Congress.
[47]"*Fellow-citizens.*"
[48]"He has incited . . . our property" deleted by Congress. ¶ inserted: "he has constrained others *falling into his hands* [then: "*taken captives,*" finally: "*taken captive*"] on the high seas to bear arms against their country & *to destroy & be destroyed by the brethren whom they love.*" The closing words replaced by: "to become the executioners of their friends & brethren or to fall themselves by their hands."
[49]"Determined . . . sold" bracketed and "and" inserted, then these changes rejected.
[50]Inserted and then deleted: "determining to keep open a market where MEN should be bought & sold."
[51]Entire ¶ deleted by Congress.
[52]Inserted: "only." [BF]
[53]"Injuries."
[54]"Free people." [Cong]
[55]"Audacity" inserted and then rejected.
[56]"Twelve."

acts of tyranny without a mask,[57] *over a people fostered & fixed in prin-*
ciples of liberty.[58] [3]

Nor have we been wanting in attentions to our British brethren. we
have warned them from time to time of attempts by their legislature to
extend *a*[59] jurisdiction over *these our states.*[60] we have reminded them
of the circumstances of our emigration & settlement here, *no one of*
which could warrant so strange a pretension: that these were effected
at the expence of our own blood & treasure, unassisted by the wealth or
the strength of Great Britain: that in constituting indeed our several
forms of government, we had adopted one common king, thereby laying
a foundation for perpetual league & amity with them: but that submis-
sion to their [parliament was no part of our constitution, nor ever in
idea, if history may] be credited: and[61] we[62] appealed to their native
justice & magnanimity, *as well as to*[63] the ties of our common kindred to
disavow these usurpations which *were likely to*[64] interrupt our *corre-*
spondence & connection.[65] they too have been deaf to the voice of justice & of consanguinity,[66] *& when occasions have been given them, by*
the regular course of their laws, of removing from their councils the dis-
turbers of our harmony, they have by their free election re-established
them in power. at this very time too are[67] *permitting their chief magis-*
trate to send over not only soldiers of our common blood, but Scotch &
foreign mercenaries to invade & deluge us in blood.[68] *these facts have*
given the last stab to agonizing affection, and manly spirit bids us to re-
nounce for ever these unfeeling brethren. we must endeavor to forget
our former love for them, and to hold them as we hold the rest of man-
kind, enemies in war, in peace friends. we might have been a free & a
great people together; but a communication of grandeur & of freedom
it seems is below their dignity. be it so, since they will have it: the road
to glory & happiness[69] *is open to us too; we will*[70] *climb*[71] *it in a separate*

---

[57]"On so many . . . a mask" replaced by: "*to lay* [then: "*build*"] *a foundation so*
broad & undisguised, for tyranny."
[58]"*Freedom.*" The passage, "future ages . . . principles of freedom," deleted by Congress.
[59]Inserted: "an unwarrantable." [Cong]
[60]"Us." [Cong]
[61]"No one . . . credited: and" deleted by Congress.
[62]Inserted: "have." [Cong]
[63]"& we have conjured them by." [Cong]
[64]"Would inevitably." [Cong]
[65]"Connection & correspondence."
[66]Line inserted: "We must therefore." [Cong]
[67]"*They are.*"
[68]In place of "deluge us in blood": "*destroy us.*" [BF]
[69]"*To happiness & to glory.*"
[70]"Must" inserted and then rejected.
[71]"*Tread.*"

state,[72] *and*[73] acquiesce in the necessity which *pronounces*[74] our *ever-lasting Adieu!*[75]

We therefore the representatives of the United States of America in General Congress assembled[76] do, in the name & by authority of the good people of these *states,*[77] *reject and renounce all allegiance & subjection to the kings of Great Britain & all others who may hereafter claim by, through, or under them; we utterly dissolve & break off*[78] *all political connection which may have heretofore*[79] *subsisted between us & the people or parliament of Great Britain; and finally we do assert and declare these colonies to be free and independent states,*[80] and that as free & independant states *they shall hereafter* have[81] power to levy war, conclude peace, contract alliances, establish commerce, & to do all other acts and things which independant states may of right do. And for the support of this declaration we mutually pledge to each other our lives, our fortunes, & our sacred honour. [4]

When Jefferson wrote his autobiography, he included the text of the Declaration before its amendment by Congress, and he prefaced the document with this statement:

Congress proceeded the same day to consider the Declaration of Independence, which had been reported and lain on the table the Friday preceding, and on Monday referred to a committee of the whole. The pusillanimous idea that we had friends in England worth keeping terms with, still haunted the minds of many. For this reason, those passages which conveyed censures on the people of England were struck out, lest they should give them offence. The clause too, reprobating the enslaving the inhabitants of Africa, was struck out in complaisance to South Carolina and Georgia, who had never attempted to restrain the importation of slaves, and who, on the contrary, still wished to continue it. Our northern brethren also, I believe, felt a little tender under those censures; for though their people had very few slaves themselves, yet they had been pretty considerable carriers of them to others. The debates, having taken up the greater parts of the 2d, 3d, and 4th days of July, were, on the evening of the last, closed; the Declaration was reported by the com-

[72]In place of "in a separate state": "*separately.*" Then: "*apart from them.*"
[73]The passage, "& when occasions . . . apart from them, and," deleted by Congress. Line inserted: "*We must theref.*"
[74]"Denounces."
[75]Inserted: "*eternal* [deleted by Congress] separation!" Then inserted: "and hold them as we hold the rest of mankind enemies in war, in peace friends." [Cong]
[76]Inserted: "appealing to the supreme judge of the world for the rectitude of our intentions." [Cong]
[77]"Colonies." [Cong]
[78]"& break off" deleted by Jefferson.
[79]"*Heretofore have.*"
[80]"Reject and renounce . . . interdependent states" deleted by Congress from the final text and, as Jefferson notes, "a different phraseology inserted."
[81]Inserted: "full."

mittee, agreed to by the House, and signed by every member present, except Mr. Dickinson. As the sentiments of men are known not only by what they receive, but what they reject also, I will state the form of the Declaration as originally reported.

Four questions . . .

1. How would you define Jefferson's seeming attitude toward the changes made by the Congress?

2. What of the necessity for such changes—why do you think that Jefferson was willing to accept them?

3. In what ways does this example model a kind of writing which you may not often do?

4. What has the example in common with your own writing?

Walt Whitman left a number of manuscript drafts which differ from the published versions of his poetry. Probably the most notable difference between manuscript and published poem can be seen in the following two versions.

Walt Whitman

from the manuscript Once I Passed Through a Populous City

Once I passed through a populous celebrated city, imprinting
on my brain for future use, its shows, with its shows,
architecture, customs and traditions
But now of all that city I remember only the man who
wandered with me, there, for love of me,
Day by day, and night by night, we were together,
All else has long been forgotten by me—I remember, I say,
only one rude and ignorant man who, when I departed,
long and long held me by the hand, with silent lip,
sad and tremulous.—

the published poem

Once I passed through a populous city, imprinting my brain, for
  future use, with its shows, architecture, customs, and traditions;
Yet now, of all that city, I remember only a woman I casually met
  there, who detained me for love of me,
Day by day and night by night we were together,—All else has long
  been forgotten by me,
I remember I say only that woman who passionately clung to me,
Again we wander—we love—we separate again,
Again she holds me by the hand—I must not go!
I see her close beside me, with silent lips, sad and tremulous.

Three questions . . .

1. Whitman's sexuality has at times been somewhat blandly described as irregular. The changes
   in this poem are frequently cited as evidence
   of that irregularity. If the changes were made
   to conceal his private feelings, they may well
   be such evidence. Can you account for the
   changes in any other way?

2. Can you overlook the question of "irregularity"
   and ask yourself which version of the poem is
   the best poetry?

3. Is it possible that neither version of the poem
   has anything to do with the "irregularity"?
   Where in the poem is the meaning of the word
   love?

Whitman's poetry usually underwent less radical change as he revised
it during his lifetime. Here are two passages from *Leaves of Grass*, one as he
first published it in 1855, the second from his last edition in 1892.

from Leaves of Grass

1855

Swift wind! Space! My Soul! Now I know it is true what I guessed
     at;
What I guessed when I loafed on the grass,
What I guessed while I lay alone in my bed . . . and again as I
     walked the beach under the paling stars of the morning.

My ties and ballasts leave me . . . I travel . . . I sail . . . my
     elbows rest in the sea-gaps,
I skirt the sierras . . . my palms cover continents,
I am afoot with my vision.

1892

Space and Time! now I see it is true, what I guess'd at,
What I guess'd when I loaf'd on the grass,
What I guess'd while I lay alone in my bed,
And again as I walk'd the beach under the paling stars of the morning.

My ties and ballasts leave me, my elbows rest in sea-gaps,
I skirt sierras, my palms cover continents,
I am afoot with my vision.

Three questions . . .

1. The most notable changes are in punctuation.
   What is the effect on the poem when the punctuation is modified?

2. Why might such changes have been made?
   Which version is most conventional? Identify
   a poetic "creation."

3. Do you find changes in language or phrasing
   which seem appropriate to the changes in
   punctuation?

Thoreau fashioned *Walden* as the composite account of a single year based on the two years he had actually lived at the pond and on later visits to it, all recorded in his journals.

Henry David Thoreau

A journal entry for March 20, 1853

Walden is melting again. It has a canal two rods wide along the northerly side and the west end, wider at the east end, yet, after running round from west to east, it does not keep the south shore, but crosses in front of the deep cove in a broad crack to where it started, by the ice ground. It is glorious to behold the life and joy of this ribbon of water sparkling in the sun. The wind blows eastward over the opaque ice, unusually hard, owing to the recent severe though transient cold, all watered or waved like a tessellated floor, a figured carpet; yet dead, yet in vain, till it slides on to the living water surface, where it raises a myriad brilliant sparkles on the bare face of the pond, an expression of glee, of youth, of spring, as if it spoke the joy of the fishes within it and of the sands on its shore, a silvery sheen like the scales of a leuciscus, as if it were all one active fish in the spring. It is the contrast between life and death. There is the difference between winter and spring. The bared face of the pond sparkles with joy. How handsome the curves which the edge of the ice makes; answering somewhat to those of the shore, but more regular, sweeping entirely round the pond, as if defined by a vast, bold sweep!

from Walden

Walden is melting apace. There is a canal two rods wide along the northerly and westerly sides, and wider still at the east end. A great field of ice has cracked off from the main body. I hear a song-sparrow singing from the bushes on the shore,—*olit, olit, olit,—chip, chip, chip, che char,—che wiss, wiss, wiss.* He too is helping to crack it. How handsome the great sweeping curves in the edge of the ice, answering somewhat to those of the shore, but more regular! It is unusually hard, owing to the recent severe but transient cold, and all watered or waved like a palace floor. But the wind slides eastward over its opaque surface in vain, till it reaches the living surface beyond. It is glorious to behold this ribbon of water sparkling in the sun, the bare face of the pond full of glee and youth, as if it spoke the joy of the fishes within it, and of the sands on its shore,—a silvery sheen as from the scales of a *leuciscus*, as it were all one active fish. Such is the contrast between winter and spring. Walden was dead and is alive again. But this spring it broke up more steadily, as I have said.

The change from storm and winter to serene and mild weather, from dark and sluggish hours to bright and elastic ones, is a memorable crisis which all things proclaim. It is seemingly instanteous at last.

Two questions . . .

1. The sentence "It is glorious to behold the life and joy of this ribbon of water. . . . " is missing from the *Walden* version. How can you account for its being cut?

2. What other generalities have undergone change?

William Faulkner published a story "Spotted Horses" in *Scribner's Magazine*, June, 1931. He included another version of this story in his novel *The Hamlet* published in 1940.

William Faulkner
Spotted Horses

It wasn't ere a man knowed yet if Flem owned them things or not. They just knowed one thing: that they wasn't never going to know for sho if Flem did or not, or if maybe he didn't just get on that wagon at the edge of town, for the ride or not. Even Eck Snopes didn't know, Flem's own cousin. But wasn't nobody surprised at that. We knowed that Flem would skin Eck quick as he would ere a one of us.

They was there by sunup next morning, some of them come twelve and sixteen miles, with seed-money tied up in tobacco sacks in their overalls, standing along the fence, when the Texas man come out of Mrs. Littlejohn's after breakfast and clumb onto the gate post with that ere white pistol butt sticking outen his hind pocket. He taken a new box of gingersnaps outen his pocket and bit the end offen it like a cigar and spit out the paper, and said the auction was open. And still they was coming up in wagons and a horse-and mule-back and hitching the teams across the road and coming to the fence. Flem wasn't nowhere in sight.

But he couldn't get them started. He begun to work on Eck, because Eck holp him last night to get them into the barn and feed them that shell corn. Eck got out just in time. He come outen that barn like a chip on the crest of a busted dam of water, and clumb into the wagon just in time.

He was working on Eck when Henry Armstid come up in his wagon. Eck was saying he was skeered to bid on one of them, because he might get it, and the Texas man says, "Them ponies? Them little horses?" He clumb down offen the gate post and went toward the horses. They broke and run, and him following them, kind of chirping to them, with his hand out like he was fixing to catch a fly, until he got three or four of them cornered. Then he jumped into them, and then we couldn't see nothing for a while because of the dust. It was a big cloud of it, and them blare-eyed, spotted things swoaring outen it twenty foot to a jump, in forty directions without counting up. Then the dust settled and there they was, that Texas man and the horse. He had its head twisted clean around like a owl's head. Its legs was braced and it was trembling like a new bride and groaning like a saw mill, and him holding its head wrung clean around on its neck so it was snuffing sky. "Look it over," he says, with his heels dug too and and that white pistol sticking outen his pocket and his neck swole up like a spreading adder's until you could just tell what he was saying, cussing the horse and talking to us all at once: "Look him over, the fiddle-headed son of fourteen fathers. Try him, buy him; you will get the best—" Then it was all dust again, and we couldn't see nothing but spotted hide and mane, and that ere Texas man's boot-heels like a couple of walnuts on two strings, and after a while that two-gallon hat come sailing out like a fat old hen crossing a fence.

When the dust settled again, he was just getting outen the far fence corner, brushing himself off. He come and got his hat and brushed it off and come and clumb onto the gate post again. He was breathing hard. He taken the gingersnap box outen his pocket and et one, breathing hard. The hammer-head horse was still running round and round the lot like a merry-go-round at a fair. That was when Henry Armstid come shoving up to the gate in them patched overalls and one of them dangle-armed shirts of hisn. Hadn't nobody noticed him until then. We was all watching the Texas man and the horses. Even Mrs. Littlejohn; she had done come out and built a fire under the wash-pot in her back yard, and she would stand at the fence a while and then go back into the house and come out again with a arm full of wash and stand at the fence again. Well, here comes Henry shoving up, and then we see Mrs. Armstid right behind him, in that ere faded wrapper and sunbonnet and them tennis shoes. "Git on back to that wagon," Henry says.

"Henry," she says.

"Here, boys," the Texas man says; "make room for missus to git up and see. Come on, Henry," he says; "here's your chance to buy that saddle-horse missus has been wanting. What about ten dollars, Henry?"

"Henry," Mrs. Armstid says. She put her hand on Henry's arm. Henry knocked her hand down.

"Git on back to that wagon, like I told you," he says.

Mrs. Armstid never moved. She stood behind Henry, with her hands rolled into her dress, not looking at nothing. "He hain't no more despair than to buy one of them things," she says. "And us not five dollars ahead of the pore house, he hain't no more despair." It was the truth, too. They ain't never made more than a bare living offen that place of theirs, and them with four chaps and the very clothes they wears she earns by weaving by the firelight at night while Henry's asleep.

"Shut your mouth and git on back to that wagon," Henry says. "Do you want I taken a wagon stake to you here in the big road?"

Well, that Texas man taken one look at her. Then he begun on Eck again, like Henry wasn't even there. But Eck was skeered. "I can git me a snapping turtle or a water moccasin for nothing. I ain't going to buy none."

So the Texas man said he would give Eck a horse. "To start the auction, and because you holp me last night. If you'll start the bidding on the next horse," he says, "I'll give you that fiddle-head horse."

I wish you could have seen them, standing there with their seed-money in their pockets, watching that Texas man give Eck Snopes a live horse, all fixed to call him a fool if he taken it or not. Finally Eck says he'll take it. "Only I just starts the bidding," he says. "I don't have to buy the next one lessen I ain't overtopped." The Texas man said all right, and Eck bid a dollar on the next one, with Henry Armstid standing there with his mouth already open, watching Eck and the Texas man like a mad-dog or something. "A dollar," Eck says.

The Texas man looked at Eck. His mouth was already open too, like he had started to say something and what he was going to say had up and died on him. "A dollar?" he says. "One dollar? You mean, *one* dollar, Eck?"

"Durn it," Eck says; "two dollars, then."

Well, sir, I wish you could a seen that Texas man. He taken out that gingersnap box and held it up and looked into it, careful, like it might have been a diamond ring in it, or a spider. Then he throwed it away and wiped his face with a bandanna. "Well," he says. "Well. Two dollars.

Two dollars. Is your pulse all right, Eck?" he says. "Do you have ager-sweats at night, maybe?" he says. "Well," he says, "I got to take it. But are you boys going to stand there and see Eck get two horses at a dollar a head?"

That done it. I be dog if he wasn't nigh as smart as Flem Snopes. He hadn't no more than got the words outen his mouth before here was Henry Armstid, waving his hand. "Three dollars," Henry says. Mrs. Armstid tried to hold him again. He knocked her hand off, shoving up to the gate post.

"Mister," Mrs. Armstid says, "we got chaps in the house and not corn to feed the stock. We got five dollars I earned my chaps a-weaving after dark, and him snoring in the bed. And he hain't no more despair."

"Henry bids three dollars," the Texas man says. "Raise him a dollar, Eck, and the horse is yours."

"Henry," Mrs. Armstid says.

"Raise him, Eck," the Texas man says.

"Four dollars," Eck says.

"Five dollars," Henry says, shaking his fist. He shoved up right under the gate post. Mrs. Armstid was looking at the Texas man too.

"Mister," she says, "if you take that five dollars I earned my chaps a-weaving for one of them things, it'll be a curse onto you and yourn during all the time of man."

But it wasn't no stopping Henry. He had shoved up, waving his fist at the Texas man. He opened it; the money was in nickels and quarters, and one dollar bill that looked like a cow's cud. "Five dollars," he says. "And the man that raises it'll have to beat my head off, or I'll beat hisn."

"All right," the Texas man says. "Five dollars is bid. But don't you shake your hand at me."

The Hamlet

When the Texan, picking his teeth with a splintered kitchen match, emerged from the house twenty minutes later, the tethered wagons and riding horses and mules extended from the lot gate to Varner's store, and there were more than fifty men now standing along the fence beside the gate, watching him quietly, a little covertly, as he approached, rolling a little, slightly bowlegged, the high heels of his carved boots printing neatly into the dust. "Morning, gents," he said. "Here, bud," he said to the little boy, who stood slightly behind him, looking at the protruding butt of the pistol. He took a coin from his pocket and gave it to the boy. "Run to the store and get me a box of gingersnaps." He looked about at the quiet faces, protuberant, sucking his teeth. He rolled the match from one side of his mouth to the other without touching it. "You boys done made your picks, have you? Ready to start her off, hah?" They did not answer. They were not looking at him now. That is, he began to have the feeling that each face had stopped looking at him the second before his gaze reached it. After a moment Freeman said:

"Aint you going to wait for Flem?"

"Why?" the Texan said. Then Freeman stopped looking at him too. There was nothing in Freeman's face either. There was nothing, no alteration, in the Texan's voice. "Eck, you done already picked out yours. So we can start her off when you are ready."

"I reckon not," Eck said. "I wouldn't buy nothing I was afraid to walk up and touch."

"Them little ponies?" the Texan said. "You helped water and feed them. I bet that boy of yours could walk up to any one of them."

"He better not let me catch him," Eck said. The Texan looked about at the quiet faces, his gaze at once abstract and alert, with an impenetrable surface quality like flint, as though the surface were impervious or perhaps there was nothing behind it.

"Them ponies is gentle as a dove, boys. The man that buys them will get the best piece of horseflesh he ever forked or druv for the money. Naturally they got spirit; I aint selling crowbait. Besides, who'd want Texas crowbait anyway, with Mississippi full of it?" His stare was still absent and unwinking; there was no mirth or humor in his voice and there was neither mirth nor humor in the single guffaw which came from the rear of the group. Two wagons were now drawing out of the road at the same time, up to the fence. The men got down from them and tied them to the fence and approached. "Come up, boys," the Texan said. "You're just in time to buy a good gentle horse cheap."

"How about that one that cut your vest off last night?" a voice said. This time three or four guffawed. The Texan looked toward the sound, bleak and unwinking.

"What about it?" he said. The laughter, if it had been laughter, ceased. The Texan turned to the nearest gatepost and climbed to the top of it, his alternate thighs deliberate and bulging in the tight trousers, the butt of the pistol catching and losing the sun in pearly gleams. Sitting on the post, he looked down at the faces along the fence which were attentive, grave, reserved and not looking at him. "All right," he said. "Who's going to start her off with a bid? Step right up; take your pick and make your bid, and when the last one is sold, walk in that lot and put your rope on the best piece of horseflesh you ever forked or druv for the money. There aint a pony there that aint worth fifteen dollars. Young, sound, good for saddle or work stock, guaranteed to outlast four ordinary horses; you couldn't kill one of them with a axle-tree—" There was a small violent commotion at the rear of the group. The little boy appeared, burrowing among the motionless overalls. He approached the post, the new and unbroken paper carton lifted. The Texan leaned down and took it and tore the end from it and shook three or four of the cakes into the boy's hand, a hand as small and almost as black as that of a coon. He held the carton in his hand while he talked, pointing out the horses with it as he indicated them. "Look at that one with the three stocking-feet and the frost-bit ear; watch him now when they pass again. Look at that shoulder-action; that horse is worth twenty dollars of any man's money. Who'll make me a bid on him to start her off?" His voice was harsh, ready, forensic. Along the fence below him the men stood with, buttoned close in their overalls, the tobacco-sacks and worn purses, the sparse silver and frayed bills hoarded a coin at a time in the cracks of chimneys or chinked into the logs of walls. From time to time the horses broke and rushed with purposeless violence and huddled again, watching the faces along the fence with wild mismatched eyes. The lane was full of wagons now. As the others arrived they would have to stop in the road beyond it and the occupants came up the lane on foot. Mrs. Little-john came out of her kitchen. She crossed the yard, looking toward the lot gate. There was a blackened wash pot set on four bricks in the corner of the yard. She built a fire beneath the pot and came to the fence and stood there for a time, her hands on her hips and the smoke from the fire drifting blue and slow behind her. Then she turned and went back into the house. "Come on, boys," the Texan said. "Who'll make me a bid?"

"Four bits," a voice said. The Texan did not even glance toward it.

"Or, if he dont suit you, how about that fiddle-head horse without no mane to speak of? For a saddle pony, I'd rather have him than that stocking-foot. I heard somebody say fifty cents just now. I reckon he meant five dollars, didn't he? Do I hear five dollars?"

"Four bits for the lot," the same voice said. This time there were no guffaws. It was the Texan who laughed, harshly, with only his lower face, as if he were reciting a multiplication table.

"Fifty cents for the dried mud offen them, he means," he said. "Who'll give a dollar more for the genuine Texas cockle-burrs?" Mrs. Littlejohn came out of the kitchen, carrying the sawn half of a wooden hogshead which she set on a stump beside the smoking pot, and stood with her hands on her hips, looking into the lot for a while without coming to the fence this time. Then she went back into the house. "What's the matter with you boys?" the Texan said. "Here, Eck, you been helping me and you know them horses. How about making me a bid on that wall-eyed one you picked out last night? Here. Wait a minute." He thrust the paper carton into his other hip pocket and swung his feet inward and dropped, cat-light, into the lot. The ponies, huddled, watched him. Then they broke before him and slid stiffly along the fence. He turned them and they whirled and rushed back across the lot; whereupon, as though he had been waiting his chance when they should have turned their backs on him, the Texan began to run too, so that when they reached the opposite side of the lot and turned, slowing to huddle again, he was almost upon them. The earth became thunderous; dust arose, out of which the animals began to burst like flushed quail and into which, with that apparently unflagging faith in his own invulnerability, the Texan rushed. For an instant the watchers could see them in the dust—the pony backed into the angle of the fence and the stable, the man facing it, reaching toward his hip. Then the beast rushed at him in a sort of fatal and hopeless desperation and he struck it between the eyes with the pistol-butt and felled it and leaped onto its prone head. The pony recovered almost at once and pawed itself to its knees and heaved at its prisoned head and fought itself up, dragging the man with it; for an instant in the dust the watchers saw the man free of the earth and in violent lateral motion like a rag attached to the horse's head. Then the Texan's feet came back to earth and the dust blew aside and revealed them, motionless, the Texan's sharp heels braced into the ground, one hand gripping the pony's forelock and the other its nostrils, the long evil muzzle wrung backward over its scarred shoulder while it breathed in labored and hollow groans. Mrs. Littlejohn was in the yard again. No one had seen her emerge this time. She carried an armful of clothing and a metal-ridged washboard and she was standing motionless at the kitchen steps, looking into the lot. Then she moved across the yard, still looking into the lot, and dumped the garments into the tub, still looking into the lot. "Look him over boys," the Texan panted, turning his own suffused face and the protuberant glare of his eyes toward the fence. "Look him over quick. Them shoulders and—" He had relaxed for an instant apparently. The animal exploded again; again for an instant the Texan was free of the earth, though he was still talking: "—and legs you whoa I'll tear your face right look him over quick boys worth fifteen dollars of let me get a holt of who'll make me a bid whoa you blare-eyed jack rabbit, whoa!" They were moving now—a kaleidoscope of inextricable and incredible violence on the periphery of which the metal clasps of the Texan's suspenders sun-glinted in ceaseless orbit, with terrific slowness across the lot. Then the broad clay-colored hat soared deliberately outward; an instant later the Texan followed it, though still on his feet, and the pony shot free in mad, staglike bounds. The Texan picked up the hat and struck the dust from it against his leg, and returned to the fence and mounted the post again. He was breathing heavily. Still the faces did not look at him as he took the carton from his hip and shook a cake from it and put the cake into his mouth, chewing, breathing harshly. Mrs. Littlejohn turned away and began to bail water from the pot into the tub, though after each bucketful she turned her head and looked into the lot again. "Now, boys," the Texan said. "Who says that pony aint worth fifteen dollars? You couldn't buy that much dynamite for just fifteen dollars. There aint one of them cant do a mile in three minutes; turn them into pasture and they will board themselves; work them like hell all day and every time you think about it, lay them over the head with a single-tree and after a couple of days every jack rabbit one of them will be so tame you will have to put them out of the house at night like a cat." He shook another cake from the carton and ate it. "Come on, Eck," he said. "Start her off. How about ten dollars for that horse, Eck?"

"What need I got for a horse I would need a bear-trap to catch?" Eck said.

"Didn't you just see me catch him?"

"I seen you," Eck said. "And I don't want nothing as big as a horse if I got to wrastle with it every time it finds me on the same side of a fence it's on."

"All right," the Texan said. He was still breathing harshly, but now there was nothing of fatigue or breathlessness in it. He shook another cake into his palm and inserted it beneath his moustache. "All right. I want to get this auction started. I aint come here to live, no matter how good a country you folks claim you got. I'm going to give you that horse." For a moment there was no sound, not even that of breathing except the Texan's.

"You going to give it to me?" Eck said.

"Yes. Provided you will start the bidding on the next one." Again there was no sound save the Texan's breathing, and then the clash of Mrs. Littlejohn's pail aganist the rim of the pot.

"I just start the bidding," Eck said. "I don't have to buy it lessen I aint over-topped." Another wagon had come up the lane. It was battered and paintless. One wheel had been repaired by crossed planks bound to the spokes with baling wire and the two underfed mules wore a battered harness patched with bits of cotton rope; the reins were ordinary cotton plow-lines, not new. It contained a woman in a shapeless gray garment and a faded sunbonnet, and a man in faded and patched though clean overalls. There was not room for the wagon to draw out of the lane so the man left it standing where it was and got down and came forward—a thin man, not large, with something about his eyes, something strained and washed-out, at once vague and intense, who shoved into the crowd at the rear, saying,

"What? What's that? Did he give him that horse?"

"All right," the Texan said. "That wall-eyed horse with the scarred neck belongs to you. Now. That one that looks like he's had his head in a flour barrel. What do you say? Ten dollars?"

"Did he give him that horse?" the newcomer said.

"A dollar," Eck said. The Texan's mouth was still open for speech; for an instant his face died so behind the hard eyes.

"A dollar?" he said. "One dollar? Did I actually hear that?"

"Durn it," Eck said. "Two dollars then. But I aint——"

"Wait," the newcomer said. "You, up there on the post." The Texan looked at him. When the others turned, they saw that the woman had left the wagon too, though they had not known she was there since they had not seen the wagon drive up. She came among them behind the man, gaunt in the gray shapeless garment and the sunbonnet, wearing stained canvas gymnasium shoes. She overtook the man but she did not touch him, standing just behind him, her hands rolled before her into the gray dress.

"Henry," she said in a flat voice. The man looked over his shoulder.

"Get back to that wagon," he said.

"Here, missus," the Texan said. "Henry's going to get the bargain of his life in about a minute. Here, boys, let the missus come up close where she can see. Henry's going to pick out that saddle-horse the missus has been wanting. Who says ten——"

"Henry," the woman said. She did not raise her voice. She had not once looked at the Texan. She touched the man's arm. He turned and struck her hand down.

"Get back to that wagon like I told you." The woman stood behind him, her hands rolled again into her dress. She was not looking at anything, speaking to anyone.

"He aint no more despair than to buy one of them things," she said. "And us not but five dollars away from the poorhouse, he aint no more despair." The man turned upon her with that curious air of leashed, of dreamlike fury. The others lounged along the fence in attitudes gravely inattentive, almost oblivious. Mrs. Littlejohn had been washing for some time now, pumping rhythmically up and down above the washboard in the sud-foamed tub. She now stood erect again, her soap-raw hands on her hips, looking into the lot.

"Shut your mouth and get back in that wagon," the man said. "Do you want me to take a wagon stake to you?" He turned and looked up at the Texan. "Did you give him that horse?" he said. The Texan was looking at the woman. Then he looked at the man; still watching him, he tilted the paper carton over his open palm. A single cake came out of it.

"Yes," he said.

"Is the fellow that bids in this next horse going to get that first one too?"

"No," the Texan said.

"All right," the other said. "Are you going to give a horse to the man that makes the first bid on the next one?"

"No," the Texan said.

"Then if you were just starting the auction off by giving away a horse, why didn't you wait till we were all here?" The Texan stopped looking at the other. He raised the empty carton and squinted carefully into it, as if it might contain a precious jewel or perhaps a deadly insect. Then he crumpled it and dropped it carefully beside the post on which he sat.

"Eck bids two dollars," he said. "I believe he still thinks he's bidding on them scraps of bob-wire they come here in instead of on one of the horses. But I got to accept it. But are you boys——"

"So Eck's going to get two horses at a dollar a head," the newcomer said. "Three dollars." The woman touched him again. He flung her hand off without turning and she stood again, her hands rolled into her dress across her flat stomach, not looking at anything.

"Misters," she said, "we got chaps in the house that never had shoes last winter. We aint got corn to feed the stock. We got five dollars I earned weaving by firelight after dark. And he aint no more despair."

"Henry bids three dollars," the Texan said. "Raise him a dollar, Eck, and the the horse is yours." Beyond the fence the horses rushed suddenly and for no reason and as suddenly stopped, staring at the faces along the fence.

"Henry," the woman said. The man was watching Eck. His stained and broken teeth showed a little beneath his lip. His wrists dangled into fists below the faded sleeves of his shirt too short from many washings.

"Four dollars," Eck said.

"Five dollars!" the husband said, raising one clenched hand. He shouldered himself forward toward the gatepost. The woman did not follow him. She now looked at the Texan for the first time. Her eyes were a washed gray also, as though they had faded too like the dress and the sunbonnet.

"Mister," she said, "if you take that five dollars I earned my chaps a-weaving for one of them things, it'll be a curse on you and yours during all the time of man."

"Five dollars!" the husband shouted. He thrust himself up to the post, his clenched hand on a level with the Texan's knees. He opened it upon a wad of frayed banknotes and silver. "Five dollars! And the man that raises it will have to beat my head off or I'll beat hisn."

"All right," the Texan said. "Five dollars is bid. But dont you shake your hand at me."

Three questions . . .

1. The nine years show remarkable changes in vocabulary. Note some examples. Does the growth in the number of "hard" words make the later version more abstract or less appealing?

2. What actual changes are made in the substance of the story?

3. Are the changes substantial enough so that Faulkner might not have had the first version before him when he wrote the second?

THE PROBLEM OF "STANDARD" ENGLISH

Throughout this book we have encouraged diversity and originality in thought. What about language? Are diversity and originality also possible in the words and forms of your writing? The history of the English language gives evidence that such diversity is possible. The outstanding qualities of English since Anglo-Saxon times have been its break with inflectional forms and its growth in word riches. Our language is the language of a diverse people, often in conflict with each other—rich and poor, native born and immigrant, Englishman and American, black and white. It has been and still is a vigorous and healthy language. It testifies to a human capacity for endurance.

Thus we cannot argue here for a "correct" English, nor do we believe in any single standard for judging writing except that each piece of writing must be such that it may also be read. That is the only way in which it may fulfill its purpose—to put one person in communication with another.

College students are most often urged to write "Standard" English, the language of educated Americans as opposed to substandard Engilsh, the language of the uneducated. It has never been the intention of the authors of this book to end the convention of what is called Standard English. It has been our desire instead to help you understand that the convention is only that—a sometimes definable area of agreement about a form of language. Writing begins with you. We need standard forms because they provide a means by which unlike persons may find something in common without interpreters.

This book is written for readers the authors have never seen, who may live in places where we could not long survive and who may speak a language at home which we could not understand. Yet if we have made proper use of a "standard" English, we should be read and understood by those readers, and our readers should be able to write to us.

Standard English is also living and changing English. It has blood in it, not whitewash. In no case should a definable Standard English be taken as some sort of absolute measure of good writing. Effective writing begins with a writer. Standard English should simply provide a means, subject to change, by which the writer may present himself, on paper, to the reader. In this book, it lets two authors appear as one.

Here are two prose pieces which deal with how the writer should appear insofar as the conventions of English usage are concerned. The two agree on one principle at least: ideas of the standard vary, and it is not the standard which makes writing effective, though it may bear directly on the fact that writing is possible.

Donald J. Lloyd

Our National Mania
for Correctness

Every now and then the editors of the university presses let out a disgruntled bleat about the miserable writing done by scholars, even those who are expert in literary fields; and from time to time there are letters and editorials in our national reviews bewailing some current academic malpractice with the English language. At present, even *PMLA* (the Publications of the Modern Language Association), traditionally the respository of some of the worst writing done by researchers, is trying to herd its authors toward more lucid exposition. And at two recent meetings of the august Mediaeval Academy, one at Boston and one at Dumbarton Oaks, bitter remarks were passed about the failure of specialists in the Middle Ages to present their findings in some form palatable to the general reader, so that he can at least understand what they are writing about.

Even admitting that a really compelling style is the result of years of cultivation, much scholarly writing is certainly worse than it needs to be. But it is not alone in this. Generally speaking, the writing of literate Americans whose primary business is not writing but something else is pretty bad. It is muddy, backward, convoluted and self-strangled; it is only too obviously the product of a task approached unwillingly and accomplished without satisfaction or zeal. Except for the professionals among us, we Americans are hell on the English language. I am not in touch with the general run of British writing by non-professionals, but I suspect that it is nothing to make those islanders smug, either.

Donald J. Lloyd, "Our National Mania for Correctness," *The American Scholar* (Summer, 1952). © 1952 by Donald J. Lloyd. Reprinted by permission.

Furthermore, almost any college professor, turning the spotlight with some relief from himself and his colleagues to his students, will agree that their writing stinks to high heaven, too. It is a rare student who can write what he has to write with simplicity, lucidity and euphony, those qualities singled out by Somerset Maugham; far more graduating seniors are candidates for a remedial clinic than can pass a writing test with honors. And freshman writing is forever the nightmare of the teachers of composition, as it would be of their colleagues if the latter could not escape to the simple inanities of their objective tests.

Yet it was not always so. I have on my desk a little manuscript from the fourteenth century written by an unknown author, which I am in the process of editing. When I read it to one of my classes, as I occasionally do, with no more modernization than my own Great Lakes pronunciation and the substitution of a word for one which has become obsolete, it is a simple, clear and engaging document. "Where is any man nowadays that asketh how I shall love God and my fellow-Christians?" it begins. "How I shall flee sin and serve God truly as a true Christian man should? What man is there that will learn the true law of God, which he biddeth every Christian man to keep upon pain of damnation in hell without end? . . . Unnethe [scarcely] is there any lewd man or lewd woman that can rightly well say his Pater Noster, his Ave Maria, and his Creed, and sound the words out readily as they should. But when they play Christmas games about the fire, therein will they not fail. Those must be said out without stumbling for dread of smiting. But if a lewd man should be smited now for each failing that he maketh in saying of his Pater Noster, his Ave Maria, and his Creed, I trowe he should be smited at the full." And so on, to the beautiful poetic line, "Then think it not heavy to dwell with thy mother in her wide house, thou that laist in the strait chamber of her womb." The spelling in the original is hectic, and the capitalization and punctuation sporadic, to say the least.

Yet there was a man who knew what he had to say and set out about saying it, with no nonsense and no fumbling. He aimed for his audience and, judging by the dog-ears and sweat-marks on the book, which is about the size of one of our pocket books, he hit it. Why cannot we do as well in our time? Indeed, the eighteenth century was about the last age in which almost any man, if he was literate at all, could set down his thoughts—such as they were—so that they did not have to be excavated by the reader. We have an abundance of letters, diaries, pamphlets, and other papers from that period, and they are well written. It was the age, we may recall, not only of Boswell and Johnson, but of Pepys and Franklin as well, and of a host of other men whose main legacy to us was a simple, direct, workmanlike style, sufficient to the man and to the occasion, which said what it had to say and said it well. With the end of that century we go into the foggy, foggy darkness, and God knows whether we shall ever find our way out of it—as a people, that is, as a nation of thinking men and women with something to say.

Nevertheless, there is no question what makes our writing bad, or what we shall have to do to better it. We shall simply have to isolate and root out a monomania which now possesses us, which impedes all language study and inhibits all mastery of our native tongue—all mastery, that is, on paper; for as speakers of English, we Americans are loving and effective cultivators of our expression. I recall the gas station attendant who was filling my car. The gasoline foamed to the top of the tank, and he shut off the pump. "Whew!" I said, "that nearly went over." "When you see whitecaps," he replied, "you better stop." "You better had," I said, lost in admiration. But if you had given him a pencil, he would have chewed the end off before he got one word on paper.

The demon which possesses us is our mania for correctness. It dominates our minds from the first grade to the graduate school; it is the first and often the only thing we think of when we think of our language. Our spelling must be "correct"—even if the words are ill-chosen; our "usage" must be "correct"—even though any possible substitute expression, however crude, would be perfectly clear; our punctuation must be "correct" —even though practices surge and change with the passing of years, and differ from book to book, periodical to periodical. Correct! That's what we've got to be, and the idea that we've got to be correct rests like a soggy blanket on our brains and our hands whenever we try to write.

This mania for correctness is another legacy from the eighteenth century, but it did not get a real grip on us until well into the nineteenth. Its power over us today is appalling. Among my other tasks, I teach advanced courses in the English language to students preparing to teach. Most of these are seniors and graduate students, and in the summer especially, there is a sprinkling of older men and women, experienced teachers, who are sweating out a master's degree. They have had courses in "English" throughout their schooling. But of the nature and structure of the English language, the nature of language habits, the relation of speech to writing, and the differences in usage which arise from dialect and from differing occupational and educational demands—of all these, they know nothing at all. Nor do they come to me expecting to learn about these. They want to know two things: what correct usage is and how you beat it into the kids' heads. That there are other considerations important to an English teacher is news to many of them. What they get from me is a good long look at their language.

To trace this monolithic concentration on usage is to pursue a vicious circle, with the linguists on the outside. The literate public seems to get it from the English teachers, and the teachers get it from the public. The attitudes and pronouncements on language of a Jacques Barzun, a Wilson Follett, a Bernard De Voto, or a Norman Lewis ("How Correct Must Correct English Be?") mean more to English teachers than anything said by the most distinguished professional students of language—such as Leonard Bloomfield, Robert Hall or Charles Carpenter Fries. Correct usage is pursued and discussed, furthermore, without much reference to the actual writing of literary men. Now and again I amuse myself by blue-penciling a current magazine such as the *Saturday Review* or *Collier's* against the rules. I have to report that error is rampant, if variation is to be considered error. The boys just don't seem to pay attention to the rules. Moreover, having seen some of their first drafts, I am pretty sure that what conformity they do display is the work of their wives, secretaries, editors, proofreaders and typesetters, rather than their own. It takes a determined effort to beat the old Adam out of a readable manuscript.

Thus it is only the determined, consciously creative professional who can build his work on the actual language of men. In a recent issue of the *Saturday Review*, I stumbled on a quotation from Wolfgang Langewiesche. "Well, it isn't crowned by no castle, that's for sure," he wrote, "and by no cathedral either." My eyes popped, and I read it again. I liked it. It looked right; it sounded right; it had a fine Chaucerian swing to it. But I bet it cost him some blood and a fifth of Scotch to get it into print. In my own limited publication, I find "a historical" changed to "an historical," all my "further's" changed to "farther" and all my "farther's" to "further," "than us" watered down to "than we," and many, many more. How E. M. Forster got by with "the author he thinks," and got it reprinted in a freshman handbook a few pages along from the prohibition of such locutions baffles me. A phony standardization of usage appears in print, the work of editors unconscious of the ultimate meaning of what they do.

The result of all this is that a wet hand of fear rests on the heart of every nonprofessional writer who merely has a lot of important knowledge to communicate. He writes every sentence with a self-conscious horror of doing something wrong. It is always a comfort to him if he can fit himself into some system, such as that of a business or governmental office which provides him with a model. It is thus that gobbledegook comes into being. I once braced a distinguished sociologist, a student of occupational myths and attitudes, about the convoluted, mainly nominal turgidity of his writing. He apparently admitted verbs into his sentences the way we admit DP's into the United States, reluctantly and with pain. In speech he was racy, confident and compelling, a brilliant lecturer. "It's the only way I can get my work into the periodicals," he told me blandly. "If it's clear and simple, they don't think it's scholarly." With what relief the pedagogues subside into pedagese!

If we really want to get good writing from people who know things, so that we can come to learn what they know as easily as we learn from their talk, we can do it in a generation or so. In school and out, in print and out, we can leave usage to its natural nurse, the unforced imitation of the practices which are actually current among educated people. We can use our English courses in school and college, not to give drill on questionable choices among common alternatives, demanding that one be taken as right and the others as wrong, but to give practice in reading and writing. We can learn to read and write for the idea, and go for the idea without regard for anything else. Then our young people will come to maturity confidently using their pencils to find out what they think and get it down on paper; then our scholars will come to write simply, clearly and brilliantly what they brilliantly know.

In our speech we have arrived, I think, at a decency of discourse which is conducive to effective expression. We listen, with a grave courteous attention, to massive patterns of speaking different from our own because they come from differences in dialect and social status; we listen without carping and without a mean contempt. Furthermore, we participate; we go with a speaker through halts and starts, over abysses of construction, filling in the lacunae without hesitation; we discount inadvertencies and disregard wrong words, and we arrive in genial good will with the speaker at his meaning. In this atmosphere, our speech has thrived, and the ordinary American is in conversation a confident, competent expressive being. In writing he is something else again.

No one flourishes in an atmosphere of repression. It is possible, of course, for a person with special aptitudes and a special drive to bull his way past the prohibitions and achieve an individual style. But with the negative attitude that attends all our writing, those whose main interest lies elsewhere are inhibited by fear of "error" and the nagging it stirs up from setting pen to paper, until the sight of a blank white page gives them the shakes. It is no wonder that their expression is halting and ineffective. They cannot fulfill the demands of a prissy propriety and trace the form of an idea at the same time. They thus arrive at adulthood victims of the steely eye of Mr. Sherwin Cody, whose bearded face stares at them from the countless ads for his correspondence school, demanding, "DO YOU make these mistakes in English?" The locutions he lists are not mistakes, and Mr. Cody knows they are not; but his readers do not know it, and they do not know that they don't matter anyway.

For usage doesn't matter. What matters is that we get done what we have to do, and get said what we have to say. Sufficient conformity is imposed upon us by the patterns of our language and by the general practices of its users so that we do not have to run the idea of conformity into the ground by carping about trivial erratics in expression. Why in this matter of language alone complete conformity should be considered a virtue—except to typists, printers and typesetters—it is difficult to see (unless, perhaps, we are using it as a covert and pusillanimous means of establishing our own superiority). In our other concerns in life, we prize individuality; why in this one matter we should depart from a principle that otherwise serves us well is a puzzle for fools and wise men to ponder, especially since there is no general agreement on what to conform to, and one man's correctness is another's error. Not until we come to our senses—teachers, editors, writers and readers together—and stop riding each other's back, will the casual, brisk, colorful, amused, ironic and entertaining talk of Americans find its way into print. We should all be happy to see it there.

H. W. Fowler

Out of the Frying-Pan

A very large proportion of the mistakes that are made in writing result neither from simple ignorance nor from carelessness, but from the attempt to avoid what are rightly or wrongly taken to be faults of grammar or style. The writer who produces an ungrammatical, an ugly, or even a noticeably awkward phrase, and lets us see that he has done it in trying to get rid of something else that he was afraid of, gives a worse impression of himself than if he had risked our catching him in his original misdemeanour; he is out of the frying-pan into the fire. A few typical examples will be here collected, with references to other articles in which the tendency to mistaken correction is set forth more at large.

Recognition is given to it by no matter whom it is displayed. The frying-pan was 'no matter whom it is displayed by,' which the writer did not dare keep, with its preposition at end; but in his hurry he jumped into nonsense; / *When the record of this campaign comes dispassionately to be written, and in just perspective, it will be found that* . . . The writer took 'to be dispassionately written' for a SPLIT INFINITIVE, and by his correction convinces us that he does not know a split infinitive when he sees it. / *In the hymn and its setting there is something which, to use a word of Coleridge, 'finds' men.* 'A word of Coleridge's is an idiom whose genesis may be doubtful, but it has the advantage over the correction of being English; *a word of Coleridge* is no more English than *a friend of me.* / *But the badly cut-up enemy troops were continually reinforced and substituted by fresh units.* The frying-pan was REPLACE in the sense 'take the place of'; the fire is the revelation that the writer has no idea what the verb SUBSTITUTE means. / *Sir Starr Jameson has had one of the*

H. W. Fowler, "Out of the frying-pan," "*A Dictionary of Modern English Usage,* 2nd ed., rev. by Sir Ernest Gowers (Oxford, England: The Clarendon Press, 1965), p. 429.

most varied and picturesque careers of any Colonial statesmen. 'Of *any* statesman,' idiomatic but apparently illogical, has been corrected to what is neither logical (*of all* would have been nearer to sense) nor English. / *The claim yesterday was for the difference between the old rate, which was a rate by agreement, and between the new.* The writer feared, with some contempt for his readers' intelligence, that they would not be equal to carrying on the construction of *between*; he has not mended matters by turning sense into nonsense; / *The reception was held at the bride's aunt.* The reporter was right in disliking *bride's aunt's*, but should have found time to think of 'at the house of.'

The impression must not be left, however, that it is fatal to read over and correct what one has written. The moral is that correction requires as much care as the original writing, or more; the slapdash corrector, who should not be in such a hurry, and the uneducated corrector, who should not be writing at all, are apt to make things worse than they found them.

Three questions . . .

1. Which piece was the harder for you to read and why?

2. On which piece does your class find the most common agreement about meaning; about appropriateness to student writing?

3. Were both pieces written by "someone"?

John Milton said it:

I cannot praise a fugitive and cloistered virtue, unexercised and unbreathed, that never sallies out and sees her adversary, but slinks out of the race, where that immortal garland is to be run for, not without dust and heat. Assuredly we bring not innocence into the world, we bring impurity much rather: that which purifies us is trial, and trial is by what is contrary.

As a writer you will have no license. You will have responsibility—the responsibility of knowing and of being known. Here are two student essays and one student poem as they were written in early drafts and as they were submitted in final version. Study the changes in them.

Comparing High School Life to College Life

One of the most difficult changes a student has to make is that of leaving high school and coming to college. He must live away from home usually and learn to stay on the college campus. In high school a student has no more than five miles to travel to school. As a result, he is able to go home every day. He always remains no great distance from his home or his parents. The student also knows many of his fellow classmates which is a great asset to his social life in school. The student in high school is able to feel a closer rapport with his teachers and principal mainly because of a rather small number of students as compared with colleges. The general class requirements are basically the same, i.e., English, foreign language, etc. Also a high school student has every class five days a week which helps in that there is no break in the learning by the student and lectures by the teacher. The usual high school course covers a whole academic year and the student's grades from his course are figured mathematically to give him his average.

The student finishes high school. He is accepted at some college. This situation immediately places the student among many problems he has to face. First of all, he must leave home and his parents. He has the responsibility of looking after himself. He has to learn to live independently of his parents. He must also study, as well as do things his parents usually do for him, i.e., washing clothes, ironing, etc. After the green college freshman has mastered these requirements he prepares to do serious study. No longer does he go to the same class every day. No longer does he have a course covering a full academic year. These are the major problems. He must learn how to study and comprehend things he learns. He must cover in a semester what he would normally cover in a year in high school. Some classes are so large that the teacher never really knows each pupil; consequently, there is no rapport established between student and teacher. In college also the student must study each teacher and give that teacher exactly what he is looking for.

College, the institution of higher learning in America, transforms the eager young teenagers from high school into men and women who will be leaders in our society in the future.

Kivy Leon Pridgen

HIGH SCHOOL AND COLLEGE LIFE

"Wow! ! I can't believe it. I really can't believe it. I'm actually going to college." This statement and many others like it are repeated each year by hundreds of high school seniors who are going to college. Many of them definitely do not know it's going to be tough. Rebellion! ! Rebellion! !

Rebellion against high school! Staying up all night, drinking, smoking, going out any time are mostly what they think about.

College life is not all freedom, not at all! ! It's hard work, good times, sadness, heartaches, and even tears. But it's all great, really great! !

In high school, a student had better go to class, or else. But in college, "Larry, I cut two classes yesterday. So what Bill I cut four, no sweat man. No one cares." College students unlike high school students must leave mom and dad and learn to stand up on their own two feet.

High school is great though, but college is even better. College is where young people come to study, share ideas and experiences both good and bad. High school—well high school is for the kids! !

Kivy Leon Pridgen

EMBARRASSMENT

The period of adolescence has often been called the "awkward age" for a young man. During this time he struggles to make the difficult change from childhood to maturity. This change involves a completely new outlook toward girls. As a child, he didn't have much use for them. His time and interests were centered around playing baseball, shooting marbles, riding bicycles, and enjoying other "boyish" activities. But then comes the day at school when one of the older boys tells him about the "birds and the bees." It confuses him at first, but this new spark of information eventually lights a fire inside him that begins his interest in girls. The period of adolescence will be filled with new situations that he will not know how to handle and he will often find himself embarrassed by his incompetence. Probably no incident is more embarrassing, however, than his first date.

It all begins when "little Johnny" falls in love with "little Sally," the "new girl who just moved into town." After building up a great deal of nerve, he asks for a date to the school dance on Saturday night. He gets Sally's "OK" and it appears everything is going smoothly until the next night at supper when Johnny's Dad asks him if he would like to go to the baseball game with him on Saturday night. Johnny finds himself in the emotional state known as embarrassment. He turns about fifteen shades of red and puts on a big act of suddenly being choked by his food. With great difficulty he then explains about his date.

Then comes the Saturday of the big dance. Sally's parents will not let her walk across town to the dance so Johnny's mother has to drive them. Johnny thinks to himself in the car, "I sure hope mother doesn't drive right up to the main entrance of the party. (What will the boys say when they see that my mother is bringing me to the dance?)" Nevertheless, Johnny's mother pulls right up to the front door where all his friends are crowded. Johnny slumps down in the seat when they look his way. He then gets out of the car, walks around to Sally's door, and lets her out. With his head down, pretending he hadn't noticed his staring buddies, he escorts Sally and a pair of scarlet ears through the main entrance.

Once inside the building, Johnny finds himself in another embarrassing situation. It seems the only music the band is playing is the fast type that he doesn't know how to dance to. He stands there with Sally waiting for the band to play a slow song so he can dance. Suddenly, the band begins Sally's favorite song. Not knowing that Johnny can't dance, she cries out, "Oh Johnny! That's my favorite song! Let's dance!" Taking him by the hand, she leads him onto the dancing floor. Without any hesitation, Sally begins a series of complicated looking dance steps. Johnny just stands there dumbfounded, until he realizes some of his friends are watching. He then tries to follow Sally's steps. I felt about as much at ease trying to dance as a cat would trying to swim. I thought that song would never end. When the band stopped I noticed my friends were laughing at me. I thought they were laughing at my dancing and it made me mad, so I asked one of them, "Just what's so funny?" With a burst of laughter he replied, "Your zipper's down." I glanced down, and sure enough, "the old barn door" was wide open. When I looked back up, Sally's eyes met mine and she giggled. I didn't know what to do. I couldn't bring myself to zip them up while she was looking at me. I felt my ears turning warm as the blood rushed in, flushing them scarlet. Turning away from her, I rushed into the bathroom and zipped up my pants. Rather than coming right back out, I decided to say there for a few minutes, hoping that everyone would have forgotten about the incident by the time I returned.

When I came out of the bathroom, everything was back to normal. Then I noticed my mother standing by the door, signalling that it was time to go. All the boys snickered when they saw me. I walked out of the building just as I had walked in—head down, and escorting Sally and my red ears.

When mom drove the car next to the curb in front of Sally's house, I got out, opened the door for Sally, and walked her to her back door so mom couldn't see me when I told her good-night. I had never kissed a girl before, and I wanted very much to kiss Sally. I didn't really know what to say and do, except for what I had seen on love movies on television. When we reached the back door, I placed my hand on her shoulder and said in all seriousness: "Sally, I have something I want to tell you. . . . I love you." I then stood, waiting for a kiss, like it always happened in the movies. But instead, she just giggled, opened the door, said good-night, and closed the door behind her. . . . Once again I felt that familiar surge of heat rushing through my ears.

David McGlohon

EMBARRASSMENT, THE FIRST DATE

The period of adolescence has often been called the "awkward age" for a young man. During this time he struggles to make the difficult change from childhood to maturity. This change involves a completely new outlook toward girls. As a child, he didn't have much use for them. His time and interests were centered around playing baseball, shooting marbles, riding bicycles, and enjoying other "boyish activities." But then comes the day at school when one of the older boys tells him about "the birds and the bees." It confuses him at first, but this new spark of information eventually lights a fire inside him that begins his interest in girls. The period of adolescence is filled with situations that he does not know how to handle, and he often finds himself embarrassed by his incompetence. Probably no incident is more embarrassing, however, than his first date.

I can still remember my first date. It all began when I fell in love with "little Sally," the "new girl who had just moved into town." I decided to ask her for a date to the school dance on Saturday night. After getting Sally's "OK," it appeared everything was going smoothly until the next night at supper when Dad asked me if I would like to go to the baseball game with him on Saturday night. I hadn't told him about my date, and I found myself embarrassed. Trying to avoid answering Dad's question, I acted as if I were being choked by my food. After regaining my composure, I broke the news rather sheepishly. Dad didn't say a word. He just smiled. I wanted to crawl under the table and hide.

Then came the Saturday of the big dance. Sally's parents would not let her walk across town to the dance, so my mother had to take us in the car. I thought to myself as we were riding, "I sure hope Mom doesn't drive right up to the main entrance of the party. What will the boys say when they see my mother is bringing me to the dance?" Nevertheless, Mom pulled right up to the front door where all my friends had gathered. I slumped down in the seat when they looked my way. I then got out of the car, walked around to Sally's door, and let her out. With my head down, pretending I had not noticed my staring buddies, I escorted Sally and a pair of scarlet ears through the main entrance.

Once inside the building, I wanted to forget about my humiliating arrival and spend an enjoyable night with Sally. Instead, I found myself in another embarrassing situation. It seemed the only music the band was playing was the fast "go-go" type that I didn't know how to dance to. I stood there with Sally waiting for the band to play a slow song so I could dance. Suddenly, the band began playing "Mustang Sally." Not knowing that I couldn't dance, she cried out, "Oh my! That's my favorite song! Let's dance!" Taking me by the hand, she led me onto the dancing platform. Without any hesitation, Sally began a series of complicated looking dance steps. I stood there dumbfounded until I realized some of my friends were watching. Very awkwardly, I then began to follow Sally's steps. I felt about as much at ease trying to dance as a cat would trying to swim. I thought that song would never end.

When the band finally stopped, I noticed my friends were laughing at my dancing and it made me mad, so I asked one of them, "Just what is so funny?" With a burst of laughter he cried out, "Your zipper is down!" I glanced down, and sure enough, "the old barn door" was wide open. When I looked back up, Sally's eyes met mine, and she giggled. I didn't know what to do. I couldn't bring myself to zip them up while she was looking at me. Once again, I felt my ears turning warm as the blood rushed in, flushing them scarlet. Turning away from her, I hurried into the bathroom and zipped up my pants. Rather than coming right back out, I decided to stay there for a few minutes, hoping that everyone would have forgotten about the incident by the time I returned.

It seemed that everything was back to normal when I came out of the bathroom. Then I noticed my mother standing by the door, signalling that it was time to go. All the boys snickered when they saw me. I walked out of the building just as I had walked in—head down, escorting Sally and my red ears. We got in the car and headed for home.

When Mom pulled up to the curb in front of Sally's house, I got out, opened the door for Sally, and walked her to her back door so Mom wouldn't be able to see me when I told her good-night. I had never kissed a girl before, and I wanted very much to kiss Sally. I didn't really know what to say and do, except for what I had seen on television. When we reached the back door, I placed my hand on her shoulder and said in all seriousness: "Sally, I have something I want to tell you. . . . I love you." I then stood waiting for Sally to wrap her arms around me and kiss me very passionately, just like the girls in the movies always kissed their lovers. But instead, she just giggled, opened the door, said good-night, and closed the door behind her. Once again I felt that familiar surge of heat rushing through my ears. . . . Dejectedly, I walked back to the car. I had had enough embarrassment for one night.

David McGlohon

NEW YEAR [first draft]

Always in the cold of night
we mark the changed year
and old things irretrievable.
Yet day waits on the night
and the fish feed beneath the ice.

NEW YEAR [second draft]

Always with the winter night
frozen around us like a lake
we mark the changed year
and old things irretrievable.
If we are lucky and drinking with friends
memories swim
like fish beneath the ice.

NEW YEAR [final version]

As winter night is frozen
like a vast lake around
our music, light and drink,
we sing the year out with friends.
But time itself is dark
and mind out there has found
memories always rising
like fish beneath clear ice.

Five questions . . .

1. In each model, how does the final version show that the writer was dealing with some abstraction from his own point of view?

2. In each piece, try to isolate the concept with which the writer began. What strategy or overall plan did this lead to?

3. What are the most significant changes in organization in each piece?

4. In the poem, what changes are made in sound effects and why?

5. Pick out several instances in which an author changes a word or phrase. What judgment made him change?

An exercise . . .

> These models were chosen not because of their final excellence but because of the kinds of changes in them. Assign a grade to each of the final versions here and write out an explanation of any weaknesses you find. Make suggestions for revision.

THE LAST WORD

To you who are still reading this book, at a late hour and from duty rather than desire, perhaps: we hope that you find writing an act in which you can get along with yourself. That might be a good thing in an education —to learn something about how you may be able to get along with yourself.

There is only one thing to do now. That is to be a better writer than you have been before: to think and act in your own way and to make your own way understood. Knowing oneself, knowing one's language, knowing how to bring the two together for recognition—your own and your reader's —those are the acts with which this book has been concerned.

You can be a writer in many times and places. You can be a writer in an examination if you have prepared in advance by meditation and free association. You can be a writer by looking at your journal and bringing it forward. You can be a writer in business or in friendship. You can write for a political group, for your community, or for yourself. Whatever kind of writing you do, you are the writer. This is what we urge: not that you write as a professional or as someone compelled to make a grade, but as an individual human being writing his own statement.

WRITING AN EXAM

If you have always felt that the reason you did not do better in exams was that you were expected simply to parrot the teacher's feelings, try writing an exam for yourself.

a) Go back through your notes in a course for which you have already had an exam. Make up an essay question or two of your own suggested by the exam you have had, or take a question already there.

b) Discover the answer to that question.

c) Write that answer as you recognize it.

> Hand it in to your English teacher if you wish, or tear out this page, put it with the exam, and turn it in to the teacher of the course involved. If your writing is effective, he should be able to recognize the value you have found in the material at hand.

FINDING ORDER THROUGH PERSONAL EXPERIENCE

The happening in Chapter 5 may have seemed artificial and remote. Test it by duplicating some part of it in everyday experience.

a)   Go to an event which is associated with people assembled—to a movie, a concert, or sports event, or any like gathering.

b)   Write an account of the experience. Emphasize two things: that you were there observing something; that being there, you saw something, but not what most people saw.

If anyone else in the class attended the same event, compare your papers. Were you the same person seeing the same thing or were your experiences unlike, just as they were in the happening? If no one else saw the event as you saw it, put yourself in someone else's place—someone very much unlike yourself. Would he have seen and felt as you did? As an extension of this assignment you might also try describing the event from the position of that other person.

USING THE JOURNAL

Look back over your journal and find an experience or event recorded there which seems now to have been a summary experience, though you may not have known it at the time. Here, for example, is a letter which appeared in *Newsweek* the week before the assassination of Robert Kennedy and which, in retrospect, provides ironic if not bitter comment on the primary campaign.

Your "RFK: Up, Up and Away?" cover of May 20 has a sequel. On May 25 Senator Kennedy spoke at the Rex-Putnam High School in Milwaukie, Ore. A large balloon broke loose and slowly floated upward. All eyes followed it, including those of the senator, who said with almost a sigh: "Sometimes I wish I were a balloon." The balloon drifted to the rafters and broke with a loud bang. The audience sat in stunned silence until RFK quipped, "I wonder if that has any special significance."

Jack D. Stevens

(Courtesy Jack D. Stevens, Milwaukie, Ore.)

Write a paper now reflecting on your summary experience. Catch the sense not only of the experience but especially of what it defines.

FINDING ORDER THROUGH DEFINITION

Read some dictionary definitions and note how often they are uninformative. For the verb *to drive*, for example, you may find simply "to operate, as to drive a car."

Write a definition which informs the reader of your own sense of the word—what it means to you to operate a car.

FINDING ORDER THROUGH COMPARISON

A primary quality of imagination is that it brings together things which do not usually seem to be relevant to each other. Comparison usually enlightens us about one of the things compared or leads us to some new general knowledge about all of the things being compared.

Choose two diverse things which you feel might be compared for the reader's benefit. An example might be comparing the dress of students with the dress of buildings or the sports page of the newspaper with the front page. You may want to start this as a sentence, a list, or a paragraph. Aim at developing the comparison into a short essay. Remember, even a comparison should be guided by your own perspective and should develop organically.

UNIFYING VICARIOUS EXPERIENCE

Reading is the most common form of vicarious experience. In school and college, most academic experience is in the form of books. As with other kinds of experience, the experience of books and their contents often has little order in it. Think about the reading and lecture and discussion in any one of your classes. What can you say about this course or about some part of the subject matter? Write a unified essay from your perspective. You may want to center your essay around a theme, a teaching method, or the class itself.

Remember thy creator in the days of thy youth. Rise free from care before the dawn, and seek adventures. Let the noon find thee by other lakes, and the night overtake thee everywhere at home. There are no larger fields than these, no worthier games than may here be played. Grow wild according to thy nature, like these sedges and brakes, which will never become English hay. Let the thunder rumble; what if it threaten ruin to farmers' crops? That is not its errand to thee. Take shelter under the cloud, while they flee to carts and sheds. Let not to get a living be thy trade, but thy sport. Enjoy the land, but own it not. Through want of enterprize and faith men are where they are, buying and selling, and spending their lives like serfs.—*Walden*

Index

A

B

C

D

20

U

T

V

W

Y

Z